Developing User Interfaces

Dan R. Olsen, Jr.

Carnegie Mellon University/Brigham Young University

MK

MORGAN KAUFMANN PUBLISHERS, INC.
San Francisco, California

Sponsoring Editor	Michael B. Morgan
Production Manager	Yonie Overton
Production Editor	Julie Pabst
Editorial Coordinator	Marilyn Uffner Alan
Copyeditor	Jeff Van Bueren
Text Design	Side by Side Studios
Illustration	Cherie Plumlee
Composition	Nancy Logan
Cover Design	Ross Carron Design
Proofreaders	Erin Milnes, Gary Morris
Indexer	Steve Rath
Printer	Courier Corporation

Morgan Kaufmann Publishers, Inc.
Editorial and Sales Office:
340 Pine Street, Sixth Floor
San Francisco, CA 94104-3205
USA

Telephone	415/392-2665
Facsimile	415/982-2665
Email	*mkp@mkp.com*
WWW	*http://www.mkp.com*
Order toll free	800/745-7323

Library of Congress Cataloging-in-Publication Data
Olsen, Dan R., 1953–
        Developing user interfaces/Dan R. Olsen, Jr.
                p. cm.
        ISBN 1-55860-418-9
        1. User interfaces (Computer systems)   2. Computer software—Development. I. Title.
        QA76.9.U83043   1998
        005.4'28--dc21   97–45231

*To my parents, who gave me values, guidance, love, a library card,
and a garage in which a boy could build dreams out of scraps of wood*

Contents

Preface

This book is intended for readers with a programming background. Unlike most of the other books on the market, this is not intended for user interface designers. Its primary target is for those who must actually program the user interface. However, those who program must also understand the world within which they work. For this reason, substantial sections are included on task analysis and functional design. These concepts are presented, however, within the context of the actual software development. I hope that this will achieve an integration between user interface design and the software architectures necessary to implement those designs. This book is intended to fill in perceived gaps in the education of software professionals. As such, the book assumes that other texts and courses will provide the broad education needed to successfully implement interactive software systems.

The field of interactive software grew out of the computer graphics community. The intrinsic ability to show the user an idealized view of some world and then to process inputs based on that world was a fundamental problem of computer graphics from the beginning. With the advent of low-cost raster-graphics workstations, the fields of computer graphics and interaction began to diverge. The computer graphics field continued down the path of ever-more-realistic 3D worlds, while the interactive software community engaged the problems of dealing with the highly varied and sometimes erratic needs of everyday users. In the development of interactive systems, software architecture problems dominate over geometry and interpretation of interactive behavior over calculus. In today's computer science departments, however, the tools of interactive systems are still frequently taught in a computer graphics course. With the growth of interactive systems knowledge, this stepchild relationship to computer graphics has become awkward.

This book is intended to break away from the traditional graphics curriculum and to address directly the issues of interactivity. The book is intended to stand alone without a supporting computer graphics text. As such, there is material on interactive devices, drawing architectures, and transformational geometry. The geometry sections have been enhanced to provide the tools necessary for interaction rather than mere rendering.

Interactive systems also owe much to the social and behavioral sciences. A good interactive system is one that meets the needs of real users on their own terms. A good education in interactive systems should include a course on usability methods and on the human characteristics of the users we serve. This book, however, contains very little of this material, except where it directly impacts the way in which the software is architected. There are already a large number of books on designing for users, participatory design, usability testing, task analysis, and functional design. Rather that rewriting these materials into this book, the reader is referred to other resources. This text focuses on the software architecture principles necessary to build the systems conceived through such user-centered processes.

This book must also exist in a world of real systems. All major computer vendors provide an operating system with support for interactive software. No computer is without its windowing and widget tool kit. For each such system, there are a large number of books of the form "Introduction to Programming in the XYZ Tool Kit" or "Advanced Secrets of XYZ Revealed." Such texts are important to being able to effectively build interactive systems, but they do not provide broad conceptual knowledge. One of the aspects of interactive systems is that a high level of systems support is required. This level of support requires a learning investment to successfully exploit the system's features.

A key aspect of such systems support for interaction is that it will change. Over the last 10 years, X Windows and NeWS fought a war for UNIX that is now becoming irrelevant due to the decline of UNIX. NeXTSTEP has risen, fallen, and in the guise of an Apple product may be rising again. OS/2 has come and gone. The once-mighty MacOS is in decline. MS Windows has failed, failed again, and then conquered the marketplace. Since the major work on this book was completed, Java has begun its rise. Readers of this paragraph five years from now will wonder what relevance any of the above systems have to their current problem, because other systems will have risen and the current ones fallen or radically changed. The goal of this text is to tease out the principles of interactive software architecture that transcend all of these systems and to present their algorithmic essence and basic principles. As each of these systems has risen and fallen, it has included 80% to 90% of its features in common with some prior system. A system-independent understanding of this common core is essential to the education of today's software professional. The examples in this book are drawn from real commercial systems rather than research prototypes. Some of those systems are in current use and some are dead. The intent is to illustrate the general principles by comparing and contrasting how various companies have implemented them.

Acknowledgments

This book owes a great deal to my colleagues in the SIGCHI community. Interaction with this community of scientists has defined most of my career. Although there are many individuals who are personal friends, the credit for this work belongs to the community as a whole. They have provided a delightful environment in which to spend my professional life.

I would specifically like to mention Bill Hays, who helped me through my MS degree and served for years as my department chair and my dean at Brigham Young University. Through all of my CS career, Bill has provided encouragement and resources for my work.

1

Introduction

1.1 What This Book Is About

Computer scientists, programmers, and other computing professionals are increasingly asked to improve the usability of their products. Through the media, the public has seen a vision of what computers might do for it and finds itself frustrated when that vision is not fulfilled. An essential part of that vision of computing power for everyone is the software that controls the human/computer interface. This book addresses the software fundamentals necessary to pursue such a vision.

1.1.1 Early Computing

In the early 1970s, when I first encountered computing as a college freshman, we were shown a special room behind a large glass window. In the room were large boxes of blue and gray metal, each with various lights and buttons. The buttons would flash, the printers would print, and cards would be read as we freshmen stared through the glass in fascination. The room was populated only by middle-aged men or older students, all wearing white or light blue lab coats.

Real programmers (not freshmen) could enter through a special door and stand behind a barrier and actually talk to those in the lab coats. Mere programmers, however, were not allowed past the barrier. They were allowed to look, talk, listen, and to feel the specially conditioned air, but never to touch (except possibly late at night when the supervisors were gone). The rest of us were left to stare through the glass.

Occasionally a loud bell would ring and those in the lab coats would spring into action. All would converge on a large box the size of a refrigerator whose front was covered with fruit-colored lights and numerous switches. The knowledgeable ones would shout something about "ABEND" and "re-IPL." The programmers would frown and wander back out through the special door to wait for a more favorable time to try their creations.

The only truly human aspect of this process were the "expediters." These were students like ourselves who accepted our decks of punched cards and assembled them into batches. Occasionally someone in a lab coat would come out to get a batch of cards to use as fodder for the machine. If you were nice to the expediters, they would go talk to someone in a lab coat to find out when your program would be done. We would talk to the expediter, who would talk to a lab coat, who would consult the machine and send back the message, "it will be done in a while." It is no wonder that gloomy futurists predicted humanity as the servants of their own machines.

1.1.2 Winds of Change

Simple economics was at the root of this world of humans serving machines. Students, expediters, programmers, operators, and supervisors were cheap. Computers were expensive. The goal was to do whatever it took to get as much as possible from the expensive machine in as little time as possible. As a student programmer, I was paid $4.00 per hour to serve a machine whose time was billed in excess of $500 per hour. The economics were obvious.

With the development of microprocessors and silicon technology, all of that changed. Most workstations cost less than one month's salary for a programmer. A personal computer costs less than a day's personnel costs for the executive who uses it. There are fewer than three machines in our entire building that cost more than six months of my salary. Even the most poorly paid full-time secretaries make more in two months than the cost of the computers on which they work. The new economics of computing dictates that people, not computers, are important. For those of us who like people, the world is more as it should be.

1.1.3 The Legacy of Lab Coats

The lab coats are gone or largely ignored by the computing community. Banks of lights, spinning reels of tape, and the ca-chunk of card readers have all disappeared. The dominant media vision of a computer is no longer a card sorter or tape drive but rather a large television with a keyboard and a mouse. The glass windows and wooden barriers are gone. The expediters have married and are raising children. Their children consider computers to be like their TV, stereo, or refrigerator rather than expensive laboratory instruments.

Although everyone is allowed to touch a computer, many people still cannot use them. Among those who use them, many cannot get done what they want. The desire for service exceeds the system's capacity to serve. In large part, this is not a hardware problem. The physicists and engineers are doubling machine capacity every 18 months without a significant increase in price.

This usability problem is primarily a software problem. Even though in the areas of voice, video, and virtual reality hardware barriers still exist, these barriers are not the ones that the average computer user is currently faced with.

The root of the software usability problem lies in the legacy of the lab coats. Even though this style of computing vanished before most current college students were born, it still influences software design and the ways programming is taught. When computers were expensive, the focus of software development was on saving time and memory. For a whole generation of programmers, the optimization of these two metrics was the grail of their profession. Much of computer software architecture was based on sequential processing of data files. When Borland introduced Turbo Pascal, the company exploited the very simple concept of combining the editor with the compiler so that compilation would all take place in memory with no disk accesses at all. The speed and usability of the product were far superior to the competition, but in its very heart it was still the same sequential parse structure found in the first FORTRAN compiler.

The legacy of lab coats is that users prepare information, the computer reads the information, and finally the computer produces a report of the computation. This batch model for using computers is taught in most introductory programming classes. Students are first taught to perform arithmetic and print the results. They are then taught to read a file, compute the sum of the numbers in the file, and write out the result. This batch model proceeds through most of their programming curriculum, with the inputs and outputs becoming more complex but the same batch paradigm remaining unchanged. The lab coats are gone but the mindset created for that computing environment remains.

1.1.4 A Question of Control

The central issues in this book are the granularity of control and the structuring of that control. In the batch model for software, the user prepares information, the computer then has complete control until it produces an output, at which point control is returned to the user. In many ways, graphical user interfaces are still the same. The difference is that the computer has control not for minutes or hours but for very small increments of time. In a good graphical user interface, the computer has control for less than 200 milliseconds between mouse movements or keystrokes. The set of actions that a user may choose to take at any point in time is widely varied rather than carefully constrained. The dominant control mechanism is human, not algorithmic. This shift of control from algorithm to user has important implications in the way that software is designed and written.

1.2 Setting the Context

The focus of this book is software architectures for user interfaces. It is intended for programmers, developers, and computer scientists. In particular, it is assumed that you understand programming and are already a good programmer. This is not a book for psychologists or user interface designers. Many such books already exist.[1,2,3]

The concepts in this book rely strongly on foundations from computer graphics and from human factors and usability. Although the problems of user interface software differ from both of these fields in major ways, the issues from both are very important to the computer scientist building user interface software.

1.2.1 Computer Graphics

Computer graphics courses have been part of the computer science curriculum for a very long time. With the exception of audio input and output, user interface software is built around graphical presentations and interactive input devices. Computer graphics courses, however, have focused on topics pertinent to their roots in computer-aided design and the rendering of realistically lighted 3D images. Most computer science students will use computer graphics not for the purpose of rendering photorealistic, 3D images but as part of the user interfaces to a variety of informational and communication tools. The software concepts needed for user interface work are very different from the mathematical concepts of splines and curves or the algorithms for hidden surfaces. The focus of interactive graphics is on the structure of control and the updating of presentations rather than on geometry and light.

This book assumes that you have not previously studied computer graphics and therefore will cover the following topics found in a traditional computer graphics course:

- basic drawing primitives such as lines and polygons
- text drawing, including fonts and international fonts
- 2D clipping of drawing primitives to regions
- color models
- 2D geometric transformations
- interactive input devices
- windowing

There are a variety of topics normally covered in a computer graphics course that will not be found in this book. Such topics include

- pixel rendering of drawing primitives such as lines and polygons
- 3D geometry and perspective viewing

- mathematics of parametric curves and surfaces
- light, shading, and texturing
- hidden surfaces
- solid modeling

For these topics, you are referred to traditional computer graphics texts such as Foley and van Dam.[4] For a broad background in user interface software, it is recommended that a computer scientist take a course in traditional computer graphics. This is particularly important as computing power puts realistic 3D rendering within the range of the average workstation.

1.2.2 Human Factors and Usability

Just as there is a large literature on computer graphics, there is also a similar background in psychology, ergonomics, and usability. There is much that has been done to study how human beings use and comprehend computer software. This material is also important to the understanding of user interface software. The primary goal of user interface software is to facilitate computers in serving their human masters. This is not, however, a book for usability experts or user interface designers. This is a book for user interface software engineers.

As much as this book is oriented toward software architecture issues, the needs of the user are of critical importance. Because of this priority, there are several usability themes that will be stressed throughout this book. In addition, frequent references will be made to human factors information. This book is not a substitute for a good background in user psychology,[5] usability testing,[6] or human factors.[7] The topics that will be covered include

- basic human factors principles of visualization and input devices
- general issues of human memory and perception
- techniques for usability evaluation

This book will not address issues such as

- cognitive modeling
- mental models
- psychology of errors
- experimental design
- usability methodologies and processes
- social and anthropological influences

An important concept to establish is that programmers are just that, programmers. They have chosen their profession because they enjoy the challenges and intricacies of the logical structures we call software. Most users do not have these interests at all. A most difficult problem is for programmers to

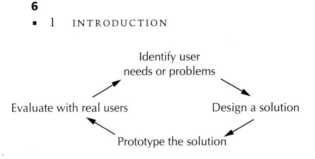

Figure 1-1   Iterative design

achieve a true understanding of the needs of the prospective user. What programmers should understand is that there are other professionals who are interested in such issues and who have trained equally long in the understanding of what people want and how people think about, perceive, and act in their world. Working collaboratively with these usability specialists, psychologists, and sociologists is essential to successful user interface development.

Building quality usable software is not a science. There are some principles and guidelines, but they are either very general or very specific. Unlike parsing or numerical methods, there is no general procedure that will produce a result of a particular quality. The dominant engineering paradigm for user interfaces is iterative design, as shown in Figure 1-1.

Programmers will notice that this looks like an infinite loop. In reality, it is. During some of the iterations of this loop, economics or patience will dictate that software must be released. The loop, however, will and must continue for as long as the software or the organization that created it remains in the marketplace.

Throughout this book, techniques for evaluating the interface design will be presented. These techniques will be discussed in an informal way. The purpose is to make you aware of the need for constant usability evaluation and to help you understand the issues involved. There will be frequent references to other works, which can fill in the details of user interface evaluation in all its facets.

1.2.3 Object-Oriented Software

Having introduced the user-centered issues, we now turn to more software-oriented subjects. Object-oriented design is all the rage in software engineering circles. It is assumed that you already have had some exposure to these concepts. For those who have not, there are a variety of texts that discuss both the principles of software engineering and the concepts of specific languages. You are referred to such texts for a more in-depth understanding of the software engineering problem as a whole. Most of these works point to a language from the 1960s called SIMULA, which is credited as one of the first object-oriented languages.[8]

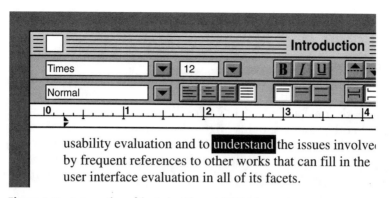

Figure 1-2   **Interacting objects in Microsoft Word**

In the late 1970s, researchers at Xerox Palo Alto Research Center (PARC) began to address the software needs of graphical user interfaces. What they found was a large space of semiautonomous visual objects being manipulated by a user whose goals and methods were not encoded in the software. The Smalltalk language was created to reflect this chaotic model of software control.[9] There have since been a variety languages developed. The power of the object-oriented paradigm has so pervaded computer science that many have forgotten that this current wave began at the user interface.

To illustrate the use of object-oriented methods in designing user interface software, Figure 1-2 shows the tool bar of a Microsoft Word document. There are a variety of objects on the bar and in the text that can be selected and manipulated by a user. Suppose you wanted to activate the icon **B** in the tool bar. The icon itself must be programmed to receive inputs from the mouse and to correctly change itself to **B** when it is selected. It must remember its selected status so that it can properly display itself. It also must inform the selected portion of the document that it must change to bold. When a different piece of text is selected, the boldness property of that text must be checked and the button updated appropriately. By modeling each interactive item as an object that remembers things about itself and that can receive and send messages, we capture the kinds of behavior that must be programmed in a user interface. Note that there are a variety of such buttons on the tool bar and each behaves in exactly the same way, except for their label and function. We will exploit such similarities in our software architectures.

This book will not address the various religious arguments concerning single- or multiple-inheritance, class-based or prototype-based, or typeless versus strongly typed languages. There is no particular programming language used in this text. Most of the algorithms are presented in a semiformal pseudocode that attempts to convey the essence of the strategy without getting bogged down in the idiosyncrasies of a particular language. In general, the syntax has the flavor of C++. There is, however, some general terminology that is required to provide coherence to the text.

Objects and Classes

An *object* is a single unit of behavior represented in computer memory. Every object has a *class*, which defines the information stored in that object and the behavior of the object. Objects have *fields*, which contain information about the object. In other models, fields might also be referred to as properties, attributes, slots, or data members. These fields each have a particular *type*. Types may be primitive, such as an integer (long or short), a floating-point number, a character, or some other atomic unit; types may also reference a class.

A class also defines a set of *methods* that can be applied to objects of that class. The set of methods defines the behavior of the class. Each method has a name and zero or more arguments, each of which has a type. Languages like LISP and Smalltalk are less stringent in their enforcement of types. The typing is still present, but it is checked at run time. For our discussion, these differences between typed and typeless are not critical.

In some models, the fields are hidden behind methods so that any access to read or set a field will in principle pass through some method. In much of the pseudocode in this book, it will be assumed that fields are directly accessible since this will improve clarity. It should be noted, however, that a major problem in user interface software is the ability to update a display whenever some aspect of a displayed object is changed. For this reason, in some discussions it will be assumed that fields are accessed through methods that can be programmed to handle the update of the display.

To illustrate some of the communication complexities in user interface software, consider the following example. In Figure 1-2, we had a variety of buttons of the form **B** *I* U . Each of these buttons behaves in exactly the same way with the exception of its label and the action it initiates. We can assemble this commonality into a class that has a field for the label and a field for the attribute (bold, italic, or underline) that is to be set. The class would also define a field for the document that these buttons control. When selected, they would send a message to the document to indicate the change of attribute. This class can have methods for receiving mouse input and for receiving notification that the selected text is or is not set according to the attribute. By defining a class of such buttons, we capture all that is common about them and create reusable objects that we can apply in multiple situations.

The most important concept about objects and classes is that each object carries with it (as defined by its class) a complete definition of how it behaves. This allows software to interact with that object while generally ignoring other concepts.

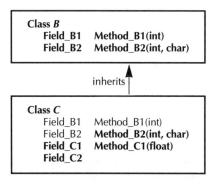

Figure 1-3   Class inheritance

Inheritance

An important part of object-oriented programming is the ability of a class to inherit from another class. If some class *C* inherits from another class *B*, we assume that the objects in class *C* possess all of the fields and methods that objects of class *B* would possess. If *C* inherits from *B*, then *B* is a *superclass* of *C* and *C* is a *subclass* of *B*. We also assume that any type that accepts an object of class *B* also accepts an object of any subclass of *B*. This works because anything that can be done to objects of class *B* can also be done to objects of any of its subclasses, because they possess the same fields and methods. Although there are many formal aspects and possible variations on this theme, this definition of inheritance is sufficient for this text.

Figure 1-3 shows an example of *C* inheriting from *B*. When a class *C* inherits from class *B*, it can provide three kinds of additional behavior. The first is that it can define new fields in addition to those provided by *B*. In Figure 1-3, class *C* has added two such fields. Second, a subclass can define new methods. In our example, *C* has added the method *Method_C1*. Finally, a subclass can override or replace the implementations of some of the methods defined on *B*. An example of this is that *C* has redefined *Method_B2*. This overriding or replacement of methods allows class *C* to modify the behavior of *B* without changing the interface (the methods and their arguments) to *B*. Within the methods of class *C*, it is still possible to invoke the original methods of *B*, even though they may have been overridden.

Many object-oriented languages allow a class to have only one superclass. This *single-inheritance* model is efficient to implement and simple to define. Many languages, however, allow a class to inherit from more than one superclass. Such *multiple inheritance* simplifies some problems in modeling the real world. There are, however, technical problems in implementation and some definitional problems in resolving conflicts between superclasses. In general, this text assumes single inheritance.

Abstract Classes

Much of the claimed advantage of inheritance is that it allows for reuse of code. By creating a subclass *C* of *B,* we can use much of the behavior and implementation of *B* by defining only what is different, rather than completely redefining and reimplementing the class. This model of reuse is very important to object-oriented interface tool kits, which will be described later. This is not, however, the most important use of inheritance in user interfaces.

Using the model of inheritance that we have defined, we can create the notion of an *abstract class.* We define abstract classes primarily for their interfaces because we can then define a variety of subclasses that will all have the same interface but may have very different behaviors.

For example, we can define the class Student, which has Name, Age, Address, and ID fields. This class also has the methods Enroll, RegisterForClass, and Expel. We may even provide a standard implementation for students in the class Student. We can, however, provide subclasses such as Senior, which has additional information relating to graduation. We might define the class Alumni, which has the RegisterForClass and Expel methods redefined to do nothing. We might also define the class ForeignStudent, which has a special implementation of Enroll and additional information about visa status. The key, however, is that the student registration system need only know about the class Student. Any subclass of Student can be entered into the registration system because they all conform to the same interface. This allows for a general registration system that can ignore much of the variety in the student body while still allowing that variety to exist.

In a user interface context, we can define the class Widget (a *widget* is a term used for buttons, scroll bars, and other interactive controls), which has a field for its Bounds (a rectangle defining the bounds of the widget in a window) and has methods for DrawSelf, MouseUp, MouseDown, MouseMove, and KeyInput. We can create a variety of subclasses for Widget such as PushButton, ScrollBar, CheckBox, or TextTypeIn. Each of these subclasses has very different behavior, but they all conform to the abstract class Widget.

Based on the abstract class Widget, we can write a window manager that can use any number of Widgets. It can assign them a Bounds based on the amount of screen space available and can forward interactive inputs to them through the various methods. It can also have them each draw themselves to create the screen display. The window manager only knows about the abstract class Widget. It need not know or care whether the Widget is a ScrollBar or TextTypeIn, as long as it has the appropriate fields and methods. We will use this concept of an abstract class extensively.

1.2.4 Commercial Tools

As the field of graphical user interfaces has grown, a variety of commercial tools have been developed. Accompanying those tools are a large number of books about programming with those tools. This is not one of those books. The goal here is to explain the root concepts that underlie such tools. The intent is to provide a framework of ideas around which the actual details of the various software packages can be learned as the need arises.

The commercial tools, however, do serve as excellent examples of various approaches to the problem. This book will not exhaustively cover the various tools, but it will reference the major approaches. There are three significant systems, which will repeatedly be referenced. These are the Macintosh tool box, Microsoft Windows, and X Windows/Motif. These systems are in such general use that references to their particular solutions are of practical importance. Occasional references are made to systems such as NeXTSTEP and NeWS.

There are also several object-oriented tool kits that provide reusable classes that can be subclassed to implement graphical user interfaces. The systems referenced most frequently are MacApp, the Borland class library for Windows, and InterViews.

1.3   An Overview of the User Interface

In order to set the stage for the discussions that follow, a discussion of the basic structure of a graphical user interface is in order.

1.3.1 The Interactive Cycle

The various software techniques discussed in this book are built around the interactive cycle illustrated in Figure 1-4. When an application appears on the screen, the user must understand what is displayed, evaluate what is presented, and formulate some desired change to the model. Having formulated a desired goal, the user will create a plan of action and generate inputs based on that action. The application software must then interpret those inputs and generate changes to the internal model that the program maintains. This internal model represents the current state of whatever the user is attempting to interact with. When the data model is modified by the code that is handling the inputs, it must generate updates that redraw those portions of the display that no longer reflect the new state of the model. The cycle then repeats.

For a concrete example, suppose that you are the author of this book and want to make corrections in the text. The application data model for your

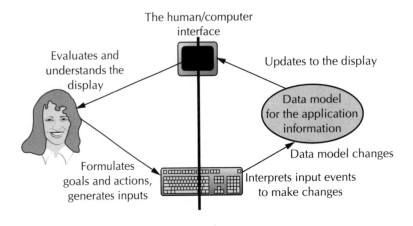

Figure 1-4   The interactive cycle

word processor consists of the document, paragraphs, sentences, characters, and drawings. In addition, there is other control information in the document, such as the current scroll position in the document and the current point for inserting characters or selected text. The word processor is responsible for presenting a clear, readable representation of the document. You as the author view the document and notice a poor phrase that needs rewording. You formulate a new phrase and then generate a series of mouse clicks and keystrokes that hopefully accomplishes the desired task. As each mouse click or keystroke is entered, some aspect of the data model is changed. In the case of mouse clicks, the selection point must be moved, and in the case of keystrokes, the text is modified. In response to each of these changes to the model, the display must be updated so the user clearly understands the new state of the document. Performing rapid updates of the display in response to user inputs is a key software problem in user interfaces.

This approach is highly simplified both in terms of the software processes and the user's cognitive and perceptual processes. It does serve, however, to lay out a broad sketch of the issues involved in user interface software.

One of the first things that becomes obvious from this approach is that the primary function of user interface software is the editing and manipulation of information. Admittedly, there are specialized applications where the primary function of the interface is to control some specialized process, but in terms of the user interface software, these are degenerate cases that are easily handled if you have mastered the concepts of interactive editing. Even in such cases, however, the model still holds because the operator is modifying the state of control variables and evaluating what is happening in the larger model of the process. Most graphical user interfaces, however, are basically information editing engines.

Gulf of Evaluation

Don Norman has identified two gulfs in a user's understanding that can cause this interactive cycle to break down. The first is called the "gulf of evaluation" and occurs when users look at the screen and must interpret what they see and then evaluate what they see relative to their ultimate goals. This evaluation of the visual state by the user and the user's memory of what has gone before forms the basis for the decisions that the user will make and the subsequent actions that he will want to take.

There are many ways in which this evaluation might fail. There are ergonomic factors that may cause evaluation problems. For example, the text may be hard to read. Important information may be presented in low-contrast colors and thus may be missed.

There are also design and layout problems that may cause evaluation to fail. Items may be ineffectively grouped so the user does not see an important relationship. The critical information may be incorrectly placed so that a quick scan of the display completely misses what is needed. All information may appear the same without emphasis or highlights, and thus important facts must be carefully searched for. (The most important role of a spell checker is to focus the user's attention on one word out of the thousands of words in a document. The word may actually be correctly spelled, but that automatic focus of attention is invaluable in proofreading a document.)

One aspect of this gulf of evaluation is timeliness. It is not enough to have the information on the screen in some form. It must be there in a form that can be evaluated without tedious analysis. Simple things must be immediately obvious.

A most disastrous form of the gulf of evaluation is when information about the relevant state is not even on the screen. In the old world of line-oriented editors, the entire document was invisible and had to be reconstructed from memory. In many current interfaces, information relevant to the behavior of the user interface may be invisible and thus may impair the user's ability to understand what should be done next to achieve a desired goal.

Gulf of Execution

The second problem is termed the "gulf of execution." Having seen and understood the visible state of the system, the user must determine what to do to accomplish the goal. The gulf of execution arises when a user does not know what sequence of input events will accomplish the desired goal.

There are many factors that cause this gulf. One of the first is lack of understanding on the part of the user as to what is even possible. For first-time users of computers, the relationship between the mouse and the objects on the screen is not obvious. Scroll bars have no meaning to people who have never used a computer. The image of a button is not sufficient for a user to understand that placing the mouse over the button and depressing a button on the mouse is the same as having pressed the equivalent physical button. Consistent interface design can help resolve this problem because users can carry over concepts of what inputs will have effects on the visual objects. For new techniques, a training and exploratory process is needed.

A second cause is inadequate feedback in response to inputs. If a user generates inputs and the resulting visual feedback does not indicate that the user is getting closer to the desired goal, confusion results. One of the tenets of direct manipulation is that users can safely explore the interface. This aids in overcoming the gulf of evaluation problem by allowing users to try out possible actions. If the feedback is poor, however, users may terminate a fruitful course of action because they do not perceive it as leading to the desired goal.

I personally faced the gulf of execution while drawing Figure 1-4. I had decided to try a new draw package that has more power than my normal tool. What I wanted to do was draw arrows. I could see where to click to draw lines but could not find arrows. I checked various menus where they were on my old system but there were no arrows. I looked at the palette of line styles but there were no arrows. After poking various places and not finding any help button, I finally noticed that the palette of line styles had a scroll bar. I scrolled the bar and there were the arrows. I clicked on one that looked like what I wanted and went happily on my way. The gulf of execution arose when I could not construct a sequence of inputs that would produce the result that I wanted.

When using this same draw package, I attempted to create centered text. I selected the text-centering option from the menu, clicked on the desired location, and proceeded to type. The text did not appear centered on my selection point as in other draw programs but extended to the right as if it were left justified. After making several attempts to solve this problem, I decided to accept left-justified text and continued to work. When I entered the second line, the text began to center on itself, not on my selection point. All that I had done was correct but the feedback did not so indicate. If the user does not understand the sequence of inputs that will produce a result, the gulf of execution appears and the interactive cycle is seriously impaired.

Model Sufficiency

A final usability problem that deserves overall attention is the sufficiency of the model that the program is actually manipulating. For example, consider the standard home VCR. The popular media have commented freely on the inability of the average consumer to program a VCR to record at a particular time. Many aspects of this problem can be identified by analyzing the gulf of evaluation (the same LEDs are used for both start time and end time) and the gulf of execution (the information is changed using a complex combination of shift, increment, and decrement buttons). There is a problem, however, with the actual model.

The normal model for VCR programming is that the user wants to manipulate the channel, day of the week, start time, and end time for a given recording session. In reality, this is not the way users think about VCR recording at all. Most users have a specific program in mind, such as "the final episode of *Star Trek: The Next Generation*," and just want it to be taped. The model, based on start and end times, is tuned to the needs of the VCR, not to the user's tasks. There are a number of proposals for VCRs that address this issue, including special codes in the program guides that the VCR would understand or interactive menus provided by the cable TV service. None of these, however, would be discovered by careful ergonomic analysis of the buttons and lights. It is of overriding importance to know and understand the user's model of the task being addressed.

There is another modeling problem when programming your VCR. If the user wants to program a particularly long movie such as *Gone with the Wind*, and has the VCR set to record on short play with highest quality, there are no videotapes capable of holding that recording. To record over a long time period on a single tape requires the VCR to be set to extended-recording mode with lower image quality. The VCR has all of the information to make such judgments and to issue a warning, but no VCR does this. Instead, the user watches the tape for two hours to the point where Ashley is wounded, Scarlett is in a tizzy, and the tape ends. Serious user dissatisfaction sets in at this point. Again, it is the underlying application model itself that is incomplete.

1.3.2 The Interactive Porthole

An important characteristic of graphical applications is that all interaction must take place through a relatively narrow view of the world. This narrow view is the interactive porthole. There are two issues here. The first is accommodating the limitations of computer displays. The second is accommodating the limitations of human attention.

Limited Display Space

For those who have grown up in the DOS and PC world, the interactive porthole is 640×480 pixels. Yes, there are better resolution displays for such machines, but it seems that such a narrow view of the interactive world is ingrained in the culture. A large amount of code for MS Windows is still written with the implicit assumption that no window could ever get larger.

Even top workstations will not provide a view of the interactive world larger than 1200×1200. The only exception to this are systems that will support multiple monitors, effectively producing a potentially large work space. A major portion of an interface design involves presenting the critical part of a potentially large application model through the interactive porthole. A simple example of this is the presentation of a large document in a window that can only display a few dozen lines. It is important to point out that the design of the interactive porthole is rarely as simplistic as a panning window on a linearly organized document. The information in application models rarely has such a uniform structure.

Designing the information porthole is critical to reducing both the gulf of evaluation and the gulf of execution. A useful example is the decision to view an American football game on television or in person. American football is a useful example because, unlike basketball or European football, the play is not continuous. Viewing the game in person, you see the entire field and can watch the play unfold as receivers and running backs execute various patterns and the defenders pursue their planned strategies. The problem is that you don't get much of a perception of the kinds of moves being done by the quarterback or the personal battle between the center and the defensive nose guard. If the quarterback fakes effectively, you may lose the play entirely by watching the wrong player. At the game, the scope is large but the focus is poor.

You can resolve this focus problem with a pair of binoculars. You can see every blow and facial expression between the center and the nose guard, but you quickly lose sight of the ball and miss the drift of the whole play. Now the focus is very fine but you have lost the global view.

An alternative is to watch the game at home on television. In this environment, the camera follows the ball through the entire play (unless the cameraman gets lost). When play stops, the announcers use instant replay to highlight the other action that occurred, which may not have been visible in the primary camera view. You are shown the crossing pattern of the first receiver that opened up an area for the second receiver. You might be shown a particularly good block by a lineman that made a spectacular run possible. The time between plays is used to fill in the informational gaps created by the highly focused television camera. Each fragment of information, however, is delivered with much greater focus than the spectators in the stands will ever get. Television is still not the same as being at the game, however, because you lose the excitement of the crowd, and the collection of analyzed fragments does not necessarily give you the grasp of the whole. One approach is to take a TV with you to the game or to rent a very expensive box seat that has TV service.

Limited Focus of Attention

A key to designing an effective information porthole is the focus of attention. This focus of attention is not necessarily an artifact of graphical user interfaces. Take, for example, the text that you are currently reading. Focus your eyes on any word on this page. Without moving your center of focus from that word, attempt to read something from three lines above or three lines below your focus point. The geometric distance between your focus word and the other text is actually quite small, and if you allow your eyes to roam freely, you skip between lines without a lot of effort.

This word focus example demonstrates the ergonomic issues in visual focus. The football example demonstrates issues in the architecture of how the information should be viewed. There are also implementation issues. Manipulation of the currently selected object allows for several optimizations in the software. In general, the loop shown in Figure 1-4 of "user generates input, the inputs are interpreted, the data model is changed, the screen is updated" can be too slow for smooth interaction. We can sometimes short-circuit that loop temporarily in order for the current focus of attention to produce acceptable response in a very local way, with the more global changes taking place when some closure or completion of the action occurs. An example of this would be the Macintosh or MS Windows directory interfaces dragging a cartoon or outline of a file icon rather than the full icon because this technique allows for more efficient dragging. When the mouse is released, the actual change is made to the directory model and the screen is more accurately updated.

1.3.3 The Interface Design Process

Based on the preceding discussion, it is now time to lay out a general process for creating a new graphical user interface. The process described in this section is open to disagreement from other development process models proposed elsewhere in software engineering. This rather cursory overview of the design process serves as the overall outline of the remainder of the text.

It is most important to point out that this process is *not linear*. You do not start at the beginning and work through, ticking off steps as you go. As shown in Figure 1-1, the user interface design process is iterative. Evaluation needs to be performed at each step, and when problems are found, decisions and implementation must be corrected in whatever phase of the design is deficient.

Analyzing the Task

The first and most important step in designing any interactive system is to analyze the tasks that users actually want to perform. If the system does not assist users in performing tasks that are of interest to them, users will not buy the product and the system designers will be out of a job. In general software engineering texts, this step is called *requirements analysis.* Among user interface folks, it is called *task analysis.* The goal of this step is to understand what the user wants to accomplish, the strategies the users use in meeting their goals, and the information and techniques that they apply to the problem. This information is essential to designing a system that solves the problems.

As a simplifying assumption, let us assume that the output of this step would be a set of task scenarios. These would be representative tasks that a user needs to be able to accomplish with the new system. These scenarios should include descriptions of the information that the user will need to accomplish this task, terminology and symbols that are already common in the user domain, and descriptions of how these tasks are currently accomplished. Also of importance is information about software that the users are currently familiar with.

Designing the Functional Model

Having in mind the things the user wants to accomplish, we must define an application model that facilitates those goals. This functional model defines the essence of what the system is capable of. This application model does not include details like command key bindings or graphical layouts. This is a definition of the data model that the user manipulates by means of the new user interface. The structure of this model, and actions that can be performed on the model, define the range of capabilities of the user interface. No amount of pretty graphics or keyboard accelerators will compensate for a lack of functionality, nor will they compensate for poorly designed functionality.

There is a chicken-and-egg problem in designing functionality and designing visual appearance. Most users can readily understand the concreteness of screen designs. The problem, however, is that in large systems, functionality lasts through many interactive incarnations of a product. A careful design of the function to be performed can allow for wide variation in proposed externals of the design. On the other hand, for many users the externals are the function. Suffice it to say that this is an iterative process. The functional model forms a useful interface between those who focus on users and those who focus on implementation.

The functional model design, in general, consists of the classes of objects that can be represented in the system. These classes are arranged into superclass/subclass relationships not only for the purpose of implementation but as a model for how the user will understand and conceptualize how the model behaves. Each class is characterized by the information stored for objects of that class (fields) and the actions that can be performed on those objects (methods). An important part of the set of actions is a representation of which information about the object can be changed by the user and how the user can do that. Much of the information represented is to inform rather than to be manipulated directly. This needs to be clear in the design.

An important point to understand is that "user friendly" does not mean "user dumb." Users who design aircraft do not use a simple drawing program like MacDraw. The nature and sophistication of their problems go far beyond putting lines on paper. The functional model must represent the complexity of the tasks such users are faced with.

Complexity is a two-edged sword. As the functionality of an application grows, the ability for the user to comprehend all of its functionality diminishes. Great application design frequently comes from reconceptualizing how the problem is structured. Design breakthroughs occur when several different task concepts can be clearly represented in a single, clear, uniform model.

Take, for example, a word processor. We might give a word processor the notion of books, chapters, sections, subsections, and paragraphs. Or we might create the notion of a hierarchy of text units with headers. The first model has five different concepts that must be implemented in the software and learned by the user. Each concept has its own unique twist. The model is also somewhat inflexible in that documents that have some other level or grouping (such as abstract or summary) must be forced into this model. The hierarchy model, however, has only the concept of units and headers. There is much less for a user to learn and much less complexity to the software.

However, the simplification of the functional model must not ignore the tasks that the user must accomplish and must not lead the user into the "Turing tar pit." All programs can be implemented on a Turing machine; however, the model is so simplistic that nothing can be implemented effectively. The same can happen to overly simplified functional models.

The only way to resolve issues of complexity versus simplistic elegance is to repeatedly evaluate the model against the task analysis and with real users. Too many specialized features may cause confusion. A few primitives that must be repeatedly and tediously composed to get anything done may cause frustration. Only repeated evaluation against knowledge of the user's needs will resolve these issues. *There is no formula for optimal design.*

The design of this functional model is not just a usability question; there are serious software architecture questions here. It is one thing to design a VCR that assumes that program information will be available over the cable TV network and can be browsed by those wanting to program their VCR; it is quite another thing to actually deliver the information necessary for the model to work. Many of us remember the bad old days of line-oriented text editors. The fact remains that wishing for full-screen editors would not have helped. There were not enough machine cycles available to update the screen to support a full-screen editor. A student using an on-line registration system may want to request "any schedule between eight and noon that is 16 credit hours and fills requirements for my major." However, the computational cost of such an algorithm would be prohibitive and the current state of expert-systems practice may render the result unsatisfying.

Designing the Presentations

Having a functional model of all information the user can interact with and all things the user can do with that information, we need to design a visual presentation of the model. The visual presentation of the information is critical for reducing the gulf of evaluation. Visual presentation of the actions the user can take is essential to reducing the gulf of execution. For example, it must be visually clear which data can be changed by the user and which are simply displayed as information.

There are a variety of usability questions related to the design of the visual presentation. There are questions of recognition. For example, in a file system, do the files look sufficiently different from the directories so that they are easily recognized? In my first experience with the Macintosh, I encountered an icon in a paint program that looked like this ⬚. For the longest time I could not understand what the "brick" icon did until someone told me that it was an eraser. For me, at least, it did not look like an eraser.

There are ergonomic questions related to how people perceive images. For example, people have a very difficult time seeing small blue objects. Blue on red is very poor for recognition. Different fonts have different readability characteristics. The number of colors that people can discriminate in terms of choices is important.

I recently used a program for retrieving text from a large CD-ROM database of religious materials. Their task analysis had shown that users of this product frequently wanted definitions and Greek, Latin, or Hebrew derivations for words. Based on their analysis, they provided a lexicon of such definitions. To access the lexicon, you double-click on a word. To reduce the gulf of execution, they highlighted every word in the body of the text that also has a definition in the lexicon. The only problem is that they chose to highlight with pale green letters on a white background. Since in some sections a large number of the words are in the lexicon, major pieces of text are very difficult to read due to the poor contrast between foreground and background. This product had shipped before its graphical presentation had been evaluated by users.

In designing the visual presentation, there are software issues that must also be addressed. One of the major parts of the software architecture is the timely update of the display in response to changes to the application data model. A large part of the efficiency of the resulting system lies in getting this display update architecture right. Implementation issues at this point may dictate a change in the presentation design. A large consideration will be the kinds of changes that a user can interactively make to the model that must then be mapped to changes to the display.

A major software problem is the handling of multiple views of the same information. A given class of objects may have a variety of ways in which it is presented. Working with mathematical formulae, the user might at various

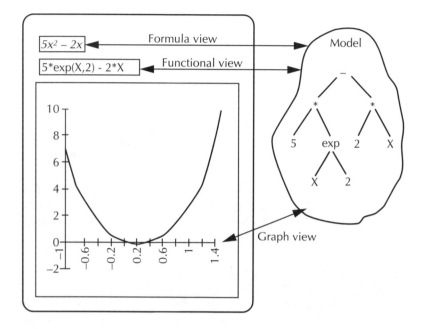

Figure 1-5   Models and views

times want to see the notational display of a formula, a functional form, or a graph of the potential values, as shown in Figure 1-5.

Each of these views supports a particular purpose and any or all of them may be displayed at the same time. If the user changes the coefficient from 5 to 6 by typing in the functional view, the functional view must notify the model of the change and the model must inform each view that it must be updated in its own way. The number of different views of an object may vary under user control and this too adds to the complexity of the software architecture.

Designing the Interactive Porthole

Having designed the model and how the information in the model is to be presented, we need to design how that information should be organized so that it fits onto the screen. There are a variety of mechanisms for accomplishing this goal. Information can be laid out on a 2D plane and a window can be scrolled over that space to select a view that will fit on the screen. This mechanism is used by drawing programs and word processors. Outline or tree models are possible, where subpieces that are not currently of interest can be replaced by ellipses. This preserves a view of the overall structure while reserving most of the screen space for the current focus of attention. A graph

Figure 1-6   Two presentations of text

model is possible, where the current object of attention is visible with various selection points that can lead to other information. In some cases, optical metaphors such as zoom in and zoom out can provide a model for touring the information.

The interactive porthole not only applies to information that is to be displayed but also to the visual representations of possible actions. For a commercial-grade word processor, the number of possible actions is so large that it would take more than a screen to completely represent them, leaving no space for the information being acted upon. Pull-down and pop-up menus were created to solve just this problem. Using menus, actions can be easily retrieved without requiring that they continuously occupy screen space.

One of the advantages of a good direct-manipulation interface is that if you can see an object on the screen, you can manipulate it. In designing the interactive porthole, this also has a down side. If you can't see it, you can't manipulate it. One of the usability issues in designing the porthole concerns how you can access and manipulate objects that are not visible at the time.

The design of the interactive porthole is driven by the task structure. As tasks are partitioned into related groups, presentations can be organized that provide the information needed for those tasks and the actions that are used in those tasks. This takes advantage of the fact that a user cannot do everything at once, and therefore the interface does not have to present everything at once. What is required is that the interface present information and capabilities in a form that closely relates to the way users would regularly use them.

Designing the Actions

Having designed the model, the way in which the model is visualized, and having organized that visualization within the constraints of screen space and user focus, we can now design the actual techniques for manipulating the objects. This is rarely a separate phase of development and will frequently be done concurrently with the presentation and organization designs. One of the reasons for designing the visuals in consort with the interaction is shown in Figure 1-6. These are two instances of the same piece of text. One looks like a static presentation of some information and the other has the appearance of a physical button that can be pressed. This button's appearance of being active is important in reducing the gulf of execution. These visual invitations to interact are called *affordances.* There are a variety of such techniques, which we will look at later. The use of standard affordances has a lot to do with the look and feel of an interactive environment.

Another usability issue that arises when implementing the actions of a user interface is the selection and use of interactive input devices. There are a variety of devices for generating input. Each of them has a certain behavior in terms of the way that users physically interact with it. Almost all graphical interfaces today are based on a mouse. The mouse is an excellent pointing and selecting device because it directly maps the natural motion of the forearm and wrist to movements on the 2D screen.

The mouse, however, is very poor for drawing, sketching, or signing your name. The large muscles of the forearm and wrist do not have the fine control for such activities. Pen input is better for these activities because it uses the fine muscles of the fingers. A pen, on the other hand, is much worse than the mouse when used in conjunction with a keyboard. This is because grasping the mouse after typing is a very simple activity that rarely requires looking at the mouse. Picking up a pen from the desktop is much slower because you have to look for the pen and carefully pick it up rather than just lay your hand on top of it.

A simple usability experiment you can do yourself is to lay a pen (with the cap off) next to your mouse. Place your hands on the keyboard and then pick up the pen and get it into writing position. Put the pen down (without allowing it to roll off the table) and put your hand back on the keyboard. Now reach over and click the mouse. Repeat this several times and the usability issues become obvious.

Actually programming the interactive behavior is difficult for most programmers who have not done previous user interface work. The problem is that the user, not the software, is in control. The difficulty is to create a software architecture that can handle any legal user input at any time the user wants to present such an input. These inputs must be assembled into coherent chunks of behavior and translated into manipulations on the application model. The architecture used in modern user interfaces is the event-dispatching model discussed in Chapter 2.

1.4 Summary

The essence of an interactive system is to 1) present a visual representation of the application model for this system, 2) interpret user inputs and translate those inputs into changes to the model, and 3) translate changes to the model into changes in the visual presentation. These are the software architecture problems that we will address in the majority of this text.

Paramount to these software problems are issues of usability. We must design our application model around the tasks that users are actually trying to accomplish. We must present the model on the screen in a way that allows the user to clearly and quickly evaluate the state of the model. We must present interactive affordances that make it easy both conceptually and physically for users to generate inputs to change the model in desired ways. If we can do all of this in cost-effective ways that serve real user needs, we will be successful.

2

Designing the Functional Model

Before designing screen layouts, widget selections, and menu organizations, we first need to understand the tasks and problems that our prospective users face. We must remember that the vast majority of the people in the world see a computer as a necessary evil that assists them in accomplishing their real goals. Those of us who pursue computing for the sheer joy of it are a very small minority. In this chapter, we will discuss task analysis, which is a process for understanding and capturing user goals and needs. We will then use this task analysis to produce a functional design of what the interface is to accomplish. We want to do all of this before we begin actual interface design so that we have a clear image of what we are trying to build.

To understand the tasks and problems of prospective users, we need to capture a description of the information that users need in order to accomplish those tasks. At this point in our design process, we want to understand all of the required information that a user needs rather than just that set of information that we intend to encode in the computer. Remember our interactive process from Chapter 1. A user will attempt to perceive what is displayed on the screen and to mentally combine that information with other required information in order to decide what to do next. If we are to design a good interactive solution, we must understand all of the information required, including items that a user must remember or obtain from other sources.

2.1 Examples of Task-Oriented Functional Design

In order to better understand the impact of functional design, we will consider several examples.

2.1.1 Line-Oriented vs. Full-Screen Text Editors

A good illustration is found in the history of text editors. In the period immediately following the demise of punched cards, there were a variety of text editors that allowed users to interactively modify text files. The dominant model
provided an interactive interface to a virtual deck of numbered cards. Based on
this functional model, users could

- specify a range of card numbers to be deleted
- specify a card number at which to start inserting new lines (cards)
- specify a range of card numbers to be listed on the screen or printer

In this functional model, the users were required to visualize the document
being edited in their mind. The task, of course, was and still is to change a text
document consisting of lines, but only the current commands and most
recent listings were visually presented to the user. There were variations on
this model to improve its usability. Some systems fixed the card numbers so
that they would remain constant outside of the range currently being modified. This technique was useful in managing large programs. Other systems
provided an automatic listing of the lines (cards) within a neighborhood of the
current editing focus. In some systems, this model was moderately improved
by modeling the file as a stream of characters, with line breaks being encoded
as special characters.

In comparison to our current full-screen editors, which use direct-manipulation techniques, this line-oriented approach was extremely painful. Text
editors were bound by available machine cycles and by the model of text files
as decks of cards or streams of bytes. No amount of tweaking, command
renaming, key accelerators, or presentation techniques could overcome the
limitations of the line-oriented model. A fundamental change in the functional model was required. Once enough machine resources were available
and developers grasped the concept of maintaining an image of the document
on the screen and directly modifying that document, modern word processing
was born and text editing was vastly simplified. Until that fundamental
change in the functional model occurred, user productivity was stuck on a
plateau.

2.1.2 Word Processors

The transition from text editor to word processor is also instructive. When we
start to include features such as italics, bold, special fonts, outlining, styles,
and figures, the functional model of application again must fundamentally
change. The first issue is that we must design a data model that represents the
information being edited. In addition to the text itself, information about the
style, font, and alignment must be stored. The design of this functional model

constrains what is interactively possible later in the design and later in the lifetime of the application.

For example, Microsoft Word 6.0, the application used to create this book, has in its functional model the concept of a style, which is a collection of settings specifying font, alignment, underlining, etc. A style can be given a name and that style can be invoked by name in a variety of places in a document. Changing the style will change all of the places in the document that have that style. This is a very nice feature and I use it frequently.

In Microsoft Word 5.0, however, styles were attached to paragraphs. Inside a paragraph, individual words and characters could have their font attributes changed, but could not be given a style. This functional model had previously prevented me from creating a style called Emphasis, which I could have put on any text that I wanted to stand out. I would have liked to do this since various journals have different requirements as to how things should be emphasized. Some want boldface, some italics, and some underlining. If I could have used a style on individual words, this would have been trivial. The functional model, however, dictated that styles were only on paragraphs and that I must interactively perform my desired task by hand without the assistance of styles. (Note that Microsoft Word 6.0 corrected this problem.)

2.1.3 Why Do Secretaries Have Typewriters?

In the days of word processors and laser printers, which can produce far better output than a typewriter, why does every secretary have a typewriter? My secretary despises the typewriter but uses it almost every day. With an obvious preference by the user (my secretary) for the word processor and obvious usability problems with the typewriter (error correction), why is this relic of the past still in common use? This is exactly the kind of question that user interface designers should be asking and answering long before any code is written or any screens are designed. This is the role of task analysis and functional model design. The answer to why users still use the typewriter is the need to create labels, envelopes, and forms.

The issue of labels and envelopes is mostly a hardware problem. Many laser printers will not accept labels or envelopes. Among those that do, loading a label or an envelope into the printer is more effort than banging it out on the typewriter. Obviously, there are solutions available to the label and envelope problem, but in terms of effort they are not effective for small jobs of one or two rather than 50 or 100. The average secretary weighs the options and types the address with the typewriter. In the case of labels and envelopes, the user has performed an almost automatic work-flow optimization.

Forms are a slightly different problem. Preprinted forms are a problem for computers because there is an unwritten law that states that the alignment of the boxes on the form must be aligned differently from most printers. This means that if you use a computer to fill out the form, you must work very hard to make sure that all of the information fits into the right places. Most secretaries optimize this by using the typewriter instead, because the alignment problems are immediately obvious and can be corrected on the fly. Functionally, however, the typewriter is terrible for forms because it cannot compute totals, taxes, fringe benefit rates, or any of a number of other things that I must do to fill out the forms in my life. As a user, I have solved this by designing spreadsheets that look almost exactly like the various forms that are required in my department. I enter data into the spreadsheet, print it, and then give the printed copy to the secretary, who types the information on the required form with the typewriter! I have optimized my personal work flow and the secretary gets paid to interface my life with the university's requirements.

We could think more carefully about this process and simply use the output of my spreadsheet as the form. At this point, we run into that curse of modern bureaucracy, the multicolored, multipart, carbonless form. The laser printer cannot compete with the typewriter in the generation of carbonless forms. We could make four copies of my spreadsheet printout and submit them stapled together. If we did that, however, the dean and various vice presidents would have to sign four times (once on each copy) rather than just once. In addition, the functionaries who originally designed the form would end up with a white rather than a goldenrod form and the whole system would be out of whack. The most disheartening part of this story is that when the form reaches its final destination, someone is paid to enter the information into a computer because the receiving organization cannot afford to manage all of that information on paper.

The point of this discussion is that the cultural and informational context in which our interactive system must exist is very important to our task analysis and functional design. It is easier for our office to pay someone to retype forms than to wrestle with the university about changing their process. These kinds of realities face potential users of interactive software in numerous ways. If the software does not solve these real problems effectively, the software will not be used. A second point is that whoever designed the university system did not take into account the total effort required. In performing their task analysis, they only considered the information management cost to their own office without evaluating the problems of all those who must generate the input to their office. Our research office, for example, accepts a single copy of their forms, which can be generated from spreadsheets, and then redistributes copies of the approved forms to those who need them. This is slightly more expensive for their office but much more effective for the university as a whole.

Considering the whole problem rather than the local manifestations can be very important for developing good solutions. The envelope/label problem can

be sharply diminished if email is possible with most corresponde
correspondence is not private and less than a page, a two-sided l
would allow printing the address on the back so that folding and s
all that is required for mailing. Automating university functions
remote entry would eliminate the forms. Optimizing only our department
office, however, leads to a frequently used typewriter.

2.2 Overall Approach

Having motivated the need for analyzing what users do and the context for
their work, we now take an overview of the process of such analysis. Following this overview, we will look at each step in detail.

Creating a functional model for an interactive application consists of essentially three steps: task analysis, evaluation of the analysis, and identifying the
objects, information, and actions that make up the model.

2.2.1 Task Analysis

The purpose of task analysis is to identify the goals and purposes of the
prospective user community and to understand what users do to achieve
those goals. Having understood how such goals are currently achieved, we
want to design ways that they might better achieve the desired results. There
are three important outcomes of this phase. The first is a set of plausible scenarios of user behavior. These are primarily goals that users might have, along
with conceptual outlines of how they might achieve those goals, augmented
by events that might cause problems along the way.

Accompanying these scenarios of use are lists of information objects that
users must have to accomplish their goals. Understanding the information
that users require for a task is essential for designing the user interface.
Clearly understanding a user's information needs is a requirement for effectively reducing the gulf of evaluation when the user is working with the user
interface.

Finally, our task analysis defines the set of actions that users can take.
These involve editing of information, making decisions, forwarding information to others, and possibly discarding unneeded materials. These actions
form the functionality that the computer is to provide.

2.2.2 Evaluation of the Analysis

Having produced sets of tasks, goals, scenarios, objects, and act
to understand how our users interact with all of these concepts
ing the users is critical to the quality of our user interface. The

aspects of our task analysis that we want to evaluate, including frequency of use, importance of various tasks, and how the system is used.

For each goal, task, object, and action it is important to understand how often each appears in everyday practice. The frequency of use of a design item impacts how we include that item in the interface. Items with a high frequency of use should be very fast, even if some training is required. Items that occur less frequently need not be optimized for speed but rather for ease of use, so that when they do arise users can quickly understand how to take the appropriate action. Very low frequency items may be omitted from the interface entirely so they do not clutter the design.

We need to evaluate the importance of each item in the overall set of tasks. Fire alarms are used very infrequently but they are very important. Likewise, critical pieces of information must receive special attention so they are not neglected or omitted by users.

It is also important to understand how the interface design fits into the context of work use. A key part of this is whether items are required or optional. Required tasks can involve training in how to perform them. My secretary must know how to process purchase orders because it is a required part of her job. Because of this, it is possible to require greater training on the purchasing process. Note that because such requirements are possible does not necessarily mean they are a good idea. Financial services organizations are notorious for requiring users to learn arcane procedures, simply because they have the power to force users to adapt. Tasks that are discretionary must be more inviting in their interfaces or they will simply be ignored. If the on-line university handbook is hard to use, individuals will either ignore it or call someone who should know the answer. Whenever people are faced with alternatives, they will select what is easiest to themselves, frequently optimizing the short term at the expense of long-term productivity.

2.2.3 Functional Design

Having thoroughly and carefully understood our users, their goals, and their environment, we finally define the functional model of our interface. This model defines the user/system boundary. We must carefully choose which information items will be modeled in the computer. These items are defined as classes of objects. For these classes, we define the items of information that our program will retain about objects in those classes and how those objects will interrelate. The actions that the system provides are defined as methods on those objects.

Note that although this functional design is couched in programming terms, it is not necessarily an implementation design. For example, we may have a list of inventory items in our functional design that has a method to search for items by supplier name. This is a functional view of what the user needs. There are still implementation issues as to how the data should be organized to perform the search. Whether we should use a B-tree or a linear list as our search structure is still to be decided but has no part in the functional interface design. The users do not care about these implementation issues, provided they are correct and performed in a timely fashion.

Having created our functional design, it must be evaluated in terms of our task analysis. We must take each of our scenarios and identify how it would be performed with our design and whether the criteria from our task evaluation have been met.

2.3   Task Analysis

With this overview of our design process in mind, we now begin our task analysis. Task analysis is the process of identifying the user tasks and how they might be addressed. This involves taking a careful look at what the users are trying to accomplish, the information they use as part of that process, the variations in the process, and the kinds of things that might go wrong. Because this book is primarily about software architecture, task analysis will only be addressed informally.

The primary lesson for software designers is that high-quality interactive software is designed around user tasks, not around simplifying the software architecture. Frequently, an elegant, flexible, and usable system will have an elegant underlying architecture, because good, consistent usability design usually has a straightforward logical structure. An elegant, consistent software architecture does not by itself lead to a usable system. A convoluted, confused, and poorly designed software architecture, however, frequently makes conceptually simple interactions very difficult to build. In all cases, however, the principle is that users are more important than algorithms in creating good user interface designs.

2.3.1   Examples of Task Analysis

The processes of task analysis and good understanding of the user have no known mathematical solution. There is no list of 12 things to do that guarantee a good design. Good designs come from wisdom, insight, careful and methodical work, and the discarding of a lot of designs that don't pan out. In this text, we discuss some example problems to illustrate the design process rather than provide formal models for that process.

In order to better understand the role and issues of task analysis, we will consider two examples. As noted before, programming a VCR to record at a later time has been widely reported as a user interface problem. In terms of goals there is only one: to have the VCR record the desired program. As another example, we will consider a student registration system for selecting courses. This is a more complicated problem because students have a wide variety of goals when planning a course schedule. In addition, the student's goals are not necessarily the same as those of the university registrar's office. Studying the differences between these viewpoints will be very instructive in understanding task analysis.

2.3.2 VCR Task Analysis

Our task analysis will proceed by answering the following questions:

- What do the users want to do?
- What information objects are required?
- What actions are required?

What Do the Users Want to Do?

Task analysis always begins with the question "What does the user want to do?" When considering the task of programming a VCR, the task is quite straightforward. If this problem is presented to the average programmer, the answer comes in terms of setting the start time, end time (or duration of the program), and channel to record. It is helpful, however, to lay out concrete scenarios for what a user wants to do. Here are several:

- I want to tape *The Cosby Show.*
- I want to tape the PBS special on Gettysburg this week.
- I want to tape a good old movie this afternoon so that I can watch it when I get home from work.

These scenarios of user goals are very instructive because they do not mention start times, end times, or channels. The scenarios are stated in terms of what users want to do rather than in terms of what the VCR needs to know in order to do them. Adopting the machine-oriented view (times and channels) rather than the user-oriented view (TV program) is a critical mistake that many programmers make in interface design.

While identifying goals, we also need to consider how the users will evaluate the quality of the solution. In our VCR example, users will make two evaluations. The first occurs at the time they complete their programming, and the second at the time they view the recorded program. The first evaluation can be stated as "Is the VCR programmed to record the show I want?" A good interface makes this evaluation by the user as straightforward as possible. The second evaluation is simple. The user watches the tape and spends his time either enjoying the show or commenting on the intellectual deficiencies of VCR designers.

When understanding how users will evaluate the results of their interface task, it is helpful to list the kinds of things that can go wrong and why. In our example, the usual problem of incorrect data entry causes some other program to be taped instead.

Another problem frequently not addressed by VCR manufacturers is when there is not enough remaining tape for the current record-mode settings. This results in heroes dangling over cliffs just as the tape ends. The fact that VCRs do not have sufficient sensors to detect how much tape is remaining does not eliminate user frustration when the tape runs out. Economics dictates that we need to eliminate some features for the sake of a cost-effective product, but task analysis is not the place to make these trade-offs. The purpose of task analysis is to understand the user's needs as clearly as possible so the impact of later implementation choices can be clearly understood.

What Information Objects Are Required by Various Agents?

Having defined our scenarios, we need to focus on agents and information. Agents are loosely defined as any processor or class of persons that can take some action. In our example, there are two agents: the user and the VCR. Every agent considers the information presented to it and takes some action. Making sure that sufficient information is available is an important part of the interface design. Considering all of the agents, in this case the user as well as the VCR, is important to the analysis.

To begin collecting information objects, we consider each scenario in turn. Let us take the first scenario, "I want to tape *The Cosby Show*." The user already knows that *The Cosby Show* comes on every weekday afternoon from 4:00–4:30 PM on channel 6. The VCR needs this same information, along with permission to actually record on the tape currently in the machine. Our information objects so far are

Start time, end time, channel

An important task-analysis question at this point is, "should the information be start/end or start/duration?" Algorithmically it doesn't matter much which is chosen. Selecting the one that users prefer is very important, however, particularly at this stage.

The second task, "I want to tape the PBS special on Gettysburg this week," is a little more complicated because the user knows that the program will be shown on PBS and presumably knows the channel (except in cities where there is more than one PBS channel). Knowing the network, however, is not the same as knowing the channel number. The user knows that the program is about Gettysburg and that it is on sometime this week. The user needs to locate and select the Gettysburg program. Based on this selection, the VCR still needs the start and end times and the channel. In addition, because the program might be on any of a number of days this week, the VCR needs to know the day of the week to do the recording.

There are several new information objects required for this task. The full list so far includes

- a listing of programs offered this week
- criteria for selecting a program
- program entries consisting of program title, start time, end time, day, and channel
- a selected program entry to be recorded
- the day of the week to do the recording

Some of the information is derived from other information. The selected program is selected from the program listing and the day of the week to record can be derived from the selected program entry.

In the last task, "I want to tape an old movie this afternoon so that I can watch it when I get home from work," the user does not even know the desired title. The user has in mind a type of movie and a time period and wants to scan a set of possible programs in order to select something to record. The additional information required is that each program entry should contain keywords for the program type and a program description.

Based on the previous analysis of the scenarios, we have the following information objects and attributes required to perform the various tasks:

List of Programs
ProgramEntry
    Name, Date, StartTime, EndTime, ProgramType, Channel
ProgramSearchCriteria
    NamePattern, DateRange, TimeRange, ProgramType
SelectedProgramEntry
RecordSession
    StartTime, EndTime, Date, Channel, RecordingMode
VCRStatus
    TapeIsEntered, RecordingEnabled, TapeLength, List of RecordSessions

What Actions Are Required?

Because we are using object-oriented design, we associate each of the actions with the class of object to which it applies. We take each object in turn and identify the actions that can be taken on that object. Many of the actions defined on objects consist primarily of editing the attributes of that object. For this reason, we specifically identify those attributes that have edit actions rather than enumerating actions for them, as follows:

List of Programs

      Search(ProgramSearchCriteria) -> List of Programs

      Select(ProgramId) -> ProgramEntry

   Editable attributes: none

ProgramEntry

   Editable attributes: none

RecordSession

      SetToProgram(ProgramEntry)

   Editable attributes: all

VCRStatus

      Insert(Tape)

      Remove() -> Tape

      EnterRecordSession(RecordSession, SessionSelector)

      DeleteRecordSession(SessionSelector)

   Editable attributes: RecordingEnabled

The task analysis for the VCR has been very informal. We have identified the goals, information objects, and actions required in programming a VCR. In particular, we have expanded our view to include the entire user task. This will be helpful later in our design process.

2.3.3 Student Registration Task Analysis

The student registration problem is more complex than our VCR example. We will not pursue this problem in as much depth due to its size. It will illustrate the value of task analysis in understanding the user's complete problem.

Who Are the Users?

In the VCR example, the fact that there is only one class of user, the owner of the VCR, simplifies the task analysis. The environment in which a student registration system must function is not so simple, because there are actually several users of a student registration system. The staff in the university records office must schedule class sections, keep the records accurate, and produce reports. The university administrators at various levels need to understand student enrollment patterns. The faculty need to know who is enrolled and need to approve adding and dropping of students in their courses after the semester starts. Finally, there are the students themselves. All of these classes of users must be considered.

After listing all of the classes of users who will be involved with the system, we can then do a more specific task analysis for each class of user. We also need to consider the relative importance of each class of user to the success of the system. In the case of student registration, the faculty are relatively unimportant because, in general, their role is only to be informed of who is in the class. Many student registration systems put the records office staff at the top of the importance list because their costs and issues are most obvious to those managing the registration system. Staff is an important class of users; however, good universities understand that students must be the top priority list since they and their supporters are the primary customers of the institution. For the remainder of this discussion, we look at the needs of the student.

What Do the Users Want to Do?

A student's goals in approaching registration are much more complicated than those of a VCR user. At a basic level, the goal of a student is to register for an acceptable list of classes. This goal is actually part of a larger set of goals that may include completing the requirements of a particular degree program, gaining specific skills for an immediate job need, pursuing a personal interest, or finding a place to enhance one's social opportunities. In general, the university registration system is not interested in the dating life of the student body, but the other goals are of interest. A university considers course offerings to be important contributions toward these life goals. In essence, that is the product that a university is selling. The university therefore wants to provide a registration system that helps students select a course schedule that meets those goals.

When a student approaches the registration system with a set of life goals (which may be very fuzzy), there are a number of issues that may be considered:

- What are the degree requirements?
- What are the university general education requirements?
- What courses are available?
- What am I interested in taking?
- How do I schedule around my part-time job?
- How do I schedule so I don't have to run back and forth across campus?
- How do I avoid taking philosophy from Schwartz?

We need to understand these issues in order to create a realistic and complete set of scenarios of how students will use our system.

Concrete Scenarios

We next create our list of concrete scenarios that a student will have when using our system. We also want to identify how students will evaluate the quality of the resulting schedule. We will also expand our study of student goals to look at what problems might arise as a student proceeds toward the goal. Identifying the set of things that might impede a user's achievement of a goal is very important in determining the breadth of functionality that real users need. These difficulties form part of the scenario set.

Goals   *I want to register for section 2 of CS 130.* In this case, the student knows exactly what he wants and simply needs a clean, obvious way to enter the information. The scenario might be to

- select CS 130
- select section 2
- complete the registration

We can take this first scenario, which allows the user to proceed directly to the desired goal, and explore the kinds of things that might go wrong. As every student knows, sections are frequently full. An alternative scenario for this goal might be to

- select CS 130
- find that section 2 is full
- select another section (based on the student's original criteria for choosing a section)
- complete the registration

Another problem faced by students trying to register occurs when all sections of a course are full or the possible alternatives conflict with previously scheduled classes. A third alternative scenario might be to

- select CS 130 and find that all sections are full
- consult degree requirements and classes previously taken
- select CS 125
- find that the only section of CS 125 is at the same time as BIO 210, in which the student is already registered
- consult the course availability and find another section of BIO 210
- select the new section of BIO 210
- select the section of CS 125
- complete the registration

The important point is that we must consider the user goals and all of the problems that may arise in attempting to meet those goals. We started out with a simple scenario for registration and identified several things that could go wrong. Using those possible problems, we created another scenario that arose when a section was not available. In working through that scenario, we considered the fact that no sections might be available. In each case, we worked out strategies that students might pursue in solving each of these problems.

This analysis is quite limited because we have not considered all the strategies that a student might use. For example, upon finding that CS 130 is full a student might prefer to get on a waiting list in case someone drops out of that section, or might get special permission to register for a section that is otherwise full. A common student strategy is to both register for CS 125 (as a backup) and still try to get into CS 130. If CS 130 becomes available, then CS 125 can be dropped; otherwise the student has the bases covered.

This process of creating scenarios cannot possibly be complete. If we take the set of student goals, the set of problems that can arise, and the set of problem-resolving strategies, the outer product of these sets is the set of possible scenarios. The difficulty is that this outer product is enormous and in many cases infinite. Even so, concrete scenarios do help in working out what the issues really are so that general solutions can be devised.

I want to take 6 hours that fill Computer Science degree requirements and 9 hours that fill university general education requirements. In this case, the goal is more general. The student is certain of what is desired, but the task is defined in terms of the life goals of the student rather than in terms of courses and sections. This complicates the scenario. Following good software design practice, we decompose this large, complex goal into intermediate goals and then work on each of them.

Goal: Register for the desired courses.

■ Select 6 hours of computer science courses for which the student already has the prerequisites and that fill degree requirements.
■ Select 9 hours of general education courses for which the student has taken the prerequisites and that satisfy requirements that the student has not already filled.
■ Select and schedule sections of the desired courses.

Subgoal: Select 6 hours of computer science courses that satisfy prerequisites and degree requirements.

■ Obtain a list of all required CS courses.
■ Filter out those courses already taken.
■ Filter out all courses for which the student does not have the prerequisites.
■ Select 6 hours of course work from the remaining list.

Subgoal: Select 9 hours of general education courses.

■ Obtain a list of the university general education requirements.
■ Filter out all requirements that are filled by classes the student has already taken.

- Replace any general requirements with specific requirements imposed by the degree program. (For example, our department requires PHYS 121, which also fills the university's physical science requirement.)
- Obtain lists of courses that might fill the remaining requirements.
- Filter out all courses for which the student does not have the prerequisites.
- Select 9 hours of courses from the remaining list.

Subgoal: Select sections for the selected courses. [This goal is similar to our previous goal of how to register for a specific section.] The goal/subgoal structure we have developed so far is very incomplete. An important problem to point out is that our hierarchical decomposition of the goal and subgoals may cause conflicts. For example, when selecting sections for the courses we may find that one of the biology classes and one of the computer science classes are only taught at the same time. The student must resolve this by reevaluating the selections made in satisfying previous subgoals.

The issue for us as interface designers is to clearly model the situation so that students can take informed alternative actions to resolve these conflicts. We may also want to enhance the capabilities of the system to warn students early in the process of making course selections that such problems might arise in satisfying the remaining goals.

Evaluation   Having completed all or part of the registration process, how will the student evaluate the result? We need to determine what a student uses as criteria for success in scheduling courses. This is important because we as interface designers must provide the user, in some form or another, with the necessary information to make these evaluations. The following is a list of questions that students might ask themselves:

- Did I get the classes I wanted?
- Do the classes fit around my job schedule?
- Do I have to run all over campus?
- Do I have my free time arranged in large chunks?
- Am I filling useful degree requirements?
- Do I have the courses I need as prerequisites for the courses I should take next semester?
- Do I like the teachers?

Creating lists of these questions is very important because we can use them later to evaluate our interface designs. If these are valid questions that users might ask, then we should look at our interfaces and ask those same questions to see if we can answer them. If those questions cannot effectively be answered given the current design, then we have a usability problem.

Note that the computer-based interface is not the only component that determines the usability of the system. Our later design may determine for various cost and organizational reasons that some of this information will not be on-line but rather in the printed university catalog. Even though the catalog may not be on-line, it is still a critical part of the usability of the registration system and it must be evaluated in that light.

Agents and Information

Having worked through a set of scenarios, we can now identify the information needed for each step in our scenarios. Note that we have not decided which agents will be responsible for this information or for the actions that must be taken.

In our scenarios, we defined a step where all CS courses already taken are filtered out of the list of CS requirements. In order to accomplish this step, a list of the courses already taken is required. Because most students know what courses they have taken, the user is the agent that performs this filter. It is also possible that the student's on-line transcript can be this information object. If the on-line transcript is to fill this role, then either the transcript is displayed so that the student performs the filtering or the computer can automatically perform the filtering.

It does not matter at this point if the student or the computer is the agent responsible for the list of classes already taken. It is also not important at this stage whether the student or the computer performs the filtering. Regardless of these agent-selection issues, the list of classes taken is the critical information object for this step in our scenario. Identifying all such objects and their actions is the critical foundation to the rest of our design. Even though we are not going to make assignment of actions and information to agents at this time, we must consider all such agents in determining what the information and actions should be.

There is a caveat to ignoring agent assignment at this stage. If some agent other than the user performs a particular task, the user needs some confidence that the right thing has been done. Take, for example, the task where all CS courses for which the student does not have the prerequisites are filtered out. If this is done automatically from the student's transcript, a particular student might be confused as to why a class does not appear in the list of possible classes.

Because the filtering was automatic, the student may or may not understand that CS 232 is not in the list of possible classes because CS 142 is a prerequisite and is not in the student's transcript. In the case of the computer as agent, it is important that the user be able to ask why particular actions are taken. In our example, CS 232 was filtered out because the transcript did not contain CS 142. Understanding this, the student may accept this and register for CS 142, or may need to point out that CIS 101, which was taken at Somewhere Tech, is equivalent to CS 142 at our university. When agents other than the user are taking action, it is frequently the case that the user needs to understand what action was taken, why it was taken, and how it can be overridden.

As a counter example to the user's need to know, we can consider aircraft flight controls. In early airplanes, every pilot knew how the stick was connected to the control surfaces by cables and what each movement of the stick did to those control surfaces and how it would affect the flight of the plane. In modern jet aircraft, there is no such clear connection between the stick and the control surfaces. Flight computers and other devices act as agents that translate the pilot's desires (as expressed through the stick) into movement of the control surfaces. Because the relationship between stick movement and plane movement is very clear to the pilot, the agent mechanism that connects the two is no longer important. How much a user needs to know about how and what computing agents have done for them is very much a part of the art of user interface design.

What Are the Objects and What Are Their Attributes?

As with our VCR example, we need to review our scenarios to determine the types of objects and what attributes they must have. The object analysis of a student registration system is far beyond this text. We can, however, work through a part of our scenarios to derive a portion of the object/attribute space.

In our first scenario for the goal "register for section 2 of CS 130," there are only a few information objects required:

List of Courses

Course

      Department, CourseNumber

List of Sections

Section

      Course, SectionNumber

Schedule

      Student, List of Sections

In the second scenario, the problem of a section being full arises and the student must select another course. This involves adding SectionSize and NumberEnrolled to a Section so that it can be determined whether or not a section is full. We also need to attach a ListOfSections to each course so students can choose alternatives, even though our scenario is not clear on what the student's criteria will be for choosing another section. At this point, we would need to refine the scenario and then continue this analysis. Suppose that students indicate they choose sections based on the time they are offered and on the instructor. We would need to add ClassTime, ClassDays, and Instructor attributes to the Section so that students would have the necessary information to make their selection.

The remainder of the analysis would proceed as described above. For each step in each scenario, we determine what information is needed to take that step. By proceeding through all of our scenarios, we can build a complete model of the information requirements of our interactive system. A complete interactive system involves more than the software in the computer. It is the complete information and action context in which users attempt to achieve their goals.

Actions

Either after or during our information analysis of the scenarios, we need to determine the set of actions that can be performed on each of our objects. For example, most of the actions performed on the list of courses consist of selections. We remove courses without prerequisites; we select courses that meet specific graduation requirements.

In the case of the Schedule object, the actions might include adding a section, deleting a section, checking for conflicts, confirming the schedule for registration, and printing the schedule. Again, by working through the scenarios we build up this list of actions that must be provided to enable the desired behavior.

In many interfaces, a majority of the actions modify information objects. Drawing programs, for example, consist entirely of creating and modifying drawing primitives. In our student registration problem, we have only considered the student's needs, so the only information that can be edited is the student's schedule. From the university registrar's point of view, we would need to provide actions to add and delete sections; and to change section times, places, days, and instructors. All such actions would need to be accounted for in our object/action model.

2.4   Evaluation of the Analysis

As with all parts of user interface design, it is critical that we evaluate our design relative to the needs of real users. It is one thing to sit in a conference room and invent plausible scenarios of how users might want to solve their problems; it is quite another thing to work with actual users in understanding their problems. In evaluating our task analysis, we must answer the following questions:

- Have we captured or characterized all of the goals of our users?
- Do we understand the relative importance of each of these goals?
- Is our set of scenarios representative of the kinds of things that might happen when users attempt to meet their goals?
- Do users really behave like this?
- In particular, have we captured all of the things that might go wrong and the strategies that users apply in solving those problems?
- Do we understand the relative frequency of the various problems that might arise?
- Have we captured all of the ways in which users evaluate the results of their work?

2.4.1 Understanding the User

The goal of a user interface is to help users meet their goals. An understanding of user goals and the strategies used to reach those goals is critical to good interface design. It cannot be stressed enough that the key to successful user interface design is to understand the needs of the prospective users.

Obtaining a clear understanding of user needs is not, however, a simple matter of watching them or asking them what they want. Most users do not spend a lot of time thinking abstractly about the way their work is accomplished. Many users have very good ideas for localized improvements to their work practice; few users can suggest a radical rethinking of their process.

A critical component of understanding the users is to obtain a clear understanding of the goals and problems they face. In our VCR example, we could interview a large number of users trying to program their VCR and get a lot of suggestions concerning new buttons or readouts on the face of the VCR. Few users would suggest providing bar codes in the TV listing that would automatically program the VCR. If, however, we get a clear understanding of what users are trying to accomplish, we can invent alternative ways to meet those goals.

As important as goals are, however, an understanding of actual work practice is also important. The way users do things now is the result of intelligent human beings adapting themselves to the actual challenges of their jobs. In any significant market for software, there has been far more user time spent trying to be successful at an application than there will ever be invested in user interface design.

A specific case is helpful in understanding user input to user interface design. A large word processing company is delivering a successful product to text-based DOS computer users. Market research shows that the installed base of computers is overwhelmingly dominated by text-only machines. To stay in touch with their users, the company provides a helpline that users can call with their problems. The company keeps careful logs of these problems as well as the features that users say they want. When new features are added to the user interface, they are always the ones for which there is a large user demand. Based on this strategy, the company is very successful at selling periodic upgrades filled with features that exactly match the needs of a large segment of the market.

What this careful market-driven approach does not account for, however, is that all of the users providing input are only responding in the context of the existing product. Users do not call hotlines to provide their blue-sky ideas for the way they wish things were. A secretary trained on a typewriter and retrained in text-based DOS will rarely say, "My boss would really like to import a segment of a spreadsheet into this document as a pie chart, with the other text flowing around the chart in Old English type to better reflect our product line." In the secretary's work context, such a concept is as unreal as "free ocean cruises every year for all employees." Without having seen such a thing done, it will not appear as a possibility to most secretaries. When windows-based graphics systems demonstrated that such a request was possible, the market realized they had such a need, which led to massive purchasing of graphics-based hardware and software and left the carefully market-driven, text-only word processor scrambling to catch up.

The moral of this story is that user-centered design is not a point in the product development cycle. User needs change in response to society, regulations, new market directions, and a variety of other things. If you deliver a successful product, your own success will change users' perceptions of what they need. Freed from early frustrations that your product has eliminated, users—and your competitors—will conceive of new possibilities of what can be accomplished. Eliminating certain barriers in the workplace will create whole new work patterns that have their own problems and frustrations.

2.4.2 Goals

Obtaining a good goal set is the most problematic part of user interface design. A simple approach is to ask a set of users what kinds of problems they face in the area your system is trying to address. If you have the right mix of users, this can quickly lead to a large list of problems and goals.

The next question is which of these goals are significant and which reflect the quirky aspects of a particular user's needs. This information can be obtained by simply ranking the goals based on the frequency with which they are mentioned. An alternative is to take the goals and have users rank them. Asking users to rank a list of 200 goals is not a reasonable request, but asking them to categorize the goals based on some scale can be helpful. Asking users to rank groups of three or four goals and then using the aggregate comparisons is also possible. There are a variety of experimental and survey techniques that can be used in this kind of study.

The selection of the goals or problems to be addressed and the quality of your solution to those problems will have a lot to do with the success of your interface design. There is no substitute for creative, intelligent, insightful, and informed thought on this matter.

2.4.3 Scenarios

Having decided on a set of goals or problems to be addressed, the scenarios are easier to develop. One can pose a goal to a user and ask him how he would solve it. Videotaping this process can be helpful so that it can be reviewed later. Having worked through a problem, the user can then be asked "What might go wrong?", "What are the problems that arise?", or "What usually messes this up?" Such questions provide the breadth of the problem space that the scenarios are intended to capture. In most cases, work practice, unlike a specific scenario, is not a straight line process. There are many choices, alternatives, and repetitions. When choices arise, ask the users how they choose one alternative over another. This information provides specific insight as to the information objects that control the user's process.

Once a set of scenarios has been identified, it can be tried out on users. Work through the scenario with the user to check whether such a sequence of events is plausible. Make sure you have captured all of the information that users use in making decisions. Check again that you have accounted for mistakes and deviations in the process.

2.4.4 Programmers and User Interface Design

The preceding discussion attempted to make concrete some of the important issues related to creating designs that will successfully meet the needs of users. This text, however, is intended for programmers and such people frequently do not address user issues well. The personality and intellect that creates elegant, efficient software designs is often not suited to sitting patiently for hours with users who have limited technical background, listening to them explain payroll or how musicians compose a musical score. The skills for good user-centered design come from anthropology, psychology, sociology, education, and the actual application domains. The techniques described above are cursory and crude. For a complete understanding of them, you should consult the large literature on human factors and user interface design.

It is critical, however, that programmers have an overall understanding of that design process. The key points that every programmer must understand are as follows:

■ The first design is never the delivered design. The design will change because mistakes will be made or design directions that look promising will not work with actual users. Because of this, the user interface software must be structured to allow change. It must be possible to discard pieces and replace them with others. It must be possible to produce quick prototypes for testing with users, which can then be solidified after they are accepted.

■ The individuals who create good designs are professionals with special skills and expertise, but they are not necessarily programmers.

■ User needs come before algorithmic elegance. There is a constant negotiation between what is possible given the current state of the software art and what is desirable from the user's point of view.

2.5 Functional Design

Having created the set of goals, the scenarios, and the information objects with their attributes and actions, it is now time to functionally design the interface that is to be implemented. In essence, this design consists of selecting from the set of objects, attributes, and actions those things for which the computing agent will be responsible. In our VCR example, this involves such questions as whether the program listing will be contained in the computer or printed in the newspaper or a magazine. If it is decided that the user interface will not be responsible for the program listing, then there is a related decision as to whether printed program listings will be part of our program offering. Most VCR manufacturers choose to leave the task of selecting a program to the print media, including the usability issues related to that task.

Similar decisions occur in the student registration system. We must choose whether the university catalog and course schedules for the current semester will be printed as books, available on-line, or both. If we choose a printed book for the catalog, then the usability of that book must be considered as part of the registration system. Universities cannot leave the publication of the catalog to some other market segment. If we choose on-line, then we may have disrupted the way a student browses the academic offerings in planning an education. The catalog serves more purposes than just registration. Most universities generate the printed version of the catalog from an on-line version and both are possible. Each must still be considered in terms of the usability of the registration system.

2.5.1 Assignment of Agency

The first step in the functional design is to assign an agent (user, book, academic advisor, or computer) to each step in each scenario as well as to each information object, attribute, and action. Which agents will know what and do what is the essential question.

Having made a tentative assignment of agency, there is a whole new set of evaluations that must be performed. We again must work our way through the scenarios and consider the capacity of each of the agents and the costs of transferring information between agents.

If in our VCR task we assign the VCR/computer the responsibility for the program listing, we must consider how that VCR will obtain, store, and manipulate such a listing. This has a substantial impact on the storage, communication, and computation capacities of a VCR and may either be technologically impossible, due to inadequate communications, or too costly to succeed in the marketplace. On the other hand, if we assign that task to a printed document, we must consider what it will take to transfer the information about a program selection from the program listing to the VCR. It is exactly this information transfer that causes most VCR programming problems for users.

2.5.2 Object-Oriented Functional Design

Having made the decisions as to what parts of the problem the computer will be responsible for and having worked through the consequences of those choices, we can complete the functional design of our interface. This design consists of creating classes for each kind of object we identified in our task analysis. The attributes become fields and the actions become methods.

This process of converting our task analysis to class definitions forces some formalization of our information objects. In particular, we must provide type definitions for everything including the fields and arguments on the methods. Working through these type definitions forces the consideration of conversions from one type to another and various other details.

One of the issues that must be considered at this time is which fields and methods will be public and which will be private. Public fields are those that the user will be able to directly manipulate through the interface. Private fields are those pieces of information that the objects need to perform their function but that are only indirectly accessible to the user.

A particular issue in this functional design is the class hierarchy, which involves organizing classes of objects into similar groups. This allows concepts, fields, and actions to be reused. Take, for example, an interface that involves drawing, such as that shown in Figure 2-1.

Our task analysis indicates that our set of information objects is a Drawing, Line, Rectangle, Ellipse, Polygon, and ControlPoint. Looking at the attributes of these objects, we discover that Line, Rectangle, Ellipse, and Polygon all have a line width, line color, fill pattern, fill color, and a list of control points.

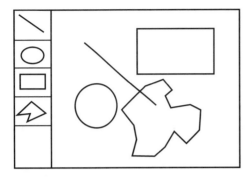

Figure 2-1 A drawing application

Using this information, we create a class DrawableObject that has all of these attributes. We then make the Line, Rectangle, Ellipse, and Polygon each a separate subclass.

Note that at this point in our design, there is nothing to differentiate a Line or Rectangle from a DrawableObject because the set of information to be managed is the same. The differences come when the presentations for these objects are designed and implemented as discussed in later chapters. Even though the information is uniform, it is obvious to any designer that Lines and Rectangles will have some differences later on and will need to be separate classes.

This organization of the functional model into a class hierarchy usually does not happen as a separate and distinct phase after task analysis. It occurs in parallel, as part of the analysis of the task scenarios. In fact, in designing this application it would become obvious very early on that DrawableObject would be a significant class. Much of the task analysis of creating and modifying Drawings would be performed in terms of DrawableObjects rather than Lines or Rectangles. As a separate part of the analysis, we would try to identify the set of DrawableObjects that will be important to the user. The class hierarchy aids us in the decomposition and organization of large problems.

A similar situation might occur in our student registration application. For most registration purposes, there is simply a class Student that has a Schedule that is a list of Sections. There may, however, be special registration provisions for honors students, international students, or seniors. One of the non-task-oriented decisions that must be made in a functional design is whether an international student is a separate subclass of Student or simply that the Student class has an attribute that indicates whether or not the student is international. One of the questions will be how significant the differences in handling an international student are versus a normal student. Seniors, for example, may be a special case only in that they are allowed to register in certain courses. This would typically not require a separate class. An international student, however, may require significant checking to verify that all regulations have been met and may warrant a separate subclass.

Such decisions concerning whether or not to form a separate subclass, however, are not part of the task analysis because they have no importance to the end user. Whether or not an international student is implemented as a separate subclass of Student is of no importance to the user. On the other hand, the class hierarchy is important to users because it forms part of the conceptual structure of the interface. The fact that Line, Rectangle, Ellipse, and Polygon are all unified under the class DrawableObject will have an important impact on how the interface is structured. Handling all such objects in a uniform way is very important in terms of how the users will mentally organize their knowledge of our user interface.

2.6 Summary

Understanding the users and their tasks is critical to good user interface design. Creating a functional model for an interface that provides the necessary objects, attributes, and actions to support those tasks is the first major step in creating a good user implementation.

The process begins by collecting a set of goals or problems that users are faced with. For each of these goals, we prepare a set of scenarios of how users might meet their goals. Each scenario is a description of a plausible set of steps a user might take toward meeting the goal.

We create new scenarios by analyzing existing scenarios to see what might go wrong or what problems might arise. By understanding what could go wrong, we can provide strategies for overcoming these difficulties so that users can still reach their goals.

In addition to creating goals and scenarios, we need to list the ways users judge the results of their work. What are the criteria that they use in evaluating their class schedule or determining if the right program will be recorded? It is important to point out that not all user evaluations of their work are captured in the classes and fields of the functional model. Many user evaluations of their work depend on the presentation or appearance of the objects.

Take, for example, early versions of the equation facility in Microsoft Word that required users to specify the formula in a textual notation such as ".\R(.\F(x+2,x))," which would produce a formula like that in Figure 2-2. Current versions of this feature provide an interface that allows users to visually lay out the formulas from templates. The underlying functional model for formulas is still the same; the difference is that a user can more easily determine if the formula is right by its correct presentation. The textual form of the equation was functionally complete but the gulf of evaluation was too wide.

$$\sqrt{\dfrac{x+2}{x}}$$

Figure 2-2   **Equation in traditional mathematical form (see text)**

The important point to be made here is that our goals, scenarios, and evaluations are not discarded once the functional model is complete. This information about user tasks must drive all aspects of user interface design.

The task analysis, to be of value, must be checked with users. Time must be spent verifying that our abstract description of what they do and what is important to them does indeed reflect their situation.

We next analyze our scenarios and evaluations to determine what information is needed to carry out the steps that users must take. This information forms the basis of our functional model. With this information, we also capture the actions that must be taken at each step.

Armed with an abstract description of all the objects and actions that are required to carry out our task scenarios, we select the portion of the task that will be the responsibility of the computer. The assignment of agency to tasks forms the basis of our functional model of the interface. Having selected what portions of the user task will be performed by the computer, we organize our objects, attributes, and actions into class definitions appropriate to our programming language. Essentially at this point we produce the class declarations for our implementation without specifying the implementation of the methods.

At the end of this process, we should have a description of the interface and its functions ready for implementation. We have not yet done anything to determine how this interface is to be organized to accomplish the tasks. No matter how beautiful our interface design or how carefully the human factors have been worked out, if the interface does not help users reach their goals, it is useless. The purpose of task analysis is to produce a functional model of the interface that will meet those goals.

3

Basic Computer Graphics

Having completed a functional design of what our user interface is to accomplish and how it is logically structured, we must lay the technical groundwork required for implementing graphical presentations. This chapter covers the basics of 2D computer graphics, involving the basic drawing techniques and hardware. Also included is the necessary 2D geometry required for interaction with primitive forms. We also discuss the issues of text, clipping a drawing to stay within a particular region, and color.

In this chapter, we focus on the basic 2D primitives that are required to present information to the users so they can interactively manipulate it. The field of computer graphics is quite diverse, and only the bare essentials are presented here. In creating realistic images of physical objects, we must consider 3D perspective viewing, realistic reflection of light and shadow, texturing physical objects, and removing hidden surfaces. The whole area of realistic physical models as well as the animation of such models is not considered here. A variety of computer graphics texts already address these issues.

In addition to ignoring high-level 3D modeling and rendering, we also ignore scan conversion. *Scan conversion* is the process of converting a geometric shape such as a line or polygon into a set of pixels that represent the shape on the screen or a printer. We assume that any user interface tool kit will provide methods or procedures that perform such tasks for us.

In this chapter, we assume that we are using a graphics package that can draw a variety of 2D shapes, given the appropriate inputs. Our problem is to understand how to invoke such methods and how to organize them in a way that will efficiently display our user's information. Understanding the various display architectures will help us understand how those architectures affect interactive software.

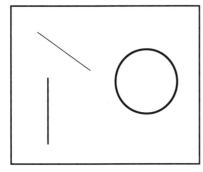

Line ((4, 5) (9, 7) thick 1)
Line ((4, 10) (4, 17) thick 2)
Circle ((19, 8) radius 3 thick 3)

Figure 3-1   Stroke representation of images

3.1 Models for Images

There are three primary ways to represent 2D images—strokes, pixels, and regions. Each model has properties that are helpful for display, modeling, or interaction, and each has its disadvantages.

3.1.1 Stroke Model

The stroke model is the earliest form used for representing geometric objects in a computer. In this model, we describe all images as strokes of some specified color and thickness. For example, Figure 3-1 shows a simple diagram and its accompanying stroke representation.

   In the stroke representation, the type of stroke and its geometry are represented. Early vector-refresh displays and direct-view storage tubes represented their images in this fashion. Special control hardware was required to translate the stroke representation into images on the screen. Plotters accept such representations and convert them into paths that the pen should follow to draw the stroke on paper. PostScript printers also accept such a representation, which they then convert to a region model and then to a pixel model for actual printing.

   The stroke model is the one that is commonly used for many interactive applications. Most graphics packages in user interface tool kits provide more complex stroked objects, including arcs, ellipses, elliptical arcs, rectangles with rounded corners, and various curved shapes.

3.1.2 Pixel Model

The stroke model, however, is not adequate for representing more realistic or complex images, such as Figure 3-2. Such images require a pixel model, which

Figure 3-2   A pixel image

divides the image into a discrete number of pixels and then stores an intensity or color value for each pixel. In addition, all of today's graphics hardware is pixel based, which means that ultimately all models must be reduced to pixels before printing or display.

There are three key aspects to the resolution of a pixel image. The number of rows of pixels and the number of pixels per row constitute the spatial resolution of the image. For good display screens, this is 1024×768, with some displays going higher. For most laser printers, the resolution varies from 3000×2400 to 6000×4800 in order to create a high-quality printed page. The third aspect is the image depth or number of bits required to represent each pixel.

There are four basic forms of pixel-based images. The first is a simple bitmap, where each pixel consists of one bit that is either on or off. Such a model is suitable for representing the black and white of a printed page. In order to represent levels of gray, several pixels are grouped together in various patterns of on and off, producing an appearance of grayness. This is the approach used in laser printers, which can either put down a spot of ink or not. With very high resolution, this halftoning or dithering process can produce acceptable gray.

In the second method, gray-scale images provide more than 1 bit per pixel. Some systems such as the early NeXT provided 2 bits per pixel. This approach only doubled the space required to store the screen image while providing four levels of gray. This 2-bit image only marginally improved the quality of photographs and other realistic images, but it significantly improved the appearance of interface items such as buttons and type-in boxes. Items that the Macintosh (using bitmaps) had to represent as grainy patterns appeared smooth on the NeXT. Most modern gray-scale systems provide 8 bits (1 byte) per pixel, which can represent 256 levels of gray ranging from 0 (black) to 255 (white). A 1024×1024 gray-scale image requires 1 megabyte of storage.

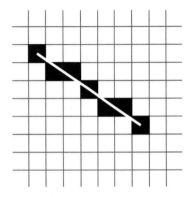

Figure 3-3 Pixel representation of a line

The third, and most flexible, representation of images is the full-color representation. Colors are assembled from the three additive primary colors, red, green, and blue. With 8 bits per primary color (3 bytes), the entire range of colors can be represented. Such an image format requires 3 megabytes for a 1024×1024 image. Space becomes a problem when dealing with highly realistic full-color images. For photograph-quality images that are 3000×2400, approximately 22 MB of storage are required. Because of these requirements, compression techniques are often used.

The fourth representation is the color-mapped image. In this case, only 8 bits are used per pixel. Instead of storing a color, each pixel stores an index into a color table that contains the full 24 bits for each indexed color. This allows many color images to be represented in the same space as a gray-scale image. Many color displays that are being used for normal interaction, rather than photograph-quality applications, are based on the lookup-table image model. In addition to cutting the storage space to a third, the smaller number of bytes also reduces the amount of computation required to manipulate the pixels.

Although the pixel model can represent any image, there are some problems when converting stroke or region objects into pixels. If the spatial resolution of the pixel image is low, as shown in Figure 3-3, aliasing can occur where smooth objects, such as a line, appear jagged.

If the resolution is very high, as with a good laser printer, the jagged edges are so small that the eye does not perceive them. In the case of lower-resolution displays, gray scale can be used to alleviate the problem by filling in some of the jagged places. This process, known as *antialiasing*, is shown in Figure 3-4. The appearance is improved, but significantly more computation is required to produce the correct gray settings. Similar effects are used with each of the primary colors in color images.

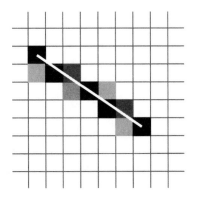

Figure 3-4   Antialiased line

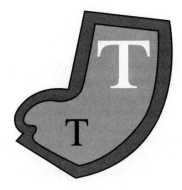

Figure 3-5   Region-based image

3.1.3 Region Model

The third image model is the region model. In this model, stroke objects are used to outline the region to be filled, as shown in Figure 3-5. There are various models by which regions are filled, including constant colors or various blendings to produce shaded effects. A major advantage of region models is that filled shapes can be represented in very little memory and in a way that is independent of the display resolution. This is very advantageous for high-resolution display devices, such as laser printers, where transferring a full page to the printer would require at least 2 MB in pixel form (thus slowing communications) and would require that the computer software be aware of the printer's resolution.

Even text is represented as regions and then converted to bitmaps inside of the printer; this method allows good clear text of any size to be generated. In

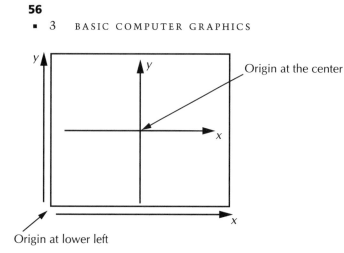

Figure 3-6   Normal Cartesian coordinates

fact, even a line that is 1 pixel wide on a screen must be converted to a region of pixels when rendered on a 600-dpi (dots per inch) laser printer. Otherwise the line would be too thin in print.

3.2 Coordinate Systems

An important consideration in drawing objects is the coordinate system of the drawing and the coordinate system in which the objects are defined in the application. These coordinate systems may not be the same; this merits careful discussion

3.2.1 Device Coordinates

Device coordinates are the coordinates of the actual display device. In most geometry texts, the origin of the coordinate system is either in the lower left or the center with positive x going to the right and positive y going up, as shown in Figure 3-6.

This coordinate system is rarely used for frame buffers, graphics displays, or laser printers, because most display devices work from the upper left and downward. For this reason, most devices use the coordinates shown in Figure 3-7. In this model, device coordinates are always positive integers, except in cases such as laser printers where additional processing of the image is done by the printer's processor before actual display.

One significant modification to the use of device coordinates in displaying graphics is the window. In most modern interface tool kits, the programmer is presented with a window as the abstraction for the display. This window is presented to the programmer as a virtual display on which the programmer is

Origin at upper left

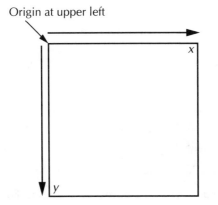

Figure 3-7 Device coordinates

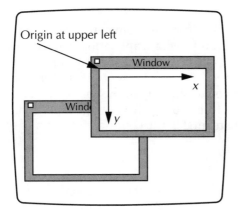

Figure 3-8   Window coordinates

free to draw. Most such systems also provide a frame around this window that allows the user to manipulate the window's location and size. The program's coordinates are placed inside of the window as if the frame did not exist, as shown in Figure 3-8. The programmer then treats the window as a display in and of itself and generally ignores the larger space of device coordinates.

Window coordinates and sizes, like display coordinates and sizes, are almost always expressed in pixels. Because some windows can receive mouse events that are outside of their boundaries, mouse events in some systems are reported in display coordinates rather than window coordinates. It is important to know how a particular system handles mouse coordinates so that the appropriate conversions are done to make the input coordinates and the drawing coordinates consistent.

3.2.2 Physical Coordinates

Pixel-based device coordinates can be a problem when dealing with display devices of varying resolutions. For example, a line that is 20 pixels long on a 1024×1024 screen appears very differently on a 600-dpi laser printer. What we need is to specify display coordinates in physical units, such as inches, centimeters, or printer points.

Let us suppose that we want to access our laser printer in terms of inches. Suppose also that we know that this is a 600 dots (pixels) per inch laser printer. The conversion from 5 inches to pixels is

$$5 \text{ inches} \cdot 600 \text{ dpi} = 3000 \text{ pixels}$$

Printer points for defining font sizes are defined as 72 points to the inch. For a 400-dpi printer, the height of 12-point text would be

$$\frac{12 \text{ points} \cdot 1 \text{ inch}}{72 \text{ points}} \cdot 400 \text{ dpi} = 67 \text{ pixels}$$

Defining devices in physical units simplifies the formatting of displays to be used on a variety of media but also requires a multiplication of every coordinate by some constant. Because these conversions can cause a performance problem on low-end machines, some tool kits still present pixel coordinates as the model for devices and leave any conversions up to the application. Laser printers, on the other hand, have been forced by their varying resolutions to present physical units as their coordinate model.

3.2.3 Model Coordinates

In many situations, the information objects are modeled in coordinates that are very different from the display coordinates. In a word processor or drawing package, the coordinates of the model are in physical units for printing because the application is modeling exactly what is going onto the page.

For an architectural drawing, however, the model units are feet or meters when designing buildings. Thus a scaling transformation is required that transforms feet, for example, into inches, which can then be used as physical display units. A possible scaling might be 10 feet to the inch. This would make the total transformation (for an example length of 22 feet) from model coordinates to a 100-pixel-per-inch display

$$22 \text{ feet} \cdot \frac{1 \text{ inch}}{10 \text{ feet}} \cdot \frac{100 \text{ pixels}}{1 \text{ inch}} = 220 \text{ pixels}$$

The constants in this formula can be combined into a simpler formula that can be used on all parts of the drawing of the building:

$$22 \text{ feet} \cdot \frac{10 \text{ pixels}}{\text{foot}} = 220 \text{ pixels}$$

If, however, the scale of the drawing changes or the display device is changed, these constants must be recalculated.

3.2.4 Interactive Coordinates

Up until now we have only considered output. When an input point is received from the mouse or other device, the mapping must work in the other direction. The following general formula maps a point in some model coordinates to a window at a particular location on the screen:

$$\text{ModelPoint} \cdot \text{DrawScale} \cdot \text{PhysicalToPixel} + \text{WindowOrigin} = \text{OutputPoint}$$

The DrawScale transforms this point into physical display units, PhysicalToPixel transforms the point from physical display units into pixels, and the WindowOrigin moves the whole drawing to where the window is located on the screen. WindowOrigin is defined in pixels.

If a mouse input is received, it will be defined in pixels relative to the upper left of the screen. The transformation must be reversed to produce a point in model coordinates. This new transformation is

$$\frac{(\text{InputPoint} - \text{WindowOrigin})}{\text{PhysicalToPixel} \cdot \text{DrawScale}} = \text{ModelPoint}$$

We need to have the input point converted to model coordinates so that we can use that point as information in changing our model of the application information.

There are many more issues involved in defining the geometric mappings between application models and actual displays. The simple analysis we have done here is only the beginning. In Chapter 10, we will discuss a more complete system based on homogeneous coordinates and matrix algebra.

3.3 Human Visual Properties

In order to interactively present information to users, we need to understand a little about the human visual system. This understanding is essential in designing presentations and interactions that are understandable and pleasing to the eye.

3.3.1 Update Rates

Early moviemakers were limited by their technology in the number of frames of film that could be presented to a viewer in a second. Consequently, early silent films appear very jerky. We perceive the movement but it does not look real. Experimentation has shown that when images are presented to viewers at more than 20–30 frames per second (fps), the images fuse together and appear to be moving continuously. This is because the frame rate has exceeded the rate at which the visual system samples the inputs to the retina. NTSC video is 29.997 fps, film is 24 fps, and PAL video is 25 fps.

On a 30-MIPS (millions of instructions per second) computer—the available rate when this book was begun—there are 1 million instructions available to update the display frame in 1/30 of a second. Although 1 million instructions seems like a lot, remember that a 640×480 display (television resolution) has 307,200 pixels, leaving 3.25 instructions per pixel if every pixel is to be manipulated between each frame. On a 300-MIPS computer—the rate in common use by the time many of you read this book—there are still only 32.5 instructions per pixel per frame. This is a serious problem for video applications.

For normal interactive use, however, we do not change every pixel in every frame; therefore the magic number of 30 fps for smooth motion is not required for most interactive uses. If the user wants to drag an object across the screen, experiments have shown that 5 updates per second to the object being dragged are sufficient to maintain the "interactive feel." Obviously, improving this update rate up to 30 updates per second will make the movement appear more smooth and natural. For dragging tasks, 5 updates per second is the lower bound for acceptable interaction. This means that our display update process, for dragging purposes, must complete in less than 1/5th of a second to be acceptable.

For interactions that are not continuous, such as displaying a new student record or finding a word in a document, delays of 1–2 seconds are acceptable. In these situations, we are not trying to create a smooth movement but are visually moving to a new context. Such context movements on the part of users are much slower because of the scanning and understanding that must occur. For important or time-consuming tasks, users will tolerate delays of much longer than 2 seconds, but beyond 10–15 seconds the feel of the interface is no longer interactive.

3.4 Graphics Hardware

A brief introduction to basic graphics devices is in order, since these are the devices for which our images will be generated.

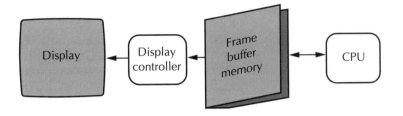

Figure 3-9   Frame buffer architecture

3.4.1 Frame Buffer Architecture

The frame buffer, shown in Figure 3-9, is the dominant architecture for display devices. The graphics package, which is part of the interactive tool kit running in the central processing unit (CPU), sets pixel values into the frame buffer memory. The frame buffer is the repository of the image that is being displayed on the screen. In many cases, the CPU can read the image out of the frame buffer as well as modify it. Various display technologies use differing techniques to convert the contents of the frame buffer into a visible image.

3.4.2 Cathode Ray Tube

The most popular display device is the cathode ray tube (CRT), which is the basis for standard televisions. For such a device, the display controller scans the frame buffer memory from top to bottom, left to right to retrieve pixel values. Simultaneously with this scan of the frame buffer, an electron beam is scanning across the face of the display in a similar pattern. The display controller modifies the intensity of this beam based on the pixel values found in the frame buffer. This produces an image on the phosphor of the screen. In most color displays, there are three beams, one for each of the primary colors, red, green, and blue.

The phosphor image decays based on the persistence of the phosphor. If a long-persistence phosphor is used, the image will not decay by the time the display is refreshed again. Too long a persistence means that fast-moving objects have ghosts of the object trailing behind. If a low-persistence phosphor is used, then the image will start to decay before the display controller can redraw it, causing the display to appear to flicker. If the display is refreshed 30 times per second, there is a conflict between ghosting from high-persistence phosphors and the flicker of low-persistence phosphors. On good displays, this is resolved by refreshing the screen 60 times per second (60 Hz) so that the user cannot perceive the flicker. On higher-quality displays, this may go up to 75 Hz.

The resolution of a huge number of such displays is 640×480. This resolution is determined by the resolution of American television. By using the same CRT hardware as a television, the development costs can be amortized over all televisions rather than just over computer displays. Good-quality CRTs for computer work have resolutions on the order of 1024×768, with some in the 1200×1000 range and experimental systems going much higher.

3.4.3 Liquid Crystal Display

Most portable computers use liquid crystal displays (LCD) because they are flat and have low power consumption. By placing a charge on the liquid crystals, the polarization of light passing through those crystals is changed. When used in conjunction with polarizing filters, such crystals can be made transparent or opaque, which produces the image.

Low-cost LCDs use a passive-matrix technique where the circuits for controlling the crystals are located at the periphery of the screen and the settings of the various pixels must be done sequentially through the screen. This results in a constant image without flicker, but the time required to change a pixel's color is much slower than 30 fps. Depending on how slow this time is, fast-moving objects, such as cursors, may "submarine" or disappear while moving quickly. This is because the cursor has moved from its location before the display was fully changed.

More expensive LCDs use an active-matrix technology that places the control circuitry for each pixel next to the crystals that are being controlled. This yields higher-contrast images, much faster times to change pixels, and eliminates the submarining behavior of cursors.

All LCDs use a frame buffer architecture similar to that of the CRT. The difference is that the display controller is controlling the opacity of crystals rather than the intensity of an electron beam. Similar technology is used by display devices that have not yet gained a wide market, such as plasma panels and others.

3.4.4 Hardcopy Devices

Hardcopy devices are only indirectly involved with the user interface. However, many of the same software techniques—and in a good software design the same code—are used to generate both hardcopy and screen output. The major difference between hardcopy devices and the screen is that the CPU does not have direct access to the memory in the frame buffer of a hardcopy device. Communication bandwidth is a large factor in drawing on a hardcopy device.

One of the oldest technologies for hardcopy graphical output is the pen plotter. This device is based on the stroke image model, except that the coordinates of stroke objects are sent to the plotter in physical coordinates. The plotter then moves a pen across the paper to draw the stroke. This process has all of the imaging limitations of the stroke model, including the inability to present realistic images.

Modern laser printers are based on the frame buffer model. The primary difficulty is that in a 600-dpi printer, the frame buffer requires 3.6 megabytes to print a standard letter-size page. Communicating this much information for each page is prohibitive. For these reasons, laser printers generally use a region model. The most popular of these is PostScript.[1] The PostScript language is based on FORTH,[2] which allows the printer to be programmed by the print driver software. The primitive elements are regions bounded by splines and straight lines, and the printer itself fills the frame buffer from these region definitions. This method allows for very compact communication of very precise and sophisticated images.

In the case of a photograph, however, the region image model is not sufficient. Most laser printers can also accept pixel-based images that are then rendered into the printer's frame buffer. Such images are usually much lower in resolution than the printer's resolution, which somewhat mitigates the communication-bandwidth problem.

From the frame buffer a laser writes an electrostatic charge on a drum or belt. Toner (powdered ink) is attracted to the charges and sticks to the surface wherever a charge has been written. The drum or belt is then rolled across a piece of paper to which the toner sticks. The toner is heat fused to the surface of the paper so that it will not rub off. In addition to the standard laser printer technology, there are ink jet printers, which use frame buffers of lower resolution, and various high-quality color printing technologies such as dye sublimation and wax transfer.

3.5 Abstract Canvas Class

In building our software architecture for the presentation of user information, we need an abstraction for a drawing surface. We will call this a Canvas. A Canvas is an abstract class that defines the methods we will use for drawing. Many user interface tool kits or graphics packages provide such a class. If they do not, it is essential that the application programmer design one.

The Canvas class defines a uniform model for drawing on a 2D surface that can be used everywhere in the application. A Canvas has a width and height and defines its physical units. From this abstract class, we can define subclasses for a window on the screen, an image in memory, various hardcopy devices, or a file in which a picture is to be saved for drawing later. Each of these subclasses is implemented differently because of the varying destinations for the output image, but through the interface defined by the abstract class they can all be treated the same.

There are some variations among the subclasses to Canvas that must be considered. The first is the actual pixel resolution of the Canvas. A screen window that is 8 inches high cannot represent the same information as a laser-printed page of the same size. In some cases, the application program may need to be aware of the resolution limitations of the screen window and may need to adapt the kind of detail it attempts to display. Another major difference is in the capacity of the pixels. It is important to know if we are drawing on a Canvas that only supports black and white or on one that supports gray scale or full color, because it makes a significant difference in the way the presentation is defined. A third difference is that some Canvases, such as a screen window, can dynamically change size while others, such as a printer page, cannot.

All modern user interface packages provide a uniform model for drawing on a 2D surface. This is independent of what or where this surface might be. In X, there is a standard interface for drawing to windows, drawing to images in memory, and saving to files. There is no such interface to hardcopy devices. In NeWS and on the NeXT, PostScript is the model for drawing on any drawable surface, including windows, memory images, files, or printers. The View class in NeXTSTEP performs the Canvas role of providing this abstraction. On the Macintosh, the basic Quickdraw package provides GrafPorts as the abstraction for drawing. In MacApp, the GrafPort features are more carefully abstracted into the View class. View has, for example, a subclass called TStd-PrintHandler that will draw on the printer using the View abstraction for drawing. Microsoft Windows provides the Graphical Device Interface (GDI), which is not object oriented but provides a uniform interface for drawing on various media including the screen. The GDI associates a particular graphical device driver with a "device context." All drawing occurs through a device context that then translates the drawing commands into appropriate output. In Visual C++, the device context concept from MS Windows is encapsulated into the abstract CDC class, which can handle printing, windows, files, and images.

3.5.1 Methods and Properties

Our drawing functionality can be defined in terms of the methods and properties that our Canvas class provides. The methods can be grouped into drawing of lines and shapes, drawing of text, clipping our drawings so that they do not go outside of specified portions of the Canvas, and controlling color and texture. Properties here are like fields of the class except that they are accessed by means of methods rather than directly. The reason for this form of access is that when they are set, most subclasses such as a printer require that additional processing be performed. Such properties include the coordinate system, the physical drawing units, the current drawing color, or the line width.

(X1, Y1) ■

■ (X2, Y2)

Figure 3-10   Properties of a shape

All of these properties are accessed by methods on the Canvas class. The actual implementation of these methods is different for each kind of output surface that we are trying to draw onto.

3.6 Drawing

A fundamental part of graphical output is the drawing of geometric shapes. This section discusses how we model such shapes and also covers some of the geometry that will be needed as we interact with these shapes. Text is such a special case that we treat it separately.

All graphical shapes have a few properties in common. These include basic geometry of the shape, line or border width, fill or line color, and a pattern or texture. For example, the rectangle in Figure 3-10 has its geometry defined by its two corner points. It has a width and color for its border as well as a color for filling in the rectangle.

We could define our rectangle facility with a single method of the following form:

void Canvas::Rectangle(X1, Y1, X2, Y2, LineWidth, LineColor, FillColor)

Such methods, however, are painful to use because of the number of parameters required. In most cases, the LineWidth, LineColor, and FillColor will be the same for a large number of rectangles and other shapes.

For this reason, most graphics packages limit their drawing methods to specify only geometric information. The other properties are handled by current settings on the Canvas object. For example, we might provide Canvas with the following methods:

void Canvas::Rectangle(X1, Y1, X2, Y2)

void Canvas::SetLineWidth(LW)

long Canvas::GetLineWidth()

void Canvas::SetLineColor(LC)

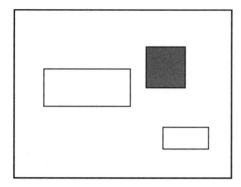

Figure 3-11 **Rectangles and their properties (see text)**

Color Canvas::GetLineColor()

void Canvas::SetFillColor(FC)

Color Canvas::GetFillColor()

Note that each property has a Set and a Get method. When a rectangle—or any other shape—is drawn, the settings of the current properties are used to supply the remaining information. In most systems, these settings are stored in the Canvas objects; thus they may be different for different windows or printers. To draw several rectangles, we might do the following:

```
Canvas Cnv;

Cnv.SetLineWidth(1);
Cnv.SetLineColor(Black);
Cnv.SetFillColor(White);
Cnv.Rectangle(50, 50, 150, 100);
Cnv.Rectangle(200, 120, 250, 140);
Cnv.SetFillColor(Gray);
Cnv.Rectangle(180, 20, 220, 40);
```

This produces the picture shown in Figure 3-11.

Current property settings are used widely in graphics packages. This method does have some drawbacks, however. If you're not careful, you may forget to set the properties before drawing the objects. In some cases this might work, because the properties are already correct. Sometime later, when the program is changed, the properties will be different and suddenly your drawing code does not work correctly.

Most drawing in graphics systems is performed in terms of geometric primitives and text. The geometric primitives can be divided into paths and closed

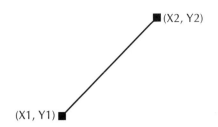

Figure 3-12   Control points of a line

shapes. We only discuss the basic geometries of these shapes in terms of how they are specified by the programmer. You must consult a graphics text for the details of how to convert these shapes into pixels on a screen or page.

3.6.1 Paths

The first set of geometric objects we discuss are paths, or 1D objects that are drawn in a 2D space. The simplest description of these objects is that they have no inside or outside; they are infinitely thin. Most of our geometric questions involve paths. When paths define the border of a filled shape, the geometry of the shape is determined by the geometry of the path, which is its border. The paths that we discuss are lines, circles, arcs, ellipses, splines, and complex piecewise paths.

Lines

Lines are the simplest of all paths and provide the easiest geometric solutions. Figure 3-12 shows a line and its control points. Control points define the line's geometry and we use them to compute the coefficients for our line equations.

Circles

The next most interesting geometric shape is the circle. The simplest model for a circle is defined by its center and its radius. The radius is not a control point but it does provide the simplest geometry. Circles can also be defined by their center and some point on the circumference of the circle, as shown in Figure 3-13.

Arcs

Arcs are fragments of circles and as such use the same equations as circles. The question is how to define the restricted part of the circle that forms the arc. This is most easily done by using the parametric equations for a circle and restricting the parameter values; this geometry is discussed in Chapter 9.

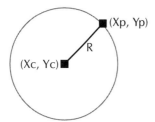

Figure 3-13   Geometry of a circle

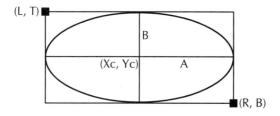

Figure 3-14   An ellipse

Ellipses and Elliptical Arcs

There are two major classes of elliptical shapes to consider. The simplest class is the set of ellipses whose major and minor axes are parallel to the x and y axes. These are computationally quite tractable and can be understood by expanding on the equations for circles. A much more difficult class is the set of ellipses that can have any orientation for their major and minor axes; this class of shapes is more computationally expensive. There are applications where the general class of ellipses is required, but we can go a long way without them. For our discussion, we restrict ourselves to the ellipses aligned with the x and y axes, as shown in Figure 3-14.

Splines

Curved shapes are frequently called splines because of the original mechanical tools used for drawing such curves by hand. Most curves are defined as parametric cubic equations. Their geometry and definitions are discussed in detail in Chapter 9.

Piecewise Path Objects

The path objects defined so far are generally not sufficient for all of our drawing needs. Paths such as those shown in Figure 3-15 are constructed by piecing together a variety of simpler path objects to construct the desired figure. A major issue with such drawings is the continuity between pieces, that

Figure 3-15   Piecewise paths

Figure 3-16   Closed Shapes

is, whether the pieces connect smoothly or whether there is a sharp corner. Issues of how to ensure continuity are discussed in Chapter 9.

3.6.2 Closed Shapes

The graphical objects described above only draw lines. Frequently we want closed shapes that can be filled, as shown in Figure 3-16. They are generally defined by a border, which is a path object. The filled shape is defined as all points lying inside of the closed shape. The definition of the inside and the outside of a closed shape will be deferred until we have a better definition of the geometry of these shapes.

3.7 Text

The drawing of text is one of the most common needs in graphical user interfaces, not only for text editors but also for a variety of labeling and information presentation needs. Unfortunately, this can be one of the more complex parts of an application, due to the wide variety of textual representations that have evolved over time and the various mechanisms used for representing them.

Courier (fixed-space font)
Avant Garde (sans serif)
Helvetica (sans serif)
Times Roman (serif)

Figure 3-17 Font families

3.7.1 Font Selection

The first task in drawing graphical text is to select the font in which the text is to be drawn. There are a variety of ways in which fonts are specified, but in general there are three primary arguments: the font family, the style, and the size. The font family defines the general shape of the characters in the font, as shown in Figure 3-17.

The Courier font family is a monospaced or fixed-space font, meaning that every character in the font has the same width. Fixed-space fonts work like typewriters and character-based terminals. Alignment and spacing of characters is very easy, but the resulting text is not as pleasant to read nor is it very space efficient, since the character "i" gets the same space as "G." The remaining fonts shown in Figure 3-17 are proportionally spaced fonts. Each character has a different width depending upon its needs.

The Times Roman font is an example of a serifed font. Each vertical stroke that reaches the baseline has a little foot, or serif, on the bottom. The Avant Garde and Helvetica fonts do not have such serifs. Compare the "i" in Times Roman with the "i" in Helvetica. When characters from a serifed font are strung together, the serifs tend to form a line, which visually defines the line of text. This facilitates eye tracking across the line while reading. In general, long lines of serifed text can be read more quickly than sans serif text because the eye has less difficulty in horizontal tracking. The advantage with serif type for reading on paper does not necessarily hold true for reading on screens due to resolution problems. With lower resolutions, the serifs may make letters harder to discriminate.

Font Style

Within a font family, there are frequently a variety of styles of font face. These styles are variations on the basic character shapes, as shown in Figure 3-18.

On some systems, various styles such as Times Roman bold are treated as completely separate fonts. On other systems, they are separate fonts but are

Times

Helvetica

Times bold

Helvetica bold

Times italic

Helvetica italic

Times bold italic

Helvetica bold italic

Figure 3-18 Font styles

9 point
10 point
12 point
14 point
18 point
24 point
36 point

Figure 3-19 Font sizes

grouped together within families. On the Macintosh, there may only be a Times Roman font, and the font system automatically distorts the base font to create bold, italic, and outline versions of the font.

Font Size

The third primary control on font selection is the font size or vertical height of characters. This is usually expressed in *points*, where 1 point = 1/72 of an inch, as shown in Figure 3-19. A point is a unit of measure that has carried over from printing. Unfortunately, in many systems the point size of a font is only loosely related to the actual vertical size of the characters as displayed on the screen. The problem lies in the low resolution of many graphics displays. Some more complex fonts are slightly larger than their point size would indicate because that is how many pixels are required to clearly display characters in the font. On most laser printers, however, the point size of a font accurately reflects its height.

The set of things that can be specified about a font is not restricted to family, style, and size even though these are the most common specifications. Other controls vary widely with the particular windowing system being used.

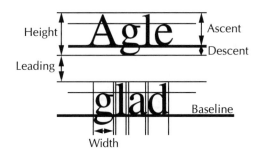

Figure 3-20   Font size information

Font selection is a major problem in developing applications that port from one system to another. In fact, porting a drawing or document between machines that are running the same windowing system can cause font problems because of the differences in the fonts actually installed on the machine.

3.7.2 Font Information

Having selected a font family, style, and size, there is a variety of information we need to know about the font in order to display text at the appropriate positions on the screen. Consider the characters in Figure 3-20.

As with the font family, style, and size, there are a variety of ways in which font geometry is represented. Figure 3-20 shows the general characteristics, although these vary among graphics packages. The most useful piece of information is the height since that indicates how much vertical space should be allocated to accommodate a line of characters in this font. The leading is the space between multiple lines of text. In some systems, the leading is incorporated into the height of the font. In some, it is an additional parameter on the font. In others, the leading has to be handled separately by programmers using the font.

In most systems, the vertical position of text is indicated by the y coordinate of the baseline. Note that in the case of the character "g," this is not the lowest extent of the line of text. The distance between the baseline and the lowest extent of any character in the font is the descent. The distance between the baseline and the highest extent of the font is the ascent. These two measures, along with the height, define all of the information normally needed to position text vertically.

Horizontal positioning of text is a little more problematic because the width of each character may vary. All windowing systems provide calls that return the width of an individual character or a string of characters, given a particular font selection. In some fonts, the space between characters is actually included in the width of each character. In others, it is specified separately. The vertical measurements are uniform for an entire font. The horizontal measures vary from character to character. The only exceptions to this are fixed-spaced fonts such as Courier.

3.7.3 Drawing Text

In most systems, drawing text is relatively simple. A current font is selected in which all following text will be drawn. For each text string to be drawn, a reference point and the string to be drawn are specified, for example:

```
Canvas Cnv;

Cnv.SetFont("Times", Bold, 10);
        Times Roman; bold; 10 point
Cnv.Text(10, 20,"This is the text");
```

In most cases, the reference point (10, 20) specifies the baseline and the leftmost position of the first character. There are other alternatives, however. We could specify that the y coordinate of the reference point defines the bottom or the top of all characters rather than the baseline. We could also specify that the x coordinate defines the center or rightmost position of the string. Some systems provide only reference points at the leftmost baseline, since all of the others are easily calculated by programmers using the system. MS Windows, on the other hand, provides a SetTextAlign routine that sets the current alignment for subsequent reference points. This allows for all of the possible variants.

Suppose we wanted to output multiple lines of text that are appropriately spaced depending on the font being used. It is never wise to hard-code font heights and widths because sooner or later some user will want a different font and all that code will need to be rewritten in order to accommodate the new flexibility. To solve this problem, we can use the font height information, as follows:

```
Canvas Cnv;
long Height;

Cnv.SetFont("Times", Plain, 12);
Height = Cnv.GetFontHeight();
Cnv.Text(10, 20, "This is the first line");
Cnv.Text(10, 20 + Height, "This is the second line");
Cnv.Text(10, 20 + 2*Height, "This is the third line");
```

For an arbitrary number of lines, this is done in a loop incrementing the y position by Height each time.

A slightly more complex problem is to output "Some **bold** text" on a single line. This string must be output as three separate strings with different fonts, and they must be correctly positioned relative to each other. This can be done as follows:

```
Canvas Cnv;
long Width;

Cnv.SetFont("Times", Plain, 12);
Cnv.Text(10, 20, "Some");
Width = Cnv.StringWidth("Some");
Cnv.SetFont("Times", Bold, 12);
Cnv.Text(10 + Width, 20, "bold");
Width = Width + Cnv.StringWidth("bold");
Cnv.SetFont("Times", Plain, 12);
Cnv.Text(10 + Width, 20, "text");
```

These two examples illustrate what is necessary when outputting strings in multiple fonts. If we were faced with multiple lines and varying fonts per line, we would need more complex calculations of line height and width.

3.7.4 Outline vs. Bitmapped Fonts

In order to draw a textual character into a frame buffer or onto some other pixel-based display, we must know the set of pixels that make up the character. In many windowing systems, fonts of characters are simply defined as the bitmaps, or set of pixels, that make up each character. This technique is very efficient but it has several problems. When the size of the font is very large, the amount of space required to store all of the bitmaps becomes a problem, especially when each font size requires a separate set of bitmaps. This is even a problem with small font sizes when drawing onto high-resolution printers. At 300 dpi, a 10-point font can take over 20 KB of space. A 72-point font at 300 dpi would take 1.4 MB. Using very many sizes of a particular font can easily consume a large amount of space.

To resolve this problem, many systems now represent fonts by storing characters as closed shapes. This means that only the outline needs to be stored, as shown in Figure 3-21. The outline of the letter A is stored as a piecewise path of lines and splines, or on some systems as lines and elliptical arcs. Such character definition can be readily scaled to any size and then converted to bitmaps as needed rather than storing all of the font sizes that might ever be required. This also allows advanced drawing packages to treat characters as geometric shapes that can be manipulated like any other graphical object.

Figure 3-21   Outline fonts

This is some text to edit

Figure 3-22   Editing a line of text

3.7.5 Character Selection

Since text is a major part of many user interfaces, editing text requires that the user interface software be able to select a given character in a text string, given a specific mouse position. Take, for example, the text type-in box shown in Figure 3-22. The problem is that the sizes of each of the characters are different. All systems that support proportionally spaced text provide a mechanism for obtaining the width of each character for a given selected font. On most systems, there is a single call that returns an array of character widths. Indexing this array with the ASCII value of a character yields the desired information. The algorithm for selecting the character, then, is as follows:

```
Canvas Cnv;
int StringLeft, =
     The leftmost location where the string was drawn.
int MouseX, =
     The X coordinate of the mouse location.
char * Str, =
     A pointer to the string being edited.
int CharWidths[256];
int I, X, StrLen;

Cnv.SetFont("Times", Plain, 12);
Cnv.GetCharWidths(CharWidths);
StrLen = Length(Str);
I = 0;
X = StringLeft;
while(I < StrLen && X < MouseX)
```

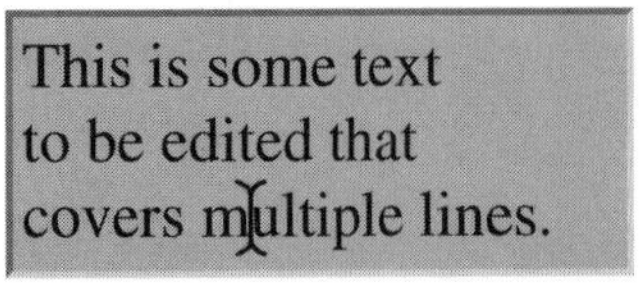

This is some text
to be edited that
covers multiple lines.

Figure 3-23   **Selecting text from among multiple lines**

```
{
    X = X + CharWidths[ Str[I] ];
    I = I + 1;
}
```
Selected character is at Str[I–1].

Sometimes, as in Figure 3-23, there is a need to select a text point from within multiple lines of text. In this case, we must take into account the text height in determining which line of text is being selected. The general algorithm for this is as follows:

1. Compute the line of text being selected using the y position of the mouse and the text height plus leading.
2. Starting at the beginning of the text string, run through the string, counting new line characters, until the beginning of the appropriate line is found.
3. Apply the single-line selection algorithm described above, starting at the beginning of the line of text.

3.7.6 Complex Strings

Our discussion so far has covered the drawing of simple strings of ASCII text. Some graphics packages support the creation of compound strings that contain additional formatting information. The simplest of these include style information such as, bold, italic, or change of font. These issues complicate selection and computation of text height.

The most complicated issues in text output arise from internationalization. The ASCII standard for representing text is an American standard and does not support the special needs of even closely related languages such as French or German. These languages, although they use the Latin alphabet, require special accents (umlaut, circumflex, etc.) over letters that are necessary to the pronunciation of those languages. Most of the Latin alphabet issues are met by extending ASCII beyond the 128 characters to use the full 256 possibilities in an 8-bit byte.

The problem is complicated slightly by languages such as Russian or Bulgarian that use the completely different Cyrillic alphabet. In such a case, Cyrillic fonts can be selected that map the 256 values in a byte into the appropriate characters; the mapping of 8-bit integers into character faces is completely different from ASCII but the software techniques are identical.

However, there are languages—such as Hebrew and Arabic—that are written right to left instead of left to right. This means that the text reference point for drawing and the algorithms for text selection are all reversed. Because of the worldwide use of English in technology, users of such languages sometimes want to embed English words in the middle of sentences. This means that such compound strings contain fragments of both left-to-right and right-to-left text.

Oriental languages, such as Chinese or Japanese, use ideographic representations that have a large number of characters, each of which represents a single word or a word fragment. Except for the fact that such languages are frequently written top to bottom instead of left to right, many of the algorithms are the same. The biggest problem is that there are far more than 256 characters. To handle such strings, 2-byte character encodings and a much larger font are required. Such languages—with thousands of characters—also have keyboard entry problems in addition to the graphics problem of drawing text strings.

In order to be truly international, an interactive application must support the mixing of a variety of languages in a single drawing, document, or database. This requires more general character representations such as UNICODE, which attempts to define a 2-byte encoding for all of the world's major written languages.[3]

3.8 Clipping

The clipping problem arises when we want to limit drawing to a particular area of the screen. There are a variety of cases in which this might occur. The simplest is clipping to a rectangle, as shown in Figure 3-24. This is a commonly used form in computer graphics for clipping displayed objects to the bounds of the window in which they are to be displayed.

The rectangular-window clipping model is not sufficient, however, for most modern windowing systems. As Figure 3-25 shows, at least rectilinear clipping regions are required. If any drawing is to be done on the window in the back, all of its output must be clipped to the rectilinear visible region that remains when other windows are laid over the top. And as shown in Figure 3-26, such rectilinear regions must allow for holes if they are to accommodate all of the cases.

Figure 3-24   Rectangular clipping

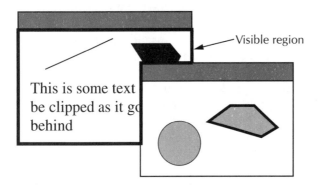

Figure 3-25   Rectilinear clipping to visible regions

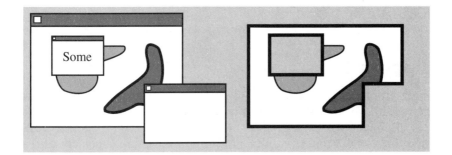

Figure 3-26   Rectilinear region with holes

3.8.1 Regions

A variety of types of regions can be used as the basis for clipping objects to the exact visible area. The critical consideration when choosing a particular type of region as the basis for clipping is the complexity involved in computing the intersections of the graphical objects that are being clipped and the boundaries of the region.

Types of Regions

As noted above, the simplest clipping region basis is rectangles. The most common region definition in current windowing systems is rectilinear. Rectilinear regions are closed shapes with their edges defined entirely by vertical and horizontal lines. Intersections with vertical and horizontal lines are just about the simplest geometry to compute; that, coupled with the general usefulness of such regions, is the reason they are used so frequently.

Some windowing systems support clipping to arbitrary polygons, which is a generalization of the rectilinear region in that the lines are not restricted to being vertical or horizontal. This form is not used very often because it only provides a limited increase in the kinds of regions that can be defined but it substantially increases the computation cost of the clipping.

PostScript-based systems, such as NeWS or NeXTSTEP, can clip to any complex shape bounded with a combination of lines and curves. This is a highly flexible and powerful model but it requires significantly more computation to do the clipping.

Some systems support clipping regions that are defined as pixel masks. A set of pixels with a 1 value is defined for the entire area within a bounding region. If a given pixel is 1, then objects drawn in the region will show at that pixel. If the pixel is 0, then drawn objects will not show at that pixel. This model is very fast when handled at the lowest levels of the system where objects are actually scan-converted to pixels. Also, the model is very powerful in that any shaped region can be defined. It is not very space efficient, however, and it has the problem of being very resolution dependent. One alternative is to define the clipping region as complex curved or polygonal shapes and then to scan-convert those shapes to a pixel map at the particular desired screen resolution.

One mechanism for reducing the space requirements of pixel-based regions is to run-encode them. For a given horizontal line of pixels, the 1s and 0s are grouped together. Instead of storing each 1 or 0 for each pixel, we can store the number of 1s and 0s in a row. Consider the shape in Figure 3-27. For any given horizontal line, there is a string of 0s for the empty space to the left, a row of 1s for the space inside the shape, and a row of 0s for the empty space to the right. By storing just three numbers, we represent all of the shape information on any given row.

Set Operations on Regions

When working with a clipping region, it is helpful to think of such a region as a set of points on the 2D plane that lie inside of the region. We can then work with the region in terms of set operations. Throughout the rest of the

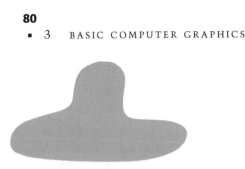

Figure 3-27   An arbitrary clipping region

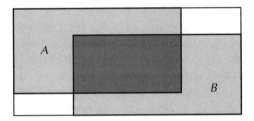

Figure 3-28   Set operations on rectangles

book, we ignore the particular style of clipping region that is supported by a given graphics package and simply treat them as abstract objects defined in terms of sets. The set operations that we are interested in are union, intersection, and difference.

Closure   A most important property when considering types of regions is closure under the set operations. *Closure* means that given some set, the result of any combination of operations on that set will yield a member of the same set. Take, for example, the rectangular regions A and B in Figure 3-28.

Note that the union $A \cup B$ is not a rectangle and that the difference $A - B$ is also not a rectangle. The intersection $A \cap B$ is a rectangle. This example illustrates that rectangular regions are closed under intersection but are not closed under union or difference. This lack of closure can be a problem in terms of the usability of a particular class of regions.

We can overcome the closure problems with rectangular regions by representing regions as a list of nonoverlapping rectangles rather than as a single rectangle. Lists of rectangles are closed under union and difference. In Figure 3-28, we can represent $A \cup B$ by dividing B into three small rectangles, one of which is $A \cap B$ and the other two of which make up the remainder of B. The result $A \cup B$ is A plus the two smaller rectangles from B. Similarly $A - B$ can be represented by slicing A into three smaller rectangles and retaining two of them. Any rectilinear region can be represented by a list of rectangles.

Abstract Class for a Region

For the purpose of this text, we assume that all regions are rectilinear and are composed of lists of rectangles. All subsequent uses of regions, however, are based on the abstract Region class that has the following methods:

Region Region::Union(Region)

> *Returns a region that is the union of the target region with the argument.*

Region Region::Intersect(Region)

> *Returns a region that is the intersection of the target region with the argument.*

Region Region::Difference(Region)

> *Returns all parts of the target region that are not in the argument.*

int Region::IsEmpty()

> *Returns true if the region is empty and false otherwise.*

Rectangle Region::Bounds()

> *Returns the smallest rectangle that completely encloses the region.*

int Region::IsInside(Point)

> *Returns true if the point is inside of the region and false otherwise.*

Region MakeRegion(basic primitive shape)

> *Constructs a region from a basic primitive object.*

In addition to the set operations, there is also a method for determining the rectangular bounds for a region, used for quick tests on the region before considering all of the complexity of the actual region definition. The IsInside method is used with mouse selection to determine if the region has been selected.

By using these methods on the abstract Region class, we can take care of most of our user interface needs. We use the difference operator extensively to handle problems with overlapping windows.

In order to use regions, we need to augment our abstract Canvas class with several methods, as follows:

Region Canvas::BoundingRegion()

> *Returns the regions that define the outside of the canvas.*

Region Canvas::VisibleRegion()

> *Returns the region of the canvas actually visible through all other canvases that might be overlapping.*

void Canvas::SetClipRegion(Region)

Sets the clipping region to the intersection of the argument and the visible region. All future drawing (until this is changed) will be clipped to this region.

Region Canvas::GetClipRegion()

Returns the clipping region.

The BoundingRegion method returns a region because windows may not be rectangular in their definitions. On some systems such as X, nonrectangular windows can be defined. The visible region for a window canvas is defined as its bounding region minus the bounding regions of all windows that lie in front. As will be discussed later, this visible region is very important for drawing information efficiently. A clipping region is used to restrict drawing to some smaller area inside of the canvas. Clipping regions will be used extensively when updating the screen in response to changes in displayed information.

3.9 Color

To understand the use of color, it is important to understand how the human eye perceives color. The retina of the eye is covered with two types of light sensors, rods and cones. The rods are sensitive to a broad spectrum of light. Because the rods are sensitive to a broad spectrum, they cannot discriminate between colors; they primarily sense light intensity or shades of gray. In contrast, there are three types of cones. Because of variations in pigment in the cones, each type is sensitive to a different band of the light spectrum. In humans, there are cones for red, green, and blue.

The eye does not directly measure all of the wavelengths of visible light. For example, yellow light, which falls in the spectrum between red and green, excites both the red cones and the green cones and thus gives a visual sensation of yellow light. The same visual sensation of yellow can be produced by simultaneously providing some light in the red band and some in the green band. The human eye is incapable of differentiating between light in the yellow wavelengths and light that consists of both red and green wavelengths. The fact is exploited by color modeling systems.

3.9.1 Models for Representing Color

There are various ways that color can be represented. Each of these models has different properties and provides a different set of controls for the user to specify color. In the end, however, they must all be converted to red, green, and blue (RGB) colors for actual display.

The RGB Color Model

The mixing of different wavelengths of light to produce the visual sensation of some particular intermediate wavelength forms the basis for all color displays. We can produce any of the human visual sensations of color by using varying intensities of the primary colors red, green, and blue. It has also been shown that the human retina can only distinguish about 64 levels of intensity. This means that we can represent all of the colors that can be sensed by the retina using 6 bits for each primary color, or a total of 18 bits.

The 64 levels of intensity, however, only account for retinal sensitivity, not the sensitivity of the total ocular system. The pupil, by varying the amount of light that enters the eye and strikes the retina, allows the eye to cover a much larger range of light intensity and allows us to function both in bright sunlight as well as in a dark basement. For most reading and other uses of a computer screen, the pupil only makes minor adjustments. This means that 256 levels of intensity for each primary color are more than adequate for human visual needs. We thus find that almost all computer displays represent colors with 24 bits (3 bytes) per pixel. There are frame buffers with a greater range than 8 bits per primary color but the additional bits are for image processing or composition functions, rather than for visual presentation of information.

Most windowing systems allow the programmer to set the current color of the canvas by specifying the RGB values of the desired color. This color is then used in subsequent drawing operations. Because a color can be represented in 24 bits, it is frequently represented by a single long word with special functions that assemble and extract the RGB components of the color. We can augment our canvas with the following methods:

```
long MakeRGB(int Red, int Green, int Blue);

int GetRed(long RGB);

int GetGreen(long RGB);

int GetBlue(long RGB);


void Canvas::SetColor(long RGB);

void Canvas::SetRGB(int Red, int Green, int Blue);

long Canvas::GetRGB();
```

For our abstract Canvas class, we have chosen to represent each of the colors red, green, and blue with an integer number between 0 and 255. In other systems that wish to remain more independent of the color resolution, red, green, and blue are each represented by a floating-point number between 0.0 and 1.0.

The HSV Color Model

Although the RGB model accurately represents what display devices must use to produce color sensations in the human eye, it is not a very good model for users to express a particular color. For example, if users are asked for the RGB values that represent the color of a manila envelope, they are very hard pressed to do so. For this reason, many user interfaces use the hue, saturation, and value (HSV) system for specifying colors.

Hue represents the primary wavelength of light. For most people, this is what they think of when they think of color. The hue might be red, yellow, orange, green, cyan, blue, or purple. The *value* is the intensity or brightness of the light. Thus we have light red or dark red. A yellow or orange hue with very low value would produce brown.

Saturation is a little more difficult to explain, it is a measure of how pure the primary light wavelength is. If there is only red light present, then the color is highly saturated. On the other hand, there may be the same amount of red light but also a lot of blue and green. The hue or primary wavelength is still red and the value or intensity is unchanged, but the color is pink rather than red. With pink, which has low saturation, there is a lot of white mixed with the red color. High saturation means a very pure color while low saturation means that a lot of white or gray has been mixed in.

The HSV model is directly linked to the RGB model, which is required for actually drawing on the display. The code for converting between HSV and RGB is somewhat complicated but not excessively.[4]

The CMY Color Model

For people trained in the visual arts, such as painting and printing, color is not defined in terms of mixtures of light but rather mixtures of pigment. A pigment gets its color from the light that it absorbs (does not reflect). For example, a green piece of plastic appears green not because it is generating green light but because it has absorbed the red and the blue light and is only reflecting green.

For mixing pigments, the cyan, magenta, and yellow (CMY) system is used. These are called the subtractive primary colors; red, green, and blue are the additive primaries. Each of these colors corresponds to the absence of one of the additive primaries. Cyan occurs when there is no red, magenta indicates no green, and yellow is what is left when blue light is removed. Mixing all of the subtractive primaries produces black rather than white because when all of the subtractive primaries are mixed, all wavelengths are absorbed.

In the printing business, it is also helpful to specify a black component in addition to cyan, magenta, and yellow. This need for black is a property of printing and ink rather than the mathematical mixing of colors. Images with greater contrast and clarity can be achieved through the printing process by actually using black ink rather than by mixing the CMY pigments to produce black. (This is the basis for four-color printing; the system acronym is CMYK, with *K* standing for black.)

3.9.2 Human Color Sensitivity

The human retina has approximately 7,000,000 cones and between 75,000,000 and 150,000,000 rods. These numbers mean that humans are 10 times more sensitive to variations in intensity than they are to variations in hue or the color wavelength of light. This also means that our ability to discriminate fine detail between two areas that have different hues but similar intensity is much worse than our ability to distinguish details that vary in intensity rather than hue.

The makeup of the human visual system has a strong impact on the use of color in a user interface. If the user is presented bright green text on a bright red background, it will be much harder to read than light green text on a dark red background. When presenting bright green on bright red, the rods cannot distinguish between the text and the background; only the cones will be able to distinguish between the two. This means that 90% of human visual capacity is useless in reading the text. In the case of dark on light, however, the rods can distinguish between text and background and can thus contribute to resolving the shape of each character.

The ability of the retina to distinguish differences of intensity is not uniform across the visible spectrum. The eye is much less capable of distinguishing intensity at the fringes of the spectrum (deep red and violet) than it is in the center where the yellows and greens are found. Reds and blues are less easy to resolve than other colors. This means that putting blue text on a dark red background will cause problems because we are forcing the eye to distinguish detail in the areas of the spectrum where it is least capable of resolving differences.

In terms of usability for all people, we must remember that many segments of the population are colorblind. In 1% of the male population, one of the primary colors cannot be sensed. A protanope (red blind) individual is not able to pick up the red primary; for such a person, bright cyan (green and blue) cannot be distinguished from white. A deuteranope cannot detect the green primary, and the very rare tritanope cannot sense the blue primary. In most situations, this is not a problem because most of our visual processing depends on the rods, which are sensitive across the entire visible spectrum. What this means, however, is that we must not present users with visual tasks that require discrimination based solely upon hue. There must also be a contrast in value or intensity.

In addition, the rods and cones are not distributed uniformly across the retina; there is a central area that has a much higher density. This high density of sensors allows much sharper resolution of images. It is this part of the eye that we use in reading. This makeup of the eye accounts for the very narrow focus of visual attention discussed earlier. We accommodate such a narrow focus by moving our eyes.

3.10 Summary

This chapter has covered the basics of drawing the images that are a central part of graphical interaction. Central to the process of drawing is the question of the coordinate system used to specify the geometry. Device coordinates are those actually supported by the device or system on which images are to be drawn. Physical coordinates provide resolution independence by specifying the physical size of the images that are drawn. Model coordinates allow an object to be specified in the size it is actually being represented rather than the size in which it is rendered. The transformations between these coordinate systems are discussed in more detail in Chapter 10.

Only a brief introduction has been given for output devices. The most common of these devices are the cathode ray tube (CRT), the liquid crystal display (LCD), and various hardcopy devices. For purposes of interactive systems, we encapsulate all of these in the abstract Canvas class; using this class, we can draw on any device regardless of its implementation. The actual details of image creation are handled in the implementations of the various subclasses of Canvas. Most of the drawing on a Canvas is done in terms of geometric primitives such as lines, circles, ellipses, arcs, and splines, or combinations of these primitives. Closed shapes are also formed from such geometries. Such stroke models for graphics objects are easy to specify and manipulate, but ultimately they must be converted to pixels for printing or display. It is also frequently the case that rectangular arrays of pixel values can be drawn on a canvas. Such direct use of the image model supports painting and image manipulations.

Of special interest is the drawing of text, which is complicated by a variety of factors related to various fonts. Outline fonts have clear geometric definitions while resolution-dependent, pixel-based fonts provide speed at some cost of space. Fonts with variable sizes and variable spacing pose additional algorithmic problems when they are being drawn and selected. International fonts, which will become increasingly important, also complicate the problem.

The concept of clipping to restrict drawing to a defined region has been introduced. This is the basis for most windowing and for a wide variety of other interactive techniques. Clipping has also been encapsulated in the abstract Region class, which provides set operations on regions of the drawable space. The geometry of regions is discussed in Chapter 9.

The specification of color is also important. We deceive the human eye in terms of color by only presenting mixtures of red, green, and blue (RGB). This physically based model for color, however, is not very intuitive. Instead, the hue, saturation, and value (HSV) model is a better way to express intended colors. For those trained in the visual arts, the cyan, magenta, yellow, and black (CMYK) model mirrors the behavior of pigments rather than light.

Throughout this chapter, human issues have also been addressed. When drawing images on the screen, the rate at which those images change is important. If we draw changes faster than 30 times per second, the changes fuse into continuous motion because this rate is faster than the sampling rate of the human eye. If we move something across the screen, a redraw rate as slow as 5 times per second preserves the "feel" of movement even if the movement no longer appears smooth to the eye. When drawing text, the notion of serifs, which aid the eye in tracking across lines of text while reading, was discussed. Finally, the issues of color perception were addressed, in particular the fact that humans differentiate light and dark far better than variations in color, and the fact that resolving detail in the blue and red areas of the spectrum is much harder than at the center of the spectrum in the green and yellow bands.

Basics of Event Handling

At the heart of user interface software is the event model for communication between interactive objects and the input/output system. This event model was developed to support the creation of direct-manipulation interfaces. *Direct manipulation* is when the user is presented with concrete objects on the display and then manipulates those objects using the interactive devices.

Before the advent of direct-manipulation interfaces, the interaction architecture was much simpler. Interfaces such as the DOS or UNIX command lines or the LISP interpreter had a very simple architecture. The software would read a line of text from the input, parse the text, evaluate the result, and repeat. Slightly more complicated question-answer dialogs had a similar architecture. Whenever the program, which was always in control, wanted some information from the user, a prompt would be written out to indicate what was wanted. The input line would then be read, parsed, and executed as before. The control architecture was simple because the program was in control. Users did what the program wanted them to do, and when the program wanted them to do it. The architecture for direct-manipulation interfaces is much more complicated than that because the user, not the program, is in control.

Before we look at exactly how user interface software is constructed, we must first understand the environment in which such programs run. It is assumed that our graphical user interfaces will run under the control of a *windowing system*. In this chapter, we will discuss the services performed by such systems and how interactive applications work within them. A modern graphical user interface communicates with other applications, with the windowing system, among parts of itself, and with the code that implements the interface's functionality. The communication is performed by means of

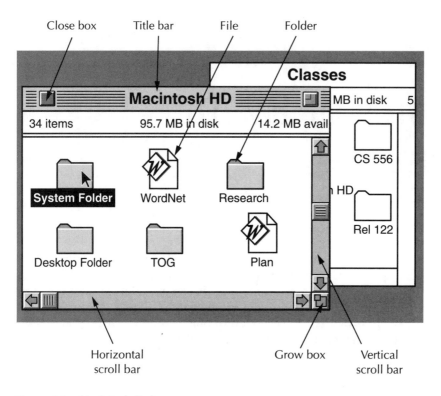

Figure 4-1   Macintosh finder

events. This communication between parts is crucial to the understanding of interactive software and is discussed in detail in this chapter.

To illustrate the kinds of problems that must be addressed, we will consider an example. Figure 4-1 shows a screen dump of the Macintosh finder that is the user interface to the file system. In this example, there are a variety of interactive options available to the user. The user can do these things, among others:

- close the window by clicking in the close box
- move the window by dragging the title bar
- bring the Classes window forward by clicking on it
- drag the WordNet file into the Classes folder

It is this complexity of what can be done that leads us to the event model architecture.

With the variety of options possible, there are several issues that must be addressed in handling events. The major issues discussed in this chapter are

- partitioning between the application and the windowing system
- the kinds of events a window might receive
- distributing inputs to the interactive objects
- models for communication between objects

4.1 Windowing System

On most graphical screens, a variety of interactive applications can be running simultaneously. Each of these applications is decomposed into smaller parts, where each performs some part of the interface functionality. In order to prevent chaos on the screen and in the software, graphical user interfaces are generally built on top of a *windowing system*. There are two aspects to such a windowing system. The first is a set of software services that allow programs to create and organize windows as well as to implement the interactive fragments within those windows. Together these fragments form the user interface. In addition to this software view of the windowing system, a user interface allows the user to control the size and placement of windows. This is called the *window manager.*

4.1.1 Software View of the Windowing System

It is almost universal in graphical user interfaces to decompose interactive objects into a tree, based on the screen geometry of the interactive objects. We can decompose our finder example from Figure 4-1 into the tree in Figure 4-2.

Notice that except for the files and folders in the folder contents area, the geometry of each of the subpieces in Figure 4-1 is a rectangle that is fully contained within the rectangle of its parent. This hierarchy of nested rectangles is the basis for the vast majority of windowing systems used in graphical user interfaces. The primary reason is that nested rectangles form a simple, consistent model for decomposing screen space and for dispatching events. It should be noted that some systems, such as X, provide for nonrectangular windows such as the two ovals required for the program X-eyes 〇〇 .

There is a wide variation in how much of this hierarchy is managed by the system software. On the Macintosh, only the top-level areas ("Macintosh HD" and "Classes") in Figure 4-1 are considered windows. All windowing systems would call these top-level items windows and would manage them in the system software. In most systems, these are referred to as *root windows.* In systems other than the Macintosh, however, there is only one root window, which is the display screen. For our purposes, we refer to the top-level windows rather than the whole display as the root windows.

Root windows are special because in most systems they provide the user interface abstraction for multiple applications. Each root window belongs to a

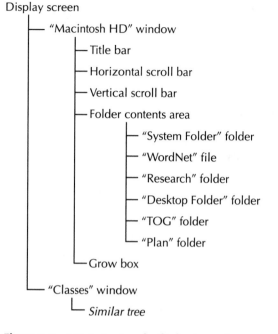

Display screen
— "Macintosh HD" window
— Title bar
— Horizontal scroll bar
— Vertical scroll bar
— Folder contents area
— "System Folder" folder
— "WordNet" file
— "Research" folder
— "Desktop Folder" folder
— "TOG" folder
— "Plan" folder
— Grow box
— "Classes" window
— *Similar tree*

Figure 4-2   Interactor tree for finder example

particular application and is managed by that application. In all modern systems, there can be a variety of applications, with each having a set of root windows. A primary purpose of a windowing system, then, is to arbitrate interactive resources and in particular screen space among these independent applications.

The concept that each root window corresponds to a given application and that all descendant windows belong to that application is generally true in all windowing systems. This distinction, however, has recently been broken down by systems such as Object Linking and Embedding (OLE) and OpenDoc. These systems allow applications to partition a piece of their window space to be managed by some other application. An example of this would be a word processor that allows a spreadsheet fragment to be pasted into a document and then allows the spreadsheet application to manage that screen space. Such architectures, which allow the embedding of one application in another, are very powerful and will be discussed much later in this text in a section by themselves.

In some systems, such as X, NeXTSTEP, or Microsoft Windows, all of the items in this hierarchy would be considered windows and would behave in the same uniform way. It would depend on the application as to whether items such as the contents of the folder contents area would be windows or would be handled in some other way by the application. In older systems, such as the Macintosh, only the root windows are considered windows. Items such as scroll bars, grow boxes, and buttons are handled under the separate concept of *controls.*

Most windowing systems provide a built-in set of interactive objects, such as text type-in boxes, buttons, scroll bars, or color selectors. These are referred to as either *widgets* or *controls.* Implementing each widget as a separate window is conceptually useful but may incur significant overhead in space and time. In systems like X or NeXTSTEP, a root window must have sufficient information to arbitrate between multiple asynchronous processes. That facility is usually overkill for a simple scroll bar. That is the reason why the Macintosh created the separate notion of controls that manage a rectangular area of screen space within a window. Sun/View has a similar notion of panes within windows. Panes have far less system overhead but provide similar interactive functionality. The Motif tool kit provides gadgets that behave similarly to widgets except that they do not have their own window.

For purposes of this text, we will refer to all of the rectangular regions known to the windowing system as *windows.* This means that windows can recursively contain other windows for the purpose of handling input events and screen space.

Since windows are an important part of the user interface system, many parts of the software must refer to them in some way. This is done by means of a window ID. In some systems, this is as simple as a pointer to the data structures that have information about the window. In others, it is a specially allocated integer that can be used to access internal tables. In almost all systems, the exact nature of this identifier is hidden from the programmer. The window ID is used in conjunction with various system calls to get information about windows and to perform operations on them.

4.1.2 Window Management

In modern windowing systems, the entire screen is viewed as a work area on which various applications can interact with a user. The management of this work area must be under the control of the user, just as a person generally has complete control over how his desk is organized. In order to manage this work space, the user must be provided with a standard user interface. On most windowing systems, root windows usually implement their interfaces using standard code provided by the windowing system. This standard code provides the user's interface for window placement and size and is known as the *window management* code. Providing a standard user interface for the manipulation of windows is very helpful to the users. On most systems such as MS Windows or the Macintosh, the window manager is fixed and standard.

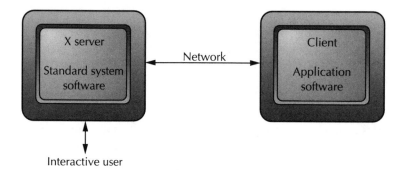

Figure 4-3   X client/server architecture

4.1.3 Variations on the Windowing System Model

There are several variations on the basic windowing system approach. The most notable of these are when the workstation serving the user is not the same as the one running the program. This network-based interaction forces several changes in the basic architecture that are addressed in different ways by X Windows, NeWS, and Java.

X Windows

There are several features of the X Windows system that impose special requirements on its implementation. The first is that the user and the application can be on separate machines, provided that there is a network connection between them, and the second is that the window manager is a separate process.

Most windowing systems are designed to allow the user of a workstation to interact with software running on that workstation. X, however, was designed so that the application software and the user do not need to be on the same machine. Figure 4-3 shows the overall architecture of X.

In the X system, there is a separate process called the *window manager* that takes care of the sizing and positioning of root windows. Notice in Figure 4-4 that there is a frame around the window with various regions that can be used to resize or reposition the window. There is also a title bar with standard buttons for opening, closing, and iconifying windows. This frame area is managed by the window manager, which in Figure 4-4 is the Motif window manager. Having the window manager as a separate process allows a variety of window managers to be used and even allows the implementation of special personal window managers.

Each system that supports X provides an X server program that can interpret X commands from the network and can send interactive events over the network. X client systems also provide Xlib, which provides the software

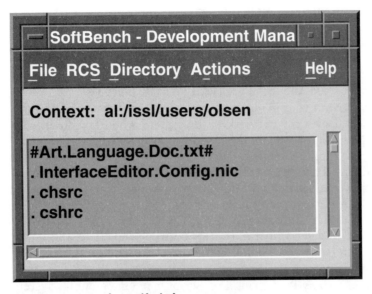

Figure 4-4   Example Motif window

interface to X. Xlib assembles the output from these routines into packets for transmission to the appropriate X server. When the user runs a program, he designates which machine on the network will be the user workstation. Xlib automatically forwards all output to the appropriate server on the appropriate workstation.

When a user generates interactive inputs, X must uniquely determine which window should receive those inputs and then forward the input events over the network to the system that is running the client software for that window. This means that, unlike the other windowing systems that must only arbitrate interactive resources among multiple applications on the same machine, X must arbitrate between applications running on different machines and possibly controlled by different users.

This client/server architecture provides great flexibility in the way that users interact over the network. It does, however, complicate the way in which X must handle input events. For the most part, however, X hides these problems from the application programmer. Therefore, we can discuss X as if the network issues did not exist.

NeWS Goes One Step Farther

There are two problems with the X system that are addressed in NeWS. The first of these is that all user interactions must make a round trip over the network. The second is the graphics model used. NeWS uses display Post-Script, which is based on splines rather than the more line-oriented model of X.[1]

Like X, NeWS is designed to handle interactive sessions over a network. To understand the differences between the two, let us consider the case of a scroll bar. When the mouse-down event occurs in the thumb area of the scroll bar, the thumb area must be redrawn to show that it is selected. As mouse-move events are received, the thumb must be drawn in a new position. When the mouse-up event is received, the scroll bar is drawn in its inactive state.

In X, the mouse-down event is received at the user's workstation and forwarded by the X server over the network to the system where the client software is running. The client software must send messages back to redraw the scroll bar thumb. For each mouse-move event, a message must be sent from the server to the client. The client software must then send one or more messages back to the server to have the thumb drawn in a new place. Every mouse movement on the scroll bar thumb involves a complete round-trip set of network messages to get the thumb moved. If there is any delay in the network, due to excessive load or the number of routers between the client and server workstations, the scroll bar acts very sluggish. This does not make for great usability.

NeWS is based on display PostScript. PostScript is itself a graphics system built around the language FORTH.[2] FORTH is a relatively fast interpretive language. PostScript defines all of its graphics routines as commands in FORTH and was originally designed to drive laser printers. Instead of sending the pixels for what is to be printed to the printer, application software sends a FORTH program with PostScript commands. The printer then executes this FORTH program to generate the printed image. This approach greatly reduces the network traffic required for high-resolution printing. FORTH also provides the ability to create new FORTH commands at run time, which can then be used by other parts of the FORTH program.

Display PostScript uses the same FORTH base and the same PostScript drawing commands. In addition, it defines commands for handling input events. A program can either download FORTH code into the NeWS server that will handle input events locally or it can have the inputs forwarded back to the client software. Remember that, as with X, the client software supports the application code and the server supports the user.

In our scroll bar example, we could do the following. When the mouse-down event is received, we can send the complete code for drawing the scroll bar as a FORTH procedure to the server. In addition, we can send code that converts the mouse-move events into invocations of the draw procedure for the scroll bar. Using this technique, there is no network traffic involved while dragging the scroll bar's thumb. When the mouse-up event is received, the client software is notified and whatever is being controlled by the scroll bar can be updated.

The key to NeWS is that, unlike X, the server can be programmed at run time using the FORTH language. This allows significant functionality to be programmed into the server by each application and thus can greatly reduce network traffic. There are problems, however, with the fact that the server may have limited resources and may be serving for multiple applications. In spite of these issues, NeWS provides a much more flexible and efficient interactive system than the simpler X model.

Java Goes Farther Still

The Java approach goes even farther than NeWS in downloading entire interactive applets into the server. The interactive server (usually embedded in a World Wide Web browser) is implemented as a virtual machine for executing Java programs. Thus, as with FORTH, Java provides a mechanism for remotely programming user interface servers. These applets function as complete interactive applications and use AWT (abstract window tool kit, the graphics layer and user interface tool kit for Java) to interact with the user. By downloading entire applets, Java user interfaces are implemented more like single-machine applications than X and NeWS because the networking is deeper in the application rather than in the user interface.

4.1.4 Windowing Summary

A windowing system breaks the screen space into semi-independent fragments. The programmer writes software for such fragments or reuses previously implemented fragments (widgets) to provide user interface functionality for an application. These fragments are then composed, generally in a tree structure, to form complete applications. The windowing system is responsible for arbitrating interactive resources such as screen space and input events among the various interactive fragments. Generally each fragment is a separate window. The window manager is software that provides a user interface for controlling placement of the root windows.

4.2 Window Events

As a user interacts with the input devices, these actions are translated into software events that are then distributed to the appropriate window. In some systems, such events are called *messages*, but the concept is the same. It is important to note that these messages or events do not always involve interprocess communication. Most message passing has the approximate cost of invoking a procedure rather than the cost of an operating system message.

Before discussing how events are distributed to windows, it is helpful to characterize the kinds of events that a window might receive. All events are identified by an *event type* that allows the receiving software to distinguish the kind of information that the event is intended to communicate. In addition to the event type, there is other information, such as the mouse position, the window to which the event is directed, or the character key that was pressed.

4.2.1 Input Events

Among the most important events are the input events generated by the user. Most such events carry with them the current mouse position, since that information is necessary to dispatch the event appropriately. In general, event records carry with them the identifier of the window that should receive the event. On older systems, such as the Macintosh, the programmer must make a separate call to convert the mouse position into a window ID.

Mouse Button Events

In mouse-based systems, the mouse button events are among the most important because they provide the point-and-click functionality found in most modern interfaces. A large amount of interactive functionality is associated with handling the mouse-up and mouse-down events. The mouse button events always carry the current mouse location with them.

To understand how these events are used, take the example of the finder application shown in Figure 4-1. If the user positions the mouse over the close box (the square box on the far left of the title) and presses the mouse button, an event signaling a button down is sent to the title bar object. The title bar must compare the mouse location with the position of the close box. If the mouse is inside the close box, the title bar interactor highlights the close box and remembers that fact. When the user releases the button, a button-up event is sent to the title bar. The close button is unhighlighted and the window is closed.

The interactive button syntax is actually more complicated than this because the mouse may have moved. The button-down event may have occurred outside of the close box, with the button-up event occurring inside the close box. Designing the complexities of button syntax is left for a later discussion.

The way in which mouse events are defined by a windowing system has a lot to do with how that system was designed relative to a particular hardware configuration. For example, the Macintosh tool box assumes that all mice have only one button and therefore there is only one event for button down (when the button is pressed) and one for button up (when the button is released). Microsoft Windows, in contrast, defines separate events for the left, middle, and right buttons of a three-button mouse.

X, however, was defined to run on a variety of platforms across the network and therefore defines a single button-down event and a corresponding button-up event. Each of these events carries with them the number of the button that was actually pressed. This allows application software to support any number of buttons. The flexibility of X is a problem, however, in that software that is written to rely on a three-button mouse is very difficult to use on hardware that only has a one-button mouse. For example, running UNIX programs—which use three buttons—from an X server program on a one-button Macintosh can be difficult.

Modifiers

Focusing so much interactive behavior through a limited number of mouse buttons has its problems. It is difficult to do 10 different interactive actions on a given object with only one or even three buttons. Many applications solve this by using special-function keys and double-clicking. All keyboards supply a Shift key and a Control key; many of them provide Alt, Meta, or Option. Many applications do different things in response to mouse button events, depending on whether or not one of these modifier keys is pressed.

There is a problem in how such modifiers should be handled relative to mouse button events. Defining separate events for each modifier key (down and up) leads to a lot of events and requires a lot of event logic for each handler. It also requires that the application software pay attention to when the modifiers are pressed relative to when buttons are pressed. Most systems define a "modifiers" or "flags" word, which is passed with the button events. This word assigns one bit to each modifier key. If a modifier key is down at the time the button event occurs, its corresponding bit in the modifiers word will be on. This simple mechanism provides the application software with great flexibility in ignoring or assigning meaning to such actions as Control-Alt-Shift-MiddleButton_Up. Many systems also add a modifier flag for the state of each of the mouse buttons. This allows applications to assign meaning to having multiple buttons pressed at the same time.

Double-Clicking

When the original Macintosh appeared with only one mouse button and only the Shift and Command keys, the set of possible mouse actions was limited. The Macintosh associated meaning with the notion of a double-click. A double-click is a second button-down event that occurs within a short amount of time from the previous button-down event. The length of time used to determine if a button-down event should be recast as a double-click event is settable by the user in all systems that define this concept. In Microsoft Windows, there is a separate double-click event for each of the three buttons.

On the Macintosh, the double-click is universally associated with opening an object or accessing more information about it. Interpreting double-clicks can be problematic because when an object receives the first button-down event it has no idea whether a double-click event will follow. This is resolved

Figure 4-5   XPaint using mouse motion

in most situations where a double-click has meaning by defining the first button-down event as a selection of the object and the double-click as the opening of the object. If the double-click never arrives, the original button-down event still has meaning. This, however, is only a convention, not a built-in feature of the system. Because of the influence of the Macintosh on graphical user interfaces, this double-click convention is widely used.

Because X was defined to run over a network on machines that—at the time—were relatively slow, the double-click was a problem. Double-clicking depends on accurate timing of the input events. With multiple processes and network delays, such timings were not practical. X, therefore, has no double-click event. Because of the Macintosh influence, however, many X applications simulate the double-click in the application code by comparing the time stamp of the events.

Function Buttons

Most hardware configurations provide many more buttons than those on the mouse. In earlier graphics systems, all buttons were treated uniformly. On most current workstations, these function buttons are physically mounted on the keyboard and so most windowing systems treat nonmouse buttons as special keys on the keyboard. In X, the resolution of this issue depends on the implementation of a particular X server. The X model is flexible enough to accommodate either choice. The client software, however, must adapt to whatever choices the actual server makes.

Mouse Movement Events

Figure 4-5 is a snapshot of XPaint in the midst of sketching a curve. In order to sketch this curve, the paint window object needs to know the position of the mouse at much more frequent intervals than on the button-down and -up events.

In very early graphics systems, mice and other locator devices were treated as sampled devices; that is, whenever the application software needed to know the location of the mouse, it would call a routine (or read a hardware I/O register) to obtain the current mouse location. With the advent of event-driven interfaces, this sampled model was no longer appropriate. In particular, user interfaces running on multitasked systems such as UNIX have problems with sampled devices.

In order to implement a tool like XPaint using a sampled approach, the application would enter a loop of reading the mouse and then updating the screen. Such a tight inner loop steals machine cycles from all other processes. This is a problem because process-time slices are on the order of 1/60 of a second and interactive input requires only about 1/5 of a second. Such a loop is extracting information and performing processing at 12 times the rate actually needed by the user interface. Thus a large amount of computing resource is wasted and cannot be used by other applications.

In the early Macintosh, only one application could be running at once. Based on this, the system provided a NULL event whenever there were no other events pending. Mouse motion dialogs such as painting would be driven by this NULL event. The advantage was that software was now entirely event driven. This simplified the software architecture. Such an approach in a multitasking system, however, would have the same problems as the sampled approach. In the Macintosh, with only one process, the system had nothing better to do. This made running through code to process NULL events as good a use of the CPU as doing nothing.

In order to resolve the mouse motion issue for multitasking, most systems now provide a mouse motion event. The windowing system generates a special event each time the mouse actually changes position. This means that if a user starts a compile while a paint program is running and walks away to talk with someone, the paint program does not compete with the compiler for cycles because there are no events being generated for the paint program if the mouse is not moving.

Our XPaint example points out an additional optimization that can be made. Most cases where a window needs continual notification of the mouse movement occur when one of the mouse buttons is currently pressed. This applies to most painting, drawing, and dragging operations. X, MS Windows, and NeXTSTEP all provide mechanisms for masking off all mouse motion events when there is no button being pressed.

In X, where the input devices may be on a different machine from where the client software will handle the inputs, further refinements become necessary. The problem is the latency in the network connection between the server and the client. X provides a PointerMotionHint option that only reports motion events when 1) the pointer (mouse) has actually moved and 2) the client software actually asks for the next event. In situations like echoing

Help

Figure 4-6   Handwriting recognition

menu selections, the exact trace of the mouse location over time is not important. What is important is the current location at the time the menu selection is to be updated.

The network and process latency can also cause a problem when very fine information about the mouse location is required. Such a case occurs when trying to recognize handwritten gestures, as in Figure 4-6. Many current handwriting-recognition algorithms sample the input devices at a much higher resolution than the screen display. Some such algorithms also use the timing of the motion events as part of their recognition. Recent versions of the X server support the concept of a motion history buffer that allows the server to accumulate motion events and to provide them in a block when they are requested by the client software.

Mouse-Enter and Mouse-Exit Events

A more common set of motion events are the mouse-enter and mouse-exit events. These events are generated whenever the mouse cursor enters or leaves a window. An example use of this is the action of a button on the screen. When a button on the screen is pressed, it must be highlighted. If, while the mouse button is still down, the user moves the mouse outside of the window associated with the screen button, then the screen button is unhighlighted. We could program this with mouse motion events but that is much more precision than is required. Sending mouse-enter and mouse-exit events to a window is relatively simple for the windowing system and has very little overhead.

Keyboard Events

Keyboard events are special for a variety of reasons. In its simplest form, a keyboard can be considered an array of buttons. Each button (key) can generate an event for key down and another for key up. There are several complications with the handling of keyboard events.

First, keyboards are not standard. In the US, the set of letters and special symbols is fairly standard; however, the placement of some special characters (physical button assignment) is not standard. When we leave the US for the UK, some symbols—such as currency—change. When we go onto the European continent, we encounter variations in the letters with various inflections and accents. When we enter Asia, we encounter nonphonetic systems such as Kanji characters in China and Japan. This array of buttons called a keyboard can have an enormous range of meanings.

A second problem is that keys tend to work together. The "A" key has a different meaning when the Shift key is pressed. This is further complicated by the Control, Alt, Meta, and Command modifiers on various keyboards. All of these combinations must be accounted for. At the extreme are computer games, in which holding various keys down simultaneously has meaning, much like playing chords on a piano.

The last problem in deciding what to do with a keyboard event is the notion of accelerator keys, as provided by most windowing systems. On most Macintosh applications, any key that is pressed in conjunction with the Command or Apple key (⌘) is not passed directly to the application windows but is captured and forwarded to the menu system as a surrogate for selecting a menu item. If no menu item has this key associated with it, then it can be forwarded to the application. In Motif, the Alt or Meta key serves the same function. In fact, in many applications a single modifier key is not sufficient for all such accelerator keys because there are more than 24 choices that could profit from a key binding.

The complexities of keyboard handling will not be discussed at this time. For our current discussion, it is sufficient to understand that each key press and release will generate an event. With the event is an accompanying *scan code*, which essentially defines the actual key that was pressed or released. All windowing systems provide a routine or set of routines that can translate these raw key events into a more acceptable form. Scan codes can be replaced by ASCII or UNICODE characters. Accelerator keys can be filtered out and appropriately handled. Modifier keys will have their actual events intercepted and instead will participate in the conversion to ASCII codes and the provision of modifiers/flags as discussed earlier.

In general, most interactive objects handle a key-down event that has been translated into ASCII. Dealing with the additional complexities of keyboards will be left for later in this chapter.

4.2.2 Windowing Events

The next major class of events that a window can receive has to do with managing the window itself. Most windowing systems will send an event when the window is first created. This event allows the window to be initialized. A corresponding event is sent when the window is being destroyed, which allows the application code to clean up any data associated with the window. A similar pair of events can be associated with opening and closing the window. In some window systems—such as X, MS Windows, or NeXTSTEP—a window can be reduced to an icon and set aside; there is a pair of events associated with iconifying and deiconifying a window. Some windowing systems such as the Macintosh have the notion of a currently selected window. A window receives one event when it is selected and another when it is deselected. These events allow the window to change its appearance depending on whether or not it is selected.

One very important event notifies the application code that the window has been resized. This event allows the software to adjust what is displayed in the window to accommodate the change in size.

4.2.3 Redrawing

An important issue is how a window's visual display gets updated in response to resizing, obscuring, data changes, and all other things that might happen. Let us again consider our example from the Macintosh finder in Figure 4-1. In this example, the "Macintosh HD" window is obscuring most of the "Classes" window. If the user were to select the "Classes" window by clicking on it, the Macintosh style guidelines indicate that the "Classes" window would be brought to the top. This would mean that the portion of the "Classes" window that is obscured by the "Macintosh HD" window would need to be drawn over the top of the "Macintosh HD" window. Such drawing actions are also required if a NeXTSTEP window is converted from an icon to a full window.

The problem is that the windowing system itself has no capability to draw what has been hidden without help from the application. Some older systems such as the AT&T Blit terminal provided off-screen bitmaps for the hidden portions and modified the drawing primitives to actually draw into these hidden areas if necessary.[3] Some form of this is provided in the X Windows concept of *backing store.* In general, however, saving copies of hidden portions of a window can be very costly in space and is not frequently done.

The windowing system needs a mechanism for having the application redraw the newly exposed portions of the window. This is done by sending the window a *redraw event.* This event carries with it a rectangle or region of the screen that should be redrawn. In X, these are called expose events; in NeXTSTEP, it is the drawSelf event; in MS Windows, it is the WM_PAINT event; and on the Macintosh, it is the updateEvt event.

One of the most confusing concepts for new programmers of window-based interfaces is the fact that you can't just draw in the window. Yes, there are routines for drawing in the window but these draw instructions must be performed in response to a redraw event. The application draws when user actions require it to draw, not when the software decides it wants to draw. The implementation of handlers for redraw events will be discussed in great detail in Chapter 5. The issue again is that an application is not in control of all of

```
Initialization
while(not time to quit)
  { Get next event E
    Dispatch event E
  }
```

Figure 4-7   Generic main program

the situations that may modify the screen display. Such applications must therefore be designed to respond to whatever might occur.

4.3 The Main Event Loop

Having discussed how windows are organized in a windowing system and the set of events that a window must be prepared to receive, we now need a general understanding of how events are actually processed. Event-driven programs are very different from traditional software architectures.

When most programmers first start working with windowing systems, they take a sample program, locate "main," and start reading to understand how the program works. This is very frustrating in interactive programs because there is little or nothing in the main program. The main program for all windows-based applications is shown in Figure 4-7.

In the initialization, the application will define windows, load information about the application, and generally set up things. This usually involves creating a main window for the application. In many systems, the main window will not appear until the event processing starts. The reason for this is that no drawing is done in the new window until a redraw event has been received and dispatched to that window, after which the window will appear.

The actual calls to create windows vary from system to system and will not be discussed in this text. Suffice it to say that the initialization must create at least one window that the user can interact with. Subsequent actions may create more windows but one is required to get started. That window may be as simple as a menu bar (as on the Macintosh), but there must be some visible object to manipulate and all such objects exist in windows.

If you read this main program with the intent of understanding the application, you find that it is fruitless. The routine to get the next event and in many cases the routine to dispatch the events are system calls that cannot be read. Reading the main program is like following a creek only to have it immediately go underground. The real functionality of the program is in the code that handles events that are being passed to windows.

Key down key 16	*The Control key.*
Key up key 16	*Oops.*
Key down key 75	*The Shift key.*
Key down key 42	*The "t" key.*
Key up key 42	*The "t" key.*
Key up key 75	*The Shift key.*

Figure 4-8 Low-level key events

4.3.1 Event Queues

There are various models for how events are distributed to objects; of prime importance is the main event queue. As the user manipulates interactive devices, input events are placed in a queue. In multitasked systems such as X or NeXTSTEP, there is one queue for each process. All windowing systems provide a routine to get the next event from the queue. In some systems like the Macintosh and X, all communication with windows must pass through this queue as events. MS Windows and NeXTSTEP have event-handling mechanisms that allow event distribution without going through the queue. These shortcuts simply invoke the dispatch mechanism directly rather than queuing the event. In almost all cases, however, events are placed on the queue and the main event loop removes them and dispatches them for processing.

4.3.2 Filtering Input Events

In many cases, the raw input events are too low level for effective use. Take the simple example of entering the letter "t." The low-level event sequence might be that shown in Figure 4-8.

What is generally wanted is the single event "Key down (t)." The mistaken pressing of the Control key and the pressing of the Shift key are generally irrelevant to getting the ASCII character "t."

This case is more complicated when dealing with foreign keyboards such as those for Kanji. The set of possible input characters far exceeds the number of keys on the keyboard. Input techniques have been devised that use multiple keystrokes and possibly a popping up of a small set of choices for selecting the right character. X provides special XIM processes that handle such input tasks and then forward the final character to the application. The low-level key events need to be filtered out by the input handler before being dispatched.

Another case is the accelerator keys associated with menus in many systems. Figure 4-9 shows a Macintosh menu where entering "Command O" is the same as selecting the "Open" menu item. The key event sequence needs

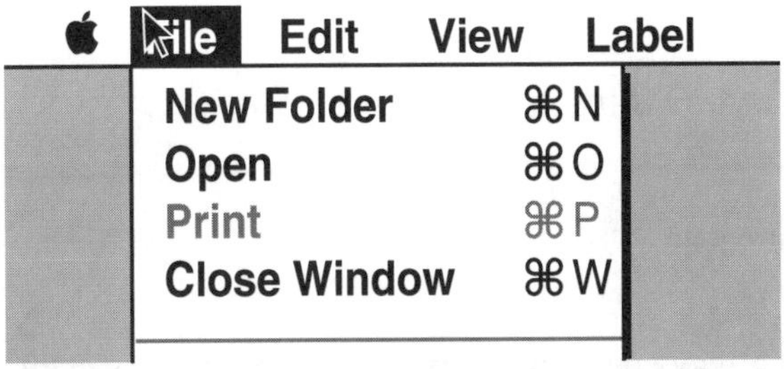

Figure 4-9   Macintosh accelerator keys

```
Initialization
while(not time to quit)
  { Get next event E
     if(not FilteredEvent(E))
       { Dispatch event E
       }
  }
```

Figure 4-10 Filtered events

to be filtered out by the menu system and replaced by an event that indicates a menu selection.

To handle all of these cases, we modify the generic main program to that shown in Figure 4-10. If the event E is filtered, then the FilteredEvent function will handle the event and return true. Using this technique, only the higher-level events (after menu handling and other chores) fall through into the event-dispatching code.

The nature of what must occur in filtering events varies widely and is very system specific. Readers are referred to the manuals on particular systems for the details. In our example of the letter "T," all of the low-level key-down events would return true from FilteredEvent with the exception of the key events on "t," which would be changed to the correct ASCII code in Filtered-Event. In our accelerator key example, all of the key events would return true and would thus be ignored. A menu-selection event would be generated, how-ever, and placed in the queue; when dispatched, it would cause the file open dialog to appear.

There is one more aspect of event filtering that may not be handled in the main event loop. This is the masking of events that particular windows actu-ally want. As windowing systems have matured, there are an ever-growing number of input events that can be generated to handle special cases. In many

```
Application myApp;
Initialize windows and application data structures.
Set any special event masks by sending messages to myApp.
myApp.Run();
```

Figure 4-11   Object-oriented main program

situations, these events are not always needed. A prime example is very accurate mouse motion events. These events consume lots of resources because of their frequency. While writing a forms-based business program, however, you have no need for finely detailed mouse movements. Most windowing systems allow the programmer to set an event mask that indicates which events are of interest. This event mask is set during the initialization. Some systems such as the Macintosh and X set an event mask for the entire application, while others provide masks per window. Such masks inform the windowing system of the events that are truly of interest to the application; all other events can be discarded in order to not waste resources.

4.3.3 How to Quit

Terminating the application main loop is relatively easy. In systems where the programmer writes the main event loop, a global variable is defined and is initialized so that the loop continues. Whenever the application wants to quit, the variable is changed so that the loop terminates. As applications got more complex, various window-closing and termination events were created to help windows take themselves down cleanly. MS Windows provides a PostQuitMessages routine that will send termination events to all necessary windows before setting the flag to indicate a quit.

4.3.4 Object-Oriented Models of the Event Loop

Various object-oriented tool kits have been developed that take over the standard functions of the main event loop. Generally there is an *application class* that is defined in the tool kit. This class has initialization methods to set up the application, although much of the standard initialization is performed automatically when an application object is created. This is the strategy used by Microsoft's Visual C++,[4] Borland's OWL library,[5] and Apple's MacApp.[6]

The application class generally provides a Run method that contains the actual event loop. There is also some kind of Quit method that takes care of cleaning up and stopping the event loop. When a simple application is being built, the program is like Figure 4-11.

The application class provides methods that take care of all of the special event-handling cases. If a programmer needs to take control of some of that special processing, the programmer can define a new subclass of the application class that can override the standard methods with special code to handle those cases. This is a classic use of object-oriented programming, which is to inherit the normal behavior and only provide extra code for what is different or special.

4.4 Event Dispatching and Handling

So far we have discussed the fact that events are the primary communication vehicle in interactive programs. We have discussed the variety of events that are possible. We have also considered the main event loop found in every windows-based program. It is now time to address how those events are dispatched to the various window objects and how programmers define application code that responds to those events. We need to answer the following questions:

■ How are events actually dispatched?
■ How does a programmer write application code that can attach to a window and handle the events that the window receives?
■ How does a programmer reuse standard behaviors such as scroll bars and push buttons, while providing the special handling that is unique to the application?
■ How do window objects communicate with each other to cooperatively accomplish a task?

These questions can be illustrated by the following example interaction. Figure 4-12 shows a window fragment from Microsoft Word. The parts of the window tree essential for this example are shown in Figure 4-13.

Suppose that the user wants to scroll the text in the text window. The set of user actions would be to

1. move the mouse over the thumb of the vertical scroll bar
2. press the mouse button
3. drag the thumb to the desired location
4. release the button

In response to this series of user actions, software must be provided that

1. directs the mouse events to the scroll bar

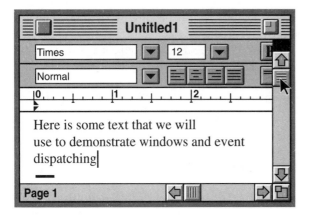

Figure 4-12   Microsoft Word window

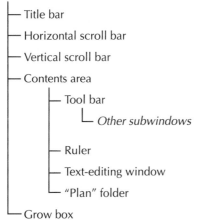

Figure 4-13   Partial window tree

2. updates the scroll bar display in an appropriate manner while the drag operation is in effect

3. notifies the text-editing window that it needs to scroll itself so that the text appears to have moved

In doing all of this, we want to reuse the standard code for managing the vertical scroll bar. All we want to modify is how that scroll bar notifies the text-editing window of the new scroll position.

4.4.1 Dispatching Events

Since very early windowing systems such as Canvas/GIGO,[7] the model for dispatching mouse events has been based on the window tree. The algorithm generally used is to select the bottom, frontmost window. In our example, the mouse position is over the vertical scroll bar in Figure 4-12. This is inside of the Untitled1, vertical scroll bar, and tool bar windows. The Untitled1 window is rejected because it is higher in the window tree than the other two. The vertical scroll bar is selected because it is in front of the tool bar at that point.

A large number of windowing systems use exactly this algorithm to select a window from the window tree using the current mouse location. Once the window is selected, the event is forwarded to the code that controls that window. This approach is referred to as a *bottom-first* event-dispatch model. The advantage of this model is that objects that control windows only need to consider their own events and the window system handles all of the arbitration between windows. A disadvantage of this model is that it is difficult to impose any high level of control over the event dispatching; the standard algorithm is all you get.

Suppose for a moment that we wanted to disallow scrolling of the text and only wanted the scroll bar as an indicator for the current location in the file. (There are strong usability reasons for not doing it this way, but we will set them aside for the moment.) What we would like to do is inhibit the vertical scroll bar from receiving any mouse events. In a bottom-first dispatch algorithm there is no way to exert this control. The events are passed directly to the window with no possible intervention by application code.

An alternative to the bottom-first algorithm is a *top-down* algorithm. The event would always be passed to the Untitled1 window as the topmost, frontmost window that contains the mouse position. The Untitled1 window is a special container window that has code to dispatch the event to one or more of its children. Standard code for container windows would provide the same functionality as the bottom-first model that users expect but would allow some portions of the event dispatching to be modified by programmers.

Key Dispatching

The algorithms described above work fine for mouse-related events that have an inherent geometric position. The question is how to dispatch keyboard events that have no such inherent position. This is a topic of much religious feeling among users of UNIX workstations. The mouse-based dispatch algorithm appends the mouse location to all key events and then uses that position to dispatch events in exactly the same way as the mouse events. This means that the key events will go to whatever window currently contains the mouse position.

An alternative key-dispatch algorithm is the click-to-type model, which will send key events to the last window where a mouse-down event occurred. This algorithm is complicated somewhat by mouse-down events in nontext areas such as scroll bars and screen buttons.

The click-to-type model is usually implemented using the concept of a *key focus*. A window can inform the windowing system that it wishes to receive all future key events. No matter where the mouse is, key events are always dispatched to the window with the key focus. When a window requests the key focus, an event is sent to whichever window previously held the focus to inform it that it has lost the focus. Using this model, any window that can accept text will request the key focus whenever it is selected.

In some forms-based dialogs, it is useful to have a tab or carriage return pass the key focus on to a different window. This allows a form to be filled out without the user's hands leaving the keyboard. (Usability issues arise again.) When a window with the key focus receives a tab (or carriage return), it can explicitly release the key focus that allows it to be passed to another window.

Mouse Focus

The concept of a mouse focus is similar to a key focus. Take, for example, our vertical scroll bar. If the scroll bar is long and narrow, it may be difficult for a user to stay inside of the scroll bar while dragging the thumb from one end to the other. In our standard model for mouse events, moving outside the scroll bar would cause a series of mouse-enter and mouse-exit events with subsequent loss of the dragging. In some systems, the programmer can request the mouse focus, which will cause all mouse events to be sent to a particular window regardless of where the mouse actually is. In our scroll bar example, when the mouse button goes down inside of the thumb, the scroll bar can request the mouse focus. It retains this focus and receives all events until the mouse button goes up. When the button goes up, the scroll bar code releases the mouse focus, which restores the standard dispatch algorithm.

4.4.2 Simple Event Handling

Having determined which window should receive a given event, we must be able to tie application code to those events. The unique behavior of a window is determined by the code that processes a window's events. Wrapped up in the issues of event-handling code are the techniques for reusing standard implementations of window objects such as scroll bars and push buttons.

The event-handling techniques used on a particular system are very much dictated by the programming language used in the original system design. The Macintosh was designed for Pascal. X and MS Windows were designed for C. NeXTSTEP was designed around Objective-C. As object-oriented programming became popular, MacApp, which is built around Object Pascal, appeared on the Macintosh. Motif was developed for X, using the Xtk intrinsics, which are a package of C library routines with some object-oriented flavor to them. The model for Motif, however, remains essentially C. Visual C++ from Microsoft and the Borland C++ libraries have appeared on MS Windows. NeXTSTEP, obviously, needed no transition to an object-oriented language.

Macintosh-Style Event Handling

Using only the functionality of Pascal to handle input events and having only Xerox as a model to follow in designing system software for graphical user interfaces, the original Macintosh event handling was quite limited. As discussed earlier, a system routine would map an input event to the information about a particular window. The window data structures provided a mechanism for the application to store a pointer to additional information about the window. When the window was initialized, the application would store some identifier as to the kind of window it was, and then the event handler could use that identifier in a Case statement to determine which code should be called to handle the event. Once the window type had been selected, the application code usually provided another Case statement based on the event type, which would select the particular code for that event. This basic convention was used by most Macintosh programmers but was not explicitly supported by the windowing system.

Event Table Model

To provide a better model for event handling, a research system called GIGO was developed for C and UNIX and was later used as the basis for the Notifier in Sun/View, which was the first windowing system on Sun workstations. This model exploits the ability of C programmers to obtain and save the address of a C procedure. Using the saved address of the procedure, other software can invoke that procedure at a later time. The use of procedure addresses is basic to a large number of windowing systems as well as to the implementation of message/method binding in C++.

In GIGO, each event has an integer event type ranging between 0 and 255. Each window has a pointer to its parent window, a data pointer, and a pointer to an event table. The event table contains the addresses for C procedures that will handle events for the various event types. The event-dispatching algorithm selects a window for the event, locates that window's event table, and subscripts the event table for that window using the event type. This subscript yields the address of a C procedure. This procedure is called using the window and the event record as parameters.

These event tables are built as part of the initialization of a window. A programmer writes separate procedures for each of the events that a window needs to handle and places their addresses in the appropriate locations in the event table. If there are several windows with the same functionality, they share an event table. The differences between windows sharing event tables are in the window data pointer where descriptions of the state of the various windows are found.

The programmer can obtain a new initialized event table from the system, where all of the indices are loaded with a standard routine that forwards the event to the parent window. This default event table provides a standard protocol whereby any event that a window's event table does not support is passed to the parent for handling.

This event table mechanism also provides rudimentary support for reusable widgets. Suppose that we want to create a push button to be used in a variety of situations. The differences between the situations are the label in the button and the code to be executed when the button is pressed.

The button widget programmer creates an event table with event procedures to handle the various input and redraw events. All of these procedures assume that the information referenced by the window data pointer has as its first word a pointer to a string with the button's label in it. GIGO allowed up to 256 types of events but actually only defined less than 20. This meant that there were a large number of event types available for application code to use. The button widget programmer could allocate one of these event types to use as notification of the button being selected. Such an application-defined event is called a *pseudoevent*. When the standard button code determines that the button is selected, it sends this new type of event back to its own window.

If you want to use this standard button code, do the following in initializing the button's window:

▪ Make a copy of the standard button event table.
▪ Write a procedure to be executed whenever the button is selected.
▪ Place the address of this procedure in the event table at the location corresponding to the selection event type reserved by the button widget programmer.
▪ Allocate window data information and make sure that the first word of this information points to a string containing the label for the button.
▪ Place a pointer to the window data in the window data structure.

Having done all of these steps, the new button behaves as the standard button did, with the exception of its label and the code to be executed when the button is selected.

Xtk/Motif Callback Model

One of the main problems with the GIGO model was that a programmer had to be very careful in setting up and managing event tables and the procedure addresses stored in those tables. This was a particular problem because if you were wrong in placing the procedure addresses, your program would end up in weird places that were very hard to debug.

To address this problem, the Xtk intrinsics were developed and simultaneously coined the term *widget*. Xtk provided mechanisms for storing information such as colors and labels in *resources* that are read from a file at run time. These resource files are easier to read than code, and things like labels are easier to change when internationalizing a user interface. Motif is built on top of Xtk and provides a standard set of widgets that are used on most UNIX workstations. Motif also provides a simpler set of routines for creating and managing widgets.

When we create a button using Motif, we do the following:

- Create an argument list containing information about the label and other information unique to the widget.
- Call a Motif routine to create an instance of the button widget using the argument list.
- Write a procedure to be executed whenever the button is selected.
- Register the button selection procedure as a callback on the widget, using the appropriate callback name defined by the button widget.

As this process describes, each kind of widget defines a set of named callbacks that it will invoke. Callbacks are similar in concept to the pseudoevents defined in GIGO. Using the routine XtAddCallback, a programmer can attach a callback procedure address to one of these named callbacks. Callbacks hide all of the event-dispatching mechanism from the programmer and provide a much more reliable facility. With the callback procedure address, the programmer can also provide a word of data (usually a pointer) that is passed to the callback procedure. This pointer to information allows for multiple buttons to use the same callback procedure with different information on each button.

Relative to Figure 4-12, we described the problem of notifying the text window to scroll itself whenever the scroll bar is moved. To accomplish this scrolling, a programmer could create a vertical scroll bar widget. A callback procedure would be written that has code to notify text windows of their new scrolling location. This callback procedure would be registered with the widget as the callback to be invoked when the scroll bar is moved. Along with the callback procedure, a pointer to the text window would be registered as the callback data. This pointer would tell the callback procedure which window was to be scrolled.

In our example, when the user presses the mouse button over the thumb of the scroll bar, the standard widget code handles the event. As the mouse is used to drag the thumb, the mouse movement events are also handled by the standard widget code. When the button goes up, the scroll bar widget code invokes whatever callback procedures have been registered with it.

Like GIGO, the Xtk/Motif model of event handling is based on programmers providing the windowing system with addresses of procedures to call in response to particular events. Xtk/Motif callbacks provide a better mechanism for handling this event process but the model is essentially the same.

WindowProc-Based Event Handling

Microsoft Windows was designed after the Macintosh, Sun/View, X, and Motif had been on the market for some time. As such, the designers had the advantage of studying the prior systems. MS Windows derives much of its windowing system architecture from the Macintosh model. The event-handling mechanism, however, is far superior. The MS Windows model—like GIGO, Xtk, and Motif—is based on storing the addresses of C procedures.

MS Windows programmers can define *window classes,* which are registered with the system under a specific name. The key component of a window class is the WindowProc. Every window has a class and every class has a WindowProc, which is similar in concept to a callback procedure. In essence, each window class defines exactly one callback procedure that handles all events. Every WindowProc has the following four parameters:

- a pointer to the window that received the event
- the integer event type of the event (called a *message* in the MS Windows system)
- wParam and lParam, which are words of information that depend on the type of event received

Whenever the event-dispatching algorithm identifies a window that should receive an event, that window's WindowProc is invoked with the appropriate information. The dispatch algorithm is thus quite simple.

Application programmers define new window behaviors by writing new window procedures, registering them as window classes, and then building windows that use the new class. The body of a window procedure is essentially a switch on the event type with each case of the switch implementing a handler for the particular event.

Because all communication in MS Windows is done in terms of events, there are over 100 standard events defined along with many more that are defined for other purposes and others that are defined by the application itself for communication. This number of events can make writing a window procedure very complicated.

In general, window procedures only handle a fraction of the possible events; most event handling is inherited from another window class. Because MS Windows was built for C, there is no language support for classes or inheritance. MS Windows uses an inheritance mechanism known as *delegation.* The idea is that each window procedure handles the events that it understands and then delegates all other events to some other window procedure.

Creating a new kind of button consists of writing a new WindowProc and registering the procedure as a window class. This procedure handles whatever events it needs to and then calls the standard button class's window procedure to handle the rest. One of the things that this new type of button can do is to forward all input events to the standard button window procedure and process only the events generated by actually selecting the button. All windows ultimately must invoke DefWindowProc either directly or indirectly through a superclass. This provides the standard window-management functionality.

4.4.3 Object-Oriented Event Handling

All of the event-handling mechanisms described so far have required that programmers either explicitly sort out events with case or switch statements or register the addresses of event-handling routines. All of these mechanisms are prone to programmer errors that can be difficult to debug. Object-oriented languages provide mechanisms that can more naturally handle the issues of passing messages between independent objects. Object-oriented languages are the basis for the NeXTSTEP windowing system, MacApp, Visual C++, Inter-Views,[8] and Java. With the exception of NeXTSTEP and Java, all of the object-oriented tools are pasted as a layer on top of a windowing system designed without the benefit of a good object-oriented model.

Abstract Class for Event-Handling Class

In order to handle windowing events, we define an abstract class that defines the behavior to which all event-handling objects must conform. We will define a simple version of such a class for discussion purposes. There are wide variations among systems on the methods used for such a class; the details are only important when programming in a given system.

We will call our abstract class WinEventHandler and give it the following methods:

SetCanvas(Canvas)
> *Sets the canvas that this event handler can use to draw on the screen.*

SetBounds(BoundsRect)
> *Sets the screen bounds allocated to this handler. This may be smaller than the bounds of the window.*

Rectangle GetBounds()
> *Returns the screen bounds allocated to this handler.*

MouseDown(Button, Location, Modifiers)
> *Invoked when a mouse-down event has been directed to this handler.*

MouseMove(NewLocation, Modifiers)
> *Invoked when a mouse-move event has been directed to this handler.*

MouseUp(Location, Modifiers)
> *Invoked when a mouse-up event has been directed to this handler.*

KeyPress(Key, Modifiers)
> *Invoked whenever a keyboard key is pressed.*

MouseEnter(Location, Modifiers)
> *Invoked whenever the mouse enters this handler's bounds.*

MouseExit(Location, Modifiers)
> *Invoked whenever the mouse leaves this handler's bounds.*

Redraw(DamagedRegion)
> *Invoked whenever some portion of this handler's screen area must be redrawn.*

These methods correspond to the major input events that we have discussed. If other events are defined by a given windowing system, other methods can be added to the abstract class. For all of these methods—with the exception of SetCanvas, SetBounds, and GetBounds—the default implementation is to do nothing.

The concept of a Canvas is described in Chapter 3. A Canvas is a drawable region that may be a window on a screen, a printer file, or an image representation in memory. For our purposes here, a Canvas is a window.

All object-oriented user interface tool kits have an abstract class similar to our WinEventHandler. In MacApp, it is TView; in Borland's system, it is TWindow; in Visual C++, it is CFrameWnd, and in NeXTSTEP, it is Responder.

Dispatching Events by the Windowing System

Based on this abstract class, we can now perform all of our handling of events based on the methods of this class. The first problem is to connect this abstract class into existing windowing systems that were not defined using object-oriented programming. The windowing system is generating events and the object model wants invocations of methods. What we need to do is associate an event handler object with each window to provide the translation between events and methods. The event handler object provides code to convert the events directed to that window into invocations of the appropriate methods on that window's event handler.

We will define a routine called NewWindow(EventHandler), which accepts a pointer to an object that is a subclass of WinEventHandler. This routine returns a newly created window. It also stores a pointer to the EventHandler in the window and stores a pointer to the window in the EventHandler using the SetCanvas method. All windowing systems provide mechanisms for storing application information in a window. In general, only a pointer is necessary. NewWindow is called as part of the initialization to set up the main windows of a program and can be called at other times whenever a new

```
Initialization
while(not time to quit)
  { Get next event E
    W = window to which E is directed
    WEH = W.myEventHandler
    switch(E.EventKind)
    {
    case RedrawEvent:
      WEH->Redraw(E.DamagedRegion);
    case MouseDownEvent:
      WEH->MouseDown(E.WhichButton,
          E.MouseLoc,
          E.Modifiers);
    case
        .  .  .  .
        .  .  .  .
    }
  }
```

Figure 4-14   Object-oriented event dispatching

window is created. The key is that EventHandler can be any of thousands of different subclasses of WinEventHandler, each of which interacts differently. It is important to point out that even windows that only display information without handling any inputs must have a WinEventHandler that implements the Redraw method to do the actual drawing.

In the case of the Macintosh or X Windows, we can modify our main event loop to that shown in Figure 4-14.

The dispatching of events now consists of finding the window that should receive the event, finding that window's event handler, and invoking the appropriate event handler method for each event. All of the other event-handling issues are taken care of by the method-invocation mechanisms of the programming language. In actuality, the callback tables used by Motif and other tool kits are very similar in function to the virtual method tables used by C++. Instead of programmers building the structures by hand, C++ does all of the work automatically and correctly.

In MS Windows, the main event loop is completely hidden inside of the operating system. In that case, we can define a standard WindowProc that contains the switch statement on the events. We then register this WindowProc with windows created by NewWindow.

NeXTSTEP is built using Objective-C as the primary model. As such, the operating system invokes the appropriate methods directly. There are no additional connections to be made by the tool kit because it is entirely integrated. This clean integration is one of the major advantages of the NeXTSTEP operating system.

Use of the Abstract Class

Once we have the abstract class, we need to use it to implement interactive behavior. Our first example is a push button. We define a class PushButton as a subclass of WinEventHandler. We give PushButton a field called Pressed that is either true or false, depending on whether the button is pressed. Initially Pressed is false. We also give the button a field called Label that is the text for the button's label. We define the method Redraw to check Pressed and Label to correctly draw the button. We override MouseDown to set Pressed to true, and we force the button to get redrawn in its Pressed state and to request the mouse focus. For this discussion, we ignore MouseMove, MouseEnter, and MouseExit; real button widgets should not. We define MouseUp to set Pressed to false and force the button to be redrawn. MouseUp also checks to make sure that the mouse is still inside of the button's bounds and, if so, it invokes a new method called ButtonSelected. The ButtonSelected method is defined to do nothing.

Our PushButton doesn't actually do anything. We might, for example, have a button that will cause the program to quit when it is pressed. We can define a new class, QuitButton, which is a subclass of PushButton. QuitButton only overrides the ButtonSelected method. Inside the ButtonSelected method, it does whatever is necessary to terminate the program. A basic technique in most object-oriented tool kits is to define a set of widget classes like our Push-Button class. Such generic classes have their major functionality defined in empty methods like ButtonSelected. Programmers use these classes by defining subclasses that override these methods to provide application-specific behavior. Programmers using such widget classes do not need to concern themselves with all of the input events, redrawing, or presentation design required to create the widget. Although this widget-design technique fits very nicely with object-oriented languages, it has problems.

Problems with the Simple Subclass Model

Using the class PushButton, we created a new subclass for each use in which we can override ButtonSelected to provide a specific action. As elegant as this model seems, it has some serious problems. In Figure 4-15, there are at least 14 separate widget objects, each of which has its own actions that must be specified. This would involve creating as many as 14 new classes. Creating a new class for every different kind of event action is not very effective for

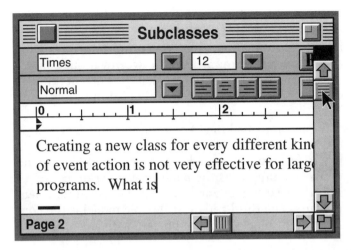

Figure 4-15   A large number of separate communicating widget objects

large programs. What is needed is a standard behavior for the built-in widgets, such as scroll bars and buttons, which can be modified slightly without creating new classes.

4.5 Communication between Objects

The final topic to be discussed relative to event handling is the communication between interactive objects. Up until now, our focus has been on the communication between the interactive devices and the window event handlers. An example of this interobject communication is shown in Figure 4-15. When the scroll bar on the right is moved by the user, the text window must be informed so that it can scroll itself vertically. If the user performs a search and locates a word at some other place in the text, the text window must scroll to that place. The vertical scroll bar must be informed of this so that it can change to reflect the new scroll location. Similar problems arise with the buttons in the control bar across the top. If the centered-alignment button is pressed, the text window must be informed so that the selected text can be realigned. If new text is selected, the alignment buttons must be notified so that they can accurately reflect the alignment of the selected text.

These communication problems are handled by *pseudoevents*. Pseudo-events are new events that have been created for communication between objects and are not real input events. In all non–object-oriented windowing systems, the event record consists of an event kind, some standard information, and any additional information provided by the originator of the event.

The event kind is an integer with a subrange of the event kinds reserved for input and system events. Other ranges are reserved for events generated by the standard controls or widgets. The remaining event kind numbers are available for use by applications programs in communicating between various components of the user interface. In object-oriented models, the event kind is encoded as the method to be called, with the remaining information being passed as parameters.

There are three basic models for this kind of communication. The first is the *simple callback model* used by Motif and all widget sets built with Xtk. This allows C procedures to be attached to widgets at run time. The second and one of the more popular techniques is the *parent-notification model* in which each widget notifies the next higher window in the window tree whenever a significant event occurs. The third and most flexible model is the *connections model,* which allows any object to communicate with any other.

4.5.1 Simple Callback Model

All of the Xtk widgets use callback procedure lists as their model for application programmers to add behavior to a widget. A callback procedure is a C procedure that has the following definition:

```
void callback(w, client_d, class_c)
    Widget w;
```
Identifier for the widget generating callback.
```
    XtPointer client_d;
```
Application data.
```
    XtPointer class_d;
```
Data from the widget class.

A programmer creates such a procedure for various actions to be performed by a widget. Once such a procedure has been defined, it can be registered with a widget using the XtAddCallback procedure, defined as follows:

```
void XtAddCallback(w, cb_name, cb_proc, client_d)
    Widget w;
```
The widget to which the callback is added.
```
    String cb_name;
```
The name of the callback.
```
    XtCallbackProc cb_proc;
```
The callback procedure.
```
    XtPointer client_d;
```
The client data.

Let us take the example of the center-alignment button. When this button is pressed, the text area needs to be notified so that the selected text can be center aligned. We first define a callback procedure called CB_Align that contains the code necessary to handle the alignment and is used for all of the alignment buttons on the tool bar. The CB_Align procedure needs to know which text widget should be notified and it needs to know what kind of alignment it should be doing. In order to handle this, we can define a structure of the following form:

```
#define LeftAlign     1
#define RightAlign    2
#define CenterAlign   3
#define BothAlign     4
struct {
   Widget WidgetToNotify;
   short Alignment;
   } Align_Client_d;
```

We can then register this callback with the push-button widget as follows:

```
XtAddCallback(CenterAlignWidget, XmNactivateCallback, CB_Align,
   ClientDPointer);
```

CenterAlignWidget is our widget created for the center-alignment button. XmNactivateCallback is the standard Motif name for the callback list that is called when a button is clicked. ClientDPointer is a pointer to one of our Align_Client_d structures that has been initialized to point to our text widget and has Alignment set to 3. When the button is clicked, our CB_Align procedure will be called. It can look in its client data to find the text widget to be notified and the alignment to use.

The mechanism for handling such callbacks is quite simple. The XtAddCallback simply takes the address of the callback procedure and the client data and adds it to the specified callback list on the widget. When the widget gets the MouseUp event, it searches its XmNactivateCallback list and invokes each procedure that it finds there. In C, it is relatively easy to store the addresses of procedures.

This sort of communication mechanism to notify one widget of what has happened to another is rather simple, but quite general. Any widget can point to any other with an associated code fragment to handle the communication. The main drawback is that this technique provides no structure to the way in which applications and their widgets interact. There is a web of interconnections that can become very difficult for programmers to understand and debug.

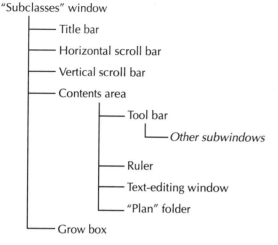

"Subclasses" window
— Title bar
— Horizontal scroll bar
— Vertical scroll bar
— Contents area
    — Tool bar
        — *Other subwindows*
    — Ruler
    — Text-editing window
    — "Plan" folder
— Grow box

Figure 4-16   Widget tree for the example in Figure 4-15

4.5.2 Parent Notification Model

The parent notification model provides more structure to an interactive application. To understand this model, consider the widget tree shown in Figure 4-16.

Widgets such as the push buttons and scroll bars are all programmed to notify their parent (the next higher widget in the tree) whenever a significant event occurs. In addition, every widget has an identifier that can be set by the application. Depending on the system, this identifier is any 4 bytes (which fit in a long integer), any string, or any integer. The key is that a widget can be uniquely identified. In our example, if the vertical scroll bar (VSCB) is moved by the user, it will send a message to the parent window. The parent window will have all of the code for deciding what to do with the fact that the scroll bar has moved. Since the parent also knows which widget generated the message, the parent can interrogate the scroll bar as to its current scroll value. The parent can then notify the text widget to move itself to the new position.

In some situations such as the dialog shown in Figure 4-17, the parent will ignore all child messages except the ones from the OK or Cancel buttons. When either of these buttons is activated, the parent will retrieve data from all of the other child widgets before taking the appropriate action. This technique allows for relatively simple dialog box code to be written.

MacApp

MacApp handles all dialogs using the parent notification model. The class TView is an abstract class that is used to contain other widgets and to manage

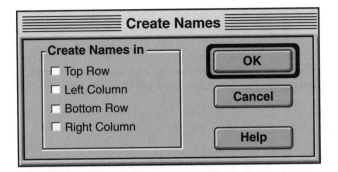

Figure 4-17   Example dialog box

a collection of interactive behaviors. One of its methods is DoChoice. Widgets—like scroll bars, buttons, and text boxes—are all programmed to invoke the DoChoice method on their parent view. DoChoice accepts two parameters: the widget that invoked DoChoice (the originator) and the type of widget (scroll bar, button, etc.).

Given the widget tree in Figure 4-16, if the user moves the horizontal scroll bar (HSCB), the HSCB will invoke DoChoice on its parent, passing the scroll bar itself and the identifier for scroll bars. Most of the behavior for the window in Figure 4-15 is encoded in the DoChoice method on the parent widget. This DoChoice method detects that a scroll bar has moved. It checks the originator's identifier and determines that it is HSCB. It then asks the horizontal scroll bar for its current value and notifies the text widget of the new scroll position.

All information about this window flows through this DoChoice method. The advantage is that the behavior is not fragmented in a variety of callback procedures. The disadvantage is that the programmer must do significant work in sorting out which of a variety of widgets needs attention.

Microsoft Windows

Microsoft Windows also uses the parent notification model. Unlike MacApp, however, a much greater variety of messages are sent. Each of the widget types generate messages unique to themselves. For example, push buttons send BN_CLICKED and BN_DOUBLECLICKED to their parent window. Scroll bars send SB_THUMBPOSITION and SB_THUMBTRACK messages to their parent whenever the scroll bar is interactively changed. The window procedure for the parent window can respond to these messages in much the same way as MacApp's DoChoice method.

In Visual C++, the standard event-handling mechanisms discussed previously can handle the events sent to the parent window. The Visual C++ event mechanism will map messages to methods on the parent window object. It is still up to the programmer to sort out which widget sent the message and how it should be handled.

4.5.3 Object Connections Model

The object connections model allows objects to communicate directly with each other. In order for the scroll bar object to communicate with the text editor object, it must have a pointer to that object. The communication is handled by the scroll bar invoking some method on the text editor object.

There are two challenges in this approach. The first is that the text editor object in Figure 4-15 will be receiving many messages for various purposes. The exact method the scroll bar should use is not known at the time the scroll bar is programmed. The second is that at initialization time, each widget must be given pointers to all of the widgets that it needs to notify.

The NeXTSTEP system provides solutions to these two problems. In order to handle communications, NeXT uses two members (fields) of a given widget class. These are the target (a pointer to the widget to be notified) and the action (a data value that identifies the method to be invoked). These two data values can be sent at run time. For example, the menu item class has two members (target and action). Whenever the menu item is selected, it takes the object referenced by its target and invokes the method identified by its action, passing the menu item itself as the parameter. This provides the same functionality as MacApp's DoChoice method except that different child widgets can invoke different methods on other objects. In addition, widgets are not restricted to their parent widgets as objects to communicate with.

It is important to point out that this object connection mechanism will not work unless the underlying programming language provides some mechanism for storing a method identifier as data. Objective-C, on which NeXT is based, provides the @selector operator, which will create such an identifier at run time. Dynamic languages such as Smalltalk,[9] CLOS,[10] or Self[11] provide such mechanisms. C++ has no such facility. All such information is discarded at compile time. This lack of reflection is a serious deficiency in the language when using it for interactive programs. This deficiency is overcome in Java and forms the basis for the JavaBeans architecture for plugging together components.

4.6 Summary

In this chapter, we have discussed how events are used as the primary mechanism for communication between the user and the interactive objects, and among the interactive objects themselves. Graphical user interfaces are generally organized in trees of windows. Whenever a user generates inputs, the inputs are translated into events that are forwarded to specific windows. A variety of mechanisms are used for determining which window should receive an event.

There are special problems with events in systems like X and NeWS. Each of these systems may have application software running on one machine with the user display on another. The involvement of multiple machines means that network traffic is required when communicating between the user and the application program. This networked implementation requires some consideration in designing interactive systems.

The main program for a graphical application is usually minimal. It consists of initialization followed by a loop that gets events and dispatches them to the appropriate objects. All application behavior is encoded in the event handling of various interactive objects.

The communication among the objects that cooperate to make up an interactive application is essential to understanding interactive software. The fact that the user is in control and that there is no uniform flow of control through the program is the defining paradigm in interactive software architectures.

5

Basic Interaction

In the preceding chapters, we have discussed the basic concepts of event handling and graphical display. In this chapter, we will assemble these basic pieces together to construct an interactive application.

5.1 Introduction to Basic Interaction

The example we are going to use is shown in Figure 5-1. This application lays out simple logic schematics. The application has two windows, one for showing the circuit layout and connectivity and the other for showing a list of chips and their names.

The window on the left is the circuit view and has a menu of two modes on its far left. If the chip icon is selected, then the user can create new chips by clicking on any empty space in the chip view area. The chip will be added to the part list window without a name. The user can select a chip by clicking on it in the circuit view or in the part list view, in which case it will be highlighted in both views. If the DEL icon is selected, the currently selected chip is deleted from both views. The user can move a chip by pressing the mouse down on the chip and then dragging the mouse to a new location. The chip will be moved and all of the wires will stay connected.

When the wire icon is selected, the user can create new wires by pressing the mouse down on one of the chip connectors and dragging the mouse to another chip connector. This will create a wire between those two connectors. If the user clicks on an existing wire, it will become the selected wire. If the user then clicks on DEL, the wire will be deleted.

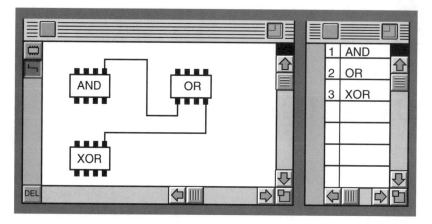

Figure 5-1   Logic schematic application

When a user selects a chip in the part list view, a character insertion point in the chip name is also selected. The user can then edit the chip name using the keyboard. The name of the chip will be updated both in the part list view and in the chip layout view.

This is a relatively simple application but it will illustrate several important concepts. In particular, we can look at how functional models are translated into model implementations. We can also look at architectures for handling multiple cooperating views. Finally, we can look at how the model and the actual user interface cooperate.

5.1.1 Functional Model

Having sketched the behavior of our example application, we need to define the functional model for the application. Since the purpose of this model is to demonstrate interactive architecture rather than to serve real users, we will skip the task analysis steps; in practice, this should never be done. There are three classes of objects in our functional model; they are Circuits, Chips, and Wires.

Circuit

A Circuit object captures the semantics of both the circuit view and the parts list view. The Circuit is the object being manipulated by both views. It is important to capture the concept of a circuit as an object rather than as a set of global variables. In any good application, it should be possible to view and edit multiple circuits at the same time. This means that there will be multiple circuit objects. A set of global variables cannot handle this concept.

The data representation of a Circuit consists of the following:

Chips

An array of chip objects.

Wires

An array of wire objects.

SelectedChip

The index into Chips for the currently selected chip. This is −1 if there is no selected chip.

SelectedWire

The index into Wires for the currently selected wire. This is −1 if there is no selected wire.

There are a variety of methods on the class Circuit that provide the semantic behavior for our application, as follows:

AddChip(CenterPoint)

Add a new chip to the circuit at the specified location.

AddWire(Chip1, Connector1, Chip2, Connector2)

Add a wire to the circuit that connects Chip1's Connector1 to Chip2's Connector 2.

SelectChip(ChipNum)

Make the chip with the specified index the currently selected chip.

MoveChip(ChipNum, NewCenterPoint)

Move the specified chip to the new location.

ChangeChipName(ChipNum, NewName)

Change the chip's name.

DeleteChip(ChipNum)

Delete the specified chip.

SelectWire(WireNum)

Select the specified wire.

DeleteWire(WireNum)

Delete the specified wire.

These are the methods that the views can use to change circuits. These methods define the functionality of our application.

Chip

A Chip is a simple object that consists of the following:

CenterPoint
> *Center of the chip in the layout.*

Name
> *Name of the chip.*

In this simple application, the class Chip has no methods of its own. The entire functional behavior is captured in the Circuit class. In general, this would not be true. Circuits would consist of a variety of classes of circuit objects, each of which would have its own behavior. We will discuss more complex models in later chapters when we have more powerful geometric and architectural tools to handle them.

Wire

Wires are also quite simple and contain only their relevant data, as follows:

Chip1
> *Chip index to which the wired is connected.*

Connector1
> *Connector index in Chip1 to which the wire is connected. All Chips have exactly 8 connectors.*

Chip2
> *Chip index for the other end of the wire.*

Connector2
> *Connector index from Chip2 for the other end of the wire.*

5.2 Model-View-Controller Architecture

The Smalltalk system was developed as a language and an environment for building interactive applications.[1] As part of that development, an architecture for interactive applications was designed. This object-oriented approach was called the model-view-controller (MVC) architecture.[2] A schematic of this architecture is shown in Figure 5-2.

The *model* is the information that the application is trying to manipulate. This is the data representation of the real-world objects in which the user is interested. In our logic diagrams, the model would consist of the Circuit, Chip, and Wire classes.

The *view* implements a visual display of the model. In our application, there are two views, the circuit view and the part list view. Anytime the

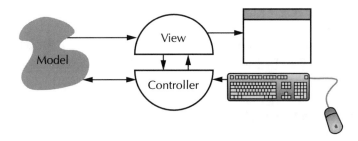

Figure 5-2   Model-view-controller

model is changed, each view of that model must be notified so that it can change the visual presentation of the model on the screen. A region of the screen that is no longer consistent with the model information is called *damaged*. When notified of a change, the view will identify the changed parts of the display and report those regions as damaged to the windowing system. In some systems, such regions are called invalid or out of date. In this text, we will use the term damaged. Reporting of damaged regions is fundamental to maintaining views on the screen.

A model, like ours, may have multiple views. In such a case, all views must be notified of the changes and the windowing system will collect them all. Later, when the main event loop looks for a new event to process, there will be redraw events waiting for any views that were affected by damage reporting and by any windowing operations. Each view must redraw the damaged areas based on information in the model. In addition to drawing the display, a view is also the location for all display geometry as will be discussed later.

The *controller* receives all of the input events from the user and decides what they mean and what should be done. In the circuit view of our example, the controller would receive a mouse-down event and must determine from the currently selected menu item whether wires or chips are to be manipulated. The controller must communicate with the view to determine what objects are being selected. For example, since the circuit view is responsible for positioning all of the chips in the window, the controller must be able to pass a mouse point to the view to determine if that mouse point is over a chip, a wire, or in empty space. Once the controller has all of the information that it needs, it will make calls on the objects in the model to make the appropriate changes. These calls by the controller on the model will cause the model to notify the views, and the displays will be updated.

Because the functionality of the controller and the view are so tightly intertwined and also because controllers and views almost always occur in pairs, many architectures combine the two functions into a single class. Recall from Chapter 4 the WinEventHandler class, which had several methods for responding to events. The Redraw method would implement the majority of the view. (The methods to handle notification from the model and object selection for the controller must be added.) The mouse and keyboard methods would implement the controller functionality. The model is implemented based on our functional design as described in Chapter 2.

5.2.1 The Problem with Multiple Parts

In simple applications, it is tempting to combine the model, view, and controller into a single class or into global variables. Such an approach will not scale up to large applications. The model classes must be separated out for two reasons. The first is that there may be multiple models that a user is working with. In our example, the user may have an old version of the circuit on the screen and may be using it as a guide to design a new version in a separate window. This scenario would require multiple models and multiple views. The implementations would be the same but different information is being manipulated in each case.

A second problem, which is frequently ignored by those building simple applications, is the fact that a model may have more than one view. In our example, the model has at least two views, the circuit view and the parts list view. Each view is very different but each must be updated when a chip is added to the circuit. There may also be multiple, similar views of the same model. Our example application does not support scrolling of the circuit view, but let us suppose that it did. Let us also suppose that the circuit was very large and the user had need to work in two separate areas of the circuit at once. An additional circuit view of the same circuit could be created at run time. Each view could be scrolled to a different part of the circuit. In such an application, there can be any number of views of the same model, depending on what the user is trying to do. Each of these views must be kept consistent with the model and the user must be able to interact with the model through the controllers of each of those views. The support for multiple views is the primary reason for the separation between the model and the view-controller.

There are also software maintenance reasons for the separation. Suppose, for example, that our users look at our first implementation and decide that it is important to have a wiring list view that shows all of the wires and that names their connections. We could implement the new view and its controller and add it to the list of views that need to be notified whenever the model changes. The existing views would not need to be changed and the model would be unaffected. With the addition of a new view, new model information may be needed; however, the old views would still respond in the same way.

Suppose that our graphics designers and marketing people decide that chips should be drawn with a 3D look rather than a flat schematic look. Only the

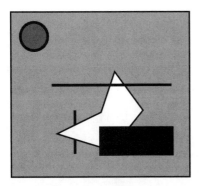

Figure 5-3   Shapes to be manipulated

view would need to be changed to draw the chips in a different way. The view would also need to be changed to select chips and contact pins in a different way, because the positions of the pins relative to the chips would be different. That is why selection tasks are handled by the view as a service to the controller. That is also why we think of the controller as conceptually different. The pattern of behavior in response to user events (controller issues) is independent of visual geometry (view issues).

5.2.2 Changing the Display

In most of our applications, any interactive work by the user will cause the model to change. In response to this change in the model, the views will need to update what is drawn on the screen. Before we go through the event flow between models, views, and controllers, we first need to work through the relationship between a view and the windowing system in handling updates to the display.

Let us consider the problem in Figure 5-3. In this example, our model consists of a list of the shapes that we want to draw, along with their colors and geometric information. We want to interact with this model by moving shapes around. The problem that our view code must solve is to change the display in such a way that the polygon stays in front of the background and vertical line as well as behind the horizontal line and the black rectangle.

One simple-minded way to solve this problem is to draw the shape being moved using the color of the background. Drawing in the background color will erase the shape in its old position. We can then draw the shape in the new position. This will work just fine in the case where we move the circle as shown in Figure 5-4.

It will not work, however, if we want to move the white polygon. The results of such an approach are shown in Figure 5-5. In this case, the drawing

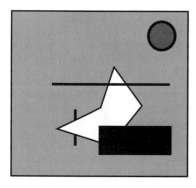

Figure 5-4 Erasing and redrawing the circle

Figure 5-5 Erasing and redrawing the polygon

of the old polygon using background color has wiped out parts of the lines and the black rectangle. In addition, the drawing of the new polygon is now in front of the horizontal line, which is not correct.

An alternative to this strategy is to move the polygon in the model to its new position and then to redraw the entire picture from the model in the following order: 1) background, 2) circle, 3) vertical line, 4) polygon, 5) horizontal line, and 6) black rectangle.

By drawing the shapes in this prescribed order, the objects that are in front are drawn last and will thus overlay any objects that are behind. Such a back-to-front drawing technique will guarantee the correct drawing. In fact, in most drawing systems, the model will maintain the list of shapes in back-to-front order so as to simplify this technique. Menu actions such as "Move to Back" or "Move to Front" found in most drawing packages simply involve changing the position of the selected shapes in the list of shapes and then redrawing.

One of the problems with this complete redraw strategy is that it is too slow for large or complex drawings. The changes required to the display are frequently very localized and redrawing the entire display is a waste. In addition, complete redrawing of the entire display can cause annoying flashes each time the redraw is done because the frontmost items are momentarily erased by the background before being redrawn. This is very bothersome to users because the human visual system is tuned to pay attention when it perceives motion.

The Damage/Redraw Technique

The common technique for handling the problem of correctly updating the display uses a pair of operations that we will call Damage and Redraw. All modern windowing systems support a variant of the damage/redraw technique. Using this technique, a view can inform the windowing system when a region of a window needs to be updated. The windowing system will then batch these updates, clip them to the portions of the window that are actually visible, and then invoke the Redraw method for the window. The Redraw method is passed the window region that needs to be redrawn. This Redraw method was discussed in Chapter 4 as part of the WinEventHandler class.

In order to accommodate this technique, we need to add the Damage method to our abstract Canvas class:

void Canvas::Damage(UpdateRegion)

When a view invokes Damage on a canvas, the windowing system will save the UpdateRegion for later. One of the reasons for saving the damaged regions is that many times a model change will cause a variety of changes to the screen, which may or may not overlap. For this reason, a windowing system will save them all until the event handler requests the next input event. At that time, the Redraw methods for all windows that have changes can be invoked.

Using this technique, we can reconsider our problem of moving the polygon. When the polygon is moved, we first damage the region where the polygon used to be, so that the area can be correctly redrawn without the polygon. We then change the polygon's position in the model and then damage the region around the polygon's new position so that the new area will be redrawn.

Before any input events are handled, the windowing system will invoke the Redraw method for this window, which will redraw the damaged regions in back-to-front order. Figure 5-6 shows the damaged regions as dotted rectangles.

In our simple set of shapes, the Redraw method may just redraw the entire model in front-to-back order because the numbers are so small. The windowing system will clip to the damaged region. This clipping prevents the circle

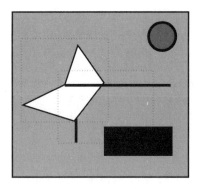

Figure 5-6   Damage/Redraw method showing damaged regions

and most of the background from actually being drawn on the screen. If, however, there were a large number of shapes in the model, the Redraw method could check groups of shapes or separate areas of the drawing against the damaged area to avoid even considering parts of the model that would not affect the damaged area. This would be much more efficient with large models.

5.2.3 General Event Flow

Having discussed the relationship between a view and the windowing system, we need to consider the entire process of handling input events, including changing the model and updating the screen. To get this overall view of the MVC architecture, we will work through a couple of interactive tasks in our example application.

Creating a New Chip

Let us first consider the creation of a new chip. We will assume that the user has already selected the chip icon on the screen and that the circuit controller has a field that remembers that the chip icon is selected. (Note that the view and the controller must share this field so that the view can highlight the currently selected icon.) The process involves the following steps:

1. To create the new chip, the user will place the mouse over the tentative position where the new chip is to go and then press the mouse button.
2. When the mouse button is pressed, the windowing system will identify which window should receive the event and locate the WinEvent-Handler that should receive the event. The WinEventHandler that implements our circuit view and controller will have its MouseDown method invoked. This is part of the controller.

3. The controller determines that it is in chip mode (based on the selected icon) and inquires of the view as to whether the mouse is over an existing chip. If the mouse is not over an existing chip, the controller decides that a new chip is to be created. It requests the view to start echoing a rubber band rectangle where the new chip will be placed and saves the fact that it is creating a new chip. The MouseDown method then returns.

4. The user can then adjust where the chip will be placed by moving the mouse while holding down the mouse button. Each time the mouse moves, the windowing system will invoke the controller's MouseMove method. The controller will then have the view move the echoing rectangle to the new position.

5. When the user finally decides that the chip is in the right position, the mouse button is released and the windowing system will invoke the MouseUp method on the view-controller. The controller will have the view remove the echoing rectangle from the screen, take itself out of chip-positioning mode, and invoke the AddChip method on the circuit model, passing in the new location.

6. When the model has its AddChip method invoked, it will add the new chip to its array of chips and will then go to the list of views that have been registered with this model. For each of these views, the model will invoke the appropriate methods to notify them that a new chip has been added.

7. When the part list view receives notification that there is a new chip, it will inform the windowing system that the space at the bottom of the list is damaged and needs to be updated. *Note that the part list view does not draw the new chip into the window at this point.*

8. When the circuit view receives notification of the new chip, it will also inform the windowing system that the region where the new chip is to go is damaged. *Note that even though the circuit view's controller initiated the request to create a new chip, the view still waits for notification from the model.* Suppose, for example, that the model was enforcing some design constraints that would not allow chips to overlap each other. The original position from the user might violate those constraints. The model may then move the chip slightly to accommodate the constraints. In such a case, the view must accurately reflect what is in the model, even if it is different from what the view's own controller specified. Also note that the circuit view must respond to notifications of new chips, no matter where such changes originate. By placing code to damage the window inside of the controller, such code would be duplicated.

9. When all views have been notified and have performed their damage processing, the model returns from its AddChip method to the controller, which then returns from its MouseDown method, leaving the windowing system in control again. The windowing system determines that there are damage requests pending and will respond to them. The first damage request is from the part list view. The windowing system determines, however, that this portion of the part list window is completely obscured by some other window. In this case, the damage request is discarded because the damaged region is not visible. This is why the part list view or any other view only damages the changed area in response to notification of a model change, rather than drawing the changed information immediately. The other damage request found by the windowing system is for the circuit view window. This area is not obscured, so the windowing system invokes the circuit view's Redraw method with the damaged area.

10. When the circuit view receives its Redraw message, it will look through all of the chips in the model and draw any chip that overlaps the damaged area. It will then look through all of the wires and draw any wire that appears in the damaged area. Because the windowing system sets the clip region to the damaged area, the circuit view may for simplicity draw all chips and all wires, leaving the clipping logic to discard anything outside of the damage area. Either strategy will work, although in very large circuits, the "redraw everything" approach may be too slow for interactive use. Let us suppose that our new chip has been placed over existing wires. In our application, we always want wires on top so that we can see them. If the circuit view had simply drawn the new chip when it received the notification from the model, the chip would have appeared over the top of the wires, which is not desired. By having the notification only report a damaged region, and then letting Redraw handle the rest, a correct presentation will always occur.

Moving a Chip

To further illustrate the issues of how the MVC and damage/redraw mechanisms work, let's look at a second example. In this case, we want to move the XOR chip to a new location. Remember that in our application, when we move a chip, the wires stay connected. We will start from Figure 5-7 where the chip icon has been selected. The process involves the following steps:

1. When the mouse button goes down over the XOR chip, the windowing system invokes the controller's MouseDown event.

2. The controller requests the view to select a chip and the view returns the index of the XOR chip as the one selected. The controller then notifies the model of the selection by calling the model's SelectChip method.

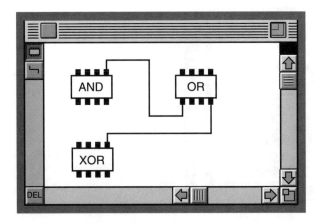

Figure 5-7 Dragging a chip

3. The model's SelectChip method notifies all views registered with that model that the XOR chip has been selected. Each view then damages its presentation of the XOR chip. In the layout view, the rectangular region around the chip is damaged; in the part list view, the chip's name region is damaged.

4. The controller then stores the fact that it is waiting to drag the chip to a new location and returns to the windowing system.

5. The windowing system locates the entries for the damaged entries and invokes Redraw methods on the appropriate views. These Redraw methods will draw the presentation of the XOR chip to show that it has been selected.

6. The windowing system then waits for more input events. Since we are dragging the chip, the next input event will be a movement of the mouse. When each mouse movement is received by the windowing system, the system calls the MouseMove method on the circuit layout view. This method must echo the new location of the chip on the screen. The normal notify/damage/redraw cycle is frequently too slow for this type of echo. Later in this chapter we will discuss faster echoing mechanisms that the controller can use without involving the model or the view.

7. When the mouse button is released, the windowing system will send a MouseUp message to the controller. The controller remembers that it is dragging a chip to a new location and invokes the model's MoveChip method.

8. The model will notify each view that the XOR chip has moved to a new location. The part list view will ignore this notice because its display does not involve the chip location.

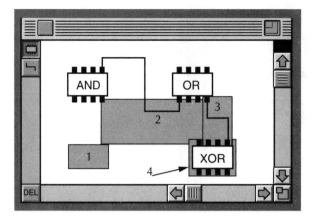

Figure 5-8   Damage regions to move a chip

9. The circuit layout view, however, has some work to do. The circuit layout view must not only move the chip but also the wires connected to it as well. When moving an object, we must damage both the old location and the new location. Because wires are moving, the areas around the wires must also be damaged. Figure 5-8 shows the chip and wires in their new locations. The gray rectangles show all of the regions that must be damaged to correctly redraw the view.

10. After the model has notified all of its views and has changed itself, it returns to the controller. The controller takes itself out of dragging mode and returns to the windowing system.

11. The windowing system locates the damaged entries and invokes the correct Redraw methods. When region 1 (see Figure 5-8) is redrawn, the view checks the model and detects that there is nothing in that region. The area is drawn in background color. When region 2 is redrawn, the view detects that a portion of the wire from the OR chip to the AND chip must be redrawn. The rest is background. These two redraws will cause the XOR chip and its wires to disappear from their old positions. When region 3 is redrawn, the wire in the new position is drawn; region 4 draws the chip in its new position.

In some windowing systems, the Redraw method would be called four times, once for each rectangle. In other systems, the process might be batched together into one large rectangle that encloses all four damaged regions. The Redraw method is then invoked only once with the large rectangle. In other windowing systems, the four rectangles would be assembled into a single complex region that exactly bounds the area specified by the four rectangles.

The Redraw method is then invoked once with this complex region. As long as the view's Redraw method can correctly redraw any region and as long as the windowing system clips to that region, the screen updates will be correct no matter what redraw/region technique is used by the windowing system.

5.3 Model Implementation

The preceding discussion focused on the various components of the MVC architecture and on the messages that flow back and forth between those components. It is now time to look at the actual implementation of those components. This example approach is not the only implementation strategy. At the end of this chapter, we will discuss variations on the theme in various commercial tool kits.

We will start our implementation discussion with the model. There are two aspects that need to be considered. The first is the interface that the model will present to the views and controllers. The second is the mechanism for the model to notify all views of changes to the model.

5.3.1 Circuit Class

As described earlier, the heart of our model is the Circuit class which, in conjunction with the Chip and Wire classes, represents everything that our application needs to know about circuits.

The methods are

```
void Circuit::AddChip(CenterPoint)
void Circuit::AddWire(Chip1, Connector1, Chip2, Connector2)
void Circuit::SelectChip(ChipNum)
void Circuit::MoveChip(ChipNum, NewCenterPoint)
void Circuit::ChangeChipName(ChipNum, NewName)
void Circuit::DeleteChip(ChipNum)
void Circuit::SelectWire(WireNum)
void Circuit::DeleteWire(WireNum)
```

and the fields are

```
Chips
Wires
SelectedChip
SelectedWire
```

These are drawn directly from the functional model that we designed earlier. The key to this model class is the methods. These are the methods that views, controllers, and other software in the application will call to make changes to the model. These methods will perform the normal data structure updates to the model, but in addition, they must also notify the views of any changes. It is this change notification that needs particular discussion here.

5.3.2 CircuitView Class

The Circuit class needs a general mechanism for notifying all of its views that some aspect of the circuit has changed. We do not want to code into our model the information about every type of view of the model. Such hard coding would seriously hamper our ability to add new views or to modify existing views. To provide this generality, we define the abstract class CircuitView. This class will define the Circuit class's interface to any of its views. The CircuitView class and its subclasses will combine view and controller functions in a single class.

The CircuitView class must be a subclass of WinEventHandler (as defined in Chapter 4), so that it can receive input and redraw events from the windowing system. Each of our views will be subclasses of CircuitView and thus will inherit both the windowing system interface methods and the view interface for the Circuit class.

Model Registration

The CircuitView class will have one attribute, which is myCircuit and is of type Circuit. This attribute provides each view with a pointer to the model that it represents. When a new CircuitView is created, it must be given a pointer to its model and a pointer to a Canvas that it is to draw upon.

Notification Methods

The methods that we add to our CircuitView class are the ones that the Circuit class will need to inform the view of any changes, as follows:

```
void CircuitView::ChangeChip(ChipNum)
```
The specified chip has been changed.
```
void CircuitView::ChangeWire(WireNum)
```
The specified wire has been changed.
```
void CircuitView::ChipMoved(ChipNum, NewLocation)
```
The chip is being moved to a new location.

These three methods will provide all of the view notification that we need. When a view receives the ChangeChip message, it will damage any regions that display information about that chip. Subsequent redraws will draw those regions with the new model information about that chip. For the same reason, the ChangeWire method will damage the region where the wire is drawn.

The ChipMoved method is special because it must damage the chip and its wires at their old locations as well as their new locations. The old locations can be determined by looking at the model. The new location can be determined from NewLocation. For this technique to work, ChipMoved notifications must be sent before the model is changed so that the old information is still available.

In the abstract class CircuitView, these view notification methods do nothing at all. Their actual behavior depends on the specific view. The damage work required for ChangeChip in the circuit layout view is very different from ChangeChip on the parts list view. When we create subclasses of CircuitView, we will provide implementations for these methods.

5.3.3 View Notification in the Circuit Class

A major function of the Circuit model is to notify the views of any changes. We need to consider this as we look at each of the Circuit methods. Before discussing those methods, however, the Circuit class needs a mechanism for keeping track of which views are attached to each model object. We need to add a list of CircuitView objects to the Circuit class, along with the following two methods:

```
void Circuit::AddView(View)
void Circuit::RemoveView(View)
```

These two methods will manage the list of views. In addition, we need a mechanism for notifying each view of the changes. To do this, we add the following methods:

```
void Circuit::ChangeChip(ChipNum)
void Circuit::ChangeWire(WireNum)
void Circuit::ChipMoved(ChipNum, NewLocation)
```

These methods are the same notification methods found on the CircuitView class. The model code can invoke these notification methods on the Circuit itself without worrying about the views that need to be updated. Each of these Circuit methods will loop through the list of views in the circuit's view list and invoke the corresponding method on each view. For example, the Circuit::ChangeChip method would be

```
void Circuit::ChangeChip(ChipNum)
  { for each V in the circuit's view list
    { V.ChangeChip(ChipNum) }
  }
```

Now that we have our view notification mechanisms designed and in place, we can discuss the actual methods that implement the circuit's functional model.

The AddChip method will first add a new chip to the end of the list at index *I*. The method will then call ChangeChip(*I*), which will notify all views that this new chip needs to be redrawn. The AddWire method works in the same way except that it calls ChangeWire(*I*) after the wire is in place. In both cases, the view can look at the model attributes to find the necessary information about the new addition.

The SelectChip and SelectWire methods change the selection from one object to another. The notification for SelectChip must first be Change-Chip(OldSelection) and then ChangeChip(NewSelection). The operation is similar for SelectWire. This can be optimized slightly by checking to see if OldSelection and NewSelection are identical, in which case no notification is required.

The MoveChip method on Circuit must use the ChipMoved notification. The reason the ChangeChip notification is not sufficient is that moving a chip requires more than just damaging the chip's bounding rectangle. The new and old wire positions must also be calculated. The CircuitView::ChipMoved method will take care of all of this for us.

When deleting objects, as in DeleteChip and DeleteWire, we must call the ChangeChip or ChangeWire notification before the deletion. Remember that views only perform damage operations, leaving all drawing to the Redraw method. The ChangeChip method will look in the model for the chip to be deleted and will damage its region. After ChangeChip returns, the chip is deleted. Later, the windowing system will process a Redraw on that region; at that time, the chip will no longer be in the model and the region will be drawn blank. The DeleteChip method is further complicated by the fact that all wires connected to the chip must be deleted. The DeleteChip method can use DeleteWire to do this, and the DeleteWire method will notify the views of the deleted wires. To accomplish all of this takes the following steps:

1. DeleteChip will call ChangeChip (for view notification).
2. DeleteChip then calls DeleteWire for all wires connected to the chip.
3. Each invocation of DeleteWire will call ChangeWire (for view notification) and will remove the wire from the model.
4. After all connecting wires are deleted, DeleteChip will remove the chip from the model.

5.3.4 Overview of the Circuit Class

The Circuit class implements the model for our application. It provides methods for registering any number of views with a circuit model and it provides methods that will send the notification messages to all views in the list. These notification messages are defined on the CircuitView class that defines the model/view interface. In addition, Circuit has methods that implement the model functionality and that notify the views of any changes.

Note that in a more complex application, there may be multiple model classes. Each of these models may or may not share the same view notification class. There may be several classes like CircuitView that each define a view notification interface for a particular type of model.

5.4 View/Controller Implementation

Up to this point, we have only defined the model and its interface to its views. With our model implementation in place, we can work on the views and controllers. The architecture used in this book will combine the concepts of view and controller into a single class. In our example application, all views are a subclass of CircuitView and as such can provide the uniform notification interface required by the Circuit class. Any view that is a subclass of CircuitView can be passed to Circuit::AddView and thus can be attached to a circuit model. Each view class also inherits from CircuitView a pointer to the circuit object that implements a view's model.

There are four issues that must be considered when implementing views. The first is the actual drawing of the view in response to a Redraw message. The second is responding to change notification messages from the model. The third is the handling of selection, which is the translation of a mouse location into some record of what should be selected. These first three issues make up what is considered to be a view in the MVC architecture. They are all concerned with the geometry of the presentation. The fourth issue is the controller implementation that translates the input events into calls on the model. The controller translates user input into the methods of the functional model.

5.4.1 PartListView Class

The PartListView class implements the view of a list of the parts in our circuit layout. It is shown in Figure 5-9. This view is simplified by its regular geometry. The chips are presented in their part number order, which is the same order as they have in the model. Each chip's presentation is exactly the same height. In fact, we can exploit the regularity by defining the following new method:

```
Rectangle PartListView::ChipArea(ChipNum)
```

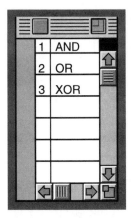

Figure 5-9   Part list view

This method will take a chip number and will return the rectangle that bounds the area of that chip. Because PartListView is a subclass of WinEvent-Handler, it has a GetBounds method that will return the bounding rectangle for this window. Let us assume that we know the height in pixels (CH) of each chip in the view. With this information, we can compute the new rectangle to be

```
B = GetBounds()
Top = B.top + (ChipNum-1) * CH
Left = B.left
Bottom = B.top + ChipNum * CH
Right = B.right
```

In most view classes, there is some essential geometry, like ChipArea, that defines the presentation geometry. This essential geometry will be used throughout the class. It is very helpful to identify these aspects of a view and to implement them as separate methods for use by the rest of the methods in the class. We will see this again in our LayoutView class.

Selection

We will address selection first because such methods can provide geometry logic that we can use in other ways. There are two selection problems that must be addressed by the view. The first is the selection of the correct chip and the second is the selection of a character in the chip's name. The following method can implement our chip selection:

```
long PartListView::WhichChip(MouseLoc)
  { return MouseLoc.Y - GetBounds().Top) / CH + 1;
  }
```

This method translates mouse positions into an index of which chip is selected.

Having selected the correct chip, we need to select the index of the character in the name that lies under the mouse position. We can implement this PartView::WhichChar method using the techniques for text selection that were defined in Chapter 3.

Presentation Drawing

The drawing of a view's presentation is defined by its Redraw method. A simple version of the Redraw method might be as follows:

```
for each chip C in the model
  { R = ChipArea(C);
    draw info about chip C in R
    draw horizontal line across the bottom of R
  }
Draw bounding rectangle for the window.
Draw the vertical line.
```

Drawing each chip is a matter of drawing the chip number and name from the model using the Canvas.

This simple version of Redraw will draw the entire window in response to every required update. It relies upon the windowing system to clip all of the output to the actual region being redrawn. Such a model will work correctly and, in the case of small numbers of parts in the list, is usually fast enough for interactive purposes. Remember, however, that the Redraw method receives as an argument the actual region that needs to be updated. Because of the simple geometry of our PartListView, we can use this region information to create a more efficient redraw.

Let us suppose that the redraw region (RR) has a method for computing the top and bottom of the region. Remember that clipping regions are not necessarily rectangles. Given such methods, we can provide the following Redraw method:

```
TC = WhichChip(RR.top)
BC = WhichChip(RR.bottom)

for each chip C from TC to BC
  { R = ChipArea(C);
    draw info for chip C in R
    draw horizontal line across the bottom of R
  }
Draw bounding rectangle for the window.
Draw the vertical line.
```

This revised version of the Redraw method will only draw those chips that may actually be involved in the region to be updated. Note that we still draw the complete border and vertical line because the clipping of such simple objects is more efficiently done by the windowing system. Our optimization exploits the additional knowledge we have of the geometry of our presentation.

Change Notification

The change notification methods inherited from CircuitView include ChangeChip, ChangeWire, and MoveChip. Our PartListView is only concerned with the ChangeChip method because it does not display wires and it does not display anything about the geometry of chips. The PartListView class will override the ChangeChip method to provide its own implementation. The other two methods will be inherited and as such will do nothing.

The implementation of ChangeChip is quite straightforward, using our ChipArea method:

```
void PartListView::ChangeChip(ChipNum)
  { myCanvas.Damage(ChipArea(ChipNum)) }
```

Controller

The controller is that aspect of the PartListView class that handles input events. Its functionality is spread across the methods inherited from Win-EventHandler that receive input events. In our simple event model, these are

MouseDown

MouseMove

MouseUp

KeyPress

MouseEnter

MouseExit

For this discussion, we will ignore MouseEnter and MouseExit.

There are only two things that a user can do in the part list view. The first is to select a new chip and the second is to change the name of a chip.

A very simple way to implement chip selection uses only the MouseUp method:

```
void PartListView::MouseUp(location, modifiers)
  { myCircuit.SelectChip(WhichChip(location)); }
```

Whenever the mouse is clicked in the part list window, the chip under the mouse position will be the newly selected chip. One of the problems our users will have, however, is that they will not always know which chip in the list relates to which chip on the layout. Being able to drag the mouse over the part list while watching the selected chip in the layout can be very helpful. We can do this by implementing MouseDown and MouseMove, as follows:

```
void PartListView::MouseDown(button, location, modifiers)
  { myCircuit.SelectChip(WhichChip(location)); }
void PartListView::MouseMove(location, modifiers)
  { if (modifiers show button is down)
    { myCircuit.SelectChip(WhichChip(location));
    }
  }
```

This new implementation will change the selection only while the mouse is down. Note that in MouseMove we need to check to see if the button is currently pressed, because the MouseMove method is called whether the button is down or not, and we don't want to change the selected chip every time the mouse casually crosses the part list.

We still have not handled the changing of the chip names, however. To change chip names, we must handle the selection of the insert point in the selected chip's name and we must handle keyboard events. Before we can handle the selection point, our PartListView class needs a new attribute, CharInsertPoint, that will remember which character was selected.

The selection point can be handled by modifying MouseUp to identify and save the selected character:

```
void PartListView::MouseUp(location, modifiers)
  { myCircuit.SelectChip(WhichChip(location));
    CharInsertPoint = WhichChar(location);
  }
```

The actual editing of the names is performed in the KeyPress method. Each time the user presses a key, the windowing system invokes the view's KeyPress method. There are several cases that the KeyPress method must handle, as follows:

1. There is no selected chip.
   Return and do nothing.
2. The current character index is 0 and the input character is a backspace.
   Do nothing; you can't delete at the beginning of a string.
3. The current character index is greater than 0 and the input character is a backspace.
   Delete the indexed character from the string, invoke the model's ChangeChipName method, and decrement the current character index.

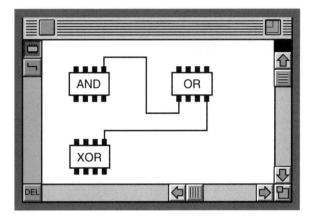

Figure 5-10   Layout view

4. The input character is not a backspace.

   Add the input character to the string, invoke the model's ChangeChipName method, and increment the current character index.

The KeyPress method illustrates the structure of most of the controller methods. A set of cases must be defined to decide what actions to take. The cases are determined by the current input (input character), the state of the model (which chip is selected), and information stored by the controller itself. In Chapter 8 on input syntax, we will discuss more precise methods for capturing these cases and translating them into code.

5.4.2 LayoutView Class

The LayoutView class is more complicated because the geometry does not have the nice array structure found in the part list. In fact, as shown in Figure 5-10, there are actually two levels of geometry in the layout view—sorting out the icons from the layout area and the actual layout of the chips and wires.

Because the layout view is more complex, we need to decompose its structure into simpler parts. At the first level of decomposition, we can think of the layout view as a drawing and a set of icons. Each icon is differentiated by its picture and by what it does when selected. Within the drawing there are chips and wires. Looking at this decomposition, we can devise several new classes from which we can build the layout view. For this design, we will create the Icon, Drawing, ChipV, and WireV classes.

Note that with most modern user interface tool kits we would not implement our own chip, wire, and delete buttons. Instead, we normally use the button widgets provided by the tool kit. We are going to delay discussion of widget design and use until Chapter 6 so as to first understand the mechanisms that underlie such tool kits.

Rather than design these classes at this point, we will work through the LayoutView class implementation to understand what we will need each of these helper classes to do for us. Our LayoutView class will need three Icon attributes and one Drawing attribute:

Icon	ChipIcon;
Icon	WireIcon;
Icon	DeleteIcon;
Drawing	CircuitDrawing;

Selection

The selection logic for the LayoutView actually consists of delegating the work to the various helper classes. Let us assume that each of the helper classes has a Select method such as

boolean   *class*::Select(MousePoint);

This method returns true if the mouse position would select the object. Based on this method, the LayoutView class can send the Select message to each of the icons and drawing area in turn. The first object whose Select method returns true is the one selected. The Drawing class can use the same approach when it needs to select chips or wires. Objects in the drawing are selected by testing the Select method on each one of them.

Presentation Drawing

The presentation drawing is the visual representation of the model in the view. The presentation drawing for the LayoutView is defined by its Redraw method. Let us assume that each of the helper classes has the following two methods:

Rectangle *class*::Bounds();

void *class*::Redraw(DamagedRegion);

If each helper class has these methods, then the redraw for the layout view is quite simple:

```
void LayoutView::Redraw(Damaged)
   { if(ChipIcon.Bounds() intersects Damaged)
       { ChipIcon.Redraw(Damaged); }
     if(WireIcon.Bounds() intersects Damaged)
       { WireIcon.Redraw(Damaged); }
     if(DeleteIcon.Bounds() intersects Damaged)
       { DeleteIcon.Redraw(Damaged); }
     if(Drawing.Bounds() intersects Damaged)
       { Drawing.Redraw(Damaged); }
   }
```

The decomposition of the problem into the helper objects greatly simplifies the complexity of our problem. We will use this technique in numerous places.

Change Notification

Remember that the model provides the ChangeChip, ChangeWire, and MoveChip notifications. In response to a ChangeChip message, the view need only damage the bounding rectangle of the chip. Since there are classes for chips and wires that support the Bounds method, we need only invoke Bounds on the relevant chip or wire view object and then damage the returned rectangle.

In response to a MoveChip notification, the old chip-bounding rectangle must first be damaged. Because wires will also be moved, the view must run through the model and damage the bounds of every wire that is connected to the chip being moved. Next, the chip-bounding rectangle is damaged in its new location. Finally, the bounds of all connecting wires are damaged in their new locations. Damaging the chip and wires is relatively easy, given the Bounds method on the ChipV and WireV classes.

Controller

Before designing the controller, we need to consider the interactive behavior of the LayoutView class. There are four interactive tasks that the layout view supports:

- selecting chip or wire mode
- deleting a chip or wire
- creating a new chip or wire
- dragging a chip to a new location

The LayoutView class is considerably more complex in its behavior than PartListView. In PartListView, each interactive task was essentially handled by one of the input-event–handling methods. In the LayoutView, each of the four interactive tasks is scattered over the MouseDown, MouseMove, and MouseUp methods. In addition, the behavior is also partitioned among the helper classes. In order to understand this behavior, we will first work through the interactive behavior of each task and then look at how the behavior is partitioned among the various class methods.

Selecting Modes   Selecting chip mode or wire mode is a process of selecting the right icon. A very simple interactive behavior is to select an icon when a MouseUp event occurs: when MouseUp is received, we test the mouse position using ChipIcon.Select and WireIcon.Select; when either of these returns true, the LayoutView must remember which one (chip or wire) was selected. We can handle this with a new field on the LayoutView class:

```
enum{ ChipMode,WireMode } IconMode;
```

Note also that if IconMode is changed, the ChipIcon and WireIcon objects must be damaged so that they can correctly draw their highlights to show the selected mode.

Normally, such damage actions would be in response to change notification from the model. The IconMode information, however, is not a property of the model; it is a property of the view. As such, the view itself must account for any screen updates. This behavior can be understood as two cases:

1. MouseUp and ChipIcon.Selected
   IconMode = ChipMode
   Damage bounds of ChipIcon and WireIcon.
2. MouseUp and WireIcon.Selected
   IconMode = WireMode
   Damage bounds of ChipIcon and WireIcon.

Deletions   Deletion can also be handled in MouseUp by adding a test of the DeleteIcon.Select method. In this case, the LayoutView will consult the SelectedChip and SelectedWire fields in the model to determine which objects should be deleted. Invoking the DeleteChip and DeleteWire methods on the model will cause the model to notify the views, which will cause areas of the display to be damaged, which will then cause the windowing system to send redraw messages to the various views.

This behavior can be represented as a third case:

3. MouseUp and DeleteIcon.Selected
   Model.DeleteChip(Model.SelectedChip)
   Model.DeleteWire(Model.SelectedWire)

Creating Chips or Wires   There are several cases involved in this task. The behavior we want is to begin drawing the desired chip or wire when the mouse button goes down. While the mouse button is being held down and the mouse moves, we want to draw the new chip or wire in the new position so that the user can see where the chip or wire will ultimately end up. When the mouse button is released, we want to notify the model to create the new chip or wire. The task is driven by the input event, the IconMode, and by whatever is being selected by the mouse location, as shown in the following seven cases:

4. MouseDown and IconMode == ChipMode and *there is no chip being selected.*
   Draw the new chip.
   Remember the new chip location.
5. MouseMove and *we are creating a chip.*
   Erase the chip in the old location.
   Draw the chip in the new location.
   Remember the new location.
6. MouseUp and *we are creating a chip.*
   Erase the chip in the old location.
   Model.AddChip(MouseLocation).
7. MouseDown and IconMode == WireMode and *there is no chip being selected and the mouse is over a chip connector.*
   Draw the new wire.
   Remember the new wire's connector.
8. MouseMove and *we are creating a wire.*
   Erase the wire in the old location.
   Draw the wire in the new location.
   Remember the new wire end point.
9. MouseUp and *we are creating a wire* and *the mouse is over a chip connector.*
   Erase the wire in the old location.
   Model.AddWire(. . .).
10. MouseUp and *we are creating a wire* and *the mouse is **not** over a chip connector.*
    Erase the wire in the old location.
    Forget that a wire is being created.

Dragging Chips   The task of dragging a chip begins with the selection of a chip upon mouse down and the redrawing of the chip with each mouse movement until the mouse is released. The cases for this task are as follows:
11. MouseDown and *the mouse is over a chip to be selected.*
    Select the chip and remember that the controller is in dragging mode.

12. MouseMove and *the controller is dragging.*
    Erase the chip in its old location.
    Redraw the chip in its new location.
13. MouseUp and *the controller is dragging.*
    Erase the chip in its old location.
    Invoke the MoveChip method on the model.

Techniques for Dragging at Interactive Speeds   The dragging and creation of chips and wires requires that objects be erased in their old location and redrawn in their new location each time the mouse is moved. As discussed earlier, the move/redraw cycle must take less than 1/5th of a second per cycle for the user to feel comfortable with continuous movement. The problem lies in getting the image redrawn and erased fast enough.

The simplistic method is to damage the old and new areas and to let the windowing system take care of the problem using redraw. Unfortunately, on many machines this is not fast enough. Even on very fast machines, some models may be too complex for fast enough redraw.

A technique that is frequently used is to not redraw the actual image of the object that is being moved but rather to use a cartoon of the object. In the case of dragging a chip, we might only drag its bounding rectangle without updating its connecting wires. This is enough of a hint to the user in placing the chip that we do not need to draw all of the details. When the model is then updated, the normal redraw cycle will correctly draw the resulting movement.

Even when using a cartoon of the object that is being moved, there is still the problem of erasing the cartoon in its old position before drawing it in its new position. On the old vector-refresh displays, this was not a problem because changing the image would change the display in one refresh cycle. On frame buffer displays, erasure as well as drawing will damage the frame buffer and mess up whatever else should be drawn underneath.

A common erase/redraw technique is the use of exclusive-OR (XOR) drawing mode. This takes advantage of the following property of the XOR operation:

for any values of D and P

$$P' = XOR(D, P)$$
$$P = XOR(D, P')$$

These properties mean that for any value D, when we draw into pixel P using an XOR, that pixel will change to P'. If we draw D again into that pixel using XOR, the value P' will change back to P. We can first draw our cartoon using D with the XOR operation, which will change all of the pixels in our cartoon to some P' depending on what the original pixel color was. When it comes time in the next cycle to erase the cartoon, we can draw it again in XOR mode and the pixels will return to their original color.

Using XOR mode to draw a white object into frame buffers that have only a single bit per pixel will complement the values of the pixels, making white appear on black and black on white. This provides a nice contrast and works very effectively. In the case of true color displays with 24 bits per pixel, this process still works well in the case of very dark or very light colors because the complement has a high contrast to the original. In the case of neutral colors, however, the complement is a very similar neutral color and the cartoon does not have sufficient contrast to be easily visible during dragging.

The contrast problem is particularly acute when using frame buffers with color-lookup tables. The XOR operation is applied to the contents of each pixel. In a lookup-table architecture, the pixel value is not a color but an index to where the color is stored. The XOR in index space may not make any visual sense at all. Again, we may end up dragging with insufficient contrast. This is very frustrating for the user because he cannot perceive what the system is doing.

There is a technique that is very fast and that can help alleviate this problem, while still allowing the use of the XOR operation. Let us assume that the color of the object we are trying to draw is C and that the normal background color we are trying to draw upon is B. What we want is to choose some color D such that $C == XOR(D, B)$. That is, whenever D is drawn over B, the resulting color will be C, which is what we are trying to draw. The color D is easily computed as $D = XOR(C, B)$. By using a D computed in this fashion, we are always guaranteed that the resulting dragging color using XOR will contrast with B. Because dragging will not always be over the background, the contrast may not always work. For example, dragging a cartoon of a chip over existing wires may not produce a contrast over the wires, but we may not care much because the contrast over the background will yield sufficient visual information to guide the user while dragging.

An alternative dragging technique is to save the portion of the frame buffer under the cartoon before drawing. The pixels are saved in a separate off-screen buffer; when the cartoon is to be erased, the pixels are drawn back as they were before the cartoon was drawn. On most modern machines, there is sufficient speed to save and restore blocks of pixels in this fashion. This pixel-saving method can provide a quite accurate erase/redraw. There are some problems, however, in network-based graphics systems, such as X, where this technique may introduce excessive network traffic into the erase/redraw cycle and may eliminate the speed advantage.

Assembling the Cases into Input Methods   The 13 cases discussed above are partitioned based on the interactive tasks that need to be performed. The approach we have taken so far is very useful in understanding how each task is designed, but it will not guide our implementation. The implementation is structured not around interactive tasks but around the MouseDown, MouseMove, and MouseUp input-event methods. Having designed our interactive tasks based on cases, we can reorganize our cases; this reorganization leads directly to an implementation for each of the input methods. Note, however, that even with our simple application, the number of cases can grow quite large. In this example application, we have also ignored the MouseEnter and MouseExit methods that account for intervals when the mouse leaves and enters the view being controlled. To handle more complex interactions, we will need more sophisticated approaches for describing and working with input behavior. Such an approach is discussed in Chapter 8, Input Syntax. The reorganized list of cases is as follows:

MouseDown

4. MouseDown and IconMode == ChipMode and *there is no chip being selected.*
   Draw the new chip.
   Remember the new chip location.
7. MouseDown and IconMode == WireMode and *there is no chip being selected* and *the mouse is over a chip connector.*
   Draw the new wire.
   Remember the new wire's connector.
11. MouseDown and *the mouse is over a chip to be selected.*
   Select the chip and remember that the controller is in dragging mode.

MouseMove

5. MouseMove and *we are creating a chip.*
   Erase the chip in the old location.
   Draw the chip in the new location.
   Remember the new location.
8. MouseMove and *we are creating a wire.*
   Erase the wire in the old location.
   Draw the wire in the new location.
   Remember the new wire end point.
12. MouseMove and *the controller is dragging.*
   Erase the chip in its old location.
   Redraw the chip in its new location.

MouseUp

1. MouseUp and ChipIcon.Selected
   IconMode = ChipMode
   Damage bounds of ChipIcon and WireIcon.

2. MouseUp and WireIcon.Selected
    IconMode = WireMode
    Damage bounds of ChipIcon and WireIcon.
3. MouseUp and DeleteIcon.Selected
    Model.DeleteChip(Model.SelectedChip)
    Model.DeleteWire(Model.SelectedWire)
6. MouseUp and *we are creating a chip.*
    Erase the chip in the old location.
    Model.AddChip(MouseLocation) . . .
9. MouseUp and *we are creating a wire* and *the mouse is over a chip connector.*
    Erase the wire in the old location.
    Model.AddWire(. . .).
10. MouseUp and *we are creating a wire* and *the mouse is not over a chip connector.*
    Erase the wire in the old location.
    Forget that a wire is being created.
13. MouseUp and *the controller is dragging.*
    Erase the chip in its old location.
    Invoke the MoveChip method on the model.

Helper Classes

Our discussion of the LayoutView class has been simplified because we have assumed the existence of the Icon, Drawing, ChipV, and WireV classes. These classes should provide a Select method that will return a true or false depending on whether the mouse position selects that object. The Select method on Drawing should return a structure indicating whether a point, a chip, or a wire has been selected. The Drawing::Select method is implemented by calls to Select on ChipV and WireV. The Select method on ChipV must return either no selection, a chip selection, or a connector of the chip that was selected.

Each of the helper classes should support a Redraw method. The Drawing::Redraw method should simply call the Redraw method on ChipV and WireV objects.

The ChipV and WireV classes pose a special problem. If we create one ChipV object for every chip in the model and one WireV for every wire in the model, each instance of a LayoutView will essentially duplicate the entire model. This not only leads to excessive memory requirements but also requires duplication of the code to manage the model's data structure. One technique to alleviate this is for the Drawing class to maintain only one

ChipV and one WireV object. Before any methods are invoked on such an object, the Drawing class first changes its chip or wire index to the correct chip or wire that the Drawing class needs help with. This simple assignment is cheap and prevents duplication of all of the chips and wires. In the case of our application, such techniques work quite well. With more complex models, we will need to be more sophisticated.

5.5 Review of Important Concepts

The overall architecture of an application is based on the Model-View-Controller (MVC) architecture designed for Smalltalk. At the heart of the architecture is the model, which is composed of those classes that implement the functional model designed for the application. The architecture used in this chapter has modified the MVC architecture by combining the view and controller functions into a single view class.

There are three basic steps in building an interactive application. The first is to design the object classes that will make up the model. The second is to design an abstract class for all views of that model. The third is to design each of the view classes.

5.5.1 Functional Model

In designing the model classes, it is very important that any changes made to the information in the model be performed by means of a method. There should be no direct modification of the model from outside of those classes, because model modification must not only change the model but must also notify all views of the changes that have occurred.

5.5.2 View Notification

The abstract view class—such as our CircuitView class—will have methods for every notification that is generated by the model. The model classes will maintain a list of CircuitView objects that are to be notified whenever the model changes. It is easiest to provide the model class with the same methods as the view class. The model's methods will invoke the view methods on every view object in the model's list of views. The purpose of this architecture is to correctly support multiple views of differing kinds to display and to interact with a given model. The model classes never interact in any way with the user or the screen. All interaction is performed by notifying the views of any changes to the model.

5.5.3 View Implementation

Each view of a particular model is implemented as a subclass of that model's view class. The view implementation consists of methods that implement essential geometry, selection methods, change notification, redraw, and the input controller methods.

Essential Geometry

In any view, there is some essential geometry that can be abstracted into a set of methods that are used by the rest of the class. It is best to first define and implement this geometry. In the PartListView, this was the location of each chip's display in the list. In the LayoutView, it was the partitioning of icons and the geometry of wires and chips. In many cases, this geometry can be broken down into classes to handle component objects that make up the view.

Selection

The selection methods provide the controller methods with essential information about the view presentation. These methods are frequently combined with the essential geometry.

Change Notification

The change notification methods are inherited from the model's view class. These methods only damage those areas of the display that need to be redrawn. Change notification methods do not do any drawing on the canvas.

Redraw

All drawing is directly performed—or indirectly performed through other methods—by the view's Redraw method. By localizing all drawing in this method, we can ensure that all drawing is done in a uniform fashion and that all display updates are consistent with the overlapping of displayed objects and with the windowing system's management of other windows.

Controller

The controller methods are inherited from WinEventHandler and manage all input events. When designing the controller, we first work out the details of each interactive task as a set of cases with their appropriate actions. We then reorder those cases by input event rather than by interactive task. These reordered cases will give us the implementation of the input methods.

The controller methods do no drawing. They use the selection methods to determine how the mouse or other inputs relate to the display and then they invoke the model's methods to make modifications to the model. The model then notifies all views, not just the one that originated the modification, of the changes that have been made. Each view's change notification methods will damage the appropriate areas of the display. The windowing system will batch up all of the damaged areas and invoke the Redraw method on any view that needs to be updated. The Redraw method will update the display based on the current contents of the model.

5.6 An Alternative Implementation

The implementation approach used in our example exploited the use of abstract classes and the message/method–binding mechanisms of an object-oriented language to do all of the event dispatching and change notification. This approach makes it quite easy to handle the variety of messages and notifications that must pass between the objects that make up the interactive architecture.

There are some drawbacks to this architecture, however. The first is that every model must have its own abstract view class, and every view must inherit both the method interface necessary to receive input from the windowing system and the method interface needed to receive change notification. This is further complicated in more sophisticated applications when views contain other views and must also communicate with them.

In some systems, the views have only one Event method. The Event method has one parameter that is a pointer to an event record, and the event record always has as its very first field an integer event type. The remainder of the record is formatted according to the type of the event. This Event method is used to handle all input events, system notification events, model change notifications, and any other communications.

When an object receives an event, its Event method must look at the type of event to sort out what should be done. Any event that it does not understand is forwarded to its superclass's Event method. This architecture eliminates the need for the abstract view class because any event-handling class can receive the Event message. Each model can then formulate its own notification events and forward them through the Event method on any view in the model's event list. This approach allows for a single Model class that contains all of the methods and fields for registering views. The Model class can also provide a ViewNotify method that will forward an event on to every view in the list of views registered on the model.

This alternative implementation is much more flexible than the strictly object-oriented model described in this chapter. In exchange for the flexibility, however, most of the type checking and event management must be done by the programmer rather than the compiler. It is a trade-off that must be carefully considered when building new applications.

5.7 Visual C++

In order to get a more commercial slant on the concepts discussed in this chapter, we can look at the View/Document architecture of Visual C++. All drawing is handled by means of the CDC (device context) class, which provides a generic superclass for all windows, printers, and other areas that a program might want to draw into. This is identical to our concept of a Canvas. The CView class is the superclass for all views and roughly corresponds to our WinEventHandler. Visual C++ does not use the abstract view classes, such as CircuitView, in its change notification model. The CDocument class defines the superclass for all models. The terminology for Visual C++ is as follows:

- WinEventHandler is a View.
- Canvas is a CDC (device context).
- Model is a Document.

5.7.1 CView

The CView class works pretty much the way we have discussed for the functioning of views. There is an OnDraw method that performs the Redraw function. The OnDraw method, however, receives a device context as its parameter rather than a damaged region. In order to determine what has been damaged, the programmer can question the device context. This allows a single view object to display on both a printer and a window because the view is not explicitly bound to a drawing surface until the OnDraw method is called.

The CView class provides an Invalidate method, which performs the same function as Damage. This directly mirrors our architecture for updating the screen.

The Visual C++ approach to change notification from the model, or document, is actually a compromise between the strictly object/method model used in most of our discussion and the alternative that uses a single Event method. The underlying MS Windows architecture supports only a single event stream because it was not designed with C++ in mind. When models, the windowing system, the menu system, or any other process sends an event to a subclass of CView, it uses the same event-dispatching method. The Visual C++ environment, however, provides a structure for mapping various events directly to methods defined on the particular view subclass. This "message-mapping" technique retains most of the flexibility of the underlying MS Windows event model while still allowing programmers to exploit the messaging mechanisms in C++. The message-mapping technique will map input events onto C++ methods in much the way we designed our example controller implementation.

There is, however, only one OnUpdate method on any view. The OnUpdate method is invoked whenever some portion of the data displayed by the view has changed. The default implementation for OnUpdate is to damage, or invalidate, the entire window. This, of course, is always correct but may be inefficient. The OnUpdate method has two parameters, a long integer and a CObject pointer. In C++, a long integer can be used for just about anything, and the CObject class is the superclass of many model objects. These two parameters allow additional information about what has changed to be sent with an OnUpdate message. This single change notification message eliminates the need for abstract classes like CircuitView, but it requires more care when programming.

In our example, we defined the following change notification methods:

ChangeChip(ChipNum)

ChangeWire(WireNum)

MoveChip(ChipNum, NewLocation)

We could map this design onto the OnUpdate method by assigning an integer code to each type of change and then defining a subclass of CObject that would hold the remaining information. This would allow implementation of our design in Visual C++ without much difficulty.

Finally, every view has a GetDocument method that provides access to the CDocument object that implements the model. In keeping with some of the ugliness of C++, this CDocument pointer must be cast to a pointer of the type of model actually being viewed. After such a cast has been performed, all of the model methods can be invoked by the view and controller methods.

5.7.2 CDocument

The CDocument class is the superclass for all models. Its most valuable function is to provide the UpdateAllViews method. Because all views are subclasses of CView, the CDocument class maintains a list of views and then invokes the OnUpdate method on each registered view. This means that subclasses of CDocument will not need to manage view registration.

In addition to CDocument, there is also a CObject class that can be used as the superclass of objects like Chip and Wire. By using the generic CObject class as the superclass, various facilities are provided in Visual C++ for managing lists of such objects. In particular, there are facilities for saving and loading documents and their objects from files and for other cutting and pasting operations.

5.8 Summary

Interactive programs are separated into models and views. A model implements the functional model of the application. A view translates the model into an appropriate image. When the windowing system receives a user input, it forwards the event to the appropriate controller method on the appropriate view. The controller collects user inputs until there is sufficient information to make a change to the model. The model then notifies all of its views whenever a significant change happens. In response to change notification, a view will damage appropriate regions of the display. The windowing system will collect all damaged regions and will then invoke the Redraw methods of appropriate views. Each Redraw method will consult the model that the particular view is displaying in order to correctly redraw the damaged portion of the screen.

6

Widget Tool Kits

In Chapter 5, we discussed the architecture of a complete interactive application. This circuit layout application was, of necessity, a small one. If every application was constructed completely by hand, as in our circuit application, the result would be very costly and would generally yield an inconsistent interface.

All modern interactive systems are built around a tool kit of widgets. A widget is a small interactive object that performs some editing or input task. User interfaces are built up by combining these widgets together. The term *widget* comes from the original X Windows tool kit. In NeXTSTEP they are called *objects*, and in MS Windows and on the Macintosh they are called *controls*. In all cases, they are the standard menus, buttons, scroll bars, and text boxes used to compose larger user interfaces from smaller pieces.

This chapter looks at the design and implementation of the widgets themselves. In Chapter 7, we discuss how they can be assembled to form more complex applications. The implementation of a particular widget set defines, for the most part, the "look and feel" of the interface. The *look* is defined as the visual presentation of the widgets. A good tool kit is composed of widgets with a uniform look so as to create a consistent appearance within an application and across all applications implemented on that particular platform. The *feel* defines the syntax of input events by which a user manipulates the information represented by each widget.

6.1 Model-View-Controller

A widget can be studied in the same model-view-controller terms that we used in designing the circuit layout application. The only difference is that the model information for each widget is very simple.

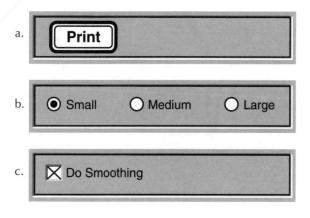

Figure 6-1   Example buttons

6.1.1 Widget Models

In general, we can group widgets according to the information in their model.

Buttons

All buttons have a single model value that can be set to one or more discrete values. Figure 6-1 shows a variety of button styles. The Print button controls a value that indicates whether or not the print function should be invoked. In this case, the model or value of the button is secondary to the command to be invoked. The three radio buttons (Small, Medium, and Large) all share a single model variable. Each button has its own value for that variable. The Do Smoothing button has a value that can be on or off. In all cases, the button is manipulating a single, discrete value or executing a command from the functional model.

Sliders

Sliders or scroll bars are designed to manipulate a continuous bounded range of values. The model for all scroll bars consists of two limits and a current value between those limits. The "thumb" or handle of the slider provides interactive control over the current value and feedback on what the current value is. Figure 6-2 shows example scroll bars.

Some tool kits provide scroll bars that can indicate a range of values or the relative size of the window of values they are scrolling through. In such cases, the model consists of two limits, the current value and the size of the visible window. For example, if a scroll bar is used to scroll through a file of 5000 lines of text, the top limit of the scroll bar would be 0, the bottom limit 5000. The current value might be 1523 and the window width might be 25 lines. Figure 6-3 shows examples of such scroll bars.

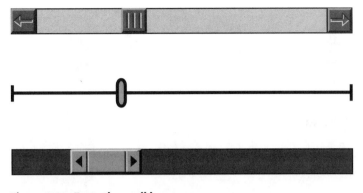

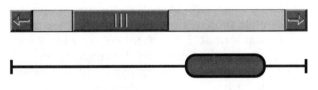

Figure 6-2   Example scroll bars

Figure 6-3   Range scroll bars

The model for scroll bars may also be extended to include page size. In the case of the top scroll bar in Figure 6-3, clicking the left arrow will cause the current value to move left by one. Clicking in the open area between the slider and the left arrow, however, causes the scroll bar to move left by one page size. This page size may vary and thus must be part of the model information for the scroll bar.

Menus

Menus are designed to select from a potentially large number of possibilities. The model for a menu is very close to that of a button. The major difference is how the large number of selections are handled. Most menus systems attempt to solve the problem of representing a range of selections that is much larger than the available screen resource. The semantic behavior of menu selection either sets model variables to particular values or issues one of the model's commands. As with buttons and scroll bars, menus frequently have the same interactive behavior and model while supporting a variety of presentations.

Text Boxes

Text entry boxes generally have as their model a single string of characters that the user is allowed to edit or type from scratch. The model may, however,

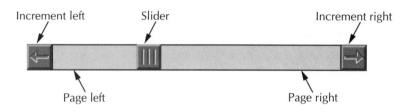

Figure 6-4   Scroll bar click areas

be a numeric value, a date, or some other value for which there is a textual representation.

There is wide variation among tool kits as to what the text box model actually should be. Take, for example, a box into which a user can type a number. Making the widget model exclusively a string greatly simplifies the widget design. The application's functional model, however, must then convert between numeric format and textual format. Since numbers are widely used in user interfaces, this mapping must be duplicated in all functional models that use text boxes. To eliminate the redundant effort, many widget sets provide text boxes that manipulate integer numbers rather than just strings.

Once we have a widget that can handle the typing of integers, what about floating-point numbers? There is also the question of supporting commas and monetary symbols in a number, such as $2,253.21. If the text box widget is going to support monetary value and floating-point numbers, why not dates and percentages? If we are going to support dates, will all of the months be in English, abbreviated, or represented numerically? Adding all of these options to the text box widget model makes for a very complex widget. Thus, many designers return to a simple character string as the model variable for the text box and let the application handle the mapping to the value that is really desired by the application's functional model.

6.1.2 Independence of View and Controller

In the preceding discussion of the model information for a given widget, we saw several ways in which buttons and scroll bars could be represented. In Figure 6-2, there are three forms of horizontal scroll bar. The only difference between them is their visual presentation. Each shares the same model information and has exactly the same input syntax.

Each of these forms of scroll bar has the clickable areas shown in Figure 6-4. Each of the other scroll bars shown in Figures 6-2 and 6-3 has similar areas. The drawing of the scroll bar and the mapping of mouse locations are properties of the view. In all of the scroll bars shown, the input syntax is the same.

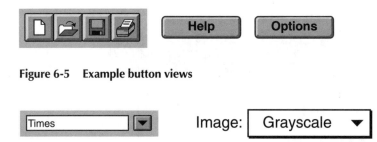

Figure 6-5   Example button views

Figure 6-6   Example option menu views

Among the scroll bars in Figure 6-2, the models are identical; only the view is different. These differences are what led the designers of the model-view-controller architecture to separate the view from the controller. All of the scroll bars shown have the same input syntax and therefore could share the same controller code. Substituting different view code produces scroll bars with differing looks but identical interactive behavior.

As with scroll bars, there are a variety of button styles that share the same input syntax but have different views of the model. Examples of various button views are shown in Figure 6-5. The buttons on the left are from Microsoft Word's tool bar, while those on the right come from the Macintosh print dialog. The input syntax for all of these buttons is identical but the views are very different. A similar relationship can be seen in the two forms of option menus in Figure 6-6. These examples are from the same sources as those in Figure 6-5.

Although there is potential for sharing controller code among widgets with multiple views, the separation of view and controller is rarely found in most widget sets. Consistent interface design dictates that objects that act alike should look alike, so that users can readily perceive the similarities and thus understand interactively how to use the widget. This consistency requirement means that in most widget sets, for a given controller there is only one view. This single-view-per-controller convention leads to the merging of view and controller, as described in our discussion of the circuit layout application.

An exception to this consistency argument is product differentiation. In the case of Word, Excel, and other Microsoft products, the marketing people wanted to clearly differentiate their suite of products from standard Macintosh applications. Adding the tool bar to the standard Macintosh menu bar was one approach to this goal. Within the tool bar, however, all buttons look and behave alike, as shown in Figure 6-7. Rather than reuse the Macintosh button controller code, it was much simpler for Microsoft to implement its own button widgets. Even with this differentiation, however, tool bar behavior is consistent across the Microsoft applications.

Figure 6-7 Microsoft Word tool bar

6.2 Abstract Devices

The notion of a widget ties into the earlier idea of an abstract device. The concept of an abstract device is useful in studying widget design. Early work in interactive software was an outgrowth of the computer graphics community. On early systems, there were a wide variety of input devices, such as knobs, sliders, tablets of many kinds, push buttons, keyboards, mice, and track balls. Each of these devices had different interfaces and behaviors. It was soon discovered that such devices could be grouped together by similar behavior and provided with standard software interfaces. It was also determined that physical input devices not present in a given hardware configuration could be simulated on the screen using other input devices. Out of this grew the concept of an *abstract device*. Most of the widgets in modern user interface tool kits are abstract devices.

In discussing abstract input devices, we consider physical, virtual, and logical devices. *Physical devices* are actual hardware input devices connected to a workstation. Example physical devices are a bank of slider controls, a row of push buttons, a mouse, or perhaps a MIDI keyboard for music.

Virtual devices are simulated on the screen rather than being actual hardware devices. The selections in a menu are virtual buttons. Many applications have buttons bars displayed across the top of some windows. These are even made to appear like real 3D buttons. In actuality, however, they are simulations of real buttons. Similarly, scroll bars simulate real slider controls. A MIDI keyboard might be simulated by an image of the piano keyboard, which can be clicked with a mouse to simulate the striking of piano keys.

A *logical device* is an abstract model of an input; the logical device defines the software's view of the input. The purpose of the logical device is to separate application software from the actual implementation of an input. For example, if an application is written to use a logical Quit button, it does not matter to the software whether that logical button is implemented as a special function button, a Control-Q from the keyboard, a Quit menu item, or a special clickable box at the top of some screen window. Some of these possibilities are actual physical devices, such as the function button or Control-Q, and some are virtual simulations. From the application software's point of view, there is no difference among them. They all indicate the logical selection "Quit."

Although the variety of implementations of logical devices may make no difference to the software, it can make a lot of difference to end users. If Quit is implemented as a function button, then special hardware must be present at the workstation. If Quit is implemented as Control-Q, users will not need to take their hands from the keyboard to activate Quit. On the other hand, if they don't know about Control-Q, they may never be able to quit. Quit in a pull-down menu has very different interactive characteristics from a standard Quit box on every window. All of these choices affect the usability of the interface. By implementing the application in terms of logical devices, designers are free to make use of device substitutions in search of good usability, without major modifications to the rest of the application. Logical devices would even allow Quit to be implemented with both a menu item and Control-Q to accommodate the variety of user needs. The application would only see the logical Quit input, regardless of which physical or virtual implementation is used.

There are several properties of logical devices that need to be identified before proceeding with their implementations. These are the concepts of acquire/release, enable/disable, active/inactive, and echo. These concepts are general across all widgets and aid our discussion of implementations.

6.2.1 Acquire and Release

Interactive resources are scarce in any user interface because there is a limited amount of screen space and there are a limited number of physical input devices. To accommodate this problem, not all logical input devices are active at any one time. For example, a pull-down menu has most of the buttons that make up the menu inactive most of the time. Only when the menu is actually pulled down is screen real estate allocated to the items in the menu. We may have an application with hundreds of logical buttons for which only 10 function buttons exist on the keyboard. To accommodate this problem, only a few logical function buttons are active at any one time.

If a logical input has its interactive resources allocated, then the device is *acquired*. If it does not have its resources allocated, then it is *released*. A pull-down menu acquires its menu items whenever the menu header is selected. This allocates screen space to the menu items. When a menu item has been selected, most pull-down menus release the items in its menu, causing the menu to disappear. By dynamically acquiring and releasing logical inputs, a pull-down menu shares screen space with adjacent menus and with the windows on the screen.

In the case of our large number of logical function buttons, the application can acquire only a few of them at any one time. In addition, no two logical function buttons that are bound to the same physical function button can be acquired at the same time. Such a strategy allows for the sharing of the physical buttons among a number of logical inputs.

Frequently, logical inputs are grouped together and managed as a group. For example, all of the items in a pull-down menu are managed as a group. Logical function buttons may also be managed as a group. Such a group is sometimes referred to as an *input context*. Acquire and release operations are frequently performed on input contexts rather than on individual logical inputs. This provides some structure to the set of logical devices that are currently available for use.

A good example of an input context is a dialog box. When a dialog box appears on the screen, all of the logical input widgets in the box are acquired. When the dialog box is removed, the widgets are released.

6.2.2 Enable and Disable

Frequently a logical device may be acquired and its interactive resources allocated, but it may not be acceptable as input. For example, a Close menu item is only acceptable as input when there is a currently open window. Similarly, the Open item may not be acceptable if the maximum number of windows are already open.

A very important principle of interactive systems is that errors should be prevented rather than reported. Preventing the logical Close input when it is not legal is much better than generating an error message or doing nothing when the user selects that input by mistake. One method of preventing unacceptable inputs is to release all such inputs. When released, they are not allocated interactive resources and therefore cannot generate inputs.

The use of acquire and release to control the set of legal inputs causes other usability problems. As users gain experience with an interface, they automatically optimize their behavior by remembering where a particular input is found. Without thinking about it, most experienced users of a system do not scan the entire File menu for the Close item. They immediately look at the location where it is normally found and never look at the remainder of the menu. This mental technique not only saves the time of scanning the menu but sharply reduces the amount of conscious attention a user must pay to the selection of Close. If logical inputs are released when they are illegal, the physical layout of the menu or other context that the items are found in will change. Items can now be found in a variety of locations, making the quick scan by an experienced user much more difficult.

The problem is even greater for infrequently used commands. For example, in the Excel spreadsheet, if the user is typing an entry, it is illegal to select the Sort menu item. If a user inadvertently goes to the Data menu, where Sort is usually found, and finds it missing, he may assume that he has forgotten where Sort is located and will search all of the menus. When he doesn't find it, he may then assume that he has forgotten the menu item's name and will then carefully and methodically search all of the menus and soon will get very frustrated.

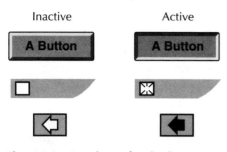

Figure 6-8   Inactive and active inputs

To accommodate illegal inputs, we use the concepts of enable and disable. A logical device may be acquired, with its interactive resources allocated, but may also be disabled and thus not accepting any input. In many menu systems, disabled items are represented in a lighter color, which is visible but has less contrast than the enabled items. Disabled scroll bars may have their sliders and buttons removed. These techniques all show the user that such an input is in its appropriate place but that the input is currently unacceptable.

6.2.3 Active and Inactive

An important part of the visual feedback of any widget is to indicate whether it is active or inactive. A user performing some input needs to know if the application is responding. Such feedback helps the user to know when he is performing correct input behaviors. A logical device is active whenever the user is currently interacting with that device. When a user presses a mouse button over the image of a virtual button, the virtual button should become active and appear to respond. When a user selects the slider of a scroll bar, the slider should become active and appear to respond. When a user selects a location in a text box, the insertion point should be highlighted and perhaps blink to show where characters will be placed. Figure 6-8 shows several examples of active and inactive inputs.

6.2.4 Echo

The last property of a widget is its echo. This is the mechanism a widget uses to display its current state. In the case of a scroll bar, the echo is provided by the location of the slider. In the case of check boxes and radio buttons, the echo is presented by whether the box or circle is filled in. For a text box, the echo is the actual text being displayed. One of the key characteristics of direct-manipulation interfaces is that the echo and the techniques for manipulating the value of the widget are visually and conceptually integrated.

Figure 6-9   Skinny scroll bar in Motif

6.3 Look and Feel

Much has been said in the research literature and in the trade press about the look and feel of various tool kits. There have been several lawsuits about such issues. For a user interface tool kit, the look and feel of the interface is determined almost exclusively by the design of the widget set. The look is determined by the visual presentation of the widgets and the feel by the way that they interactively behave.

There are three primary issues related to look and feel. The first is ease of learning. In particular, it must be obvious to prospective users what each widget is for and how such widgets are manipulated. This can be a challenge because the feel is not visible. For example, new users who have never used a mouse with a graphical interface do not know how to drag the slider in order to manipulate a scroll bar, nor do they automatically know how to resize a window. The key is to make such techniques as uniform as possible across the tool kit and to make them as simple and obvious as possible so they are easily explained and remembered.

A second issue in widget design is ease of use. Once the user has learned how to manipulate portions of an interface, will it be easy and effective or will it be a constant challenge? In some implementations of Motif, the scroll bars are very thin to reduce the amount of screen space required (Figure 6-9). The look is fine because they are easily seen and understood. Ease of learning is fine because they function like most other scroll bars. The ease of use is terrible. In particular, it is very hard to hit the little arrows at the end. If the user misses an arrow, instead of single stepping, the bar starts page stepping because the user has selected the shaft of the bar rather than the little arrow.

The last issue is that the widget set must be attractive and engaging. The essence of this requirement is that look sells software. Figure 6-10 shows a palette of drawing tools taken from Aldus Intellidraw by Silicon Beach Software. The look of this palette is similar to those found in most drawing packages. Figure 6-11 shows a similar palette from Dabbler by Fractal Design. The set of functions is very similar and the way they are used is also very similar. The attractiveness of the Dabbler palette is much greater than that of Intellidraw. Looks are not everything but engaging visuals—particularly when they do not interfere with the usability of the system—can go a long ways toward creating a more enjoyable interface. Remember, however, that a pretty face on shabby functionality will not survive for long in the market.

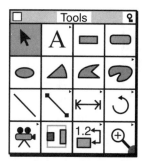

Figure 6-10   Draw palette from Intellidraw

Figure 6-11   Draw palette from Dabbler

6.4 The Look

We first consider the look or visual presentation of widgets. The issues here include the information that must be presented visually, the conserving of screen space, a consistent look across the tool kit, and the software architecture issues required to implement the look.

6.4.1 What the Look Must Present

The look must be able to represent affordances, enable/disable status, active/inactive status, a widget's echo, widget structural groupings, and the particular distinctive style of a given commercial product line.

Affordances

An affordance is a property of the visual appearance that makes objects appear as though they can be manipulated. Affordances also provide visual cues as to what might happen if the object is manipulated. It is important to remember that since images on the screen are not real objects, many of the affordances must be learned. Consider, for example, the Macintosh dialog box in Figure 6-12. In this case, most of the affordances must be learned. Free-standing text without borders is just text and is not active. Buttons that can be

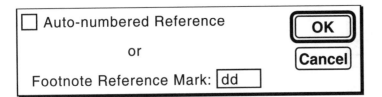

Figure 6-12   Macintosh dialog box

Figure 6-13   Microsoft Word button bar

pressed are always shown in round-cornered rectangles. Text that can be edited, such as "dd," is always shown inside a rectangle. This set of conventions was designed when personal computers were slow and graphics screens only had 1 bit per pixel.

Figure 6-13 shows the more recently designed button bar from Microsoft Word. In this case, text that can be edited is set off from other parts of the button bar by a lighter background color. In addition, any button that is pressable (can be clicked) is shown with a 3D appearance. This 3D look takes advantage of the user's experience with the physical world, where objects that stick out from a control surface usually can be pressed to make some appliance function.

This use of metaphor from the real world can be seen in Figure 6-11, which shows Dabbler's palette of drawing tools. The small figure at the top center of the palette looks like the handle of a drawer. In addition, the entire palette is set off by a 3D-appearing groove much like the crack people would see around a drawer in their kitchen or bathroom. Clicking on this handle icon causes the drawer to open and reveals additional drawing tools that can be placed in this palette. In many ways, this has similar functionality to an ordinary pull-down menu. However, the drawer metaphor draws very literally on the user's (most likely an artist's) real-world experience.

To gain further understanding of the value of affordances, consider the two banks of sliders shown in Figure 6-14. Both banks of sliders control RGB values in exactly the same way and both present the same information. The set on the right, however, has additional tracks that provide a visual cue that each of the ovals can slide up and down. The set on the left has no visual indication as to how the ovals might move. In fact, it is not clear from the image on the

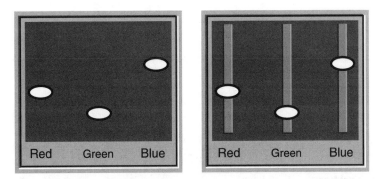

Figure 6-14   Slider affordances

left that the ovals are actually movable controls. Note also that the presence of the tracks clearly delineates the range of movement for each of the ovals.

In designing affordances into the look of a set of widgets, it is important to consider how humans visually perceive foreground and background. When we look at the world around us, we are constantly trying to decide what is important and worthy of special attention and what can be ignored for the moment. There are many issues in this area, but a few simple points are as follows:

- Light objects take precedence over dark objects.
- Objects with detail and texture take precedence over plain or uniform objects.
- Objects with high contrast take precedence over objects with little contrast.
- Large objects take precedence over small objects.
- Varied objects take precedence over regular or uniform objects.

In Figure 6-14, the ovals are much lighter and have a higher contrast with the background than the other objects. In the Microsoft Word button bar in Figure 6-13, the text that can be typed is set in a light-colored box and thus stands out. The current selection for justification of text is much lighter than its companions. All of the visual detail is inside the button icons, therefore drawing attention to them.

Figure 6-15 shows an example of a poorly designed affordance. This figure shows the tool for splitting a window horizontally into two separate views of a document. To split the window, the user must drag the black rectangle down across the scroll bar. What the user sees is simply the black rectangle shown on the left, which does not at all appear like something that can be manipulated. Its dark, flat appearance makes it recede into the background. The only indication that it is active is that the cursor changes shape when placed over

Figure 6-15   Window splitter

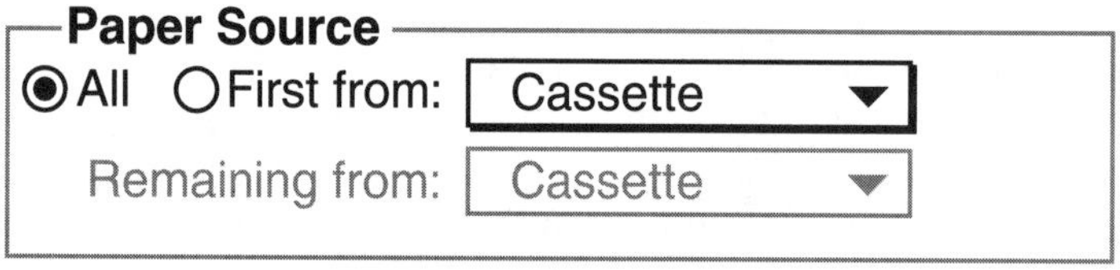

┌─ **Paper Source** ─────────────────────────┐
│ ◉ All   ○ First from: [Cassette   ▼] │
│   Remaining from: [Cassette   ▼]   │
└───┘

Figure 6-16   Disabled widgets, shown by reduced contrast

the rectangle, as shown on the right. This cursor, with its arrows, provides a much clearer affordance as to what we might do with this rectangle. Note that there may be other considerations (such as lack of screen space or too many controls competing for user attention) that would lead to this design. However, as a visual affordance, this design is rather poor.

Enable/Disable

As discussed earlier, there are times when certain widgets cannot provide acceptable inputs. At such times, it is not helpful to make such widgets disappear because this loss of continuity confuses the user. What is needed is to visually indicate that the item is disabled. One of the most common methods is to reduce the contrast of the item with its background. Users can still see the item, but it visually recedes so as not to draw attention to itself. An example of such a dialog is shown in Figure 6-16. Unless the "First from:" item is selected, the value of the "Remaining from:" widget is useless. The useless widget is disabled and is displayed in gray. The fact that the item is still visible is very helpful in communicating that the "First from:" option will select paper first from one tray and then from another. If the "Remaining from:" widget were not visible, it would be very unclear what "First from:" really does. On the other hand, displaying in gray helps "Remaining from:" recede visually so that the user is not distracted by unusable items.

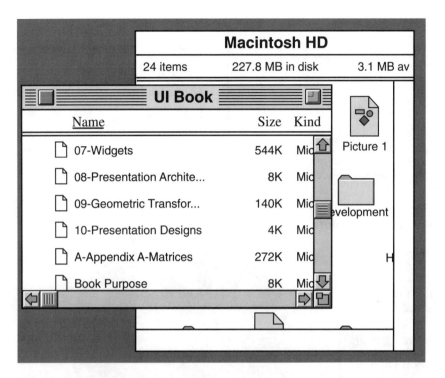

Figure 6-17　Enabled/disabled windows

Compare, for example, the two windows from the Macintosh finder, shown in Figure 6-17. The window entitled "UI Book" has a header with line detail and active widgets. The disabled "Macintosh HD" window has no such detail and displays no widgets. Note the enabled scroll bar down the right side of "UI Book," as opposed to the disabled scroll bar in the same position on "Macintosh HD." It is immediately clear which widgets are accepting inputs and which are not.

Active/Inactive Status

Active/inactive status must be visually displayed when a widget is engaged in the input. When a user clicks on a button, it should visually react so the user knows the button is active. Much of the display of active and inactive is an animation in response to user input. When a Macintosh file is opened, there is a growing-rectangle animation that grows out from the file. This clearly shows the user that the file is opening, even if the application that manages that file is slow to get started.

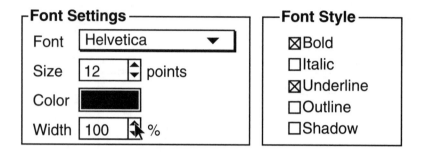

Figure 6-18   Widget echoes

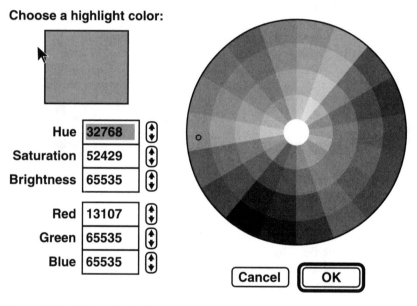

Figure 6-19   Color wheel echo

Echo

The purpose of a widget's echo is to visually display its current value. In Figure 6-18, there are several widgets, each displaying its own values. The Size and Width widgets use textual numbers. The widgets in the Font Style group all display their binary value as either checked or not checked. The Font widget displays its current font and the Color widget displays its color. For a more unique display of a widget's value, consider the color wheel from the Macintosh's color picker dialog, shown in Figure 6-19. In this case, the small spot on the wheel shows the color in the context of the set of possible colors. The

Figure 6-20   Selected-states echo

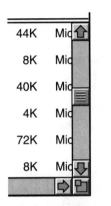

Figure 6-21   Echo of a scroll bar

large rectangle at the upper left echoes the current color of the widget, while the text boxes below echo the current color's value in each of the HSV and RGB color spaces.

An important value to be echoed in many cases is the current selected states of objects. Consider the echo of the currently selected tool from the palettes in Figures 6-10 and 6-11. Note in Figure 6-20 how the currently selected widgets in the button bar are both brighter and have higher contrast, which visually helps them to stand out from their peers. One of the more obvious echoes of a widget's value is the echo of a scroll bar, as shown in Figure 6-21.

Structural Groupings

Widgets rarely occur alone. They are generally grouped to support a complex task. Such structural groupings include menus, palettes, button bars, dialog boxes, and property sheets. These structural groupings are very important to the usability of an application. There are three issues that drive this need for visual structure. First, widgets frequently work together to accomplish a particular goal. For example, the palette in Figure 6-11 allows the user to select from a set of possible drawing techniques. These widgets form a group because they are all tied to the same object in the application's functional model, namely, the currently selected drawing pen. Other widgets are more conceptually than implementationally related, as demonstrated by the list of font styles in Figure 6-18. Each of the check boxes has its own model variable, but together these settings define how a text character should be rendered.

A second issue is screen space. In a large, complex application there are far more controls than can possibly fit on the screen at one time. Even if they could fit, their numbers would create a terrible searching problem as users try to find the widget they need for a particular task. Many widget groups are defined for the purpose of conserving screen space; the pull-down menu is a prime example of this. The menu bar takes up very little screen space, yet it provides well over 100 widgets for selection in many applications. By functionally grouping the items that are in the menu, a user's task in finding those items is greatly simplified and screen space is conserved.

The last issue is that the human cognitive process cannot handle large lists of items. People regularly handle large lists, but they do it by chunking large collections of objects into smaller groups or by imposing some organizing order on the list. For example, the specification of text styles contains close to 20 different controls. However, if we group these controls into styles, font face, and font size, the user has three groups that can easily be remembered. Within font styles we have bold, underline, italic, shadowed, outlined, and hidden, again a relatively small group of things. This grouping process can continue throughout the widget set related to text. In fact, the widgets related to text themselves form a group separate from other widgets in an application.

One of the advantages of direct-manipulation interfaces is that users do not need to remember all of the controls for an application. All controls are displayed visually on the screen where the user can recognize them rather than remember them. To effectively use a complex application, however, the user still needs a mental model of the widget structure so that the desired widget can easily be found again. Even if all widgets are displayed at once, a user must visually search through this set of widgets looking for the desired control. Visual structure aids this searching process.

Designing a good visual structure is a complex process that requires a great deal of training in visual design. Programmers generally do not have this training. The problem is alleviated to some extent by a well-designed widget set that has many of the elements of good visual design preprogrammed into the set. There are a few simple rules that programmers should be aware of, however.

User interface designers must be aware that users are continually engaged in a search process. The user has a task in mind and is searching for the widget, control, or technique that will accomplish this task. In a direct-manipulation interface, this search is primarily visual. In performing this search, the visual perception system groups together things that are close to each other and that have a similar appearance. For example, in the button bar in Figure 6-22, the widget grouping is actually defined by the open spaces

Figure 6-22   **Visual grouping**

between widgets. The small down arrows are visually associated with the type-in boxes because there is less space between them than there is between the down arrows and the widgets to their right. Note that the font and style widgets on the left visually group themselves together because of their similar structure, even though there is a dividing line between them. Visual grouping is thus defined by closeness and visual similarity.

An alternative grouping mechanism is shown in Figure 6-18, where the groups are enclosed in a labeled boundary box. Some designers and users have criticized this particular grouping technique on the grounds that the lines attract the eye's attention without contributing any information, the principle being that empty space rather than lines is preferred for separating groups.

Product Differentiation

In many cases, the look of an interface is purposely modified to produce a distinctive differentiation from other product lines. The button bars shown in Figures 6-7, 6-20, and 6-22 are a distinctive Microsoft feature. Other applications have button bars but the Microsoft bars have a distinctive style that is found in both the Macintosh and the Windows versions of Microsoft products. This style carries product recognition across platforms. An even more distinctive example is Dabbler's button drawers in Figure 6-11. Although these buttons behave in a substantially similar way to those in Microsoft products, there is no confusion between the two visual styles.

6.4.2 Economy of Screen Space

Although knowledge workers can work effectively on a desk that is 30" × 60" —disregarding storage space for reference materials and other stored resources—a very good computer screen provides less than 19" × 19" of working space, with much less resolution than the documents found on a desk. This means that screen space is a scarce resource that must be used effectively. Figures 6-23 and 6-24 show pairs of widgets that share the same model and substantially the same interactive behavior. The difference between them is in how screen space is used. The dial in Figure 6-23 takes up much more screen space and is much harder to integrate spatially with other widgets than the scroll bar. While scroll bars can be placed out of the way on the borders of

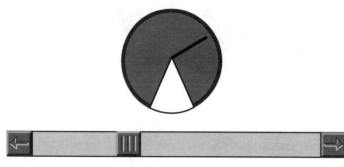

Figure 6-23   Sliders and dials

Figure 6-24   Choice widgets

a window, the dial requires a large, odd-sized space of its own. The same is true of the switch vs. the check box in Figure 6-24. The check box requires far less screen space while providing similar visual feedback and functionality. Well-designed widget sets provide strong functionality with minimal use of screen real estate.

Note, however, that economy of screen space is not the only goal in widget design. For particularly prominent functionality, the larger widgets draw the desired attention. In the case of a flight simulator application, replacing an artificial horizon widget with two scroll bars would save screen space but would be much less effective.

6.4.3 Consistent Look

A consistent look in a set of widgets is important for two reasons. The first is ease of learning. When a user faces a new interface, the look is the only clue the user has as to what items are interactive and how they behave. A second purpose is ease of use. It must be possible to readily locate needed functionality.

Ease of Learning

Users expect widgets that look alike to behave alike. With a consistent look across all buttons, for example, users can quickly learn which items are press-

Figure 6-25 A Macintosh menu bar

Figure 6-26   A pop-up widget

able and which are only visual. Similarly, a common scroll bar design makes it readily understood which items can be scrolled. The key value of a consistent look is that it allows users to transfer prior knowledge from different but similar situations. For example, in MS Windows, a user who has used other button widgets in one application readily recognizes similar shapes on a new application and understands that those locations can be clicked with the mouse to invoke some function. The words in Figure 6-25 are just words, but if they appear at the top of a Macintosh screen, users understand that pressing the mouse on one of these words causes a menu of selectable items to appear. Macintosh users know this even if they have not used this particular application before.

MS Windows and X Windows provide a similar consistency for their menus, except that the menu always appears at the top of each window. The key is that once a particular convention is learned, users can transfer such understanding to new situations.

For example, to someone not familiar with Microsoft products, the widget in Figure 6-26 seems to be a place to type a number. On the other hand, the 3D look of the arrow seems to indicate that you can click on the arrow. The knowledge that 3D objects can be pressed by the mouse is not innate; it is certainly not innate knowledge that pressing the mouse button while the cursor is over the object simulates the pressing of the object with your finger. Users who have mastered this concept in prior situations carry this knowledge with them to new situations. The text looks like other text that can be selected and typed; therefore the user is likely to try such an activity. The 3D arrow looks like it can be pressed; therefore, because of prior experience, the user is likely to try such a thing. Pressing on the arrow causes a menu of font size selections to appear. Because this menu of choices is normally invisible, only the similarity of the arrow's look to previous experience invites a user to press the arrow and find the additional help that is available.

Once a user has experienced this particular combination of type-in box and pressable arrow, this knowledge can be applied to other such lists of choices. The user recognizes which such strategies are likely by the similarity of the look between instances. A similar look encourages transference of user knowledge to new situations. Exploiting this transference enhances the learn-ability of new user interfaces.

Ease of Use

When faced with about 225 square inches of displayed image, some of which represent interactive controls that can be manipulated, a user must constantly locate and select those controls that will achieve the desired goals. The ease with which users can visually scan a screen to locate a desired control is critical to long-term ease of use of a product.

This visual scanning process can take two forms. The simplest and fastest is to have an image template in mind that is then matched against each image on the screen to locate a similar image. This is similar to the visual activities involved in pulling only the weeds from a garden or finding a paper clip in a drawer. A more complex scan is to visually identify each item and then to study that item to discern its conceptual similarity to the desired function. For example, a user might read every item in a list of topics to determine whether the item in any way relates to Tibet.

The image-matching scan is far faster than the concept-matching approach because it is "prewired" into the human visual perception mechanisms. The concept-matching approach is far more flexible in adapting to new situations. The key importance of a consistent look is that it exploits the speed of image matching to help users locate desired functionality. If all buttons have a similar look, the visual system automatically discards large sections of the images on the screen because they do not look like buttons. On the other hand, if every button is a uniquely crafted visual object, such a scan is not possible.

In some computer games, the user is presented with a screen filled with interesting shapes and objects. The user must study each object to see if it can be poked, prodded, turned, or ignored so as to manipulate the game environment. In such cases, this puzzle-solving activity is part of the fun of the game. In a user interface where the goal is to get work done, however, presenting such visual puzzles is counterproductive. A consistent look can reduce such puzzlement.

Consistency of look is not only a matter of visual appearance but of spatial location. Macintosh users trying to open a file rarely actually read the File menu title. In many cases, they hardly look at it at all. The File and Edit menus are always in the same place and therefore require almost no visual attention from the user in order to take advantage of them. Consistent placement of information and controls simplifies the process of locating and using them. The more often the user can replace a visual scan with an automatic habit, the easier the interface will be to use.

Figure 6-27   A text button

6.4.4 Architectural Issues in Designing the Look

The look of a widget is defined entirely in its view. In particular, the look is defined inside of the Redraw method of that class. A problem arises, however, because programmers in general are not particularly skilled in visual design. Creating consistent visual images that are attractive, interesting, and clearly convey a particular meaning falls within the training of artists and visual designers. On the other hand, artists cannot be expected to design the look of a widget by writing the C++ code of a Redraw method.

Most modern tool kits support the concept of resources. *Resources* are data objects that contain information about various aspects of a program and in particular about the user interface to that program. In the Macintosh, resources are specially provided for by the operating system's file structure.

For example, as shown in Figure 6-27, the textual label on a button is rarely hard-coded in the Redraw method but rather is stored as a resource. When the Redraw method for the button is invoked, the appropriate resource is identified, the text is extracted, and the label is drawn. There are a variety of properties about a button that can be defined as resources. These include the label text, the label font, the width of the border, the color of the foreground and background, and so on.

There are two great advantages to a resource-based view architecture. First, it is possible to create more general widget implementations. For example, the style of button shown in Figure 6-27 can be implemented once and serve a variety of button instances. Each instance would have different resources. In particular, they each could have a different text label, such as "Open," "Close," or "Cancel." Because such information is not hard-coded into the button implementation, the widget has much wider applicability. The use of resources also clearly defines the variability of that class of widgets. In our example button, drawn from the Macintosh, the font and rounded rectangle button are not variable. These features are hard-coded in the implementation. The net result is that all buttons have a similar and consistent look, while allowing them to have differing labels and sizes.

The second advantage of the resource-based architecture is shown in Figure 6-28. Because the resources are data objects, which are not embedded in the code, it is possible to create special *resource editors* that allow designers to visually create new widget instances. With such an editor, a designer could

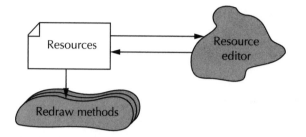

Figure 6-28   Resource editing

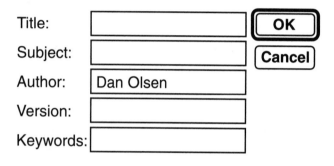

Figure 6-29   Dialog box

specify the label, size, and location of a button without entering the code at all. This also aids the internationalization of an interface because translators can work with the resource editor to change the labels without entering the code. In the case of iconic buttons, such as those in Figure 6-22, the icons can be drawn in an editor, similar to a paint program. This allows artists to create icons without writing any code. Widget properties, such as colors or textures, can use color-picking dialogs that show RGB and HSV controls as well as some color space from which colors can be selected. The use of such editors places the design of a look in the domain of taste and visual appeal rather than in that of programming.

Resources can also be used with menu widgets to define the menu's structure and the labels found in that menu. Dialog boxes, such as that shown in Figure 6-29, use resources to define which widgets should appear in the dialog box and where each should be placed. Each widget in the dialog box recursively has it own resources to define its label, style, and other properties.

A given interactive application will have many widgets and consequently many resources. For a given widget instance, the problem arises of identifying

Figure 6-30   Two types of buttons

which resources go with which widget. Almost all widgets fall in the context of some larger composite, such as a dialog box or a menu. Such composites are given names that can be referenced inside of the view code. Most tool kits provide special routines for creating a new instance of such a collection.

Suppose the dialog box in Figure 6-29 was given the name "SummaryInfo." The dialog has an MVC unit associated with it that handles the interaction. Such a unit could instantiate "SummaryInfo," which would locate the resources for the dialog box and load those resources into a dialog box widget instance. In the process, new text box, label, and button widgets would be created and have their resources loaded recursively and be instantiated as part of the dialog box. The MVC unit for summary information would not know or care what these widgets look like or where they are placed in the dialog box. Such an MVC unit would simply receive events when information is changed or buttons are pressed and then respond accordingly. Changing the labels or the widget organization can be done by visual designers working through the resource editors without changing the code.

6.5 The Feel

The feel of a widget or a set of widgets is determined by the sequence of input events that a user must generate in order to manipulate the widget. This sequence of inputs is determined by the implementation of the controller for that widget. Consistency in feel is even more important than consistency in look. The reason for this is that the input syntax of a widget is invisible and must be remembered. Take, for example, the two types of buttons shown in Figure 6-30. Even though these button styles look very different, users can quickly recognize that they are buttons. Based on that recognition, all Macintosh users know that such buttons are activated by placing the mouse pointer over the button, depressing the mouse button, and then releasing it. Experienced Macintosh users know that moving the mouse pointer off of the button while still holding down the mouse button causes the button not to be activated. This behavior is the standard button feel.

There is nothing about the appearance of either set of buttons that indicates the sequence of input events required to activate the buttons. This information must be remembered. By using a consistent feel, there is very little that

 File   Edit   View   Insert   Format   Font

Figure 6-31   A Macintosh menu bar

users must remember, and therefore users are much freer to explore the capabilities of a new interface, knowing at all times what inputs to generate.

The input behavior of a widget is very quickly relegated to "muscle memory" by most users. Experienced users rarely think about the input sequence required to activate a button or to move a scroll bar. These activities are learned and then remembered as reflex actions that require little or no cognitive thought. Changing this input behavior would require that such processes be thought about rather than performed automatically. This not only slows down a user's ability to get things done but can clash with behaviors already learned in the muscle memory.

This feel behavior must be learned. At the top of every Macintosh screen is a menu bar with words across it, as shown in Figure 6-31. There is nothing about this image that indicates the fact that pressing the mouse button over one of these words will open a list of choices. Once a menu is open, there is nothing to indicate that holding the mouse button down, dragging it over the choices, and then releasing it will select the choice. This lack of feel information is also complicated by the fact that moving the mouse across the menu bar or outside of an open menu causes other behaviors. Macintosh users with any experience do not think about these issues because they have been learned. Changing the menu feel, however, would make any new Macintosh application very difficult to use.

The menus in MS Windows are not at the top of the screen but at the top of each window. This causes some problem for Macintosh users who are moving to Windows. They must look for a menu bar in a new place. Finding such a menu bar is straightforward; however, a Macintosh user would expect it to behave in a similar fashion. Early releases of MS Windows had a very different feel. In MS Windows, the user was expected to click on the menu header, which would then open and stay open. The user would then click on the correct choice. If a user substituted the Macintosh input behavior—dragging down to choose an item without releasing the mouse button—the menu disappeared. Similarly, an MS Windows user attempting to use a Macintosh would click on a menu header, only to see the menu flash and disappear. In either case, experienced users moving from one system to the other had a worse time than new users because not only did they need to learn a new feel for the new menu system, but they needed to continually fight against their muscle memory, which was trained for a different behavior.

A similar problem arises in the X Windows system. In this system, the widget set is not standardized and each application is free to use its own widget set. There are only a few widget sets that have been widely used, but there is definitely more than one. Among these widget sets, buttons, menus, text type-in, and other widgets all behave quite similarly with almost identical input behaviors. Scroll bars, however, seem to have drawn out a creative streak in widget designers. All scroll bars have a similar basic look; however, they have very different input syntax. Users of X constantly struggle with differing behaviors of scroll bars and many users resort to the arrow keys rather than struggle with the differences.

6.5.1 The Alphabet of Interactive Behaviors

In designing a widget set, it is very important to create a small alphabet of interactive behaviors. In fact, on most systems there is a very limited set of such behaviors, including

- drag (mouse down; mouse moves; mouse up)
- click (mouse down; mouse up)
- double-click (two rapid clicks)
- drag select (mouse down at the beginning and mouse up at the end)
- click to select
- shift-click for multiple selection
- type
- menu accelerator keys (variable among widget sets)

These eight input behaviors are sufficient for most widget sets. Most experienced users have learned to explore new interfaces by simply trying one or more of these behaviors in places where they appear likely to apply. In fact, the restricted size of this set invites users to explore the interface. If it is expected that one of this limited set of behaviors will work, the task of exploring all of the possibilities is much smaller than digging your way through a user's manual.

6.5.2 Perceived Safety

There are two keys to the learnability of a graphical user interface. The first is that the range of possible functions is visually present on the screen where the user can find it. The second is that the user can freely and safely explore the interface without permanent damage to the system or the work product. Most of this safety must be provided at a higher level than the widget design. There are, however, some features that the widgets themselves can provide. The key is that anything that is done can be easily and directly undone, and if not, that the user is warned before permanent changes are made. Such features include the following:

■ Scroll bars can always be returned to their previous position.

■ A button that is depressed is not activated until button release, allowing users to change their mind.

■ Moving or clicking outside of a menu will deactivate the menu without making a choice.

It is critical that a user believe that any action is safe—that no permanent damage is done. Without this safety, users will not explore an interface's behavior. The only alternative to exploration is reading the user's manuals, and training.

6.6 Summary

In this chapter, we discussed the concept of a set of widgets, which are predefined interactors that can be assembled to form interfaces. The goals of widget tool kits are to reduce the amount of programming required by reusing predefined pieces and to create a consistent look and feel for all interfaces on a particular computing platform or across a product line.

The structure of widget sets was discussed in terms of the model-view-controller architecture. The view component defines the visual presentation of the widgets and thus defines the look of all widgets built with that set. The controller component of each widget class implements the interactive behavior or feel of the tool kit.

Widgets were also discussed in terms of abstract input devices that can be acquired, released, enabled, or disabled. The echoing of the widget state was also discussed. All of these conditions must be clearly and consistently handled by the visual presentation or look.

We concluded with a brief discussion of the interactive behavior, or feel, of a widget set. Still remaining for later chapters are the mechanisms for specifying and assembling widgets into complete interfaces and the ways in which these widgets can communicate with the application. We have also glossed over how the input behavior of widgets is implemented; this will be discussed in Chapter 8.

7

Interfaces from Widgets

In Chapter 6, we discussed the various ways in which widgets can be implemented. We discussed widgets as independent entities. Interfaces, however, are built by assembling together a variety of widgets to form a coherent whole. In this chapter, we will discuss the tools and techniques for assembling interfaces out of widgets.

Because designing using widgets is more visual than logical, it is frequently helpful to create interface editors that allow a designer to see how the resulting implementation will look. Interface editors also provide for a more flexible implementation that will allow rapid changes to the design of an interface. For example, if, during usability testing, it is determined that a pop-up menu of five items is more confusing than just listing the five items as radio buttons, we want interface designers to be able to make the change without having to learn how to program in C++ or some other language. To accommodate these needs, a data-driven approach to widget implementation will be discussed.

Widgets do not work alone and we need to discuss the mechanisms for assembling them together. The first issue is to determine how screen space will be allocated among the widgets that make up an interface. This involves using algorithms that are simple for designers to understand, that accommodate the needs of individual widgets, and that adapt to available screen space. A second issue is how the widgets communicate with each other and with the model values that they are supposed to be manipulating. We need mechanisms that bind widget model values to values in the application's model.

7.1 Data-Driven Widget Implementations

In previous discussions on how to implement controllers, we have focused on creating subclasses for WinEventHandler that will implement the view and

Figure 7-1   An example button

controller for a widget. The problem with this architecture is that it requires a special subclass for every different kind of push button. It also requires that a variety of kinds of information be embedded in code. As a way to simplify the use of general widgets, we will develop a data-driven model for widgets.

In the data-driven model, many aspects of the widget are represented as data fields rather than code. Take, for example, the button in Figure 7-1. There are several items that could be simply represented as data items. They might include any of the following:

- label
- font
- color
- border width
- border style (single line or double)
- enable/disable status
- position of the button in the window

If we implement a Button class that has the public fields described above, a programmer could create a new Button object, fill in the fields with the desired information, and thus create a new button without having to create a new class. Similarly, we could define a generic ScrollBar class with its set of fields that define how the scroll bar should look and function. We can create such generic classes for all of the basic widgets in a tool kit. Fields that control the appearance and behavior of widgets are called *resources* or *properties.*

There is a minor complication in this data-driven approach. When these fields are set, they affect the appearance of the widget and the widget must be at least partially redrawn. The problem lies in the fact that the resource fields are set one at a time but the appearance should only be redrawn after they are all set. One approach is to create the Button object, fill in its fields, and then attach it to a window. At the time it is attached, it is drawn on the screen (using its Redraw method). Another problem arises, however, when some of these fields change during the course of a program's execution. For example, the enable/disable status of a button may change frequently over the course of a program. If the program simply sets the Enabled field, there is nothing to update the screen so the button looks Enabled.

One approach is to make these fields private and to only allow them to be set by special methods that not only set the field but that also notify the view that changes are required. A second approach is to have a single Update-Property method that can be called after changing any of the desired fields. Invoking UpdateProperty notifies the widget view and controller to check the fields for changes and to make any necessary adjustments.

7.1.1 Collections of Widgets

The data-driven widget architecture is more complicated for classes that manage collections of widgets. The simplest such collection is the menu. In fact, menus are so simple that frequently their components are not implemented as separate widgets. The data description for a simple menu implementation might include the following fields:

- menu header label
- menu header font
- menu item font
- list of
    { menu item label
      menu item is checked
      menu item id
    }

This data structure represents the essential information about a simple textual menu. If we replace the font and label information in this menu descriptor with icons, then we have the descriptor for a button bar widget. If, however, more complex menus are desired—or trees of menus or menus of various optional techniques—then this simple structure is not adequate.

An alternative descriptor structure for a menu is a list of widgets. The menu will place the widgets vertically. To create a simple menu, all of the widgets would be buttons. For more complex menus, including menus of menus, other widgets could be used. The descriptor structure for such a menu would be the fields to describe the menu header and a field that contains a list of widget descriptors. Each widget descriptor would contain an identifier for the type of widget and the data to be placed in the properties of that widget.

The second most popular collection of widgets is the property sheet or dialog box, as shown in Figure 7-2. The descriptor for a dialog box is a list of widgets and information about their positions. In the widget list are the descriptors for each of the widgets. This example dialog box is composed of two Group widgets. Group widgets work almost the same as DialogBox widgets except that they provide a border and a label. Inside of each Group widget is a list of other widgets that compose the group. A most important issue in handling DialogBox or Group widgets is the placement of the widgets within the box. This layout problem will be discussed later.

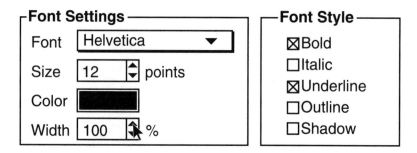

Figure 7-2   A dialog box

7.2 Specifying Resources

Having defined our widgets as generic classes with data descriptors that specify how the widgets are to function, we next need to address how those resources or descriptors get set. The simplest—and least effective—way is for the program code to set the resources at the time that the widget objects are created. The problem with this approach is that the look (which is most of what is specified in the descriptor resources) is specified in code. The people most capable of doing good visual interface design, however, are not programmers. What we need are interface design tools that allow designers to interactively specify these descriptors. The problem then arises as to where the descriptors should be stored, since they are no longer part of the code, so that they can be edited by design tools but used directly by the program at run time.

A final variation is to let users specify parts of these descriptors. Many programs have preferences that the user can set to control colors, fonts, and which menus will actually appear. Such preferences are implemented by the application, providing the user with an interface to some of the resources used by program widgets.

7.2.1 Resource Organizations

If widget descriptor resources are going to be set by users or other interface design programs, then there needs to be some mechanism for storing the resource values in a place where programs can readily find them and hopefully in a way that they won't get separated from the program itself.

There are two ways the resource values for a particular widget can be stored. The first is to create a record structure that can be declared in most of the programming languages that will be used to implement user interfaces on a particular platform. Each class of widget would have its own structure for the resource values that it needs. The binary representations of the memory for such a structure define a resource layout for that class of widgets. This greatly simplifies the code because a resource for a text box, for example, can be read straight from disk into memory and then accessed using the appropriate record or struct declaration. The problem with this approach is that it is not very flexible and it is very hardware dependent.

An alternative way to handle the resource values of a single widget is to define attribute names for each widget and to create a resource mechanism that maps attribute names to values. This can be hardware independent and can be much more flexible. This is the approach taken by X Windows. It is slightly less space and time efficient than the memory-mapping method, because the name/value mapping must be handled.

It is frequently helpful to not specify every attribute for every widget as a separate resource. It is helpful to be able to specify resources for groups of widgets and then to have specific widgets override only the resource values unique to that widget.

X provides a very flexible resource mechanism. Every attribute of a widget has a name. Every widget also has a name and a class. Every widget is placed in the interactor tree and can be referenced using a path expression containing the name of each item in the tree from the root to the widget itself. For example, we might refer to a particular widget as "drawprog.fontsheet.style." This reference indicates a widget named "style" in a dialog box called "fontsheet" in a program called "drawprog." We could specify its background color in a resource file as follows:

```
drawprog.fontsheet.style.backgroundcolor: red
```

This form of resource specification explicitly names every attribute of every widget. Let us suppose, however, that for all widgets in the program except this one we want the background color to be blue. We could specify the following:

```
drawprog*backgroundcolor: blue
```

This identifies blue as the value for any background color on any widget path in the drawprog program except for the fontsheet.style that has a more specific specification. Suppose, however, that we want all of our text boxes to have white backgrounds, even though all other widgets are blue. We could do this as follows:

```
drawprog*TextBox.Backgroundcolor: white
```

The capital letters indicate a class name instead of a widget name. This specifies the color of all widgets of class TextBox, except where a more specific attribute has been specified.

There are a number of rules in X that determine which specifications bind more tightly than others. This creates a very flexible system for specifying large groups of attributes but can be somewhat daunting to learn to use effectively. Similar approaches using widget classes and superclasses have been devised in other research systems. This inheritance or loose/tight binding model for resources does not have a clear and simple interface and has not been widely used on more popular systems like MS Windows or the Macintosh. On those systems, the simplicity of a graphical user interface has outweighed the flexibility of a resource-specification syntax.

Resource/Code Linkage

When an interface is defined by the data in the resources as well as by the actual program code, two problems arise. The first is that of keeping the resources and the code together because both are required to make the application work together. The second is identifying which resources should be used in which instances.

The Macintosh was the first to address the problem of keeping code and resources together. In the Macintosh file system, every file has a data fork and a resource fork. The data fork behaves like a stream of bytes, just as in other file systems. The resource fork contains resources that are tagged with a 4-byte name and a 4-byte type. The operating system provides calls that can access resources by name and/or type. A resource is simply a sequence of bytes. For each of the widgets, there is a resource type defined. The sequence of bytes has the same format as the memory layout for the data descriptor of that widget. The resource mechanism is quite general and can be extended beyond the built-in widgets supplied by Apple. By having resources and code tied together in a single file, the resources don't get lost.

In X, there is no strict binding between a program and its resources. X follows the UNIX model of defining a sequence of directories in which to look for information. The program follows this search path, trying to find the file that contains the appropriate resources. This search path mechanism is one of the features that makes UNIX harder to install and manage. If the resources are not placed in the correct place, nothing will work, but there is less help in getting things put in the right place.

In MS Windows, there is a resource compiler that puts together the resources and then adds them as data segments to an executable module. They are given linker names that allow the widgets to find and link to the resources. Because the resources are added into the executable code, they do not get separated and lost.

In all of these systems, when a program creates a widget, it can specify the resource that describes the widget. In the case of complex widgets such as menus or dialog boxes, these resources will contain the names of other resources that are to be used by the widgets contained in the complex widget.

7.2.2 Interface Design Tools

Having created a data-driven architecture for widgets, we now need mechanisms for defining the contents of the resources. When such tool kits are first created, they are almost always provided with resource compilers. These are programs that convert a textual language into data of the correct format for the resource. The resource languages are quite primitive. They are simply provided as an initial mechanism for defining resources.

Soon after the completion of a tool kit, developers will build an interface design tool. Such a tool is simply an interactive program for which widget resources constitute the model. This tool allows designers to lay out interfaces visually. In some systems, the interface design tools will edit the resources directly. In others, they will create textual source code that is fed to the resource compiler. The advantage of interposing the resource compiler is that the interface design tools are now independent of the format of the resources in memory.

7.3 Layout

One of the key issues for an interface design tool is the layout of the dialog boxes or property sheets. The key piece of information is the position of each of the widgets in the containing window and the key problem is what to do when the window changes size. Consider, for example, the two windows in Figure 7-3.

These two windows are the same window with different sizes. Note that the buttons for closing and maximizing the window (at the top) have remained close to their respective corners. Also note that the scroll bars have remained attached to their edges and the grow box remains in the lower right-hand corner.

On most systems, every widget has a bounding rectangle defined in the coordinates of the window that contains it. Widgets are implemented so that they will draw and interact inside of this rectangle; they depend on other widgets to handle the rest of the interface. In the case of container widgets, such as dialog boxes, the container is responsible for setting this rectangular position for each of its child widgets. In Figure 7-3, the folder window's controller is responsible for defining the rectangles for each of the buttons and scroll bars that it is using.

The problem is to define widget positions in a way that is easy for designers to control, easy to implement, and that will flexibly handle the layout needs of the user interface. There are a variety of ways in which this is done. In this chapter, we will discuss a sample of three techniques. The most popular technique is fixed-position layout. This is very simple to implement and easy for designers to understand. The other two methods are struts and springs and

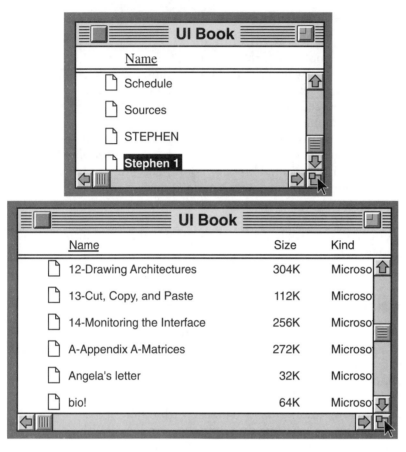

Figure 7-3   Resized windows

intrinsic size. These two techniques provide more flexible layout models than the simple fixed-position technique.

7.3.1 Fixed-Position Layout

The fixed-position model is simple to implement because all that is necessary is to store a rectangle in the resource for each child widget. This rectangle is defined in the coordinates of the container window. These container-relative coordinates allow the same layout to be used in multiple instances of the same dialog box. Designing a resource editor for this model is also quite simple. It is a matter of dragging out the rectangle for each widget and dragging widgets around to new positions. This layout model is also simple for designers because widgets stay where you placed them. Fixed position is the layout

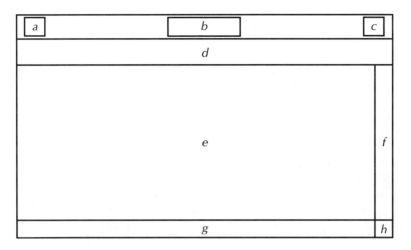

Figure 7-4   Widget layout

model used by the majority of tool kit implementations because of its simplicity.

The fixed-position model, however, cannot answer the needs of the window in Figure 7-3. If the scroll bars are placed in a fixed position, they will not move when the window is resized. The second window would look quite ugly using a fixed-position layout. The solution adopted by many tool kits is to use fixed layouts in the design tools and then to send an event to the container window when the window size changes. Upon receiving the event, the programmer must implement special code to place child widgets in new fixed positions. This would handle the resizing problem posed in Figure 7-3.

7.3.2 Struts and Springs

We would like to have a layout model that is as easy to use as the fixed-position model but that handles the resizing automatically. One model for such resizing was originally devised by Cardelli.[1] This model has been expanded over time. The idea is to draw the user interface in much the same fashion as the fixed-position model and then to add additional constraints that define the geometric relationships between the widgets. Take, for example, the schematic of the window in Figure 7-3 that is shown in Figure 7-4.

In the original Cardelli scheme, each edge of a widget could be defined as a fixed distance from any other widget edge (including the containing widget) or as a proportional distance between the edges of the containing widget. In Figure 7-4, for example, the edges of widget a would be a fixed distance from the top and left side of the container. The edges of widget f would be a fixed

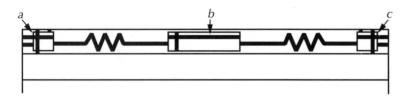

Figure 7-5   Struts and springs

distance from the top, bottom, and right side. The top and bottom of widget *b* would be a fixed distance from the top of the container, while the left and right edges would be a proportional distance between the left and right edges of the container. This proportional distance keeps widget *b* centered.

These fixed and proportional distances are simple cases of a more general technique called *constraints*. In constraint systems, equations for all of the variables are defined and the system must solve the set of equations to determine what the variables' values should be. An example constraint for Figure 7-4 would be "e.right = f.left." The variables in these constraint systems are the edges of the widget rectangles. Using the Cardelli model, all constraints are simple linear equations.

One problem with constraint systems is that specifying visual properties of an interface by writing equations is not a very satisfying technique. One way to resolve this is with the notion of struts and springs. A *strut* is a rigid object that does not change its length. A *spring* is an object that will push as much as it can. Each is a visual representation of a constraint equation. Take, for example, the title bar portion of our window as shown in Figure 7-5.

Widget *b* has solid bars from the top edge of the container to *b*'s top and bottom. These are struts that indicate a fixed distance between the ends of the strut. There is also a strut from the left to the right edge of widget *b*. This specifies a fixed width for the widget. There are springs connecting the left and right of widget *b* to the edges of widgets *a* and *c*. Each of these edges in turn has struts connecting them to the container edges. This combination of struts and springs defines the constraints that keep widget *b* in the center, pressed between the two springs. By placing struts and springs onto the layout of a user interface, the designer can control the geometric specification of the layout. This specification is reevaluated each time the container window is resized and thus automatically recalculates the positions of the widgets.

7.3.3 Intrinsic Size

An alternative method for laying out interfaces uses the intrinsic size of each widget as a guide for how to allocate space. A menu is the simplest case of such a technique. Take, for example, the two menus in Figure 7-6.

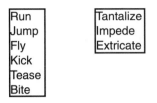

Figure 7-6   Sizing of two menus

The size of the entire menu is determined by the sizes of each of the menu items. The number of items multiplied by the font height gives the total height of the menu and the width of the widest string gives the width of the menu. The constraints that define the position of each item are also quite simple. The top of each menu item is equal to the bottom of the preceding item plus one. The bottom is equal to the top plus the height of a string. Adding an element to the menu or changing the string for a given menu will automatically resize everything that is dependent on that item. In this situation, designers don't think about positioning constraints or resizing problems because the size and positions are completely determined by the intrinsic size of each menu item.

The layout mechanism described for menus is a strictly "bottom-up" mechanism. Each character determines its own width and height. From the character sizes, each string computes its size and the positions of the characters. From the sizes of the strings, the menu computes its own size and the position of the strings. The size at any level is solely dependent on the size and arrangement of the component objects.

7.3.4 Variable Intrinsic Size

The bottom-up approach will not, however, handle the resizing problem in Figure 7-3. In this case, the size is determined by the user (by a resizing of the window), and the widgets must adjust themselves to those desires. To resolve these problems, we use a variable intrinsic-size algorithm. This algorithm was first used in TEX.[2] It was first used for user interface layout in the InterViews system.[3] A variant of this algorithm is also used in Java's Abstract Window Tool Kit (AWT). The algorithm has a bottom-up phase where each widget can report on its size needs and compute those needs from any child widgets. The bottom-up pass is followed by a top-down phase that takes the available space, partitions it among the child widgets according to their needs, and then recursively has each child do the same.

Each widget has a method that will report the size (height and width) that the widget would like to be. In addition, each widget will report on how much it is possible to squeeze the widget smaller and how much it can reasonably be stretched bigger. Take, for example, the layout shown in Figure 7-4. Widget h (the grow box) would report its height and width and then report that it cannot squeeze or stretch. It must remain exactly that size. On the other hand, widget g (the horizontal scroll bar) would report that it cannot squeeze or stretch vertically but that it can squeeze a little and stretch a lot horizontally. Widget e, the main content area, will report that it can squeeze and stretch a lot, both vertically and horizontally.

When the window is resized, the container widget will give widgets g, h, and f the fixed space that they want. Because widget e can stretch—and the others cannot—it is given all of the interior space. The squeeze and stretch components tell the layout algorithm how to balance the available space among the contending child widgets. We still have the problem of how to get widget b centered in the middle. We do this by introducing two special "glue" widgets between a and b and between b and c. Each of these glue widgets will stretch a lot horizontally and not at all vertically. Because there are now two stretchy widgets pushing on either side of widget b, the layout algorithm will compromise by letting each take half the space. This forces b into the middle. These stretchy widgets behave like springs in the previous model.

The effectiveness of this model is that each widget knows its own needs and its own ability to squeeze or stretch. Upon arranging the widgets, they naturally work out their own placement. The down side is that the designer has only indirect control over how widgets are placed. This indirect control can cause problems when the designer is trying to force a particular widget layout.

Algorithm for Variable Intrinsic-Size Layouts

The first step is to create a representation for "squeezability" and "stretchiness." For each widget, we define the following values:

- minWidth
- desiredWidth
- maxWidth
- minHeight
- desiredHeight
- maxHeight

The desiredWidth of a widget is the width that it normally wants to be, the minWidth is the limit of its squeezability, and the maxWidth is the limit of its stretchiness. For "infinite" stretchiness, we use a very large number.

Based on these values, we can define container widgets that assemble other widgets into groups. A simple container widget is the vertical stack shown in Figure 7-7. This vertical stack takes a list of widgets and arranges them vertically. It performs all layout of the stack based on the minimum, desired, and maximum values of the widgets it contains.

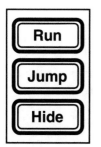

Figure 7-7   Vertical stack widget

Because the vertical stack is itself a widget, it needs to be able to report its size values to any container that it is placed in. The vertical stack computes its size values from those of its components. The formulas are as follows:

- minWidth = Maximum(component's minWidths)
- desiredWidth = Maximum(component's desiredWidths)
- maxWidth = Maximum(component's maxWidths)
- minHeight = Sum(component's minHeights)
- desiredHeight = Sum(component's desiredHeights)
- maxHeight = Sum(component's maxHeights)

Similar formulas can be defined for a horizontal stack by reversing the roles of the width and height.

We now need an algorithm for assigning locations and boundaries for widgets, given the bounding rectangle of the container. Assigning each widget its left and right bounds is easy because the limits are the left and right bounds of the stack's bounding rectangle. There are four cases for the vertical calculations:

1. height < vstack.minHeight
2. vstack.minHeight < height < vstack.desiredHeight
3. vstack.desiredHeight < height < vstack.maxHeight
4. vstack.maxHeight < height

In case 1, we can either use the minimum height of each widget and then clip any widgets that don't fit, or we can give each widget a proportional amount of what is available based on the widget's minHeight. The calculation for this would be as follows:

```
Scale = (vstack.bottom - vstack.top) / vstack.minHeight
widget(1).top = vstack.top
widget(I).bottom = widget(I).top + widget(I).minHeight * Scale
widget(I).top = widget(I - 1).bottom + 1
```

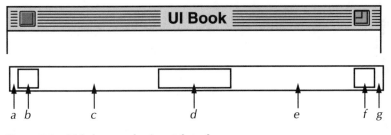

Figure 7-8   Title bar as a horizontal stack

In case 2, we have enough space to give each widget its minimum amount but not enough to give each one its desired amount. What we will do is give each widget a proportional amount of the difference between its minimum and its desired space. This gives each widget at least its minimum and then fairly shares the rest. The formulas are as follows:

```
Scale = (vstack.bottom - vstack.top - vstack.minHeight) /
    (vstack.desiredHeight - vstack.minHeight)
widget(1).top = vstack.top
widget(I).bottom = widget(I).top + widget(I).minHeight
    + (widget(I).desiredHeight - widget(I).minHeight) * Scale
widget(I).top = widget(I - 1).bottom + 1
```

In case 3, we have enough space to give each widget its desired height but not enough for each to have its maximum. We can use formulas similar to those for case 2 that give each widget its desiredHeight and then add on a proportional amount of what is left.

In case 4, there is more height than any widget wants. We can either give each widget its maximum and let the bottom part of the stack go empty or we can apply the formulas of case 3 that will apportion space based on the maximum height of each widget.

Using the Stack-Layout Algorithms

In order to see how these formulas can work with normal widgets and "glue" widgets, consider the title bar and layout schematic in Figure 7-8. The close button *b* and the maximize button *f* each are the same size no matter what. These widgets will have their minimum, desired, and maximum values the same in width and height, and thus will not squeeze or stretch. Although the label *d* is not a button, it too does not have any squeeze or stretch.

To achieve the layout of the title bar, we also insert special glue widgets into the stack. In this case, the glue widgets (*a, c, e,* and *g*) simply draw themselves with a fill of horizontal lines. Their value comes in their size values. All of these glue widgets will report their vertical size as 1, because they do not want to contribute to the vertical size of the title bar. Even though their sizes are reported as 1, the horizontal stack will still tie their top and bottom to its own top and bottom. The glue widgets on the ends (*a* and *g*) are "spacers." The designer fixes their width at the desired spacing. The widgets then report this value for minimum, desired, and maximum. The "spreader" widgets (*c* and *e*) report a small minimum and desired width but report a very large maximum.

Given the reported sizes of each of the widgets, the layout shown in Figure 7-8 fits case 3. There is more width than the desired widths of all the widgets, but there is less than the maximum. In this arrangement, however, only the spreader widgets (*c* and *e*) want any more space. For all of the other widgets, their (maximum – desired) is 0 and they will not get any space beyond their desired size. The spreaders, however, want an equal amount of additional space. The formulas for case 3 will share the available space equally between the two. The result is to center the label widget.

Composite Stacks

We can use vertical and horizontal stacks recursively to produce more complicated layouts. Consider the window shown in Figure 7-9 and its accompanying layout schematic.

Grids

Although recursive use of vertical and horizontal stacks, along with spreader and spacer widgets, can accomplish a variety of flexible layouts, the recursion is somewhat confusing to some users and there are certain kinds of alignments that are not possible. Most of these problems can be solved using a grid container. A grid provides a set of cells arranged in rows and columns. Each widget is placed in one of the cells.

For each column of the grid, we compute the minimum, desired, and maximum width by taking the maximum of the minWidth, desiredWidth, and maxWidth components of each widget in that column. We can compute the minWidth, desiredWidth, and maxWidth for the entire grid by summing up those values for all columns. (We perform height calculations in a similar fashion across all of the rows.) Once we know the minWidth, desiredWidth, and maxWidth of each column, we can allocate space for each column in the same way we allocated widths for the horizontal stack. We handle the rows like a vertical stack. Once we know where all of the rows and columns are to be placed, we place each widget according to the row and column to which it is assigned.

Grids allow for simultaneous vertical and horizontal alignments. In addition, vertical and horizontal stacks are simply single-column or single-row cases of the grid.

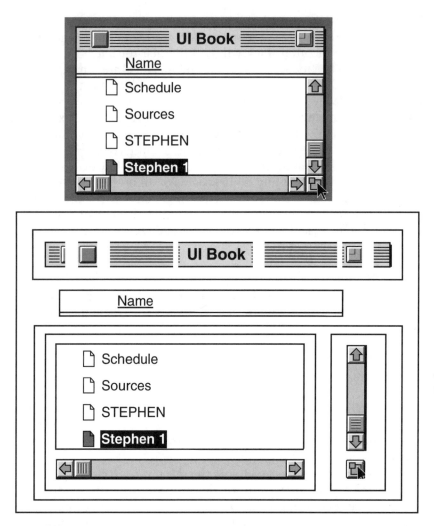

Figure 7-9   Recursive stack layout

7.4 Communication

The second major problem in organizing widgets together is the communication between widgets. Consider, for example, the spreadsheet fragment in Figure 7-10. The key widgets have been outlined in bold rectangles. If the vertical scroll bar on the right is moved by the user, the row number widget on the left and the central spreadsheet widget must both be notified so that they can scroll themselves to show different rows than before. A similar thing must occur when the scroll bar at the bottom is moved. If the user hits the

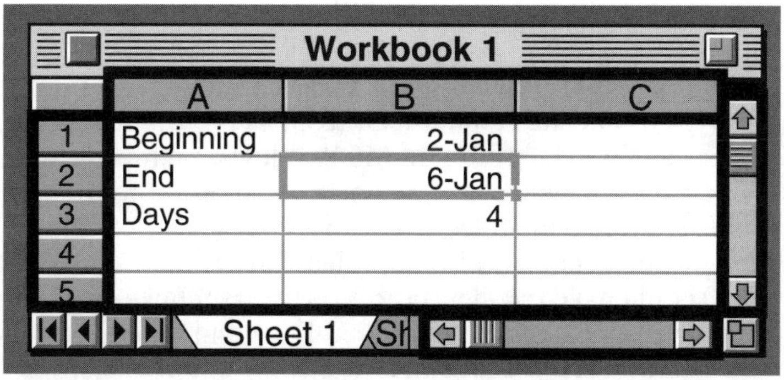

Figure 7-10   Spreadsheet example

right arrow key twice (to column D), the central spreadsheet must scroll itself. In addition, it must notify the column header widget at the top and the scroll bar at the bottom so that they will remain synchronized. A similar thing occurs when the user searches for a string that is in a cell that is not visible in Figure 7-10. The central area must scroll to show the correct row and column, and all of the other widgets must be notified so that they can scroll to match. All of this requires that these widgets communicate with each other. This communication is handled by extending the event mechanism discussed in Chapter 4 to include whatever additional events are necessary for communication between widgets.

One alternative for handling all of this communication is to create subclasses of the various widgets and to override the appropriate methods. Inside of these methods we provide the code that will handle updating the model and notifying all other widgets that need to know. This technique uses the object-oriented method invocation mechanism to handle communication events.

This subclassing of widgets strategy is problematic because a large number of unique widget classes must be created. This creation of new classes interferes with our ability to create general interface editors since such editors cannot know about new classes yet to be created. In addition, the actions for the entire window are scattered throughout the code in the action routines for each widget.

7.4.1 Parent Notification

An approach used by many tool kits is to have widgets notify their parent widget of any changes that have occurred. The parent widget then has responsibility to determine what should be done. In almost all tool kits, each widget has a pointer to the parent widget that contains it. When some user event occurs that changes the status of a widget, the widget will send a notification event to its parent.

In order for parent notification to work, each widget must have a unique identifier associated with it. On the Apple Macintosh, as mentioned before, each control (widget) has a 4-byte identifier. In MS Windows, each widget has a unique number. Whenever the parent is to be notified, a pointer to the widget that caused the notification is included in the message. In some tool kits, an additional "what happened" code is also included. For example, the right scroll bar in Figure 7-10 could have the identifier 7. If the user clicks on the up arrow, the parent window is sent a pointer to the scroll bar and a code (such as 4) that identifies the up arrow. The parent can now ask the child widget what its identifier is and switch on the identifier to know what to do. At that point, the parent can either ask the scroll bar for its new value or do something special based on the fact that the up arrow was pressed.

There are a variety of ways in which parent notification is handled. One way is to have a single ChildChanged method that receives the child widget pointer and the action code. This approach is very straightforward. Any control widget that is changed by the user in some way will invoke its parent's ChildChanged method. An alternative technique is to send a message to the parent through the tool kit's event mechanism. The parent window will now simply respond to all such events. The widgets themselves do not need to be modified in any way. Their standard behavior is to notify their parent and to store their identifier. The parent then can use the identifier to determine what exactly should be done.

Most tool kits, however, were not so simply designed. In addition, most tool kits were designed to accommodate slow workstation processors. For this reason, there are usually several methods for notifying parents. Controls such as buttons or menu items will generate Command events or invoke the DoCommand method on the parent. Scroll bars will use different events or methods to notify parent windows of their changes. In some systems, scroll bars will generate different events for different actions.

The net result is that a parent window must usually implement a variety of methods or respond to a variety of events in order to process all of the actions that a child widget might take. In a few more modern tool kits, there is only one event or method that a parent must handle.

In some cases, a widget lies inside of another widget, either for layout purposes (as described above) or simply for localization of behavior. Such structural containers frequently have no meaning to the application itself. In such cases, the default behavior of such container widgets is to forward any notifications they receive from their child widgets on to their own parent; the notifications work their way up the widget tree until they find a widget that will handle the notification. This approach allows for great freedom of organization without scattering the code around the interface.

For example, in a case where the user scrolls the horizontal scroll bar at the bottom, the horizontal scroll bar will notify its parent that it has changed. The parent will check the widget's identifier and discover that it is the ScrollCol widget. Based on this information, the parent can take action to determine the new value of the scroll bar, notify the spreadsheet widget to change its column to the new value, and notify the column headers widget to move to a new leftmost column. All of this communication is handled in one place by the widget that is managing the entire window.

7.5 Summary

Widgets do not operate by themselves. They must be organized together to form complete interactive windows. In order to facilitate the specification of how widgets behave, large portions of their functionality are controlled by data values, or resources. This data-driven approach allows widgets to be easily customized by changing their resource values without implementing any new code. We can take the specification of these data values and incorporate them into a visual design tool that provides a user interface for designers to manipulate widgets without writing any code.

One of the key issues when assembling widgets together is the assignment of screen space. The simplest mechanism is to give each widget a fixed location relative to its parent window. This is too restrictive for many uses. An alternative is the struts and springs model where a designer can add additional information about how the edges of widgets are related to each other. This information can be used automatically by the system to recompute a widget's location when its parent's size changes. Another alternative is the intrinsic-size mechanism, where each widget is programmed to report its desired size and how much it can squeeze or stretch. This information can be used to fairly apportion the space available in a resized window.

The last issue has to do with how a widget actually informs the interface that it has changed. If we are using visual layout tools to specify the interface, we don't want to force new subclasses of widgets for every use. The approach used in many such systems is for each widget to inform its parent of any changes and then to localize all code to process the notifications in the parent widget.

8

Input Syntax

In Chapter 7, we discussed the look and feel of widgets and the tool kits that assemble them together. In particular, we discussed the look, or visual presentation, of a widget set and its feel, or behavior in response to user inputs. We did not, however, discuss how the input behavior of these widgets actually works and how to define and implement such behavior. The set of legal user inputs and what they mean is called the *input syntax*. Input syntax is actually much broader than the simple widgets, but in this chapter we will discuss the handling of inputs in the context of the widgets that we have already looked at. The likelihood of someone using these techniques for widget implementation is rather low because most such widgets come prepackaged for use, as described in Chapter 7. Most programmers will use these techniques to implement the interaction in the core part of an application. The widgets, however, form a good example set for exploring input syntax and are therefore used in this chapter.

8.1 Syntax Description Languages

Before we can talk further about widgets, we need a notation for the sequence of inputs and how they are interpreted. Such a notation will help us to more precisely specify the interactive behavior of a widget and will help us to work out such behavior before implementation. In a later section, we will discuss how to transform this notation into actual controller code.

In the early days of user interface software, many researchers proposed the finite-state machine as a model for defining inputs.[1] There are several significant flaws with this approach, however. The most notable problem with finite-state machines is the n-input problem, where an interactive task requires n inputs to be received in any order with each input being received exactly once. A finite-state machine requires 2^n states to solve this problem.

The most effective models today are production systems. There are several variations of this notation, including Hill's Sassafras system,[2] the User Action Notation (UAN),[3] and Propositional Production Systems (PPS).[4] All of these systems are similar in power; their differences are not relevant to our purpose here. We will use a variant of the PPS in our discussion.

8.1.1 Fields and Conditions

All actions are taken within some range of possibilities. In a PPS, this range of possibilities is called the *state space*. At any particular time, a controller is said to have a state that lies within that space. Based on the inputs and other information, transitions are made from state to state and actions are taken in response to some of those transitions. The state space of a widget is defined by a set of *fields*, each of which consists of a set of *conditions*. All conditions within a particular field are mutually exclusive of each other and are independent of the conditions in all other fields.

Take for example the following two fields, `Color` and `Size`:

```
Color { Black, White, Red }
Size { Small, Medium, Large }
```

The conditions in the `Color` field are Black, White, and Red. A color cannot be both black and white. Even if you could blend them, which is not possible in this model, the result would be gray. Each of the colors is exclusive of the other. On the other hand, the color of an object is independent of the size of the object. A white object can be small, medium, or large without affecting the color. `Color` is a field with Black, White, and Red being the conditions of that field. All of the situations that might arise in a widget controller will be modeled using fields and conditions.

8.1.2 Special Types of Fields and Conditions

Although the model of fields and conditions is quite general, it is useful to distinguish various types of fields and conditions. The types that we will consider are input events, actions to be taken, state information, messages to and from other parts of the interface, and queries.

Input Events

There is generally one field whose conditions represent all of the input events that the widget might receive from the windowing system. So as to more easily distinguish these from other events, we precede all event condition names with a bullet (•). In Chapter 4, we defined the following input events:

```
Input { •MouseDown, •MouseMove, •MouseUp,
   •KeyPress, •MouseEnter, •MouseExit }
```

As was discussed in Chapter 4, many events are accompanied by modifiers such as the Shift, Control, Command, and Option keys. These can be modeled with additional fields, each of which has two conditions, such as the following:

```
ControlKey { Cntl, noCntl }
ShiftKey { Shift, noShift }
```

It is also helpful to refer to the state of the mouse buttons. We can handle each button with a separate field:

```
LeftButton { LeftUp, LeftDown }
MiddleButton { MiddleUp, MiddleDown }
RightButton { RightUp, RightDown }
```

With these six fields, we can model most of the input conditions that can affect widget behavior. In a real system, there might actually be many more events but the concepts of how to handle them would be the same.

Actions

Every widget controller has a set of actions that it can perform on itself, its model, or its view. These actions can be represented in a single field if only one action is possible at any one time, or in several fields when multiple simultaneous actions are possible. Action conditions are organized into fields to show when actions are mutually exclusive. This organization allows checks to be made on the specification for conflicts in the design. To distinguish action conditions from the other conditions, we precede them with an exclamation point, for example, !PrintTheFile, !DeleteObject, or !SaveMousePoint.

State Information

In many situations, it is necessary to remember information about previous input so that the sequence of inputs is understood. For example, a scroll bar might have the field Thumb{ IsDragging, NotDragging }. Whether or not we are currently dragging the thumb will make a difference in handling •MouseMove events.

Outside Events

Frequently, other parts of the interface will want to communicate with the controller, and this controller will also need to communicate with other parts of the program. For example, a widget may want to allow outsiders to tell it when to enable or disable itself:

```
EnDis { >Enable, >Disable }
```

We prefix events from the outside with a greater than (>) symbol. In addition, a scroll bar widget may want to notify its parent window when it has scrolled. This might be modeled as

```
ParentEvents { Scroll>, StepUp>, StepDown>, PageUp>, PageDown> }
```

We will use one field for each kind of destination for the events. The output event conditions themselves are suffixed with a greater than (>) sign.

Query Fields

Sometimes the controller needs information from the model or the view. For example, a scroll bar controller needs to know whether the mouse is over the thumb or over one of the stepping arrows. Only the view has this information. We model this with query fields whose conditions return the result of the query. Query fields represent methods that must be invoked before the controller can make a decision, for example,

```
MouseLocation { ?InThumb, ?InPageUp,
   ?InPageDown, ?InStepUp, ?InStepDown }
```

Query field conditions are by convention prefixed by a question mark.

8.1.3 Productions

The core of the PPS behavior definition is in the productions. Each production has a list of conditions on the left that must hold (the antecedent) and a list of conditions on the right to be asserted (consequent). For example,

```
•MouseUp, Shift -> !DoMultipleSelect, InSelectMode
```

This production will only fire if the input event is •MouseUp and the Shift key is held down. If these conditions hold, then the action !DoMultipleSelect is performed and the state is modified by setting the condition to InSelect-Mode. A controller's behavior is defined by many productions. It is possible that several productions are eligible to fire at the same time. They may all fire, provided that they do not attempt to set any field to more than one condition. This is called a *conflict.* A very important use of the notation is recognizing and resolving conflicts before implementation.

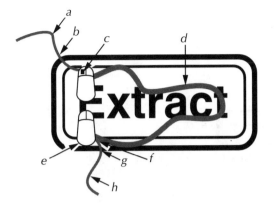

Figure 8-1   **Example input sequence**

8.1.4 Input Sequences

Now that we have a model for defining how widgets should behave in the presence of inputs, we need a simple visual notation for describing a sequence of input events. This notation will help clarify the interplay between inputs and the visual components of the interface. Figure 8-1 shows an example of such a notation.

The curved line indicates the path that the mouse is following. The sequence starts with the user moving the mouse around the outside of the button (*a*). In this section, •MouseMove events are generated. The mouse enters the button region (*b*) and a •MouseEnter event is generated. A series of •MouseMove events are generated until the mouse reaches *c* and the user depresses the left button, as shown by the mouse icon with the left button darkened. At point *c*, a •MouseDown event is generated and the LeftButton field is changed from LeftUp to LeftDown. In section *d*, the left button is held down and the mouse is moved by the user, generating •MouseMove events. Note that the LeftDown condition holds throughout this time. At location *e*, the user releases the left button, generating a •MouseUp event and changing LeftButton from LeftDown to LeftUp. This is indicated by the mouse icon with no buttons darkened. The input sequence proceeds through section *f* with a series of •MouseMove events, followed by a •MouseExit event at point *g*. The sequence ends with a series of •MouseMove events through section *h*. Throughout the rest of this chapter, we will use diagrams like this to show input sequences and to study the behavior of our syntax definitions in response to those sequences.

Figure 8-2   A simple button

Inactive   Active   Disabled

Figure 8-3   Visual states of a button

8.2 Buttons

The simplest widget is the on-screen button. In its simplest form, it is an image that will invoke an action whenever •MouseUp occurs inside the button boundaries. Consider the image in Figure 8-2.

There is one action condition and one production for this button's controller:

```
Action { !Extract }
•MouseUp -> !Extract
```

We can apply this simple definition to the input sequence in Figure 8-1. No rules can fire in any part of the input sequence until point *e* is reached. At this point, the one rule will fire and the !Extract action is performed.

The problem with this simplistic button is that it does not give the user any feedback when the user presses the mouse button inside of the Extract button's boundary. Without this feedback, the user is not sure if anything is happening. We also need to be able to enable and disable a button. If a button is disabled, it should not respond to any input events. Figure 8-3 shows the three visual states of a button.

We need to model this with an additional field for our button and a modification of our action field, as follows:

```
VisualState { Inactive, Active, Disabled }
Action { !Extract }
DAction { !DamageAll }
OutsideActions { >Enable, >Disable }
```

Note that the VisualState field will need to be read by the view so that the button can be drawn correctly according to the state. The !DamageAll action will perform a damage on the entire bounds of the button. This will cause the view to redraw the button in a new state. Note also that the !DamageAll condition is in a separate field from the !Extract action. This is because it is possible to change the visual state of the button at the same time as invoking the !Extract action. These two actions are independent and thus are represented in separate fields. Since a button does not decide for itself whether it is enabled or disabled, two events are provided to handle this issue. Other controllers or the application can send these two events and so control the state of the widget.

With these new fields, we can define a more complete syntax for our button:

1. •MouseDown, LeftDown, Inactive -> Active, !DamageAll
2. •MouseUp, LeftUp, Active -> Inactive, !Extract, !DamageAll
3. >Disable -> Disabled, !DamageAll
4. >Enable, LeftDown -> Active, !DamageAll
5. >Enable, LeftUp -> Inactive, !DamageAll

Note that in production 1, if the button is disabled, this rule will not fire because Disabled and Inactive are mutually exclusive. Note that in production 2, if the button is not active the !Extract action cannot be performed. Note that rules 3–5 use the >Enable and >Disable events to control the enabled status of the button. In rules 4 and 5, the status of the left mouse button is used to determine what the enabled state of the Extract button should be. Note that rules 3, 4, and 5 are driven by outside events rather than by input events.

We still have not captured all of the behavior of a button, however. If the mouse enters or leaves the bounds of the button, what should happen to its state? We can resolve this with the following additional rules:

6. •MouseExit, Active -> Inactive, !DamageAll
7. •MouseEnter, LeftDown, Inactive -> Active, !DamageAll

When the mouse exits the button bounds, the button becomes inactive because a mouse release should not cause the button to execute its action. When the mouse enters the button, we must decide whether the button should be activated. If the left mouse button is not down, then the button should not be activated. If the button is not inactive, it is probably disabled and should not be activated. Note that it is much easier to work with these productions in considering the possibilities than it is to work in the implementation of the event-handling methods. If we are using an object-oriented implementation to handle these events, every production, except 4 and 5, will be in separate methods. Considering them together like this is much easier than checking the code of six different methods.

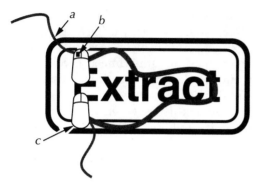

Figure 8-4 **Button input sequence**

We can now consider our definition in light of the input sequence in Figure 8-4.

We start off in the inactive state with no buttons pressed. Since we have no rules that fire on •MouseMove or •MouseEnter, nothing happens until point *b* where a •MouseDown is generated and rule 1 is activated. The visual state is set to Active and the !DamageAll action is performed, which will cause the button to be redrawn in its darkened Active state. Again nothing happens until point *c* where a •MouseUp is generated and rule 2 fires. This causes the state to change to Inactive. The !DamageAll action is performed to redraw the button and the !Extract action is executed.

Suppose that we receive a >Disable event before the input sequence begins. Rule 3 will fire, the state will be set to Disabled, and the button will be redrawn. Now as the input proceeds to point *b* and the •MouseDown event is generated, rule 1 cannot fire because the button is not in the Inactive state. Because no rule fires at point *b*, nothing happens and the button stays in its Disabled state. As the input proceeds to point *c* and •MouseUp is generated, rule 2 cannot fire because the widget is not in the Active state. Again, nothing happens and the input sequence proceeds.

8.2.1 Check Buttons

A check button is a little more complicated than a simple push button. A check button can have six visual states, as shown in Figure 8-5.

To represent all of these states in a single field would be a mistake. In fact, there are two independent states involved here: selectedness and activity. These can be represented by the following fields:

```
Selectedness { Selected, Unselected }
Activity { Inactive, Active, Disabled }
```

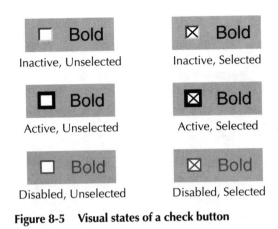

Figure 8-5 Visual states of a check button

Unlike the Extract button, whose function was to invoke a particular action, the purpose of the check button is to manage its own Selected/Unselected state. It is important, however, that this button notify any model attached to the button whenever the button's state changes. If the Bold status is turned on, a word processor application must be notified so that selected items can be set to bold. It is also important for the model to be able to notify the widget of a change of state. If a word processor selects some normal text, it must make sure that this widget is not showing bold. We will still need the !DamageAll action to notify the view of the change in state. We also need the enable/disable conditions. Note that the view will check both Selectedness and Activity when it draws the check button. We can model all of this with the following fields:

NotifyAction { !NotifyModel }
    Notify the model that selectedness has changed.
DAction { !DamageAll }
    Notify the view to redraw the entire button.
OutsideActions { >Enable, >Disable }
    Outsiders tell the controller to enable or disable.
ModelControl { >SetSelected, >SetUnselected }
    The model can set selectedness.

With these fields defined, we can specify the input behavior of our check button, as follows:

1. •MouseDown, LeftDown, Inactive -> Active, !DamageAll
2. •MouseUp, LeftUp, Active, Selected ->
      Inactive, Unselected, !DamageAll, !NotifyModel

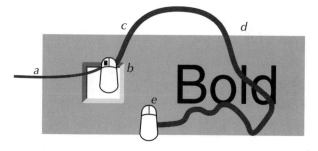

Figure 8-6   Check box input sequence

3. •MouseUp, LeftUp, Active, Unselected ->
       Inactive, Selected, !DamageAll, !NotifyModel

4. Disable -> Disabled, !DamageAll
5. Enable, LeftUp -> Inactive, !DamageAll
6. Enable, LeftDown -> Active, !DamageAll

7. •MouseExit, Active -> Inactive, !DamageAll
8. •MouseEnter, LeftDown, Inactive -> Active, !DamageAll

9. SetSelected -> Selected, !DamageAll
10. SetUnselected -> Unselected, !DamageAll

We now have a complete definition of how our check button should behave. Looking at the set of fields and productions for this button, it is obviously that they are mostly independent of the actual visual appearance of the button. The only relationship between the view and the controller portions of this widget is found in the Selectedness, Activity, and DAction fields. We can change the view any way we like as long as it clearly represents the six visual states. This independence is what encouraged early systems designers to make the view and the controller separate components. The goals of visual consistency in a tool kit, however, limit most check buttons to a single view and thus, in most systems, the view and the controller are combined together.

Now we can use our definition to work through the example sequence of inputs in Figure 8-6. We start out with the conditions Inactive and Unselected. At point *a*, a •MouseEnter event is generated; however, because no buttons are pressed, rule 8 does not fire. Because there are no rules for •MouseMove events, nothing happens until point *b* when the •MouseDown event occurs. At this point, rule 1 fires, changing the state to Active and causing the button to be redrawn in the (Active, Unselected) state shown in Figure 8-5. Input continues to point *c* where a •MouseExit event is generated and

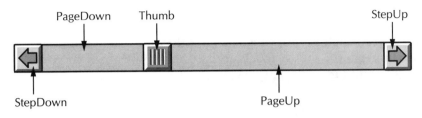

Figure 8-7   Areas of a scroll bar

rule 7 fires. This sets the state to Inactive and causes the button to be redrawn in the (Inactive, Unselected) state. No inputs are received by the widget (they are sent elsewhere by the windowing system) until point *d*. At this point, a •MouseEnter event is received. Note that LeftDown still holds because the mouse button has not been released. Rule 8 fires and the widget becomes active again and is redrawn. The •MouseMove events are ignored until point *e*, when a •MouseUp event is generated and LeftButton changes to LeftUp. This causes rule 3 to fire. The Activity field is set back to Inactive, Selectedness is set to Selected, the button is redrawn in its new (Inactive, Selected) state, and the model is notified of this change using the !NotifyModel action.

8.3 Scroll Bars

The interactive behavior of a scroll bar is a little more complicated than that of a button. In actuality, there are five separate behaviors that all manipulate the same model value. The user discriminates among these behaviors by the area of the scroll bar where the mouse button is pressed. These areas are shown in Figure 8-7. In our widget architecture, only the scroll bar's view knows where these regions are. We will need to use a query field to determine which area is selected.

We also have the problem that if the user holds down the mouse button over the page or step regions, the bar will continue to scroll as long as the button is held down. While that button is held down and not moving, there are no input events generated and the bar will not scroll. We can handle this by adding •Timer to the set of input events. The •Timer event is automatically generated on a periodic basis. On true multitasking operating systems such as UNIX, NT, or OS/2, the •Timer event is generated from the system clock. On nonmultitasking systems such as MS Windows or the Macintosh, timer events can be generated any time the software accesses an empty event queue. In such cases, they are frequently called NULL events. In either case, the important point is that events are generated on a periodic basis so the scroll bar can scroll continuously.

A final problem with scroll bars is that they are long and thin and require a user to drag the thumb along this narrow path. Most users cannot do this without being very careful or straying outside of the scroll bar. To resolve this, we will need to grab the mouse focus so that the scroll bar can continue to receive input events during dragging operations.

With these issues in mind, we can define the state space for our scroll bar behavior. All user-initiated actions on a scroll bar consist of mouse press, drag or hold, and then mouse release. The differences depend on where the initial mouse press occurred. The controller needs to know where the •MouseDown occurred and needs to remember that location so that we can discriminate future operations. This is done with the following fields:

```
ViewQuery { ?InStepUp, ?InPageUp, ?InThumb,
   ?InStepDown, ?InPageDown, ?Outside }
Status { Disabled, Inactive, PressingStepUp,
   PressingPageUp, DraggingThumb,
   PressingPageDown, PressingStepDown }
```

There are also several actions that must be taken. Each of these actions modify the model. Unlike with the button, we will allow the model to request the view to damage itself so that the scroll bar position is updated correctly. The only exception to this is when the thumb is dragging. We need the view to echo the thumb position without changing the model. We can handle this with the following action fields:

```
ModelAction { !StepUp, !PageUp, !Scroll, !PageDown, !StepDown }
ViewAction { !StartThumbDrag, !MoveThumbDrag, !StopThumbDrag }
```

We will also need external events to enable and disable as well as to set the current scroll position and the maximum and minimum values for the scrolling range:

```
External { >Enable, >Disable, >SetMin, >SetMax, >SetPos }
SetActions { !SetMin, !SetMax, !SetPos }
```

We are also going to need actions that grab and release the mouse focus:

```
Focus { !GrabMouseFocus, !ReleaseMouseFocus }
```

Based on this state space definition, we can now define the rules that will control our scroll bar, as follows:

1. •MouseDown, LeftDown -> !GrabMouseFocus
2. •MouseUp, LeftUp -> !ReleaseMouseFocus

3. •MouseDown, LeftDown, Inactive, ?InThumb ->
   DraggingThumb, !StartThumbDrag
4. •MouseMove, DraggingThumb -> !MoveThumbDrag
5. •MouseUp, LeftUp, DraggingThumb ->
   !StopThumbDrag, !Scroll, Inactive

Rules 1 and 2 handle the issue of the mouse focus. Since this is the same for all of the interactive behaviors, we place the mouse focus in separate rules of its own. Note that rules 1 and 3 may both fire at the same time. This is not a problem because the actions that they assert are independent of each other.

Rules 3–5 handle the standard dragging of the thumb to adjust the scroll bar. The model action to scroll is performed when the mouse is finally released. At this point, we can look more carefully at the view actions. In some scroll bar implementations, the actual image of the thumb is moved as the bar is scrolled. In such an implementation, the !StartThumbDrag and !StopThumbDrag actions will do nothing. The !MoveThumbDrag will damage the old position, set the new position based on the mouse location, and then damage the new location. This will cause the thumb to be redrawn correctly. In other tool kits, a simpler and cheaper echo is used such as an outline rectangle. Using this simpler version of the thumb improves the speed and also leaves the original thumb image so that the user knows where the drag started. In such cases, the !StartThumbDrag action sets up the simple image and the !StopThumbDrag takes it down. Note that rules 1 and 2 will also apply to this situation and will grab and release the mouse focus, which will prevent the widget from losing the mouse events when the mouse moves outside of the widget boundaries.

We next consider the step up and step down behaviors that occur when the arrows at the ends are pressed. In most systems, holding down the mouse button will cause the bar to scroll continuously. Moving the mouse outside of the step arrow will cause scrolling to stop. If the mouse button is not released, moving the mouse back in will cause it to continue scrolling. This behavior is modeled as follows:

6. •MouseDown, LeftDown, Inactive, ?InStepUp ->
   PressingStepUp, !StepUp
7. •Timer, PressingStepUp, ?InStepUp -> !StepUp
8. •MouseUp, LeftUp, PressingStepUp -> Inactive

Note also that when receiving the timer events, we must check to make sure that the mouse is still positioned inside of the step arrow.

The remainder of the scroll bar behaviors work almost the same as rules 6–8. They are only varied by the area of the scroll bar that activates them and the actions that they perform. The remaining rules are as follows:

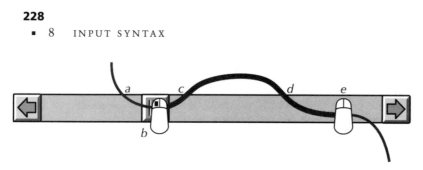

Figure 8-8   Scroll bar input sequence

9. •MouseDown, LeftDown, Inactive, ?InPageUp ->
    PressingPageUp, !PageUp
10. •Timer, PressingPageUp, ?InPageUp -> !PageUp
11. •MouseUp, LeftUp, PressingPageUp -> Inactive

12. •MouseDown, LeftDown, Inactive, ?InStepDown->
    PressingStepDown, !StepDown
13. •Timer, PressingStepDown, ?InStepDown -> !StepDown
14. •MouseUp, LeftUp, PressingStepDown -> Inactive

15. •MouseDown, LeftDown, Inactive, ?InPageDown ->
    PressingPageDown, !PageDown
16. •Timer, PressingPageDown, ?InPageDown -> !PageDown
17. •MouseUp, LeftUp, PressingPageDown -> Inactive

All that remains for our scroll bar behavior are the housekeeping chores represented by the external events:

18. >Enable -> Inactive
19. >Disable -> Disabled

20. >SetMin -> !SetMin
21. >SetMax -> !SetMax
22. >SetPos -> !SetPos

We can now use our definition to work through the input sequence shown in
Figure 8-8. Our initial state will be Inactive.

Up until point *a,* the scroll bar will receive no input events because the
windowing system will send them elsewhere. At point *a,* a •MouseEnter
event is generated but is not used by any of our rules. The •MouseMove
events generated between points *a* and *b* are ignored by rule 4 because the
scroll bar is not in the DraggingThumb state. At point *b,* a •MouseDown
event occurs and LeftButton is changed to LeftDown. This causes rule 1 to

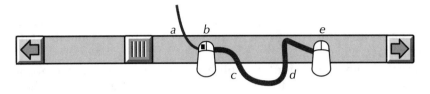

Figure 8-9   PageUp scrolling input sequence

fire, which grabs the mouse focus. It is possible that rules 3, 6, 9, 12, and 15 could also fire but that would depend on the value of the ViewQuery field. Before a query field can be used, some code must be evaluated to test the query. In this case, the view must be asked where the current mouse position is located. This is done and the view reports ?InThumb, which allows rule 3 to fire but not rules 6, 9, 12, and 15. The state is changed to DraggingThumb and the view is told to !StartThumbDrag.

As the input proceeds, •MouseMove events are generated. Because the widget is in the DraggingThumb state, rule 4 will fire each time, causing the !MoveThumbDrag action to be executed. At point *c*, the mouse leaves the widget boundaries and a •MouseExit event occurs, which is ignored by all of our rules. Because we have grabbed the mouse focus, however, this widget will continue to receive •MouseMove events even though the mouse is located outside of the widget. In the section between *c* and *d*, rule 4 will continue to fire and the thumb will continue to move. At point *d*, a •MouseEnter event is received and ignored. Rule 4 continues to fire on each •MouseMove event until point *e*, when the button is released. At point *e*, rule 2 will fire, which releases the mouse focus, and rule 5 will fire, which will cause !StopThumbDrag, notify the model by means of the !Scroll action, and set the state to Inactive. The model will notify the view of the change, which will cause the thumb to be redrawn in its new position.

The input sequence in Figure 8-9 will demonstrate the behavior of the other areas of the scroll bar. We start in the Inactive state and nothing happens until point *a*, when a •MouseEnter is generated. Successive •MouseMove events are received but no rules fire because we are in the Inactive state. At point *b*, when the •MouseDown event is received, rule 1 will fire and grab the mouse focus. Rules 3, 6, 9, 12, and 15 are dependent on ViewQuery, which is evaluated and returns ?InPageUp. This query result causes rule 9 to fire, which will execute !PageUp and set the state to PressingPageUp. Between points *b* and *c*, the •MouseMove events are ignored because rule 4 will not fire while in the PressingPageUp state. The •Timer events, however, will cause rule 10 to fire periodically, which will invoke !PageUp each time. In the section between points *c* and *d*, rule 10 will not fire even though •Timer events are received, because in this section the ViewQuery field will evaluate to ?Outside instead of the ?InPageUp that rule 10 requires. Between points *d* and *e*, rule 10 will continue to fire on each •Timer event. At point *e*, the •MouseUp event is generated, causing rules 2 and 11 to fire. The mouse focus is released and the state is returned to Inactive.

An alternative input behavior for scroll bars uses the three-button mouse rather than the view areas to control the behavior. In this case, the middle button drags the scroll bar and the right and left buttons do the paging. The only function of the view is to echo the position of the thumb. Some people prefer this because they can click the middle button anywhere in the scroll bar to move the thumb immediately to that position, without having to actually drag the thumb to that position. This behavior is defined in the following rules:

```
State { Inactive, Scrolling, PagingUp, PagingDown }
1. •MouseDown, LeftDown, Inactive -> PagingDown
2. •MouseUp, LeftUp, PagingDown -> Inactive, !PageDown

3. •MouseDown, MiddleDown, Inactive ->
      Scrolling, !Scroll, !GrabMouseFocus
4. •MouseMove, Scrolling -> !Scroll
5. •MouseUp, MiddleUp, Scrolling -> Inactive, !ReleaseMouseFocus

6. •MouseDown, RightDown, Inactive -> PagingUp
7. •MouseUp, RightUp, PagingUp -> Inactive, !PageUp
```

One important issue concerning scroll bars is the geometry computations required to map between the thumb's screen position and the current value of the scroll bar. This is not trivial and sometimes is quite frustrating to get right. In this section, we have concentrated on the inputs. The classification of such geometry occurs in query fields. The actual implementation issues for the geometry are discussed in Chapter 9.

8.4 Menus

No matter how extensive a workstation may be, there are never enough function buttons to handle the needs of all applications. This shortage is particularly a problem if the buttons need to be labeled. On commercial-grade applications, there is rarely enough screen space to represent all such buttons. This is resolved by a menu system that organizes sets of buttons so that users can easily find them.

Various styles of menus have been proposed. Rather than go into them all, we will address the standard pull-down menus found in most tool kits. We

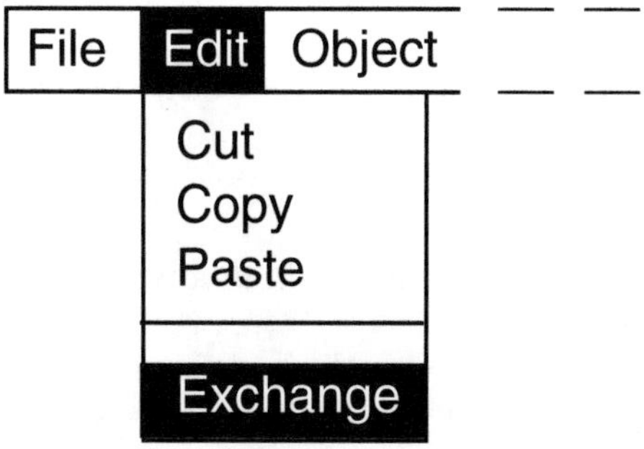

Figure 8-10   A pull-down menu

will use the Macintosh menu input model as an example. We will use the same look throughout, as shown in Figure 8-10. This discussion will also ignore the hierarchical pull-down menus that most tool kits now provide. These are an important feature but there are no additional concepts involved.

In working with our pull-down menu, we will need the following actions:

```
Actions {
    !OpenNewMenu,
```
This will pull down the menu under the mouse and highlight the menu header.
```
    !CloseMenu,
```
This will remove the pull down of the current menu and unhighlight the header.
```
    !ChangeItem,
```
This will unhighlight the old item and highlight a new menu item based on the mouse position.
```
    !DoSelectedAction
```
This will execute the action associated with the currently selected menu item.
```
}
```

The menu behavior is controlled mostly by the mouse position, for which we must use a query field so that the view can classify the position:

```
ViewQuery {
    ?OverNewHeader,
```
Mouse is over a menu header that is not highlighted.
```
    ?OverCurHeader,
```
Mouse is over the currently highlighted header.

?OverNewItem,
> *Mouse is over an enabled menu item that is not highlighted.*

?OverCurItem,
> *Mouse is over the currently highlighted menu item.*

?Outside
> *Mouse is outside of the menu bar and the current pulled-down menu.*

}

The state of our menu is very simple because all inputs are based on dragging to select items:

```
State { Inactive, Dragging }
```

Based on these fields, we can now define the input rules that control Macintosh-style menus. For the moment, we are going to ignore command-key accelerators that can substitute a keystroke with appropriate modifiers for the menu selection. The rules are as follows:

1. •MouseDown, LeftDown, Inactive ->
   !GrabMouseFocus, Dragging, !OpenNewMenu
2. •MouseUp, LeftUp, Dragging ->
   !ReleaseMouseFocus, Inactive, !CloseMenu
3. •MouseUp, LeftUp, Dragging, ?OverCurItem ->
   !DoSelectedAction

4. •MouseMove, Dragging, ?OverNewHeader ->
   !CloseMenu, !OpenNewMenu
5. •MouseMove, Dragging, ?OverNewItem -> !ChangeItem
6. •MouseMove, Dragging, ?Outside -> !ChangeItem

We can study the behavior of this definition using the input sequence shown in Figure 8-11. Nothing happens at the beginning of the sequence through point *a* because the events are directed elsewhere. Even at point *a*, where the •MouseEnter event is generated, there is no activity. It is not until point *b*, where a •MouseDown event is generated and the LeftDown condition is activated, that rule 1 is fired. This rule changes the state to Dragging, grabs the mouse focus, and opens the menu under the File menu header. •MouseMove events continue to be received that might cause rules 4–6 to fire. Each of these, however, is dependent on the ViewQuery field; until point *c*, the result of ?OverCurHeader is returned that does not allow any of these rules to fire. At point *c*, the mouse has moved over the Edit menu header. At this point, ViewQuery returns ?OverNewHeader, which allows rule 4 to fire. The

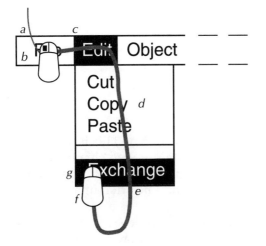

Figure 8-11   Menu input sequence

!CloseMenu action will close the current menu, which is the one under File. The !OpenNewMenu will open the menu under Edit and make it the current menu because that is the header currently referenced by the mouse location. Successive •MouseMove events will be ignored because ViewQuery will return ?OverCurHeader until the mouse moves into area *d*, which is the menu itself. As the mouse moves over the Cut menu item, ViewQuery will return ?OverNewItem, which will cause rule 5 to fire and invoke the !ChangeItem action. This will highlight Cut. As the mouse moves down, ViewQuery will return ?OverCurItem until a new menu item is entered. At such a point, ?OverNewItem is returned and rule 5 will fire again, causing !ChangeItem to update which item is highlighted. At point *e*, the mouse leaves the menu. However, because the menu has the mouse focus, it will continue to receive •MouseMove events. However, ViewQuery will return ?Outside, which will cause !ChangeItem to be invoked. Because the mouse is ?Outside, !ChangeItem will simply turn off any highlighted items. It will not, however, take down the menu. At point *f*, a •MouseEnter event is generated and ignored. The next •MouseMove events will cause rule 5 to fire because the mouse is over the Exchange item again. Finally, at point *g*, the •MouseUp event is generated. Rule 2 is fired, which releases the mouse focus and sets the state to inactive. Rule 2 will also close the open menu. Because the mouse is over a current menu item, rule 3 will also fire and cause the selected action to be performed.

a   *b*

Figure 8-12   **Text selection as *a*, a position, or *b*, a range**

8.5 Text Box

The last widget that we will review is the text type-in box. This is a primary mechanism for entering information and has some unique characteristics related to proportionally spaced fonts. A key feature of the type-in box is the currently selected text position. This can either be a position or a range, as shown in Figure 8-12.

The behavior of the text box in response to key events depends on the selection point and on whether a range or a point is selected. In response to mouse events, the text box must determine what changes should be made to the selection point. In studying the syntax of a type-in box, we can consider text selection and text entry separately.

The text box's view maintains two integer variables: SelectStart and SelectEnd. These are the indices of the characters immediately following the selection point. Let us assume the C string convention that the first character is at index 0. In this case, the variable settings for box *a* in Figure 8-12 would be (SelectStart = 8, SelectEnd = 8). When the start and the end are the same, then a location is selected. In box *b*, the values would be (SelectStart = 8, SelectEnd = 13). In this case, a range is indicated. This matter can be addressed by the following query and action fields, which are supported by the view:

```
SelectionQuery { ?SelectedPoint, ?SelectedRange }
SelectionActions {
  !SetSelectStart,
    Use the current mouse position to compute a value for SelectStart.
  !SetSelectEnd,
    Use the current mouse position to compute a value for SelectEnd.
  !OrderSelection
    If SelectEnd is less than SelectStart, exchange their values.
}
```

We need to take some time to consider how the view will support these two fields. The SelectionQuery field is quite easy. If SelectStart == SelectEnd, then return ?SelectedPoint, otherwise ?SelectedRange. The selection actions are more complicated. The problem is the use of proportional fonts. When every character in the string can have a different width, it becomes complicated to determine which character is selected by a given mouse point. In Chapter 4, we discussed the drawing of text using our abstract Canvas class. The canvas has a method for setting the font and also a method for inquiring as to the width of some string in the current font. We will use these methods to compute the selection position. Consider the following algorithm.

```
CurX = the leftmost position on the screen where the text string is dis-
         played
Len = the length of the string in the type-in box
Str = the string being edited
Canvas Cnv = the canvas on which we are drawing
Idx = 0;
Cnv.SetFont (the text widget font);
while (Idx < Len)
   { CurX = Cnv.CharWidth(Str[Idx]) + CurX;
     if (CurX > MousePosition)
     { return Idx; }
     Idx = Idx + 1;
   }
return Len;
```

The state information for selection is quite straightforward, as shown in the State field:

```
State { Inactive, Dragging }
```

Using the fields we have defined so far, we can address the text selection syntax:

1. •MouseDown, LeftDown, Inactive ->
     !GrabMouseFocus, !SetSelectStart, Dragging
2. •MouseMove, Dragging -> !SetSelectEnd
3. •MouseUp, LeftUp, Dragging ->
     !ReleaseMouseFocus, !SetSelectEnd,
     !OrderSelection, Inactive

Consider the input sequence in Figure 8-13. Because the text box starts in the Inactive state, all •MouseMoves and other events are ignored until point *a*. When the •MouseDown occurs, rule 1 fires to grab the mouse focus, set the start of the selection, and change the state to Dragging. Between points *a* and *b*, the •MouseMove events will cause rule 2 to fire. At each firing, SelectEnd is set. Note that until the mouse crosses to the letter "o," the SelectStart and SelectEnd values will both be 8. The view will echo this situation as a selection point rather than a range. As soon as the mouse moves over the "o,"

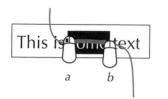

Figure 8-13 Text selection input sequence

SelectEnd will be 9 and the range will be echoed. As •MouseMove events cross additional characters, the selection range will continue to grow until point *b* is reached. When the •MouseUp event is received, rule 3 fires, the mouse focus is released, and the select end is set. It may sometimes be the case that the user selected the range by starting at point *b* and moving to point *a*. In this situation, SelectStart will be greater than SelectEnd. The !OrderSelection action in rule 3 will take care of this situation.

To handle the text input, we must pay attention to the key focus. Unlike the mouse focus where a widget will grab the focus until it is done and then release it, a text widget will grab the key focus and hold it until some other widget takes it away. We also need a query field to help us classify the characters that we are receiving, and an additional action field is required to control the editing, as follows:

```
KeyQuery { ?DeleteKey, ?LeftArrow, ?RightArrow, ?NormalKey }
EditActions {
   !DeleteSelectedRange,
```
Delete all characters between SelectStart and SelectEnd. SelectEnd = SelectStart.
```
   !DeletePreviousChar,
```
If SelectStart > 0, delete the character at (SelectStart – 1) and decrement SelectStart and SelectEnd.
```
   !InsertChar,
```
Insert the current input character at SelectStart. Increment both SelectStart and SelectEnd.
```
   !DecrementSelection,
```
Decrement SelectStart and set SelectEnd = SelectStart.
```
   !IncrementSelection
```
Increment SelectStart and set SelectEnd = SelectStart.
```
}
```

For each of the edit actions, the view must update the display to reflect the new state of the string and the changes in the selection variables.

Input	Rule fired	Result
Starting case		This is ▮some▮ text
"a"	9	This is a|text
"t"	10	This is at|text
Delete key	6	This is a|text
" "	10	This is a |text
Left arrow	7	This is a| text

Figure 8-14   Text input

The following rules control text input:

```
 4. •MouseDown, LeftDown, Inactive -> !GrabKeyFocus
 5. •KeyPress, ?DeleteKey, ?SelectedRange ->
       !DeleteSelectedRange
 6. •KeyPress, ?DeleteKey, ?SelectedPoint -> !DeletePreviousChar
 7. •KeyPress, ?LeftArrow -> !DecrementSelection
 8. •KeyPress, ?RightArrow -> !IncrementSelection
 9. •KeyPress, ?NormalKey, ?SelectedRange ->
       !DeleteSelectedRange, !InsertChar
10. •KeyPress, ?NormalKey, ?SelectedPoint -> !InsertChar
```

The input sequence notation that we have used on the other widgets is not sufficient because it does not account for key input. Because the mouse position is not important to key input, we need only list the inputs and show the results (Figure 8-14).

8.6 From Specification to Implementation

In the previous sections of this chapter, we have discussed how to specify the behavior of a widget using a PPS. In future chapters, we will use a PPS to define the input behavior of a variety of interactive techniques. What we need to discuss here is how to convert a PPS input specification into working code.

There are automatic algorithms for doing this,[5] but in many practical situations the automatic tools are not available or are not integrated with the required development environment. In this section, we will show how to carry out the necessary transformations by hand.

As an example, we will implement the text box widget from the rules defined above. We first define the class TextBox, which has Controller as its superclass. We must next define how all of the fields are to be handled and then how the production rules are encoded.

8.6.1 Fields

We first need to account for all of the fields that contain information that will control the production rules of our PPS. Remember that we have input fields, state fields, query fields, and action fields.

Input Field

Earlier in the chapter, we defined the Input field as follows:

```
Input { •MouseDown, •MouseMove, •MouseUp,
   •KeyPress, •MouseEnter, •MouseExit }
```

This field defined all of the input events. We also defined several fields that contained additional information about the state of the input:

```
ControlKey { Cntl, noCntl }
ShiftKey { Shift, noShift }
LeftButton { LeftUp, LeftDown }
MiddleButton { MiddleUp, MiddleDown }
RightButton { RightUp, RightDown }
```

Remember that we are defining the implementation of the controller, which is a class that has methods for each of the input events, as was discussed in Chapter 4. Each of these methods has certain parameters that provide additional information about the input event. Let us consider the event methods in Figure 8-15 as the basis for our controller implementation. These are virtual methods that we inherit from the abstract class Controller.

Each of the Input field conditions corresponds to one of these methods. In addition, there are the fields for the Shift/Control keys and the button state fields. All of this information is encoded in the Modifiers parameter. Almost all windowing systems provide a Modifiers parameter, which is a 16- or 32-bit word in which various bits correspond to the states of the Shift/Control/Meta keys and the mouse buttons. We test for these modifiers by ANDing the

```
MouseDown(Button, Location, Modifiers)
MouseMove(NewLocation, Modifiers)
MouseUp(Location, Modifiers)
KeyPress(Key, Modifiers)
MouseEnter(Location, Modifiers)
MouseExit(Location, Modifiers)
```

Figure 8-15   Controller input event methods

Modifier word with a mask that contains a 1 in the bit position for the desired information. If the result is 1, then the desired bit is on; otherwise the result will be 0.

Since the handling of modifiers is uniform across all of our tool kit, we can assume that there is some header file that contains the macro definitions necessary to test the modifiers. Such a tool kit would first contain a definition of all of the modifier conditions, such as the following:

```
#define noCntl 0
#define Cntl 1
#define noShift 0
#define Shift 2
  . . .
#define LeftUp 0
#define LeftDown 8
  . . .
```

Note that each field has its own number for the conditions, because each field is independent of the others. This header file might then contain macros of the form

```
#define ControlKey() (Modifiers & 1)
#define ShiftKey() (Modifiers & 2)
  . . .
#define LeftButton() (Modifiers & 8)
#define MiddleButton() (Modifiers & 16)
#define RightButton() (Modifiers & 32)
  . . .
```

Using these macros, we can test for "ShiftKey() == noShift," "if(Shift-Key())," or we might switch in the following way:

```
switch (ShiftKey())
  {
  case noShift:

    . . .

    break;
  case Shift:

    . . .

    break;
  }
```

State Fields

Almost every widget has one or more state fields. These are easily implemented as data members on the controller class. Each such field also has its
own enumeration of its conditions. In our TextBox example, there is only one
state field with two conditions. We can add the following code to the TextBox
class definition:

```
typedef enum { Inactive, Dragging } TextBoxState;
TextBoxState State;
```

Because the State field is now a member of the class TextBox, every
instance of a text box widget will have such a field. We should also add code to
the TextBox constructor that initializes State to Inactive.

Query Fields

Query fields are not stored but rather are computed as needed. As with the
state fields, each query field has an enumerated type that defines all the conditions on the field. We then add a method to the controller for the query field
that will compute the desired information and return the result. In our
TextBox specification, there are two query fields: SelectionQuery and Key-
Query. We can add the following definitions to the class of TextBox:

```
typedef enum{ SelectedPoint, SelectedRange } SQT;
SQT SelectionQuery();

typedef enum { DeleteKey, LeftArrow, RightArrow, NormalKey } KQT;
KQT KeyQuery(char Key);
```

Note that SelectionQuery and KeyQuery are defined as methods. The
implementation of these methods can be provided in the class body. In our
PPS, we only considered the conditions that were to drive our rules. We

ignored a number of implementation details that must be addressed now. The first is that SelectionQuery functions by comparing two values, SelectStart and SelectEnd, that are not part of the PPS specification but must be included in the TextBox class definition. They are essential to communication between the various semantic actions of the PPS and also to control how the view will display selections. The PPS provides us with a mechanism for sketching out the input control. There is still additional information required for a full implementation. Note also that KeyQuery has a parameter, the key value being tested, which is also ignored in the PPS definition.

Action Fields

In implementing actions, we generally ignore the field structure. The field structure of actions will, however, come into play when we work out the rule implementations. For each action condition, we provide a method on the controller class whose body will implement the desired action. To our view/controller TextBox class, we add the following methods:

```
void SetSelectStart(MouseLocation);
void SetSelectEnd(MouseLocation);
void OrderSelection();
void DeleteSelectedRange();
void DeletePreviousChar();
void InsertChar(char theChar);
void DecrementSelection();
void IncrementSelection();
```

Note again that parameters have been added to the actions SetSelectStart, SetSelectEnd, and InsertChar. In our PPS definition, we ignored this information because it did not control the sequence of legal inputs. In our controller implementation, however, such information must be accounted for.

Other TextBox Information

As was mentioned earlier, there is other information beyond the PPS fields and conditions that must be managed by a controller. In the case of our TextBox, we have the SelectStart and SelectEnd values. In addition, we have the TextString value that we are actually editing. We can add the following data members to our TextBox class:

```
int SelectStart;
int SelectEnd;
char TextString[256];
```

8.6.2 Productions

In the previous section, we used the field information to produce a class definition for TextBox. As programmers, we must implement each of the methods defined for query and action fields so that they provide the specified behavior. All that remains is to convert our PPS rules into implementations. The PPS rules define how the various input event methods are to be implemented.

Let us begin with the rule set for text boxes shown below (this rule set has been modified slightly from that shown earlier to better illustrate the implementation steps):

```
 1. •MouseDown, Inactive, LeftDown ->
       !GrabMouseFocus, !SetSelectStart, Dragging
 2. •MouseMove, Dragging -> !SetSelectEnd
 3. •KeyPress, ?DeleteKey, ?SelectedRange ->
       !DeleteSelectedRange
 4. •MouseUp, LeftUp, Dragging -> !ReleaseMouseFocus,
       !SetSelectEnd, !OrderSelection, Inactive
 5. LeftDown, •MouseDown, Inactive -> !GrabKeyFocus
 6. •KeyPress, ?DeleteKey, ?SelectedPoint -> !DeletePreviousChar
 7. •KeyPress, ?LeftArrow -> !DecrementSelection
 8. •KeyPress, ?RightArrow -> !IncrementSelection
 9. •KeyPress, ?NormalKey, ?SelectedRange ->
       !DeleteSelectedRange, !InsertChar
10. •KeyPress, ?NormalKey, ?SelectedPoint -> !InsertChar
```

The first step is that the left-hand side of every rule must be ordered in the following order:

1. input event conditions
2. input modifier conditions
3. state conditions
4. query conditions

Looking at this rule set, we see that rules 1 and 5 need to be reordered. The resequenced rules are as follows:

```
 1. •MouseDown, LeftDown, Inactive ->
       !GrabMouseFocus, !SetSelectStart, Dragging
 5. •MouseDown, LeftDown, Inactive -> !GrabKeyFocus
```

We then group all of the rules with the same input events together. This will factor the rule set into groups that relate to each of the input methods. For our TextBox example, this factoring is shown below; note that each group now defines the implementation of one of the input methods:

---

1. •MouseDown, LeftDown, Inactive ->
   !GrabMouseFocus, !SetSelectStart, Dragging
5. •MouseDown, LeftDown, Inactive -> !GrabKeyFocus

---

2. •MouseMove, Dragging -> !SetSelectEnd

---

4. •MouseUp, LeftUp, Dragging -> !ReleaseMouseFocus,
   !SetSelectEnd,

---

3. •KeyPress, ?DeleteKey, ?SelectedRange ->
   !DeleteSelectedRange
6. •KeyPress, ?DeleteKey, ?SelectedPoint ->
   !DeletePreviousChar
7. •KeyPress, ?LeftArrow -> !DecrementSelection

---

9. •KeyPress, ?NormalKey, ?SelectedRange ->
   !DeleteSelectedRange, !InsertChar
10. •KeyPress, ?NormalKey, ?SelectedPoint -> !InsertChar

Our next step is to further factor the rules for each method until we have a complete decision structure that selects the appropriate rules for each situation.

Rule Factoring of Each Method

Once we have factored our rules into groups according to the methods that should handle the rules, we need to factor the rules again so that we can decide among the rules as to which one should be executed in a given situation. This step may need to be repeated several times before each rule's situation has been identified. To show how this can be done, let us take each of the rule sets in the preceding list one by one.

•MouseDown   In the •MouseDown rule set (which corresponds to the MouseDown event method), both of the rules have the same left-hand side. In this case, both rules can fire in the same situation. However, we do need to continue verifying that we have the correct situation, as follows:

```
MouseDown(Button, Location, Modifiers)
    { if (Button == LeftButton)
        { if (State == Inactive)
            { do rule 1
              do rule 5
              return
              }
        }
```

beep or generate some other warning of an inappropriate event
```
    }
```

Since we have two rules that are executed in exactly the same situation, we must check to make sure there is no conflict. We do this by checking for two different conditions from the same field. Since field conditions are mutually exclusive, having two from the same field would be an error. In our case, there is no problem. We can, therefore, write down the code from the right-hand sides of the rules. This will produce the following code:

```
MouseDown(Button, Location, Modifiers)
    { if (Button == LeftButton)
        { if (State == Inactive)
                { GrabMouseFocus();
                  SetSelectStart(Location);
                  State = Dragging;
                  GrabKeyFocus();
                  return
                  }
        }
```

beep or generate some other warning of an inappropriate event
```
    }
```

Note that state fields are handled by assigning new values to the state and that action fields are handled by invoking the method associated with the action. Also note that SetSelectStart has a parameter.

•MouseMove   The MouseMove method has only one rule but we must check for the appropriate conditions for that rule, as follows:

```
MouseMove(Location, Modifiers)
    { if (State == Dragging)
            { SetSelectEnd(Location);
              return
              }
```

beep or generate some other warning of an inappropriate event
```
    }
```

Note that again we have the beep or warning. In this case, we probably do not want to warn the user on every mouse movement that is not a dragging movement. In fact, we have not completely specified the legal behavior of the mouse; the following additional rule also applies:

•MouseMove, Inactive ->

If we include this rule, the result is the following code (note that because both conditions of State are present, we use a switch to discriminate between them):

```
MouseMove(Location, Modifiers)
    { switch(State)
        {
        case Dragging:
            SetSelectEnd(Location);
            return;
        case Inactive:
            return;
        }
```
beep or generate some other warning of an inappropriate event
```
    }
```

In our syntax design process, we focus on all of the correct situations that users should generate to accomplish their goals. By carefully factoring the rules, we frequently detect other situations that we have not accounted for. The additional MouseMove rule is an example. Careful rule factoring will help greatly in accounting for all of the situations that can arise.

•MouseUp   As with MouseMove, the MouseUp method has only one rule (rule 4). Our only processing is to check for the correct situations and to invoke the right-hand side of the rule, as follows:

```
MouseUp(Location, Modifiers)
    { if(LeftButton()== LeftUp)
        { if(State == Dragging)
            { SetSelectEnd(Location);
              return
            }
        }
```
beep or generate some other warning of an inappropriate event
```
    }
```

•***KeyPress***   We must work a little harder in the KeyPress method because there are six rules that must be handled. If we look carefully at these rules, we can factor them on the `KeyQuery` field, as follows:

```
3. •KeyPress, ?DeleteKey, ?SelectedRange ->
      !DeleteSelectedRange
6. •KeyPress, ?DeleteKey, ?SelectedPoint ->
      !DeletePreviousChar
```

```
7. •KeyPress, ?LeftArrow -> !DecrementSelection
```

```
8. •KeyPress, ?RightArrow -> !IncrementSelection
```

```
 9. •KeyPress, ?NormalKey, ?SelectedRange ->
      !DeleteSelectedRange, !InsertChar
10. •KeyPress, ?NormalKey, ?SelectedPoint -> !InsertChar
```

We can handle this factoring of the KeyPress rule set using a switch or case statement (depending on your language) that chooses among the conditions of the `KeyQuery` field, as follows:

```
KeyPress(Key, Modifiers)
{    switch(KeyQuery(Key))
     {
     case DeleteKey:
       rules 3 and 6
     case LeftArrow:
       rule 7
     case RightArrow:
       rule 8
     case NormalKey:
       rules 9 and 10
     }
     Warning beep
}
```

Having factored the rule set and having translated that factoring into a switch statement on KeyQuery, we then work on each of the smaller rule sets that have resulted. With each of these smaller rule sets, we apply the same techniques used previously, as follows:

```
KeyPress(Key, Modifiers)
{ switch(KeyQuery(Key))
  {
  case DeleteKey:
    switch(SelectionQuery())
    {
    case SelectedRange:
      DeleteSelectedRange();
      return;
    case SelectedPoint:
      DeletePreviousChar();
      return;
    }
  case LeftArrow:
    DecrementSelection();
    return;
  case RightArrow:
    IncrementSelection();
    return;
  case NormalKey:
    switch(SelectionQuery())
    {
    case SelectedRange:
      DeleteSelectedRange();
      InsertChar();
      return;
    case SelectedPoint:
      InsertChar();
      return;
    }
  }
  Warning beep
}
```

8.7 Summary

In this chapter, we have introduced the concept of input syntax and we have discussed Propositional Production Systems (PPS) as a mechanism for specifying that syntax. As examples, we have worked through the syntax of the common widgets and shown how to generate a PPS specification for each of these widgets. A PPS allows us to work through the set of information required to control a widget—and the variety of things that should happen in handling input—without concerning ourselves with actual implementation.

Having generated a PPS for a particular situation, we have shown how to translate that PPS into the object-oriented event methods that implement the PPS functionality. We have also discussed the checking and verification of the rules to locate conflicts or neglected situations.

9

Geometry of Shapes

The preceding chapters have involved the implementation of widgets for performing low-level tasks. Most applications, however, have much more to them than collections of widgets. The central part of most applications consists of a display of the objects that the user is trying to manipulate. In interacting with those objects, the programmer must work in terms of the geometry of the shapes that represent the objects. In our widget implementations, almost all of our geometry was in terms of rectangles. Rectangle geometry is far too restrictive in dealing with a broad range of applications. In this chapter, we will cover the basic geometry of the most popular primitive drawing shapes. From these geometric concepts we will acquire the tools for interacting with most 2D objects.

All of our drawing shapes are based on elementary geometry. In order to write code that will interact with those shapes, we need to understand that geometry. We will first discuss the geometric equations for the primitive shapes that will form most of our images. We will then take an overview of the kinds of geometric problems that we will face when interacting with these shapes and discuss two formulations for geometric shapes, namely, implicit and parametric equations. These two formulations will be used extensively. Having done this, we can then work through the geometry of paths and filled shapes.

In reading through this chapter, it is not as important to understand the specific equations as the techniques used to derive them. These general techniques can be applied to a variety of other shapes that are not included here and will serve as a foundation for addressing other geometric problems.

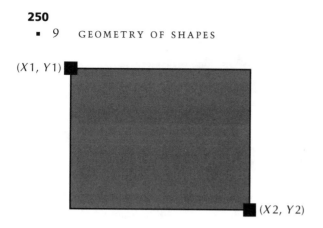

Figure 9-1   Rectangle control points

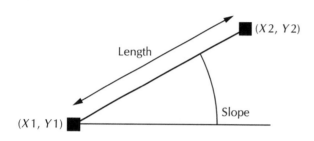

Figure 9-2   Formulations of a line

9.1 The Geometry of Interacting with Shapes

The geometry of almost all drawing objects is based on a set of control points. These are points on the 2D plane that can be used to define the geometry of the desired shape. Control points are not the only way in which geometry can be defined. Take, for example, the rectangle in Figure 9-1. We have defined its geometry in terms of $(X1, Y1)$ and $(X2, Y2)$. We could just as easily have defined it as (Left, Top) and (Width, Height). The two models define the same spatial region. The difference is in the *handles* that we provide for specifying that geometry. In some applications, the width and height properties of a rectangle may be more important than the position of the lower-left corner. In such a case, the width and height would be the geometric handles the programmer should use.

As another example, consider the line in Figure 9-2. This line can be formulated as $(X1, Y1)$ and $(X2, Y2)$; or as $(X1, Y1)$, Length, and Slope. Again, the difference is in the handles we provide for specifying the geometry.

There are a large number of controls that can be used to specify geometry. In this book, we will consider formulations that are defined entirely by control points. The reason for this choice is the interactive nature of such models. If a geometric object is shown on the screen with small handles at the control points (as in Figures 9-1 and 9-2), the user can interactively change that geometry by dragging those control points to new positions. This style of interface is not appropriate for all applications, but it is widely used.

Although most of our examples will use small squares (■) to indicate control points, there are a variety of other representations possible. In many applications, the control points are not explicit but instead are represented by portions of an image that are draggable. Regardless of the visual presentation, most 2D interaction with geometry involves the manipulation of such points. Other interactive handles can be readily derived from control point models.

Regardless of the handles used to express the geometry, the equations for lines, circles, and other shapes remain the same. Most of our geometric needs can be expressed in terms of those equations. This section will focus on expressing geometry by means of control points and on solving the equations for interactive purposes. Other applications need only map their handles onto the basic geometry in order to solve for the other needed information.

9.1.1 Scan Conversion

A most important computer graphics problem is to take the geometric specification of an object and to derive the set of pixels in some frame buffer that corresponds to that object. For example, we need to convert a line defined by two end points into the set of pixels that represent that line. This process is called scan conversion. Because this is essential to the drawing process, it must be quite fast and carefully tuned to the underlying hardware. All interactive tool kits provide routines that perform this task for us. In this book, we will assume that such drawing routines are available and leave discussions of their implementation to graphics texts.[1,2]

9.1.2 Distance from a Point to an Object

Consider the line and mouse position in Figure 9-3. The user is trying to select this line with the mouse. Our problem is to use the geometry of the line to determine if the line should be selected or not.

The key to this problem is being able to determine the perpendicular distance between the mouse point and the line. If this distance is 0, then the mouse is definitely over the line and should be selected. In many applications, however, it is interactively very difficult to position the mouse exactly over a line. Instead, we want to select the line if the mouse is close to the line, where close is defined as a maximum distance. The essential geometry required is to compute the perpendicular distance between a point and a line or any other shape. Once we know the distance, we can check to see if it is close enough

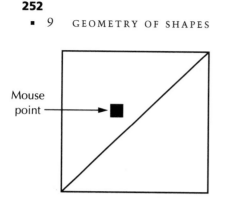

Figure 9-3 **Selecting a line with the mouse**

for selection. In some cases where we are only interested in selection, we will use measures that are less exact than perpendicular distance but that are much cheaper to compute.

9.1.3 Bounds of an Object

In most applications, there are a large number of lines, circles, rectangles, and splines. When a mouse event occurs, we must determine which of all these objects the user is actually referencing. Solving for the perpendicular distance to every object in a drawing can be quite expensive. The check for whether or not a point lies inside of a rectangle, however, is quite cheap. If we know the bounding rectangle for every object, we can use this as an initial check on the mouse point and then perform the more expensive geometry only if the mouse actually lies inside of the bounding rectangle. Computing the rectangular bounds for an object is quite simple in most cases, given the control points of the object.

9.1.4 Nearest Point on an Object

In some cases, we are not trying to select an object but rather some point on the object. If our mouse is exactly over the object, selection is not a problem. If, however—as in Figure 9-3—the mouse is near but not on the object, we also need to determine the point on the line that is nearest the mouse position. We also need this information when connecting objects to each other. For example, if we want to draw a line that exactly touches a circle, then as we are dragging the control point for our line we want it to "snap" to the circle whenever it gets nearby. Such snapping requires computing the nearest point on the circle.

9.1.5 Intersections

It is sometimes the case that we need to compute the intersection of two objects. In the case of lines, we have two linear equations and the intersection is simple algebra. Shapes such as circles, arcs, and ellipses require quadratic equations. Intersections of most shapes yield polynomials of degree 2 and can be solved directly using the quadratic equation from basic algebra. In the case of rotated ellipses, the intersections may become quartic polynomials and require numerical rather than algebraic methods to be solved. This is one reason why many drawing systems do not provide rotated ellipses as one of the drawing primitives. Most splines and curves require cubic equations whose intersections can rarely be solved algebraically; numerical methods are required. This text will not cover all of the possible methods for solving simultaneous equations; you can refer to an algebra, analytic geometry, or numerical methods text for this information.

9.1.6 Inside/Outside

Our preceding geometry discussion has focused on line-drawn objects such as lines, arcs, and curves. However, we frequently use filled shapes such as circles, rectangles, or polygons. To select such objects interactively, we need to determine if a point is inside or outside of the shape. In cases such as polygons, this check is rather expensive. We optimize this check by first checking the point against the bounding rectangle of the object. If the point is inside of the bounding rectangle, then the more expensive check is performed.

9.2 Geometric Equations

Having discussed various geometric requirements, we need equations that we can solve to answer our questions. We will use implicit equations and parametric equations.

9.2.1 Implicit Equations

The implicit equations that we are interested in are all of the form

$$F(x, y) = 0 \tag{9-1}$$

An example of this is the equation of a line in 2D, which is

$$Ax + By + C = 0 \tag{9-2}$$

where A, B, and C are constants. Note that in an implicit equation, the constants are not necessarily unique for a given geometric form. Because the

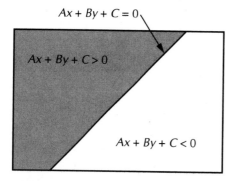

Figure 9-4   Two half-spaces

equation is set to zero, we can multiply all of our coefficients by any nonzero constant and produce an equation that describes the same set of points.

One of the advantages of the implicit form is that such equations divide the 2D plane into two half-spaces. Take for example the line in Figure 9-4. Applying $F(x, y)$ to any point in the plane will produce a result that is less than, greater than, or equal to 0. We can use this to divide the plane into two parts. This works for any function and can serve us well in determining whether a point is inside or outside of some region.

The ability to multiply the coefficients by any constant can also be useful. With many implicit equations, we can normalize the equation so that $F(x, y)$ actually returns the distance from the object. This does not work for all shapes but it does work for some of them and will thus solve one of our geometric problems.

9.2.2 Parametric Equations

An alternative description of a set of points is a set of parametric equations. In 2D, these are of the form

$$x = G(t)$$
$$y = H(t)$$

(9-3)

where t is a parameter that can be any real number. G and H are arbitrary functions of the parameter t. Equations with only one parameter will describe a 1D path. 2D shapes can be described using two parameters such as

$$x = K(s, t)$$
$$y = L(s, t)$$

(9-4)

The kinds of paths or shapes that can be described in this manner are determined by the kinds of functions used for G, H, K, and L.

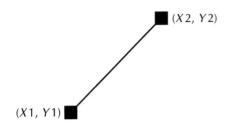

Figure 9-5   Control points of a line

In many cases, we don't want an infinite shape such as an entire infinite line. Sometimes we only want to describe a line segment. In such cases, we can formulate our parametric equations so that if the parameter ranges between 0 and 1, the points produced will lie on the line segment that we desire. This will be clearer when we discuss lines and line segments.

9.3 Path-Defined Shapes

The first set of geometric objects we will discuss are paths, or 1D objects that are drawn in a 2D space. The simplest description of these objects is that they have no inside or outside; they are infinitely thin. Most of our geometric questions involve paths. When paths define the border of a filled shape, the geometry of the shape is determined by the geometry of the path that is its border. The paths that we will discuss are lines, circles, arcs, ellipses, curves, and complex piecewise paths.

9.3.1 Lines

Lines are the simplest of all paths and provide the easiest geometric solutions. Figure 9-5 shows a line and its controls points. These control points define the line's geometry and we will use them to compute the coefficients for our line equations.

Implicit Equation of a Line
The implicit equation for a line is of the form

$$Ax + By + C = 0 \tag{9-5}$$

This is the 2D form of the linear hyperplane equation. This class of equation is found in spaces of all dimensions and will linearly divide the space into two half-spaces. In 3D, an equation such as this would define a plane. This is a very important equation in computer graphics and has many uses.

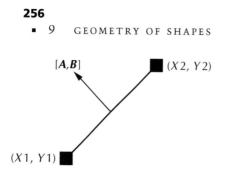

Figure 9-6   Perpendicular vector to a line

One of the interesting properties of this equation is that the vector [**A,B**] is always perpendicular to the line. In fact, given a point and a vector perpendicular to our desired line, we can derive this equation by substituting the perpendicular vector for A and B and by using the x and y values from the point. We can then simply solve this equation for C. The result is an equation of a line that is perpendicular to [**A,B**] and passes through the point (x, y).

Let's use this property to derive our implicit equation from the control points. Given the points (X1, Y1) and (X2, Y2), we can produce a perpendicular vector with the equations

$$A = Y1 - Y2$$
$$B = X2 - X1$$
(9-6)

This is shown in Figure 9-6. Note that the order of the points is important in determining the direction of the normal vector. If we are standing at point (X1, Y1) and looking at point (X2, Y2), then the vector [**A,B**] as defined above will be pointing to the left and will have the same length as the line segment.

We then substitute any point on the line into our equation and solve for C. If we choose the first end point, then we have

$$AX1 + BY1 + C = 0$$
$$C = -AX1 - BY1$$
(9-7)

Given our control points, the implicit equation of our line would be

$$Line(x, y) = (Y1 - Y2)x + (X2 - X1)y - (Y1 - Y2)X1 - (X2 - X1)Y1 = 0$$
(9-8)

Substituting any x and y into Line(x, y) will yield the distance from the line in multiples of the length of [**A,B**]. To calculate the actual distance from the line, we must divide the entire equation by the length of [**A,B**]:

$$Length(\,[\textbf{A,B}]\,) = \sqrt{(Y1 - Y2)^2 + (X2 - X1)^2}$$
(9-9)

The full definition for Line(x, y) is therefore

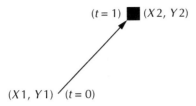

Figure 9-7   Parametric form of a line

$$\text{Line}(x, y) = Ax + By + C \qquad\qquad (9\text{-}10)$$

where

$$\text{len} = \sqrt{(Y1 - Y2)^2 + (X2 - X1)^2}$$

$$A = \frac{(Y1 - Y2)}{\text{len}}$$

$$B = \frac{(X2 - X1)}{\text{len}}$$

$$C = -\left[\frac{(Y1 - Y2)X1 + (X2 - X1)Y1}{\text{len}}\right]$$

We can use the function Line(x, y) to solve several geometric problems. The test Line(x, y) = 0 will indicate whether a point lies on the line. The Line function itself will give the distance from a point to a line. This can be used for testing a point for being close to the line.

To compute the nearest point on a line, we can use Line(x, y) and the perpendicular vector [**A,B**]. For a given point (x, y), the value of Line(x, y) is the number of multiples of [**A,B**] that the point is from the line. We can use the vector [**A,B**] and go in the opposite direction to find the nearest point (Nx, Ny) on the line. This would be

$$Nx = x - A \cdot \text{Line}(x, y) \qquad\qquad (9\text{-}11)$$
$$Ny = y - B \cdot \text{Line}(x, y)$$

Note that this solution for the nearest point does not require that the line equation be normalized to actual distances. Any formulation of the hyperplane equation will do.

Parametric Equation of a Line

The parametric formulation of a line is illustrated by Figure 9-7. If our parameter t is equal to 0, then we want the point (X1, Y1). If the parameter is 1, then we want the point (X2, Y2). For a parametric value of 0.5, we want a point halfway between (*X*1, *Y*1) and (*X*2, *Y*2) and lying on the line. For various values of *t* between 0 and 1, we want points lying on the line segment.

In creating our parametric form, we consider a vector starting at point (*X*1, *Y*1) and proceeding toward (*X*2, *Y*2). We use *t* to indicate what fraction of the distance we want to move along this vector. The resulting equations are

$$x = (X2 - X1)t + X1$$
$$y = (Y2 - Y1)t + Y1$$

(9-12)

Note that if *t* = 0, these functions will produce (*X*1, *Y*1); if *t* = 1, the result is (*X*2, *Y*2). Fractional values of *t* will produce points in between. The parametric form of the line is not used as often as the implicit form. It helps, however, to illustrate parametric equations, which we will use with the other path geometries.

Bounding Rectangle for a Line

The bounding rectangle for a line is rather simple. We frequently represent bounding rectangles as (left, top, right, bottom). Using this model, the bounding rectangle for a line is

left = Min(*X*1, *X*2)
top = Min(*Y*1, *Y*2)
right = Max(*X*1, *X*2)
bottom = Max(*Y*1, *Y*2)

(9-13)

In fact, for shapes whose control points satisfy the *convex-hull* property, the bounding rectangle can be computed from the control points by

left = Min(*X* coordinates of all control points)
top = Min(*Y* coordinates of all control points)
right = Max(*X* coordinates of all control points)
bottom = Max(*Y* coordinates of all control points)

The convex hull of a set of points is the smallest polygon that will contain all of the points. The convex-hull property of a geometric object is that all points on that object are guaranteed to lie in the convex hull of that object's control points. We will not discuss how to compute convex hulls for sets of points because we never need the convex hull in actual practice. What we do need to know is whether a geometric object defined by a set of control points has the convex-hull property; if it does, then the calculation of the bounding rectangle is easy. Our model for lines and their control points does satisfy the convex-hull property.

9.3.2 Circles

Our next most interesting geometric shape is the circle. The simplest model for a circle is defined by its center and radius. The radius is not a control point

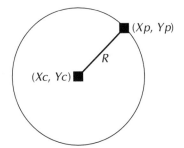

Figure 9-8 **Geometry of a circle**

but it does provide the simplest geometry for our first discussion. Circles can also be defined by their center and some point on the circumference of the circle, as shown in Figure 9-8.

The relationship between the control point model and the radius model for a circle is quite simple. Given the control points, we can derive the radius with the following equation:

$$R = \sqrt{(Xp - Xc)^2 + (Yp - Yc)^2} \tag{9-14}$$

Implicit Equation for a Circle

The implicit equation for a circle is based on the fact that a circle is the set of points some fixed distance from a center point. A circle of radius 1 centered at the origin has the equation

$$(x^2 + y^2) - 1 = 0 \tag{9-15}$$

The term $(x^2 + y^2)$ provides the square of the distance between the point (x, y) and the origin. We can describe a circle at center (Xc, Yc) that has radius R with the formula

$$(x - Xc)^2 + (x - Yc)^2 - R^2 = 0 \tag{9-16}$$

Subtracting Xc and Yc from the point (x, y) translates it to the origin. Note that equation 9-16 for a circle works in terms of the squares of the distances to the center. For some of our distance calculations, we want a formula that works in actual distances. This can be done with equation 9-17:

$$\sqrt{(x - Xc)^2 + (y - Yc)^2} - R = 0 \tag{9-17}$$

Parametric Equations for a Circle

The parametric equations for a circle are based on trigonometry. Consider Figure 9-9.

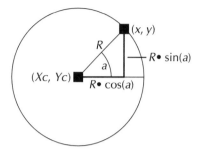

Figure 9-9   Parametric form of a circle

Given the angle a as shown, the two sides of the triangle with hypotenuse R would be $R \cdot \cos(a)$ and $R \cdot \sin(a)$. If we use a as a parameter, we have the parametric equations 9-18:

$$x = Xc + R \cdot \cos(a)$$
$$y = Yc + R \cdot \sin(a)$$
(9-18)

If sine and cosine are defined in terms of radians, then a must vary between 0 and 2π. We can reformulate our equations using parameter t, which varies from 0 to 1:

$$x = Xc + R \cdot \cos(2\pi t)$$
$$y = Yc + R \cdot \sin(2\pi t)$$
(9-19)

Distance from a Point to a Circle

The distance from some point to a circle is simply derived from equation 9-17; the function is shown in equation 9-20:

$$\text{dist}(x, y) = \sqrt{(x - Xc)^2 + (y - Yc)^2} - R$$
(9-20)

Careful examination of this equation will show that points with negative distances lie inside of the circle while points with positive distances lie outside of the circle.

Nearest Point on a Circle

The nearest point on a circle can be derived by considering Figure 9-10.

We could solve for the intersection between the circle and the line from (Xc, Yc) to (x, y). Instead, we will use a vector model. Consider that (Xn, Yn) is at distance R from (Xc, Yc) along a vector in the direction of (x, y). The vector from the center to (x, y) is

$$[(x - Xc), (y - Yc)]$$
(9-21)

A vector in the same direction that has length 1 would be

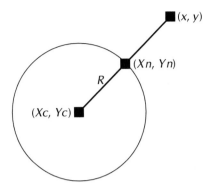

Figure 9-10   Nearest point on a circle

$$\left[\frac{(x - Xc)}{\sqrt{(x - Xc)^2 + (y - Yc)^2}}\ ,\ \frac{(y - Yc)}{\sqrt{(x - Xc)^2 + (y - Yc)^2}}\right] \qquad \text{(9-22)}$$

Once we have a vector going in the right direction that is of length 1, we can get a vector in the same direction, with length R, by multiplying by R. If we add this to the center, then we will get the point (Xn, Yn) as shown in equations 9-23:

$$Xn = Xc + \frac{R \cdot (x - Xc)}{\sqrt{(x - Xc)^2 + (y - Yc)^2}} \qquad \text{(9-23)}$$

$$Yn = Yc + \frac{R \cdot (y - Yc)}{\sqrt{(x - Xc)^2 + (y - Yc)^2}}$$

Bounds of a Circle

The bounding box of a circle is easy to calculate, as shown in Figure 9-11. The rectangular bounds can also be computed using the parametric equations by computing the points for t = 0.0, 0.25, 0.5, and 0.75. Computing the bounding rectangle for these points will yield the bounding rectangle for the circle. These are the extreme points of the circle in x and y.

9.3.3 Arcs

Arcs are fragments of circles and as such they use the same equations as circles. The question is how to define the restricted part of the circle that forms the arc. This definition is most easily specified using the parametric equations for a circle and then restricting the parameter values.

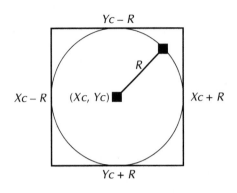

$Y_C - R$

$X_C - R$ (X_C, Y_C) $X_C + R$

R

$Y_C + R$

Figure 9-11   Bounds of a circle

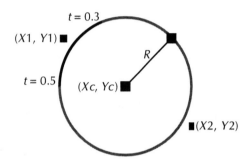

$t = 0.3$

$(X1, Y1)$

$t = 0.5$ (X_C, Y_C)

R

$(X2, Y2)$

Figure 9-12   Parametric form of an arc

Consider Figure 9-12. Using this form, we can describe the black arc using a center (Xc, Yc) and radius R with a starting parameter of 0.3 and an ending parameter of 0.5. We can describe the gray arc using the same center and radius, starting at 0.5 and ending at 0.3 or 1.3 (because of the cyclic nature of sine and cosine, a parameter of 0.3 in equations 9-19 will yield the same point as 1.3). To simplify our definition of an arc, we can reformulate our black arc as shown in equations 9-24 and our gray arc as shown in equations 9-25:

$$x = Xc + R \cdot \cos(2\pi(b0.2 + 0.3)) \tag{9-24}$$
$$y = Yc + R \cdot \sin(2\pi(b0.2 + 0.3))$$

$$x = Xc + R \cdot \cos(2\pi(g0.8 + 0.5)) \tag{9-25}$$
$$y = Yc + R \cdot \sin(2\pi(g0.8 + 0.5))$$

Note that if $b = 0$, then our angle will be $2\pi \cdot 0.3$ radians; if $b = 1$, then the angle will be $2\pi \cdot 0.5$. We have mapped the parameter b so that as it ranges from 0 to 1, it will have the same effect as t ranging from 0.3 to 0.5. The gray arc is handled in a similar manner, using parameter g. The result is that we can define an arc in the same manner as a circle while imposing the 0-to-1 limit on the parameter. By reformulating the parametric equation, we have mapped the range 0 to 1 onto a portion of the circle.

Selecting a Point on an Arc

In Figure 9-12, there are two points $(X1, Y1)$ and $(X2, Y2)$ that the user may have entered as selection points. Suppose we want to test these points to see if they would select the black arc. Taking $(X1, Y1)$ as our first case, we use equation 9-20 to calculate the distance to the circle. If it is close enough, we would consider the arc to be selected. The problem is that the point $(X2, Y2)$ will yield an almost identical distance, but as we can see, it is nowhere near the black arc. The key is that we have only considered the equation of the circle, not the restricted region of the circle that belongs to the arc.

We can solve this by first computing the nearest point (Xn, Yn) on the circle using equations 9-23. Taking Xn, we can solve equations 9-19 to calculate the parameter value of t for the nearest point on the arc. This is shown in equation 9-26:

$$t = \frac{\cos^{-1}\left[\dfrac{Xn - Xc}{R}\right]}{2\pi} \tag{9-26}$$

Once we know the parameter t, we can check to see if it falls between 0.3 and 0.5.

Selecting the gray arc in Figure 9-12 is a little more complicated since it spans the origin of the parameter. Most math libraries will have $\cos^{-1}$ return a value between 0 and 2π. This means that using equation 9-26 we will need to check t for the ranges 0.0 to 0.3 and 0.5 to 1. This case is easy to detect because the starting parameter (0.5) is larger than the ending parameter (0.3).

Bounds of an Arc

The rectangular bounds of an arc are more complicated because its control points do not define a convex hull for the arc. We can get a bounding rectangle by computing $t = (start, end, 0.0, 0.25, 0.5,$ and $0.75)$. Any point that does not lie between $start$ and end should be eliminated from the list. Using the remaining set of points, we can compute a bounding rectangle. Note that the black arc in Figure 9-12 will only use $t = (0.3$ and $0.5)$ while the gray arc will use $t = (0.0, 0.3, 0.5,$ and $0.75)$.

On some occasions, for simplicity, we don't need an exact bounding box; instead, we only need any relatively small bounding box that is guaranteed to contain the object. In such cases, we may use the bounding box of the arc's circle rather than the smaller bounding box for the arc itself. If all we are

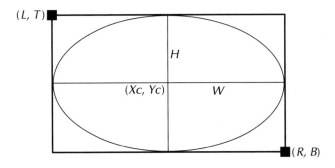

Figure 9-13   An ellipse

trying to do is make a quick test of a point before making more extensive calculations, the circle's bounding box is cheaper and faster. The fact that it includes more points than are necessary may be worth the cost because of its reduced complexity.

9.3.4 Ellipses and Elliptical Arcs

There are two major classes of elliptical shapes that we need to consider. The simplest class is the set of ellipses whose major and minor axes are parallel to the x and y axes. These are computationally quite tractable and can be understood by expanding on the equations for circles. A much more difficult class is the set of ellipses that can have any orientation of their major and minor axes. This class of shapes is computationally painful. There are applications where the general class of ellipses is required, but we can go a long way without them. For our discussion, we will restrict ourselves to the ellipses that are aligned with the x and y axes. Figure 9-13 shows just such an ellipse. We can think of this ellipse as a circle of radius 1 (a unit circle) that has been stretched in x for a distance W and stretched in y for a distance H.

In many systems, an ellipse is defined by its bounding rectangle. In such a model, we would specify the two control points (L, T) and (R, B). Since most of our equations are defined in terms of (Xc, Yc), W, and H, we can use equations 9-27 to perform the conversion, as follows:

$$Xc = \frac{L + R}{2} \qquad\qquad Yc = \frac{T + B}{2} \qquad\qquad \text{(9-27)}$$

$$W = \frac{R - L}{2} \qquad\qquad H = \frac{B - T}{2}$$

Implicit Equation for an Ellipse

To create our implicit equation for an ellipse, we can first reformulate our implicit equation of a circle by dividing by R^2, yielding equation 9-28:

$$\frac{(x - Xc)^2}{R^2} + \frac{(y - Yc)^2}{R^2} - 1 = 0 \tag{9-28}$$

We can modify this equation into an equation of an ellipse by thinking of W as the radius for the x axis and H as the radius for the y axis. Thinking of an ellipse as having two radii, we get equation 9-29:

$$\frac{(x - Xc)^2}{W^2} + \frac{(y - Yc)^2}{H^2} - 1 = 0 \tag{9-29}$$

Parametric Equations for an Ellipse

We can similarly create parametric equations for an ellipse from the equations for a circle. By substituting W and H, respectively, for the radius in each dimension, we get equations 9-30:

$$x = Xc + W \cdot \cos(2\pi t) \tag{9-30}$$
$$y = Yc + H \cdot \sin(2\pi t)$$

Note that the equations for a circle are special cases of the equations for an ellipse. Because of this, many systems provide only ellipses. This approach helps to simplify the software.

Other Geometry of the Ellipse

Calculations for nearest point on an ellipse and the distance from a point to an ellipse are problematic. The reason is that the equations for such calculations are polynomials of degree 4, for which there is no closed-form solution. The only geometrically accurate solution is to use a numerical approximation. In most interactive situations, this is slower than we would like.

One advantage of interactive selection, however, is that geometric accuracy is not absolutely essential. Take, for example, our problem of determining how close a point is to an object. The reason we are doing this is to select the object if the point is close enough. If we loosen our definition of "close enough" slightly, we can achieve an acceptable solution.

Let us take the transformation shown in equations 9-31:

$$x' = \frac{x - Xc}{W} \tag{9-31}$$

$$y' = \frac{y - Yc}{H}$$

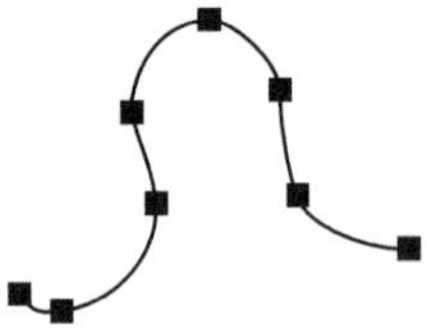

Figure 9-14   Piecewise cubic spline

This transformation, if applied to equations 9-30, will yield equations 9-32, which show the parametric definition of a unit circle (radius 1 around the origin):

$$x' = \cos(2\pi t)$$
$$y' = \sin(2\pi t)$$

(9-32)

If we apply the transformation equations 9-31 to our input point, it will be in the same coordinates as the unit circle. We can use our circle geometry to solve for the nearest point (Xn', Yn') on the unit circle. Using the inverse of equations 9-31, we can get (Xn, Yn) in our original coordinates, which we can use to calculate the distance. The next chapter will discuss the use of homogeneous coordinates and matrix transformations, which will simplify this process. Note that (Xn, Yn) is not actually the nearest point on the ellipse, but it is very close to it.

9.3.5 Curves

In many cases, users want shapes that curve in arbitrary ways. There are several ways to approach this problem. One of the most common is the piecewise cubic spline. Figure 9-14 shows such a curve with its control points.

Note that this curve has six inflection points where the curvature changes. This normally would require a polynomial of degree 7 or higher to represent such a curve. (Representing more complex curves with higher-degree polynomials is very problematic; it might be possible, but such equations would be difficult to control interactively.)

Rather than use a single polynomial curve of high degree, the curve in Figure 9-14 is composed of seven separate cubic curves that have been pieced together so that they are smoothly connected. There is a separate curve between each adjacent pair of control points.

Cubic Equations

Because of the arbitrary nature of cubic curves, there is no implicit form for these curves. Splines are always represented by parametric equations and are most frequently described by cubic polynomials. Polynomials are used

Figure 9-15   Connecting two lines with a curve

because they are computationally and algebraically easy to work with. Quadratics are rarely used because there are many things that they cannot do. To understand this, consider Figure 9-15.

The goal in this figure is to smoothly connect two lines with a curve. Note that this curve has two inflection points, which will require a polynomial of at least degree 3. Polynomials of degree 4 and above become hard to control and polynomials of degree 2 or lower cannot supply useful blending shapes.

The parametric equations for a single piece of a cubic curve are given in equations 9-33:

$$x = at^3 + bt^2 + ct + d \tag{9-33}$$
$$y = et^3 + ft^2 + gt + h$$

The curve is described by two cubic polynomials of the parameter t. These equations are frequently described in matrix form as shown in equation 9-34:

$$[t^3\ t^2\ t\ 1] \cdot \begin{bmatrix} a & e \\ b & f \\ c & g \\ d & h \end{bmatrix} = [xy] \tag{9-34}$$

Handles on the Splines

The parametric form of the cubic spline is very flexible, but requiring users to select eight coefficients (a through h) to create a curve is unreasonable. What we need is a good user interface to describe the form of the curve that can then be converted into the coefficient matrix so that the polynomials can be used to define the curve.

Control Point Definition   In most cases, these interactive handles are defined as control points. By manipulating the positions of the control points, a user can define the coefficient matrix for the curve. For cubic splines, four control points are required to define the curve. In some cases, such as the Hermite curve, two control points and two tangent vectors are used. In all of our examples, we will only discuss control point models because they have the best interactive properties.

To create a general definition for a control point, let a matrix **C** be the matrix of polynomial coefficients, as shown in equation 9-35:

$$\mathbf{C} = \begin{bmatrix} a & e \\ b & f \\ c & g \\ d & h \end{bmatrix} \tag{9-35}$$

Let matrix **G** be a matrix of control points $P1$–$P4$, where each row of the matrix is one of the control points, as shown in equation 9-36:

$$\mathbf{G} = \begin{bmatrix} P1 \\ P2 \\ P3 \\ P4 \end{bmatrix} = \begin{bmatrix} P1x & P1y \\ P2x & P2y \\ P3x & P3y \\ P4x & P4y \end{bmatrix} \tag{9-36}$$

Let matrix **S** be a matrix that defines the type of curve being used. For each type of curve, there is a 4×4 matrix of constant coefficients, **S**, that defines that curve.

The coefficient matrix **C** is composed of the spline matrix **S** and the geometry matrix **G**, as shown in equation 9-37:

$$\mathbf{C} = \mathbf{S} \cdot \mathbf{G} = \mathbf{S} \cdot \begin{bmatrix} P1 \\ P2 \\ P3 \\ P4 \end{bmatrix} = \mathbf{S} \cdot \begin{bmatrix} P1x & P1y \\ P2x & P2y \\ P3x & P3y \\ P4x & P4y \end{bmatrix} \tag{9-37}$$

The complete definition of a cubic parametric curve based on control points is shown in equation 9-38:

$$[t^3 \ t^2 \ t \ 1] \cdot \mathbf{S} \cdot \begin{bmatrix} P1 \\ P2 \\ P3 \\ P4 \end{bmatrix} = [x \ y] \tag{9-38}$$

Our interactive problem, then, is to determine what the control points are and then to multiply them by the characteristic matrix of the spline model that is being used to compute the coefficients of the polynomials. The polynomials then can be used for all of our geometric needs when dealing with such curves.

We will only briefly describe the spline definition matrices, **S**, in this chapter. For more information, please refer to computer graphics texts such as Foley and van Dam, or to more specialized spline texts.[3] In such texts, you will find many more spline curve formulations than can be discussed here, as well as detailed derivations of the geometry. Our goal in this chapter is to give an understanding of how the geometry relates to interactive problems.

Continuity Requirements   It is not enough to define the geometry of a single cubic curve; it is also necessary to define how curves are pieced together to create more complex curves. To do this, it must be interactively

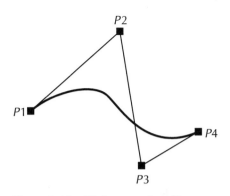

Figure 9-16   Bézier curve handles

possible to ensure that certain continuity requirements are met where two curves join.

C(0) continuity is the property that two adjacent curves share the same point where they join; that is, the zeroeth derivative (no derivative at all) is the same for both curves at the join point. This is relatively easy to ensure for all splines.

C(1) continuity is where the first derivatives are identical at the join point. This will ensure that there is a smooth transition between curves with no sharp points, because the tangent vectors of each curve are aligned at the join point. This is the most common requirement for piecing together smooth curves.

C(2) continuity is where the curvatures are the same across the join point. This is a rather specialized requirement that is imposed by some engineering problems.

Various Spline Forms   We will consider three common forms of cubic splines that are found in a variety of situations. Note that each of these is based on the same parametric definition for cubic curves. The only differences are in their characteristic matrix **S** and in the way their four control points are defined.

Bézier curves: The Bézier curve is one of the simplest and is defined by the two end points of the curve and by two intermediate control points, as shown in Figure 9-16.

The points *P*1 and *P*2 form a line tangent to the curve at point *P*1. The points *P*3 and *P*4 form a tangent at point *P*4. The intermediate control points also control how much curvature there is. By pulling *P*3 out farther, the inflection point near *P*4 can be made more pronounced, as shown in Figure 9-17.

The Bézier curve gives interactive users a very simple model for controlling cubic curves by manipulating the control points. The parametric form of this

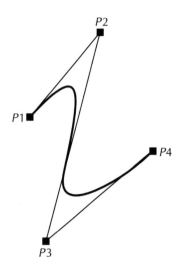

Figure 9-17   Adjusting Bézier control points

curve is shown in equation 9-39, where the matrix **Bz** is the characteristic matrix for cubic Bézier curves:

$$[t^3 \ t^2 \ t \ 1] \cdot \mathbf{Bz} \cdot \begin{bmatrix} P1 \\ P2 \\ P3 \\ P4 \end{bmatrix} = [xy] \qquad\qquad \textbf{(9-39)}$$

or

$$[t^3 \ t^2 \ t \ 1] \cdot \begin{bmatrix} -1 & 3 & -3 & 1 \\ 3 & -6 & 3 & 0 \\ -3 & 3 & 0 & 0 \\ 1 & 0 & 0 & 0 \end{bmatrix} \cdot \begin{bmatrix} P1 \\ P2 \\ P3 \\ P4 \end{bmatrix}$$

In connecting two Bézier curves to form a more complex curve, $C(0)$ continuity is easily obtained by making $P4$ of the first curve the same point as $P1$ of the second. Getting $C(1)$ or tangent continuity is done by making $P3$ and $P4$ of the first curve collinear with $P1$ and $P2$ of the second, as shown in Figure 9-18. Many interactive drawing packages will maintain this continuity automatically. This is usually done by adjusting the position of $P2$ on the second curve whenever $P3$ on the first curve is moved. By piecing together many such curves, it is very easy to create complex curved shapes. $C(2)$ continuity, however, does not come in any easy fashion using the Bézier handles on the curve.

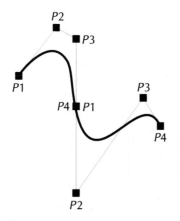

Figure 9-18   Continuity of Bézier curves

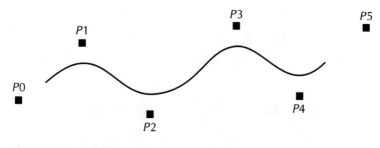

Figure 9-19   B-spline curve

One important characteristic of the Bézier curve is that the control points have the convex-hull property. If we take the maximum and minimum of x and y for all four control points, we will have a bounding rectangle for the curve.

B-spline curves: To simplify our interaction with complex curves, we want to use an arbitrary number of control points from $P0$ to Pn, such as in Figure 9-19. This curve is actually made up of three cubic curves. Each cubic curve is characterized by one of the points $P1$ through $P3$. For each of these three curves, the geometry matrices are shown in equation 9-40. The general B-spline equation is shown in equation 9-41.

$$\begin{bmatrix} P0 \\ P1 \\ P2 \\ P3 \end{bmatrix}, \begin{bmatrix} P1 \\ P2 \\ P3 \\ P4 \end{bmatrix}, \begin{bmatrix} P2 \\ P3 \\ P4 \\ P5 \end{bmatrix} \qquad \textbf{(9-40)}$$

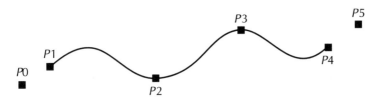

Figure 9-20   Catmull-Rom spline

$$[t^3\ t^2\ t\ 1] \cdot \mathbf{Bs} \cdot \begin{bmatrix} P(i-1) \\ P(i) \\ P(i+1) \\ P(i+2) \end{bmatrix} = (x\ y) \qquad \text{(9-41)}$$

or

$$[t^3\ t^2\ t\ 1] \cdot \frac{1}{6} \begin{bmatrix} -1 & 3 & -3 & 1 \\ 3 & -6 & 3 & 0 \\ -3 & 0 & 3 & 0 \\ 1 & 4 & 1 & 0 \end{bmatrix} \cdot \begin{bmatrix} P(i-1) \\ P(i) \\ P(i+1) \\ P(i+2) \end{bmatrix}$$

Bs is the characteristic B-spline matrix and i varies from $P1$ to $P(n-2)$ where n is the total number of control points.

Continuity between the cubic curves that make up the total shape is achieved automatically in a B-spline. In fact, a B-spline will guarantee $C(2)$ continuity. This continuity is possible because any two adjacent cubic pieces in the total curve share three control points between them. The $C(2)$ continuity comes at a price, however. Notice in Figure 9-19 that none of the control points are on the curve itself. This makes it hard to create curves that go through particular points.

The B-spline curve has the same convex-hull property as the Bézier curve. We can thus compute the bounding box by taking the maxima and minima of the control points.

Catmull-Rom curves: In many cases, we do not care about $C(2)$ continuity. Instead, we want our curve to pass through some specified points. We can do this with a Catmull-Rom spline, as shown in Figure 9-20.

The formulation for a Catmull-Rom curve is similar to the B-spline and is shown in equation 9-42; the matrix **CR** is the characteristic Catmull-Rom matrix:

$$[t^3 \; t^2 \; t \; 1] \cdot \mathbf{CR} \cdot \begin{bmatrix} P(i-1) \\ P(i) \\ P(i+1) \\ P(i+2) \end{bmatrix} = [x \; y] \tag{9-42}$$

For a given segment of a Catmull-Rom cubic, the end points of the curve are $P(i)$ and $P(i+1)$. Control points from adjacent curves are used to preserve $C(1)$ continuity where curve fragments connect. Note that $C(1)$ continuity comes automatically for a series of points without any further interactive effort. Note also in Figure 9-20 that $P0$ and $P5$ are not on the curve. These additional controls provide the tangent information for the ends of the curve.

The control points of a Catmull-Rom spline do not have the convex-hull property. This can be easily solved, however, by converting any Catmull-Rom geometry into the Bézier geometry for the same curve. Take equation 9-43, where the matrix $\mathbf{Gbz}$ is an unknown Bézier geometry matrix:

$$\mathbf{CR} \cdot \begin{bmatrix} P(i-1) \\ P(i) \\ P(i+1) \\ P(i+2) \end{bmatrix} = \mathbf{Bz} \cdot \mathbf{Gbz} \tag{9-43}$$

By multiplying both sides of the equation by $\mathbf{Bz^{-1}}$, we get equation 9-44:

$$\mathbf{Bz^{-1}} \cdot \mathbf{CR} \cdot \begin{bmatrix} P(i-1) \\ P(i) \\ P(i+1) \\ P(i+2) \end{bmatrix} = \mathbf{Gbz} \tag{9-44}$$

We now have $\mathbf{Gbz}$, which contains four Bézier control points for the same curve described by the Catmull-Rom control points. We can use these Bézier control points to compute the bounding rectangle for the curve.

Nearest Point

The nearest point on a cubic curve to some arbitrary selection point is a problem to calculate. The simplest formulation of the square of the distance is shown in equation 9-45:

$$\begin{aligned} d^2 &= (X - Xn)^2 + (Y - Yn)^2 \\ &= (X - (at^3 + bt^2 + ct + d))^2 \\ &\quad + (Y - (et^3 + ft^2 + gt + h))^2 \end{aligned} \tag{9-45}$$

Note that this is a polynomial of degree 6 in t. We minimize this distance by taking the first derivative with respect to t and setting it equal to 0. This requires solving a polynomial of degree 5, for which there is no simple formula like the quadratic equation. Solving for the nearest point requires approximate numerical methods such as Newton's method; you should refer to a numerical methods book for appropriate techniques.[4]

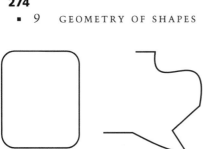

Figure 9-21   Piecewise paths

Finding the nearest point is further complicated by the fact that setting the first derivative of equation 9-45 equal to 0 solves for local minima, of which there may be as many as five. Not all of these are equally close to the desired point.

9.3.6 Piecewise Path Objects

A last form for creating path objects to be drawn is to piece together simpler objects. The rounded rectangle in Figure 9-21 is composed of four lines and four elliptical arcs. The other shape is a concatenation of straight lines and cubic curves. At some joints, $C(1)$ continuity is preserved and at others it is not. A large variety of shapes can be created by connecting up more primitive shapes. The essential geometry of such complex shapes is determined by the component shapes from which the whole was assembled.

9.4 Filled Shapes

In the preceding section, we discussed paths, or line-drawn shapes with various geometries. A second major class of drawing geometries is filled shapes, in particular, the set of 2D shapes that have an inside. Figure 9-22 shows a variety of examples of such shapes. Our primary geometric question is to determine whether or not a specific point is inside the shape or outside of it. If a mouse is positioned inside of a shape when a button is pressed, then the shape is selected. If the mouse is outside the shape, then the shape is not selected. As shown by point P in Figure 9-22, this decision can become quite complex. In fact, the package used to draw Figure 9-22 incorrectly claims that point P is inside of the shape.

9.4.1 Rectangles

The simplest of all filled shapes is the rectangle. Given its left, top, right, and bottom coordinates, we can easily determine if a point is inside of the rectangle using the inequalities in equations 9-46:

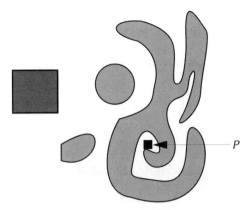

Figure 9-22   Filled shapes; point _P_ is outside the shape

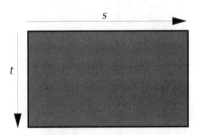

Figure 9-23   Parametric form of a rectangle

left $\leq X \leq$ right   **(9-46)**
top $\leq Y \leq$ bottom

Because this test is so simple, it is used on the bounding box of more complex shapes before performing more complex inside/outside tests.

Parametric Definition

We can create a parametric definition for points that are inside and outside of a rectangle by using two parameters instead of the one used with path objects. Given the rectangle in Figure 9-23, we can define an axis for each of the two parameters s and t, with the origin of this parametric space at the upper-left corner of the rectangle.

The parametric form for this rectangle is given in equations 9-47:

x = left + s (right − left)   **(9-47)**
y = top + t (bottom − top)

such that

$0 \leq s \leq 1,\ 0 \leq t \leq 1$

Note that the limits on s and t will cause x and y to range within the bounds of the rectangle. To determine if a point (x, y) is inside of a rectangle, we might solve for s and t and then determine if s and t lie in the range of 0 to 1. This is shown in equations 9-48:

$$s = \frac{x - \text{left}}{\text{right} - \text{left}} \tag{9-48}$$

$$t = \frac{y - \text{top}}{\text{bottom} - \text{top}}$$

This parametric form for rectangles is trivial and not very useful but it does illustrate techniques for more complex shapes.

9.4.2 Circles and Ellipses

The space inside of a circle also has a parametric equation just as does the circumference of the circle. As with rectangles, this equation has two parameters rather than one. The equations are shown as follows:

$$x = Xc + s \cdot R \cdot \cos(2\pi t) \tag{9-49}$$
$$y = Yc + s \cdot R \cdot \sin(2\pi t)$$

Note that the t parameter goes around the circle while the s parameter moves radially in and out. If $s = 0$, then the point is always the center. If $s = 1$, then the equations are the same as equations 9-19 for the circumference.

More general equations for the space inside of an ellipse are shown in equations 9-50:

$$x = Xc + s \cdot W \cdot \cos(2\pi t) \tag{9-50}$$
$$y = Yc + s \cdot H \cdot \sin(2\pi t)$$

In the case of an axis-aligned ellipse, we have an x-axis radius of W and a y-axis radius of H.

If we know x and y, we can solve the ellipse equations for s and t. If the resulting s and t lie within the range 0 to 1, then the point (x, y) lies within the ellipse; this is shown in equations 9-51:

$$s = \sqrt{\frac{(x - Xc)^2}{W^2} + \frac{(y - Yc)^2}{H^2}} \tag{9-51}$$

$$t = \frac{\sin^{-1}\left(\dfrac{y - Yc}{s \cdot H}\right)}{2\pi}$$

With these equations, we can test any ellipse for selection by a point.

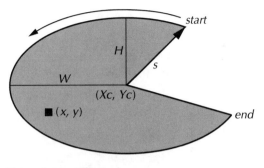

Figure 9-24 Elliptical arcs

9.4.3 Pie Shapes

A slightly more complex problem is to determine if a point lies within a pie shape such as that shown in Figure 9-24. Again s is the radial parameter and t goes around the circumference, as shown in equations 9-52:

$$x = Xc + s \cdot W \cdot \cos(2\pi(t(end - start) + start)) \qquad \text{(9-52)}$$
$$y = Yc + s \cdot H \cdot \cos(2\pi(t(end - start) + start))$$

To determine whether a point (x, y) is inside this elliptical pie shape, we must solve equations 9-52 for s and t as shown in equations 9-53:

$$s = \sqrt{\frac{(x - Xc)^2}{W^2} + \frac{(y - Yc)^2}{H^2}}$$

$$t = \frac{\sin^{-1}\left(\dfrac{y - Yc}{s \cdot H}\right) - 2\pi \cdot start}{2\pi(end - start)} \qquad \text{(9-53)}$$

With these equations, we can compute s and t for any point and then check s and t for the range 0 to 1.

9.4.4 Boundary-Defined Shapes

The preceding closed shapes are all defined by very regular geometric equations. There are a variety of shapes that do not have such regular geometry; examples of such shapes are shown in Figure 9-25.

Each of these shapes is defined by a closed boundary consisting of a number of pieces, each of which is a path-defined shape. The rounded rectangle a is defined by a sequence of straight lines and circular arcs. Polygons such as b

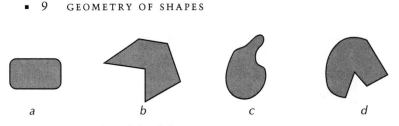

Figure 9-25 Boundary-defined shapes

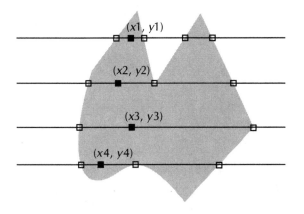

Figure 9-26 Inside/outside test

consist entirely of straight lines. The boundary for object *c* is composed of cubic curves, and object *d* is a combination of cubic curves and straight lines.

Our problem is to determine whether a given selection point is inside or outside of the shape. Before trying for an exact solution, we always first test the point against the bounding box for the shape. The bounding box is a cheap test and will quickly discard a large number of shapes that cannot possibly enclose a given selection point. The bounding box is constructed by taking the union of the bounding boxes for each object on the shape's boundary.

If the selection point is inside of the bounding box, then we use the odd/even inside/outside test. This is shown in Figure 9-26.

To compute whether a selection point (x_i, y_i) is inside or outside of a closed shape, we construct a horizontal line through the point. We next intersect that line with all of the edges of the shape. Finally, we count the number of intersections to the right of our selection point. If the number is odd, then the point is inside the shape; otherwise it is outside. In Figure 9-26, point $(x1, y1)$ has three intersection points to the right and is therefore inside the shape.

A problem arises, however, with point $(x2, y2)$ because there are only two intersection points to the right but the point is obviously inside. The problem is that the first point to the right is actually on two different edges and therefore should count as two points. With this adjustment, there are now three points to the right and the point is inside.

Using the two-edge rule, however, causes point $(x3, y3)$ to have two points to the right, if we count both edges that encounter its intersection point. We need to be a little more careful with points where two edges are joined together. In the case of $(x2, y2)$, the boundary is tangent to our construction line, whereas in the $(x3, y3)$ case, the boundary is passing through our line. Therefore, in cases of tangency, the point should be counted twice; in cases where the boundary passes through the point, it should be counted once.

In order to determine tangency, we will first assume that we can traverse the boundary in counterclockwise order. At each point where edges join, we can compute dY or the local change in Y at that point. Note that computing dY is easier for lines than for circles or cubic curves. As we are traversing, if the sign of dY for the first edge is equal to the sign of the second edge, then the boundary is passing through; otherwise it is tangent at that point. In the case of the point to the right of $(x2, y2)$, in traversing counterclockwise we get a positive dY (down) for the first edge and a negative dY (up) for the second edge. The point is a tangent point and should be counted twice. In the case of the point to the right of $(x3, y3)$, dY for the first edge is negative (up) and for the second edge is also negative. The boundary is passing through the horizontal line and therefore is counted only once.

Selection point $(x4, y4)$ poses an additional problem. In the case of linear edges, we only had tangent points where two edges join. In the case of curved edges, tangent points can occur in the middle of an edge. Having computed an intersection point with the curve, we can test the first derivative dY/dX at that point to see if it is 0. If it is 0, then we count the point twice rather than once.

In order for the odd/even inside/outside test to work, we must be able to compute the intersections of the edges with our horizontal line. For selection point (x_i, y_i), we use the equation for each edge and set $y = y_i$. For lines, this is quite simple. For circles and ellipses, we use the quadratic equation and get one or two solutions. In the case of one solution, we know that it is a tangent point. In the case of cubic curves, we use the parametric equation $y_i = et^3 + ft^2 + gt + h$ and solve for t. Once we know t, we can compute the x coordinate for the intersection point. This requires solving a cubic polynomial, which must be done using numerical approximation and may yield up to three intersections. This is one of the reasons why some systems substitute multiple quadratic segments for a single cubic segment. The calculations for inside/outside with quadratics do not require numerical approximations.

9.5 Summary

This chapter is concerned with the essential geometry of the graphical objects used in our user interfaces. Objects are composed of one or more simple geometric objects. The geometry of most such objects can be defined by a set of control points, and users can interactively manipulate those objects by dragging the control points around the screen. Depending on our purpose, we may define an implicit equation for the shape or a parametric equation. It is important to understand both forms because each has its uses when working with shape geometry.

Interactively, it is important to be able to select a geometric object by specifying some point. In the case of path-defined objects, we need to know if a point is close enough to the shape to accept it as being selected. In the case of closed shapes, we need to know if the point is inside or outside.

The shapes that have been discussed will cover most of the geometries encountered in user interface work. The implicit and parametric equations used in this chapter will provide guidance in addressing other geometries.

10

Geometric Transformations

In Chapter 9, we discussed the geometry of the major shapes used in interactive graphics. In this chapter, we will cover geometric transformations of those shapes. These transformations and their combinations provide a general geometry for manipulating a variety of shapes. We also need to discuss the special case of the viewing transformation that maps objects in an arbitrary geometric world onto the 2D space of a window. Building up from the basic transformations, we can then model complex objects as compositions of simpler objects. We will discuss how combinations of the basic transformations provide a simple framework for such compositions.

10.1 The Three Basic Transformations

There are three basic transformations that, when taken together, provide almost all of the geometric manipulations that users want to perform. They are as follows:

1. Translation—moving an object from one place to another
2. Scaling—changing the scale or size of an object
3. Rotation—rotating an object around the origin

Each of these transformations has two equations that define how to map a point (X, Y) into a new transformed point (X', Y').

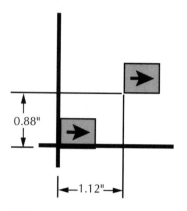

Figure 10-1   Translation

10.1.1 Translation

Translation is the simplest of the transformations. It moves an object from one place to another, as shown in Figure 10-1. Translation simply adds the distance to both x and y. The equations are as follows:

$$X' = X + dx$$
$$Y' = Y + dy$$

Each of the transformations discussed in this chapter has a set of coefficients that control the transformation. In the case of translation, the coefficients are dx and dy. The set of all possible values for the coefficients defines the set of possible transformations. In Figure 10-1, the coefficients are $dx = 1.12$ and $dy = 0.88$.

10.1.2 Scaling

Scaling is used to change the size of an object. In the scaling transformation, each of x and y are multiplied by their respective scale factors. In Figure 10-2, the dark rectangle is changed to the lighter one by multiplying x by 2 and y by 3. The equations for this transformation are as follows:

$$X' = X \cdot sx$$
$$Y' = Y \cdot sy$$

Note that the scaling transformation is defined relative to the origin. If the object being transformed is not at the origin, then the object will not only change size, it will also move. This is shown in Figure 10-3.

Because the lower-right corner of the rectangle is also multiplied by sx and sy, it moves to a new position. Only the origin stays fixed. In many cases, we

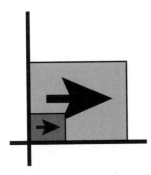

Figure 10-2   Scaling

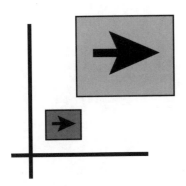

Figure 10-3   Non-origin scaling

want the rectangle to change size without moving. We will show later how this can be achieved using a combination of the simple transformations.

The coefficients *sx* and *sy* need not be positive numbers, nor do they need to be greater than 1.0. Coefficients between 0.0 and 1.0 will reduce the size of an object. Negative coefficients will produce reflections of the object about some axis, as shown in Figure 10-4. Note that we sometimes want to reflect about some axis other than *x* or *y*. We can accomplish this with combinations of transformations, as shown later.

10.1.3 Rotation

By convention, all rotations occur counterclockwise. The equations for rotation are as follows:

$$X' = \cos(a) \cdot X - \sin(a) \cdot Y$$
$$Y' = \sin(a) \cdot X + \cos(a) \cdot Y$$

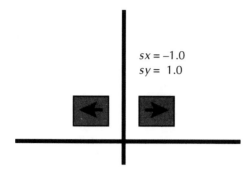

Figure 10-4   Negative scaling

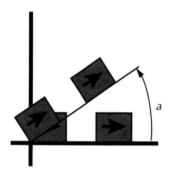

Figure 10-5   Rotation about the origin

Rotation, like scaling, occurs around the origin, as shown in Figure 10-5. The leftmost box has its corner at the origin, which does not move. The rightmost box is not only rotated but also changes its position because it was not at the origin.

10.1.4 Combinations

These three transformations are the basis for almost all manipulations of objects. These three alone, however, are not very interesting. What we need is a mechanism to combine these transformations in sequence. With such combinations, we can perform a variety of geometric tasks. Consider the transformation in Figure 10-6. This transformation is created by the following sequence of primitive transformations, which convert the dark rectangle into the light one:

1. Scale by (0.5, 0.5) to make the object half its original size.
2. Rotate the object by 35 degrees.
3. Translate the object to its new position.

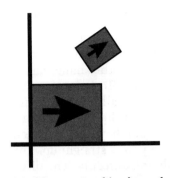

Figure 10-6   Combined transformations

10.2 Homogeneous Coordinates

Each of our primitive transformations is defined by a set of equations for x and y. If we are going to combine sequences of transformations together, we need a mechanism for combining these equations. Since we don't want to put an algebraic solver into our interactive systems, we need a better solution.

Each of the equations for our primitive transformations is a special case of a general set of linear equations. These general equations are as follows:

$$X' = aX + bY + c$$
$$Y' = dX + eY + f$$

Each of our primitive transformations can be cast into this form, as follows:

Translation:
$$X' = 0X + 0Y + dx$$
$$Y' = 0X + 0Y + dy$$

Scaling:
$$X' = sxX + 0Y + 0$$
$$Y' = 0X + syY + 0$$

Rotation:
$$X' = \cos(a)X - \sin(a)Y + 0$$
$$Y' = \sin(a)X + \cos(a)Y + 0$$

Because each of these equations is a special case of the two general linear equations, we can use matrices and linear algebra to provide our combination mechanism.

10.2.1 Introduction to the Homogeneous Coordinates Model

The particular model that we will use is called *homogeneous coordinates*. In homogeneous coordinates, we differentiate between points and vectors. A point has a particular position in space. A vector, on the other hand, has no position; it only represents a direction and a magnitude. To illustrate this, consider a map with a Mercator projection (one in which all longitude lines are straight and vertical). There are points on the map that locate places such as Provo, Utah, or Fresno, California; these are points and they have a particular position. We can consider the vector North, which points straight up. This vector points up no matter whether we are in Utah or California. The direction North is always up, just as the direction West is always to the left. These direction vectors are independent of where we are on the map.

In homogeneous coordinates, we represent a point (X, Y) as the row vector $[X\ Y\ 1]$. We can represent a vector (dx, dy) as the row vector $[X\ Y\ 0]$. The reasons for these differences will be discussed later. We represent the general linear equations using the following matrix:

$$\begin{bmatrix} a & d & 0 \\ b & e & 0 \\ c & f & 1 \end{bmatrix}$$

Using the point matrix, the transformation matrix, and matrix multiplication, we get the following equations:

$$[X\ Y\ 1] \otimes \begin{bmatrix} a & d & 0 \\ b & e & 0 \\ c & f & 1 \end{bmatrix} = [(aX + bY + c)\ (dX + eY + f)\ 1]$$

Note that the equations on the right are exactly our general linear transformation equations. Having this general matrix for our transformations, we can define each of the primitive transformations as a homogeneous matrix.

Translation:

$$[X\ Y\ 1] \otimes \begin{bmatrix} 1 & 0 & 0 \\ 0 & 1 & 0 \\ dx & dy & 1 \end{bmatrix} = [(X + dy)\ (Y + dx)\ 1]$$

Scaling:

$$[X\ Y\ 1] \otimes \begin{bmatrix} sx & 0 & 0 \\ 0 & sy & 0 \\ 0 & 0 & 1 \end{bmatrix} = [(sx \cdot X)\ (sy \cdot Y)\ 1]$$

Rotation:

$$[X\ Y\ 1] \otimes \begin{bmatrix} \cos(a) & \sin(a) & 0 \\ -\sin(a) & \cos(a) & 0 \\ 0 & 0 & 1 \end{bmatrix} = [(\cos(a)X - \sin(a)Y)\ (\sin(a)X + \cos(a)Y)\ 1]$$

10.2.2 Concatenation

We now have a matrix representation for each of our primitive transformations. Based on these representations, we can develop a mechanism for combining these transformations together. Let us suppose that we have a transformation Q that we want to use to transform point P into point P'. The equation for this is $P \otimes Q = P'$. Suppose that we then want to transform P' into P'' using transformation T $(P' \otimes T = P'')$. Since we already have an equation for P', we can substitute into this new equation to get $(P \otimes Q) \otimes T = P''$. We can use the associative property of matrix multiplication to get $P \otimes (Q \otimes T) = P''$. To transform P by the combined transformations of Q and T, we simply multiply $Q \otimes T$. Matrix multiplication becomes our mechanism for combining transformations.

Note that any sequence of such transformations can be multiplied together to produce a single transformation matrix. This ability to concatenate matrices means that the computational cost of transforming a point by any combination of transformations is the same as the cost of transforming the point by one transformation. This ability is very important for efficient handling of geometry.

The general concatenation for 2D linear transformations is as follows:

$$\begin{bmatrix} a & d & 0 \\ b & e & 0 \\ c & f & 1 \end{bmatrix} \otimes \begin{bmatrix} g & k & 0 \\ h & l & 0 \\ j & m & 1 \end{bmatrix} = \begin{bmatrix} (ag + dh) & (ak + dl) & 0 \\ (bg + eh) & (bk + el) & 0 \\ (cg + fh + j) & (ck + fl + m) & 1 \end{bmatrix}$$

As we have already shown, matrix multiplication is associative: $(Q \otimes (T \otimes U)) = ((Q \otimes T) \otimes U)$. Matrix multiplication is not, however, commutative: $(Q \otimes T) \neq (T \otimes Q)$. Therefore, the order of the transformations is very important; changing the order will change the transformation. For example, if we rotate an object and then translate it, it is not the same as translating it and then rotating. Because rotation leaves only the origin unmoved, translation followed by rotation will cause the object not only to rotate but to again change position. *Remember!* The order of transformations is very important and cannot, in general, be changed.

10.2.3 Vectors

When we first introduced homogeneous coordinates, we represented vectors by the row matrix [X Y 0]. Let us consider the multiplication of a vector by our general transformation matrix, as follows:

$$[\boldsymbol{X\ Y\ 0}] \otimes \begin{bmatrix} a & d & 0 \\ b & e & 0 \\ c & f & 1 \end{bmatrix} = [(aX + bY)\ (dX + eY)\ 0]$$

Note that the result is the same as with points, except that the coefficients c and f are missing (they were multiplied by 0). If we look at our matrix for translation, we see that c and f are the coefficients for translation, or change of position. By using 0 instead of 1 for the homogeneous coordinate, we transform vectors independent of their position. The transformation is now dependent only on the coefficients a, b, d, and e. These coefficients are the ones used in the scale and rotation matrices. With vectors, we do want to rotate (change direction) and scale (change magnitude) but not translate (change position). Using the 0 homogeneous coordinate for vectors accomplishes exactly those goals.

10.2.4 Inverse Transformations

There is a special transformation called the identity transformation that does nothing to our points and vectors. This transformation is represented by **I** and is encoded as the matrix

$$\begin{bmatrix} 1 & 0 & 0 \\ 0 & 1 & 0 \\ 0 & 0 & 1 \end{bmatrix} = \mathbf{I}$$

Any transformation that we want to do, we may also want to undo. We can do this with an inverse transformation. In the general case, we can use linear algebra to compute the inverse matrix for our transformation. Given a transformation **T**, its inverse transformation is denoted $\mathbf{T}^{-1}$. The property that we are most interested in is that $\mathbf{T} \otimes \mathbf{T}^{-1} = \mathbf{I}$. Multiplying a transformation by its own inverse produces the identity transformation, or undoes the original transformation.

The inverses for each of the primitive transformations are quite straightforward:

$$translate(dx, dy)^{-1} = translate(-dx, -dy)$$

$$scale(Sx, Sy)^{-1} = scale\left(\frac{1}{sx}, \frac{1}{sy}\right)$$

$$rotate(A)^{-1} = rotate(-a)$$

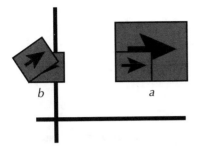

Figure 10-7   Transformation about a point; *a*, scaling, and *b*, rotation

We can also compute the inverse of a combination of transformations. Let us suppose that we have a transformation that scales, rotates, and then translates. We can represent this as $\mathbf{S} \otimes \mathbf{R} \otimes \mathbf{T}$. The inverse of such a transformation is computed by multiplying the inverses of each individual transformation in reverse order:

$$(\mathbf{S} \otimes \mathbf{R} \otimes \mathbf{T})^{-1} = \mathbf{T}^{-1} \otimes \mathbf{R}^{-1} \otimes \mathbf{S}^{-1}$$

We can think of this as walking backwards along a path. If we want to undo how we got to some place, we undo each step that led us there, only in reverse order. The same is true of combinations of transformations.

In some cases, we only have a transformation matrix. For these cases, we can use the generalized inverse for 2D transformations, as represented by the matrix

$$\begin{bmatrix} a & d & 0 \\ b & e & 0 \\ c & f & 1 \end{bmatrix}^{-1} = \begin{bmatrix} \dfrac{e}{(ae-bd)} & \dfrac{-d}{(ae-bd)} & 0 \\ \dfrac{-b}{(ae-bd)} & \dfrac{a}{(ae-bd)} & 0 \\ \dfrac{(bf-ce)}{(ae-bd)} & \dfrac{(cd-af)}{(ae-bd)} & 1 \end{bmatrix}$$

10.2.5 Transformation about an Arbitrary Point

Our primitive scaling and rotation transformations are defined to function around the origin. As was illustrated in Figures 10-3 and 10-6, objects that are not at the origin will be moved as well as scaled or rotated. Figure 10-7 shows a scaling of object *a* and a rotation of object *b*, two objects centered around points that are not at the origin.

We can accomplish a transformation about a point (Xc, Yc) by first translating the point to the origin. For scaling, this general transformation about the point (Xc, Yc) is composed by the transformation sequence

$$translate(-Xc, -Yc) \otimes scale(sx, sy) \otimes translate(Xc, Yc)$$

or

$$translate(-Xc, -Yc) \otimes scale(sx, sy) \otimes translate(-Xc, -Yc)^{-1}$$

In essence, we translate the desired point to the origin, perform the scaling, and then translate back. We can apply the same trick to rotation, as follows:

$$translate(-Xc, -Yc) \otimes rotate(a) \otimes translate(Xc, Yc)$$

This is a general technique for working with transformations. We transform the object to some simple location (such as the origin or aligned with some axis), perform the desired transformation at the simple location, and then put the object back with an inverse of the transformation that brought the object to the simple location.

10.2.6 Generalized Three-Point Transformation

A last approach to constructing a transformation is to take three points (or vectors) and three new points (or vectors) that we want to transform the first three into. We can then solve for a transformation matrix **T** that will produce the desired result, as follows:

$$\begin{bmatrix} P1 \\ P2 \\ P3 \end{bmatrix} \otimes \mathbf{T} = \begin{bmatrix} P1' \\ P2' \\ P3' \end{bmatrix}$$

$$\mathbf{T} = \begin{bmatrix} P1 \\ P2 \\ P3 \end{bmatrix}^{-1} \otimes \begin{bmatrix} P1' \\ P2' \\ P3' \end{bmatrix}$$

This approach for working with three examples of transformed points is quite general.

10.3 A Viewing Transformation

One of the most important geometric transformations is to bring objects from their native or world coordinates onto the screen at a particular location with the coordinates appropriate for the windowing system. This is called the viewing transformation. Consider the situation in Figure 10-8. A circuit is defined in the coordinate system of the circuit itself. The circuit coordinate system is

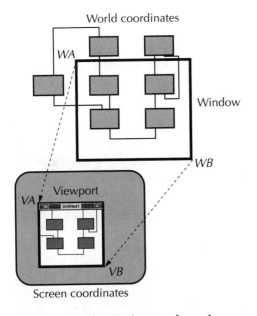

Figure 10-8 The viewing transformation

any system that the engineers feel comfortable with. Our problem is to transform the section of the circuit indicated by the "window" rectangle into the coordinates of the "viewport" rectangle on the display device.

Note that what most users—and most tool kits—consider a window is more precisely called a *viewport*. The concept of a window onto world coordinates is ignored by most windowing systems. We use the original terminology here to differentiate between the two roles of window and viewport. Together they make up a windowing, or viewing, system. A viewport is the actual location on the screen where the image is to appear. The viewport is defined by the points *VA* and *VB* in screen coordinates. The window is defined by *WA* and *WB* in world coordinates.

In most windowing systems, the window and viewport are not defined by two points but rather by the rectangle defined by these two points. We will use the point formulation so that we can derive our viewing transformation more directly. The problem in specifying viewports and windows is that not only do world coordinates and screen coordinates have differing sizes, aspect ratios, and differing origins, but they also may have their axes pointing in differing directions. Because of the influence of geometry textbooks, most world coordinate systems have y pointing up. Because of the influence of display hardware and memory, many windowing systems have y pointing down. By adopting the notion that *WA* must be transformed to *VA* and *WB* must be transformed to *VB*, we can ignore all of these variations and derive a simple viewing transformation.

If we look carefully at Figure 10-8, we see that our viewing transformation involves only scaling and translation. There is no rotation being performed in this transformation. Because of this simplification, we can use the following set of equations:

$$VA.x = a \otimes WA.x + c \qquad VA.y = e \otimes WA.y + f$$
$$VB.x = a \otimes WB.x + c \qquad VB.y = e \otimes WB.y + f$$

Since we know *VA*, *VB*, *WA*, and *WB*, we can solve each set of equations for the coefficients *a*, *c*, *e*, and *f*. Solving each pair of equations, we get the following:

$$a = \frac{(VA.x - VB.x)}{(WA.x - WB.x)} \qquad c = VA.x - \frac{(VA.x - VB.x)}{(WA.x - WB.x)} \, WA.x$$

$$e = \frac{(VA.y - VB.y)}{(WA.y - WB.y)} \qquad f = VA.y - \frac{(VA.y - VB.y)}{(WA.y - WB.y)} \, WA.y$$

We can assemble all of this into a transformation matrix that has coefficients for both scaling and translation, as follows:

$$
\begin{bmatrix}
\dfrac{(VA.x - VB.x)}{(WA.x - WB.x)} & 0 & 0 \\[2ex]
0 & \dfrac{(VA.y - VB.y)}{(WA.y - WB.y)} & 0 \\[2ex]
VA.x - \dfrac{(VA.x - VB.x)}{(WA.x - WB.x)} \, WA.x & VA.y - \dfrac{(VA.y - VB.y)}{(WA.y - WB.y)} \, WA.y & 1
\end{bmatrix}
$$

10.3.1 Effects of Windowing

All of the panning and zooming effects that we want in many applications can be handled by manipulating the world window. The movement of screen windows is handled by manipulating the viewport. The problems of aspect ratios or pixels that are not square can all be handled by this transformation.

Panning effects are achieved by moving the position of the window in world coordinates. Panning controls the portion of the window that will be visible. To zoom in on an object, we reduce the size of the window; the result is that a much smaller segment of the world is displayed on the same viewport size. Reducing the window size causes the objects that do appear in the viewport to be magnified. To zoom out, we increase the size of the window, which causes a larger number of objects to be shown, each at a smaller size.

10.3.2 Alternative Controls of Viewing

In our derivation of the viewing transformation, we have used the corner points of the window and viewport rectangles as our "handles," or parameters, for controlling the transformation. There are several other ways to control the same transformation. An important alternative is where the user is controlling the shape of the viewport and scrolling the window. Some zooming factor is used to control the scaling. In this case, we want the window and the viewport to have the same shape. Instead of the corner points, we want the following handles:

WC—the upper left-hand corner of the window in world coordinates

VC—the upper left-hand corner of the viewport in screen coordinates

Z—the zoom factor

Using these parameters, we can derive the transformation matrix. We need the transformation sequence

$$translate(-WC.x, -WC.y) \otimes scale(Z, Z) \otimes translate(VC.x, VC.y)$$

This transformation will take the window corner to the origin, apply the zoom factor, and then translate the origin to the corner of the viewport. The complete transformation matrix is

$$\begin{bmatrix} Z & 0 & 0 \\ 0 & Z & 0 \\ Vc.x - Z(WC.x) & Vc.y - Z(WC.y) & 1 \end{bmatrix}$$

This transformation is slightly more restrictive because it does not allow us to change the aspect ratio of the image, but in most cases, users only want scrolling and zooming, which is what this transformation will perform.

10.4 Hierarchical Models

Using our transformation facilities, we now have the opportunity to create more complex geometric models of objects that we wish to interact with. A very common desire is to compose objects from simpler objects. We can use our transformations and their concatenation to accomplish this goal. Consider the circuit diagram in Figure 10-9. We start with drawings of a chip body, a lower pin, and an upper pin. We compose these three parts together to produce a chip. We then compose *instances* of the chip to produce the circuit. Our task of drawing circuits is simplified by our creating one master for each

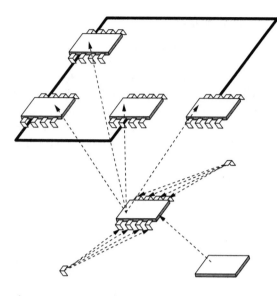

Figure 10-9 Hierarchical model

piece that we need and then creating multiple instances. For the chip, there are four instances of the lower pin and four instances of the upper pin. There are then four instances of the whole chip that make up the circuit. Each of the dotted arrows in the diagram denotes an instance of some master object. If we look closely at all of the arrows that leave the master chip, we see that the only differences between the instances of the chip are the transformations applied to the chip master. The same is true for the lower pin; each instance of the lower pin on the chip differs from other instances only by the transformation applied to the pin. The same is also true for the upper pin.

Note that each master object—lower pin, body, upper pin, and chip—has its own coordinate system. To make an instance of a master, we define an *instance transformation*. The instance transformation converts an object from *master coordinates* to *instance coordinates*.

Consider the case of the leftmost lower pin on the topmost chip in the circuit. In order to draw this pin correctly on the screen, we must do the following:

1. **T1**—Transform the pin from its own coordinates into chip coordinates for the leftmost lower pin on the chip.
2. **T2**—Transform the chip from chip coordinates into circuit coordinates for the topmost chip.
3. **V**—Apply the viewing transformation to transform from circuit (world) coordinates to the viewport for display.

Using our matrix machinery, we can compute the transformation as

T1 ⊗ T2 ⊗ V

This single combined transformation will carry the lower pin master into the appropriate coordinates on the screen so that it can be correctly drawn. Note that no matter how deep the nesting of masters and instances and how complex the model, a single 3×3 matrix will define the entire transformation from the master to the screen. This fact greatly improves the efficiency of our graphics operations.

10.4.1 Standard Scale, Rotate, Translate Sequence

In many systems, we do not use arbitrary transformations from master to instance. In fact, a large number of operations can be provided using a standard scale, rotate, translate (SRT) sequence. We scale first while we are aligned with the master coordinate axes; this simplifies the expression of the scale factors. We then rotate so that our origin is in the appropriate place, and then we translate to place the object in the correct position. We can then create an SRT transformation with the arguments SRT(*sx, sy, a, dx, dy*), which provide the scale factors, rotation angle, and translation distances. This provides a very simple mechanism for creating almost all instance transformations. *Note that if you do not want any scaling, the appropriate scale factor is 1, not 0. A 0 scale factor will shrink your image down to a point.*

10.5 Transformations and the Canvas

Having acquired the mathematical machinery for performing transformations, we now need to integrate such machinery into our graphics facilities so that we can actually draw objects using our transformations. To do this, we can augment our Canvas class with a *current transformation*. Before any line or circle is drawn, it is first passed through the current transformation matrix. This allows us to set up a transformation and then to draw in coordinates of our choosing. It is then up to the Canvas to apply the transformation so as to bring drawn objects into screen coordinates.

In many tool kits, the class that corresponds to Canvas will not handle the kinds of transformations described in this chapter; most will only support translation. If the application requires more sophisticated transformations, a new class can be created to wrap around the system class. This new class can override the drawing methods and perform the transformations before calling the methods of the system class. As processors become faster, this lack of transformation capability in the system classes will disappear.

10.5.1 Manipulating the Current Transformation

Let us assume that the class Transform exists, has a 3×3 matrix, and stores a transformation. Let us also assume that Transform has methods for multiplying two transforms, transforming a point, transforming a vector, and computing its inverse. We can give the Canvas a current transform (CT) field that is used to transform all control points before an object is drawn. We can define the following two methods:

```
void Canvas::SetCT(Transform NT)
```
   This will set the current transformation to **NT**.

```
Transform Canvas::GetCT( )
```
   This will return the current transformation.

We can also give the Canvas a method to set the viewing transformation; we will want to set this transformation before doing any drawing, so that objects will be transformed from world coordinates to screen coordinates:

```
void Canvas::View(Point WA, Point WB, Point VA, Point VB)
```
   This will compute the viewing transformation matrix and put it in the current transformation.

We can now add methods that will handle all of our primitive transformations. Each of these methods will compute the appropriate transformation matrix and then multiply that matrix by the current transformation to produce a new current transformation, as follows:

```
void Canvas::Translate(float dx, float dy)
```
   Compute a translation matrix **T** *and set* **CT = T ⊗ CT**.

```
void Canvas::Scale(float sx, float sy)
```
   Compute a scaling matrix **S** *and set* **CT = S ⊗ CT**.

```
void Canvas::Rotate(float a)
```
   Compute a rotation matrix **R** *and set* **CT = R ⊗ CT**.

To simplify a variety of things, we can also add the SRT method that performs scale, rotation, and translation in one call:

```
void Canvas::SRT(float sx, float sy, float a, float dx, float dy)
```
   Compute a transformation **T** *that will do scale, rotate, and translate in that order. Set* **CT = T ⊗ CT**.

Example

Before proceeding further, we need to work through an example to show how these methods work in conjunction with the drawing methods to provide the transformations that we need. Consider the series of models in Figure 10-10.

Figure 10-10   Three transformed houses

Suppose we have written a procedure called DrawHouse that will draw the polygons and rectangles necessary to create the image of the leftmost house. Suppose we want to create a cheap subdivision from this same house plan. We can use the following code sequence, which shows the contents of **CT** for each step in the code:

`Transform ST;`	**CT** = *viewing* **V**
`ST = GetCT();`	
`DrawHouse();`	*draws the first house*
`Translate(10, 0);`	**CT** = **T***(10, 0)* ⊗ **V**
`DrawHouse();`	*draws the second house*
`SetCT(ST);`	**CT** = **V**
`Translate(40, 0);`	**CT** = **T***(40, 0)* ⊗ **V**
`Scale(-2,1);`	**CT** = **S***(–2, 1)* ⊗ **T***(40, 0)* ⊗ **V**
`DrawHouse();`	*draws the third house*
`SetCT(ST);`	**CT** = **V**

In this example, each time the DrawHouse procedure is called, the current transformation is different. Before the polygon and rectangles of the house are drawn, the Canvas multiplies their points by the current transformation matrix. Thus, each time the same procedure is called, a different house is drawn. Note also that with the third house, a negative scale factor is used to flip the house around (a standard practice in cheap real estate development). Note also that when this happens, our origin point for the house is now on the lower right of the house instead of the lower left. This movement of the house origin means that we need to translate much farther to get the house where we want it.

Also note that for the third house, we want to first scale the house and then translate it. The current transformation just before drawing the house shows the transformations in this desired order. We got that order by calling Translate first and then Scale. The reason for the reversal is the way in which the transformation methods are multiplied onto **CT**. This kind of confusion of order is one of the reasons that the SRT transformation is included. A standard transformation sequence is built in the correct order without the user having to think about it.

The third house was drawn without the transformation used in the second house because the current transformation was saved in **ST** before the drawing process began. Before the third house's transformation was constructed, we used SetCT to restore **CT** to the value it had before we started.

10.5.2 Modeling with Display Procedures

Using the methods and techniques just demonstrated, we can create a general architecture for hierarchically modeling objects. We will use, as an example, the series of models shown in Figure 10-11.

For each of our models, we will define a procedure that, when called, will draw its model using the current transformation. Some models are defined in terms of other models and can accomplish this by setting up the current transformation and calling the procedure for the desired model.

Before trying to program these models, we first need to work out the transformations involved. Understanding the transformations is essential to being able to make calls in the correct order. Let us first look at the transformations required in building these models:

```
Rect -> Comb
```
$$rotate(-90) \otimes translate(0, 5)$$
```
Tri -> Comb
```
$$rotate(-90) \otimes translate(2, 5)$$
```
Comb left-> Join
```
$$rotate(90) \otimes scale(-3/5, 2/4)$$
```
Comb right-> Join
```
$$rotate(90) \otimes scale(3/5, 2/4) \otimes translate(3, 0)$$

The code that implements these models is shown below:

```
void Rect(Canvas Cnv)
  { Cnv.Rectangle(0, 2, 5, 0); }
void Tri(Canvas Cnv)
  { Cnv.Triangle(0, 0, 0, 2, 3, 0); }
void Comb(Canvas Cnv)
  { Transform ST = Cnv.GetCT();
    Cnv.Translate(0, 5);
    Cnv.Rotate(-90);
    Rect(Cnv);
    Cnv.SetCT(ST);
    Cnv.Translate(2, 5);
    Cnv.Rotate(-90);
    Tri(Cnv);
  }
```

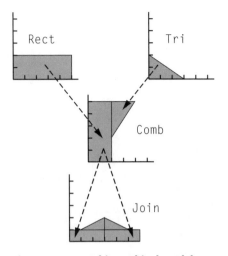

Figure 10-11   A hierarchical model

```
void Join(Canvas Cnv)
  { Transform T = Cnv.GetCT();
    Cnv.Scale(-3/5, 2/4);
    Cnv.Rotate(90);
    Comb(Cnv);
    Cnv.SetCT(T);
    Cnv.Translate(6, 0);
    Cnv.Scale(3/5, 2/4);
    Cnv.Rotate(90);
    Comb(Cnv);
  }
```

Notice that for every call to a display procedure, we must set up the transformations in opposite order so that they will come out correctly after premultiplication by the current transformation. We can show how this will work using the following trace of the execution. The current transformation is in the right column.

```
Join
   T = Cnv.GetCT();            V
   Cnv.Scale(-3/5, 2/4);       S(–3/5, 1/2) ⊗ V
   Cnv.Rotate(90);             R(90) ⊗ S(–3/5, 1/2) ⊗ V
Comb
   ST = Cnv.GetCT();           R(90) ⊗ S(–3/5, 1/2) ⊗ V
   Cnv.Translate(0, 5);        T(0, 5) ⊗ R(90) ⊗ S(–3/5, 1/2) ⊗ V
   Cnv.Rotate(-90);            R(–90) ⊗ T(0, 5) ⊗ R(90) ⊗ S(–3/5, 1/2) ⊗ V
```

```
  Rect
  Cnv.Rectangle(0, 2, 5, 0);
  Cnv.SetCT(ST);
  Cnv.Translate(2, 5);
  Cnv.Rotate(-90);
  Tri(Cnv);
Cnv.SetCT(T);
Cnv.Translate(6, 0);
Cnv.Scale(3/5, 2/4);
Cnv.Rotate(90);
Comb(Cnv);
```

Cnv.SetCT(ST); $\mathbf{R}\textit{(90)} \otimes \mathbf{S}\textit{(–3/5, 1/2)} \otimes \mathbf{V}$

Cnv.Translate(2, 5); $\mathbf{T}\textit{(2, 5)} \otimes \mathbf{R}\textit{(90)} \otimes \mathbf{S}\textit{(–3/5, 1/2)} \otimes \mathbf{V}$

Cnv.Rotate(-90); $\mathbf{R}\textit{(–90)} \otimes \mathbf{T}\textit{(2, 5)} \otimes \mathbf{R}\textit{(90)} \otimes \mathbf{S}\textit{(–3/5, 1/2)} \otimes \mathbf{V}$

10.6 Summary

In this chapter, we have presented the notion of linear transformations using matrices. For our 2D transformation, we have used homogeneous coordinates and 3×3 matrices. There are standard matrices for the primitive transformations translate, scale, and rotate. These transformations can be composed together to form more complex transformations. We have shown how to transform vectors (which are independent of position) as well as points. We have also shown how the primitive transformations can be combined to provide transformations about an arbitrary point. These new transformations use the general technique of transforming our object to a simpler location (such as the origin), performing the desired transformation, and then transforming it back using the inverse of the original transformation.

The viewing transformation was presented as a general model for mapping sections of a model world into the limited space of an onscreen window or viewport. This general transformation supports both panning and zooming.

Finally, we have shown how transformations can be built up to support hierarchical models, in which objects are defined in terms of other objects. Instances of an object are created by transforming them from the coordinates of the model into the coordinates of the instance. These can be built up using the notion of a current transformation.

This transformational machinery allows programmers to manipulate the geometry of objects or groups of objects. These matrices embody most of the object movement and manipulation that is needed in an interactive setting. In Chapter 11, we will show how to connect interactive behavior to these manipulations.

11

Interacting with Geometry

In previous chapters, we have studied the geometry of individual shapes as well as a basic set of linear transformations that can be used to manipulate geometry. We have also studied how to express interactive behavior in production systems. In this chapter, we will look at how all of these pieces can be put together to create interactive dialogs for a variety of interactive shapes.

We will look at lines, circles/ellipses, rectangles, and polygons. The interaction techniques used on these four shapes can be widely used in other situations. For example, Figure 11-1 shows a variety of shapes that all interact in the same way as a line, while Figure 11-2 shows shapes that interact using the basic rectangle model.

11.1 Input Coordinates

In Chapter 10, the viewing and modeling transformations were presented. Modeling transformations are matrices that transform an instance of an object from its model coordinates into world coordinates. These modeling transformations may be built up hierarchically, but they can all be composed together into a single transformation matrix. The viewing transformation converts world coordinates into window coordinates using a second matrix. These two matrices can be combined into a single display transformation D, as shown in Figure 11-3. In some applications, the model is actually defined in world coordinates without any modeling transformation. In such a case, the display transformation D is simply the viewing transformation.

When the mouse is over the rectangle, its coordinates are window coordinates. The user may want to select this rectangle and change its size. There

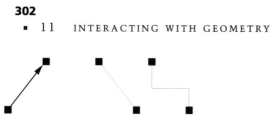

Figure 11-1   Line interaction

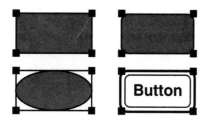

Figure 11-2   Rectangle interaction

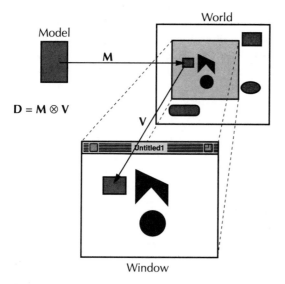

Figure 11-3   Viewing transformation

are two ways we can define this operation; it very much depends on where our interaction coordinates are defined. If, for example, we have a standard rectangle that we want to move around in the world by changing the modeling transformation **M**, then our interaction coordinates are in the world. If, however, we want to directly change the size of the original model rectangle, then our interaction coordinates are in model coordinates.

In either case, the mouse position that we receive from the windowing system is in window coordinates. We need to transform our input points from window coordinates into interaction coordinates. In the first case, where interaction coordinates are in the world, this transformation is

$$\text{InteractPoint} = \text{MousePoint} \otimes \mathbf{V}^{-1}$$

In the second case, where we want to interact in model coordinates, the transformation is

$$\text{InteractPoint} = \text{MousePoint} \otimes \mathbf{D}^{-1}$$

or

$$\text{InteractPoint} = \text{MousePoint} \otimes \mathbf{V}^{-1} \otimes \mathbf{M}^{-1}$$

The computation for these inverses is given in Chapter 10. It is very important that we carefully define what the interaction coordinates for our model really are, so that everything works out correctly.

There are short periods during which we will interact in window coordinates for speed and for local handling by the controller. All manipulation of the model, however, must occur in interaction coordinates. Otherwise there will be problems with multiple views of the model. Remember that other views will likely have differing windowing transformations.

11.2 Object Control Points

In Chapter 9, we defined the equations for shapes in terms of a set of control points. Figures 11-1 and 11-2 show a variety of shapes and their control points. We defined our shapes in such a manner as to simplify the user's interactions with those shapes. In most geometric interactions, we will define our input syntax based on what is happening to the control points. In fact, the interactive behavior is almost identical for all control points. Many shapes, such as lines and circles, have only the control points necessary to define the equation of the shape. Other shapes have more control points than are mathematically necessary. For instance, the rectangle shown in Figure 11-4 has eight control points, but only two are required to define its geometry. The additional control points aid users in interactively transforming the rectangle. The control points are dependent on each other; when one control point is moved, several others also need to be adjusted to maintain consistency with the geometry. In our rectangle example, if the upper-right control point is moved farther up and to the right, the top, upper-left, right, and lower-right control points all must be changed to maintain the rectangle geometry.

We need to work out how all of these issues fit within the model-view-controller architecture. The model for one of these shapes will only contain

Figure 11-4   Rectangle control points

Figure 11-5   Two-point shapes

the essential geometry information. For all of the shapes in Figure 11-5, the models would differ only in the type of line being drawn. In addition to the two control points, the model must also keep information about line thickness, color, and what kinds of arrowheads to use. For all four of these two-point shapes, however, the geometric controls and controller code are identical.

The view for these shapes, however, is different. The way that the shape is drawn is different for each type. The view is also responsible for selection. The view must perform the geometry of computing the nearest point to a mouse selection point and then checking the distance to see if it is close enough. Based on the similarities, we could write a single view/controller class for two-point shapes and then define subclasses that override the methods for redrawing, selection, bounds, and other geometric issues.

With the rectangle-based shapes in Figure 11-2, the controllers are identical to each other but somewhat different from those of the two-point shapes. In the case of rectangle-based shapes, everything is the same in the view and the controller except for the drawing and selection of the shape.

11.3 Creating Objects

The first interactive task to consider is the creation of new objects. We can start with the simplest case, which is the creation of two-point shapes. While the user is interactively creating a shape, we want to echo what the shape will look like so the user understands what is being created. In earlier chapters, we discussed the use of XOR while dragging such shapes. We will use that tech-

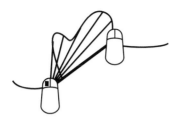

Figure 11-6   Creating a line

nique here. We start with lines because they are the simplest form. The following PPS state space can be used when creating line objects:

```
State { Idle, DraggingLine }
Actions { !SaveP1P2,
```
   Sets P1 and P2 to the current mouse position.
```
   !XORLine,
```
   XORs a line from P1 to P2.
```
   !SaveP2,
```
   Sets P2 to the current mouse position.
```
   !CreateLine
```
   Notifies the model to create a line object from P1 to P2.
```
}
```

The rules for this controller are as follows:

```
1. Idle, •MouseDown -> !SaveP1P2, !XORLine, DraggingLine
2. DraggingLine, •MouseMove -> !XORLine, !SaveP2, !XORLine
3. DraggingLine, •MouseUp -> !XORLine, !SaveP2,
      !CreateLine, Idle
```

Based on these rules, the input sequence in Figure 11-6 might occur. At each of the lines shown, the line is XORed, which will show the line, and then on the next •MouseMove, the line is XORed again before P2 is changed so as to erase the old line from the screen. The darker line is the one actually created when the •MouseUp event is received.

Let us assume that we create a controller that can accept any current two-point view object. Let us also assume that all actions are methods defined on this two-point view object. Based on this, we can generalize our PPS as follows:

```
State { Idle, DraggingObj }
ViewObjMethods { !SaveP1P2, !XORObj, !SaveP2, !CreateObj }
```

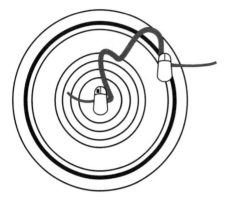

Figure 11-7 Creating a circle

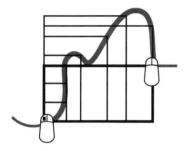

Figure 11-8 Creating a rectangle

Given any view of a two-point object, this controller syntax will create a new object of that form. For example, Figure 11-7 shows a typical input sequence using a circle object.

Let us consider the case of rectangular objects. With a rectangle, there are still only two control points required to define the geometry. The points must be opposite corners of the rectangle. With these two points, we can completely define the rectangle. Based on this observation, the syntax for creating rectangles is identical to that used for two-point shapes. This is shown in the input sequence in Figure 11-8.

There obviously is a difference between creating a circle and creating a rectangle, even if their input syntax is the same. An architecture for capturing both the similarities and the differences is described in Chapter 12.

11.3.1 Line Paths

Line paths create a new challenge in that multiple points are required to define their geometry. Take, for example, the line path shown in Figure 11-9.

Figure 11-9 A line path

In our controller syntax for two-point shapes, we use •MouseDown and •MouseUp to define the two points. This worked quite well for two points but will not work for an arbitrary number of points; we will need to have the user click on each point. Whether we use the •MouseDown or the •MouseUp event for each click doesn't really matter. For our example, we will use •MouseDown as the trigger for a new point. Rather than do a specialized line-path controller, we will use a current view object as we did with two-point shapes. In this case, however, the path view object must accept different methods.

If we click on each point in the path as it is created, we will need to know when to stop adding points to the path. We will also need to allow for a delete key so that users can remove points from the path that they added unintentionally. Our new state space is as follows:

```
State { Idle, Drawing }
PathViewMethods {
  !StartPath,
    Starts the first control point at the current mouse position.
  !XORSegment,
    XORs the current path segment being drawn at the end of the path.
  !ChangeLastPoint,
    Sets the last control point of the path to the current mouse position.
  !StartNewSegment,
    Starts a new segment on the end of the path.
  !DeleteLastPoint,
    Removes the last point from the path and restarts the previous
    segment. A damage will be performed so as to redraw without the
    previous segment.
  !CreateObj
    Creates the path in the model.
}
KeyQuery { ?DeleteKey }
```

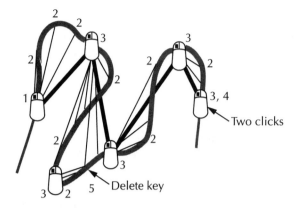

Figure 11-10   Path-creation inputs

```
PointQuery { ?SamePointAsBefore,
```
> *Is true if the current mouse position is near the start of the current segment.*

```
    ?DifferentPoint
```
> *Mouse position is not near the start of the current segment.*

```
    }
```

Based on this state space, we can now define a set of rules for drawing paths:

1. `Idle, •MouseDown -> !StartPath, !XORSegment, Drawing`
2. `Drawing, •MouseMove ->`
   `!XORSegment, !ChangeLastPoint, !XORSegment`
3. `Drawing, •MouseDown, ?DifferentPoint ->`
   `!XORSegment, !StartNewSegment, !XORSegment`
4. `Drawing, •MouseDown, ?SamePointAsBefore ->`
   `!XORSegment, !CreateObj, Idle`
5. `Drawing, •KeyPress, ?DeleteKey ->`
   `!DeleteLastPoint, !XORSegment`

The input sequence in Figure 11-10 shows an example of how this syntax actually works. The numbers along the mouse path indicate the rule that is firing at each point. At the far left, the first click of the mouse will cause rule 1 to fire and start the whole process. Rule 2 will echo the rubber band line on •MouseMove (as shown by the fine lines) until the next click of the mouse, which will cause rule 3 to fire. The !StartNewSegment action will add the segment between the two clicks (as shown by the heavy line). Further mouse moves will be echoed using rule 2 until the third click of the mouse causes rule 3 to add a second segment to the path (this segment is not shown). Rule 2 will echo a rubber band line until the point where the Delete key is pressed and rule 5 fires. When rule 5 fires, the !DeleteLastPoint action removes the second segment (which was not shown) and rule 2 will start echoing rubber band lines from the second mouse click rather than the third. Subsequent mouse clicks and movements use rules 2 and 3 to create additional segments. At the last mouse click position, rule 3 fires to add the fourth segment to the path. When the second mouse click occurs at the same position, rule 4 fires and the path is ended.

Note that this input behavior ignores all •MouseUp events that must occur between each of the •MouseDowns. This additional event information is not useful in this particular situation.

11.3.2 Splines

Catmull-Rom splines and B-splines are also defined by a series of points. If we take the state space and production system from line paths and generalize it to use a current view object with methods, as we did for two-point shapes, this controller syntax can be used for splines. In fact, we can use this method for any shape that is defined as a series of control points.

11.3.3 Polygons

Polygons have a similar syntax to that used with line paths and splines. The only difference is that we replace the ?SamePointAsBefore condition with ?SamePointAsFirst. The ?SamePointAsFirst condition compares the mouse position with the first point in the path rather than with the last to determine if the polygon is closed. In some systems, the path and polygon tools are merged into a single object type. Using the following production system with a sixth rule (4'), we can create either polygons or line paths from the same input syntax:

```
1. Idle, •MouseDown -> !StartPath, !XORSegment, Drawing
2. Drawing, •MouseMove ->
      !XORSegment, !ChangeLastPoint, !XORSegment
3. Drawing, •MouseDown, ?DifferentPoint ->
      !XORSegment, !StartNewSegment, !XORSegment
4. Drawing, •MouseDown, ?SamePointAsBefore ->
      !XORSegment, !CreatePath, Idle
4'.Drawing, •MouseDown, ?SamePointAsFirst ->
      !XORSegment, !CreatePolygon, Idle
5. Drawing, •KeyPress, ?DeleteKey ->
      !DeleteLastPoint, !XORSegment
```

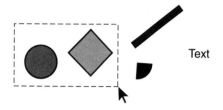

Figure 11-11   Rectangle selection

11.4 Manipulating Objects

Once objects have been created, we frequently need to manipulate or change them in some way. We do this by selection, dragging the object, and dragging control points.

11.4.1 Selection and Dragging

In almost all systems, the syntax of selection is merged with the syntax of dragging an object. This is a basic syntax structure that was worked out in the early systems and that has been used almost universally in graphical applications since then. Selecting an object by clicking on it with a mouse and dragging the object by moving the mouse while the button is down are fundamental behaviors in any direct-manipulation system. These two behaviors, more than anything else, give the user a sense of physically grasping and manipulating objects. Because these two actions are so common, their behaviors have been merged so as to minimize the number of inputs that a user must generate to accomplish the task.

Sometimes we want to select and/or drag a single object and sometimes several at once. Our dialog needs to allow for both conditions. Selecting a single object is usually performed by clicking the mouse on the object. If this is followed by clicking the mouse on a different object, the first object is unselected and the new object is selected. Selecting multiple objects is performed either by clicking on other objects using a different mouse button or by using a modifier key such as the Shift key. In either case, we must differentiate between adding a new object to the set of selected objects and starting a new selection. Most systems also allow users to select a set of objects by drawing a rubber band rectangle around all of the objects to be selected, as shown in Figure 11-11. The inclusion of rectangle selection also complicates our input syntax because we must differentiate between dragging out the selection rectangle and the dragging of an existing object.

Our state space for this behavior is as follows:

```
State { Idle, Selected, DraggingObj, DraggingSelect }
MouseLoc { ?MouseOverObject, ?MouseOverSpace }
MouseMove { ?IsLargeMove }
```
True if the mouse has moved more than a few pixels from the original selection point.
```
Actions {
  !SetStartLoc,
```
Sets the starting location to be the current mouse position.
```
  !NewSelectObject,
```
Starts a new selection set with the object under the mouse.
```
  !AddSelection,
```
Adds the object under the mouse to the selection set.
```
  !StartSelectRect,
```
Starts a rubber band rectangle at the current mouse position and clears the selected set.
```
  !StretchSelectRect,
```
Stretches the rubber band rectangle to the current mouse position.
```
  !EndSelectRect,
```
Ends the rubber band rectangle and sets the selection set to all objects inside of the rectangle.
```
  !StartDrag,
```
Begins dragging all selected objects.
```
  !Drag,
```
Continues dragging selected objects.
```
  !StopDrag
```
Stops dragging selected objects and translates all selected objects by (MouseLoc – StartLoc).
```
}
```

We can accommodate all of the selection and dragging behaviors described above, using the following rules:

1. `Idle, •MouseDown, ?MouseOverObject, noShift ->`
   `!SetStartLoc, !NewSelectObject, Selected`
2. `Idle, •MouseDown, ?MouseOverObject, Shift ->`
   `!SetStartLoc, !AddSelection, Selected`
3. `Selected, •MouseUp -> Idle`
4. `Selected, •MouseMove, ?IsLargeMove ->`
   `!StartDrag, DraggingObj`
5. `DraggingObj, •MouseMove -> !Drag`

```
6. DraggingObj, •MouseUp -> !StopDrag, Idle
7. Idle, •MouseDown, ?MouseOverSpace ->
     !SetStartLoc, !StartSelectRect, DraggingSelect
8. DraggingSelect, •MouseMove -> !StretchSelectRect
9. DraggingSelect, •MouseUp -> !EndSelectRect, Idle
```

Note that in this rule set we differentiate between selection and dragging, depending on where the •MouseDown event occurs and whether the user moves the mouse a significant amount.

Consider the selection in Figure 11-11. The •MouseDown event occurs at the upper-left corner of the dotted rectangle. Because this is not over any object, rule 7 will fire. This will cause the dotted rectangle to be drawn over a single mouse point, and the mouse-down position will be saved. As the user moves the mouse down and to the right, rule 8 will fire repeatedly. At each firing, the !StretchSelectRect action will update the selection rectangle so that it is drawn between the starting position and the current position. When the final position is reached and •MouseUp occurs, rule 9 fires to cause !EndSelectRect. This action will remove the selection rectangle and check all shapes against that rectangle, selecting all of those that are inside.

Note that if a user simply clicks in an empty space, rule 7 will fire, followed by rule 9. This first firing will produce a very small selection rectangle with nothing in it, which results in all objects being unselected.

Suppose that instead of •MouseDown occurring in empty space, it occurs over the line. In this case, rule 1 will fire instead of rule 7. This is differentiated by the query field MouseLoc. The code that implements this query must check the mouse position against every shape in the drawing. This is where the equations from Chapter 9 are involved. The firing of rule 1 will cause the !NewSelectObject action, which will select the line.

Once rule 1 fires, the user can release the mouse without moving it or moving it only a little. This will cause rule 3 to fire, which will return the controller to its idle state. If the user moves the mouse more than a few pixels, rule 4 will fire, causing the !StartDrag action. We don't want to start dragging on the first •MouseMove, because any little tremor in the user's grip on the mouse after •MouseDown would initiate a dragging of the object. By waiting for a move of more than a few pixels, we can accommodate the limitations of the human hand. If only a 1-pixel move is desired, the user can still move the object back after dragging is initiated.

Figure 11-12   A selected rectangle

Once dragging of the line is started, further •MouseMove events will cause rule 5 to fire. Each firing of rule 5 will cause the !Drag action to echo the line in its new position. When the mouse button is finally released, rule 6 fires, which causes !StopDrag. The !StopDrag action will remove the echo and notify the model of the line's new position. The new position is a translation of the line. The model can then notify the views so that the old and new positions of the line can be damaged.

It is very important to note that all of the selection points are being received from the mouse in window or screen coordinates. The transformations to interactive coordinates must be done by the semantic actions in each case.

We have only discussed selection by clicking and by dragging out a rectangle. There are other techniques for selection. Some systems provide a "lasso" that allows users to draw a line around all of the shapes to be selected. This defines a region that must be compared against all the shapes to determine which are inside and which are outside. There are also searching techniques such as finding all red lines and selecting them.

11.4.2 General Control Point Dragging Dialog

The interactive syntax that we have defined so far will only select or drag objects. To manipulate the actual object, we need to be able to drag its control points. Consider Figure 11-12. The gray rectangle has been previously selected, which is indicated by the four black control points on the corners of the rectangle. Users can manipulate this rectangle either by dragging it or by dragging one of its control points. Dragging control points is a primary mechanism for manipulating geometric shapes and can be applied to a wide variety of situations.

To allow for the dragging of control points, we must augment our input syntax definition as follows:

```
State { Idle, Selected, DraggingObj, DraggingSelect,
    DraggingControl }
MouseLoc { ?MouseOverObject, ?MouseOverSpace,
    ?MouseOverControl }
Actions {
    !SetStartLoc, !NewSelectObject, !AddSelection,
    !StartSelectRect, !StretchSelectRect, !EndSelectRect,
    !StartDrag, !Drag, !StopDrag,
    !SelectControl,
```
   Makes the control point under the mouse the current control point.
```
    !DragControl,
```
   Moves the control point and modifies the echo for that point's object to reflect the change of that control.
```
    !SetControl
```
   Notifies the model of the new control position.
```
}
```

Using this new state space information, we can add the following rules:

10. `Idle, •MouseDown, ?MouseOverControl ->`
        `!SetStartLoc, !SelectControl, DraggingControl`
11. `DraggingControl, •MouseMove -> !DragControl`
12. `DraggingControl, •MouseUp -> !SetControl, Idle`

With these new rules, a •MouseDown over the upper-right control point of the selected rectangle in Figure 11-12 will cause rule 10 to fire, invoking the !SelectControl action. The view will then start echoing the outline of the rectangle. As •MouseMove events are received, the !DragControl action of rule 11 will be invoked. This will cause the view to update the echo of the rectangle's outline to reflect the new shape indicated by the new control point position. Note that the upper-left, lower-left, and lower-right control points may also be moved because their positions are directly related to the position of the upper-right point. The !DragControl action must perform the following steps:

■ remove the old echo from the screen
■ update the control point
■ update any other control points that are dependent on the control point that was just moved
■ present the new echo on the screen, reflecting the changed shape and control point positions

When the •MouseUp event is finally received, the !SetControl action is fired by rule 12. This causes the echo to be removed and the model to be notified of the new control position. The model must then notify all of the views.

11.5 Transforming Objects

In the previous sections, we have discussed basic creation and manipulation of drawable objects. We have created a variety of manipulations from the simple "mouse down, drag, mouse up" sequence. We differentiated between manipulations based on the objects or on the controls under the initial mouse-down position. In this section, we will look at interactive techniques for performing the basic geometric transformations.

Translation has already been discussed as a dragging operation that moves objects around the screen. Scaling, however, is a little more complicated because not only must the scale factors be expressed interactively but also the center of scaling and the relative axes for scaling must be identified. Rotation has a similar problem in that the center of rotation must be expressed as well as the angle.

When expressing translation as a dragging operation, the user can select a particular point on the object and move that point to some new position. Basing translation on any point on the object is very helpful when the user is trying to align some object with another one. By selecting, for example, a point on the left edge of a rectangle, the user can drag that edge into alignment with some other object.

11.5.1 Transformable Representations of Shapes

Before we discuss the interactive techniques for transformations, we need to consider how we will represent our shapes in the model. A very important consideration is the issue of *closure* under a set of transformations. A shape representation R is closed under a set of transformations T if any sequence of transformations from T will produce a shape that can be represented in R.

Consider, for example, the use of MaxX, MinX, MaxY, MinY as a representation for rectangles. This representation is closed under translation because we just add the translation distances to our representation to get a new representation for the rectangle. This representation is closed under scaling because with two scale factors and a center of scaling, we can compute a new representation using maxima and minima. This representation is even closed when rotations in 90-degree increments are introduced. In Figure 11-13, however, we can see that this representation is not closed under general rotation and the set of rectangles themselves is not closed under rotation and scaling together.

Figure 11-13   Lack of closure under rotation and scaling

Figure 11-14   Closure of ellipses

A similar problem with circles is shown in Figure 11-14. The set of circle shapes is closed under translation and rotation, but not under scaling. The set of ellipses, however, is closed under all combinations of scale, rotate, and translate.

Closure is very important because, given a set of transformations provided to the user, we must correctly handle all of the combinations.

There are two basic ways to deal with transformational closure. The first is to restrict the set of transformations that can be performed. Systems that lay out interactive widgets using their bounding rectangles rarely allow rotations. Without rotation, the maximum/minimum representation for rectangles is closed. For widgets, this is entirely acceptable. The other option is to choose families of shapes that are closed under all of the transformations. Ellipses and polygons fit this criterion.

One possibility is to use transformational matrices and unit shapes as the representation for shapes. Take, for example, a unit square with its lower-left corner at 0.0, 0.0 and its upper-right corner at 1.0, 1.0. This gives a parametric definition of a square. If we form our shape model by combining this square with a transformation matrix, we can represent any rectangular shape. We can transform such a shape by multiplying the transformation matrix times the transformation that defines the shape. By definition, this representation is closed under all transformations. We can draw the shape by transforming the four corners of the square by the transformation matrix and then drawing the resulting polygon. We can select such a shape by multiplying the selection point times the inverse of the transformation and testing to see if the result is between 0.0 and 1.0. If we use a circle centered at the origin with a radius of 1, we can apply the same technique to produce the set of all ellipses.

Figure 11-15   Control point transformations

Some shapes—such as lines, polygons, and splines—are defined completely by their control points. In such cases, a representation that stores the control points will be closed under all of the transformations. We simply transform the control points to produce a new set of control points that defines the new transformed shape of the object.

We must be careful, however, that our control point representation is a true one. Take, for example, the set of circle shapes. We know from high school geometry that three points can define a circle; we can represent a circle using three points from its circumference. Suppose we transform those control points using a scaling in x. The circle defined by the new control points is not the same shape as that obtained by scaling the original circle, as shown in Figure 11-15. Scaling the circle in the x direction should yield the gray ellipse. Scaling the control points only will actually yield the hollow circle. Control points are only a sufficient representation when the underlying shape is closed under the allowed transformations.

11.5.2 Interactive Specification of the Basic Transformations

In using our mouse to specify a transformation of an object, we only have two degrees of freedom to work with (x and y). Some of our transformations have more variables than that. This limited number of variables poses a special interactive problem.

Translation

Specifying a translation is normally done by dragging. In the !StartDrag action, we save the mouse location (Stx, Sty). In the !StopDrag action, we again save the mouse location ($Endx$, $Endy$). The translation of the object is then Translate($Endx - Stx$, $Endy - Sty$). Translations are easy because the number of parameters matches the number of degrees of freedom on the mouse.

Scaling

Remember that the scaling transformation is defined relative to the origin. In most interactive applications, the user has no idea where the origin is. In fact, we don't want the user to know because it is generally not relevant to the

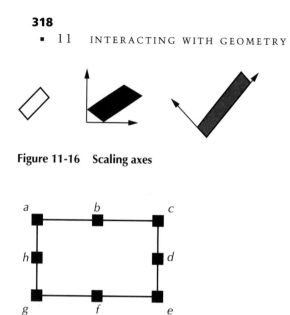

Figure 11-16   Scaling axes

Figure 11-17   Control point scaling rectangle

user's problem. What we need is scaling about points that are part of the object(s) the user is working on. Scaling has four parameters, (Centerx, Centery) and (Scalex, Scaley). Our mouse only has two variables. This means that for any particular interactive manipulation, two of the parameters must be implied rather than directly controlled by the user. Scaling is also complicated by the orientation of the axes. Take, for example, the objects in Figure 11-16. If we scale the white rectangle relative to the *x* axis, we get the black polygon. If, however, we scale the same rectangle along an axis parallel to the long edge of the object, we get the long gray rectangle. This additional information must also be accounted for in expressing a scaling operation.

The Scaling Rectangle   A large number of our scaling operations are defined relative to the *x* and *y* axes. As such, we can use the scaling rectangle as our mechanism for expressing the scaling parameters. The form of the scaling rectangle made popular by the Macintosh is shown in Figure 11-17. It is based on dragging eight control points.

Each control point makes an assumption about what is being scaled and what the scaling origin should be. Each control point implies a particular scale factor to be changed and the center of scaling to be used. The corner controls (*a*, *c*, *e*, and *g*) scale in both *x* and *y*, with the opposite corner as the center of scaling. (Note that the center of scaling will remain fixed.) The edge controls (*b*, *d*, *f*, and *h*) scale in only one dimension, holding the opposite edge fixed. Remember that to scale by (*sx*, *sy*) about a point (*px*, *py*), the transformation is

$$translate(-px, -py) \otimes scale(sx, sy) \otimes translate(px, py)$$

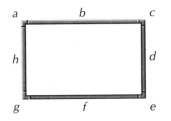

Figure 11-18   Border-scaling rectangle

For a given control point, let p be the point's location before dragging and let p' be the location after dragging. The following equation shows the transformation specified by dragging point a:

$$translate(-eX, -eY) \otimes scale\left(\frac{a'X - eX}{aX - eX}, \frac{a'Y - eY}{aY - eY} \right) \otimes translate(eX, eY)$$

Similar transformations can be created for all of the other corner points.

The next transformation is specified by the dragging of the edge point b:

$$translate(0, -fY) \otimes scale\left(1, \frac{b'Y - fY}{bY - fY} \right) \otimes translate(0, fY)$$

Similar transformations can be created for the other edge points.

Figure 11-18 shows an alternative version of the scaling rectangle—found in some windowing systems—to control the size and shape of windows. In this case, the control points have been replaced by 3D borders. Each border and corner behaves like the corresponding control points in Figure 11-17.

Dragging a Point   An alternative scaling method is to allow a user to drag any point on the object to a new location and to scale the object an appropriate amount to transform the original point to the final point of the drag. This scaling technique requires that the scaling axes and origin be previously defined and usually assumes that the scaling axes are parallel to x and y. The scaling origin is defined either by clicking on the origin point before scaling or by defining some natural origin for the object, such as its center. Assuming that we know the origin point o, the drag start d, and the drag end d', then the transformation is

$$translate(-oX, -oY) \otimes scale\left[\frac{d'X - oX}{dX - oX}, \frac{d'Y - oY}{dY - oY} \right] \otimes translate(oX, oY)$$

Interactively, this technique has a problem in that it clashes with the normal dragging operations for translating an object. In terms of input events, there is no distinguishing difference between dragging to translate and dragging to scale. With the scaling rectangle, we recognized a scaling operation

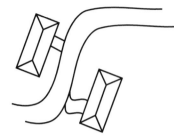

Figure 11-19 Example of a drawing that is not aligned with the *x* and *y* axes

when the •MouseDown occurred over a control point. Without the control points of the scaling rectangle, we cannot make such a distinction. We can resolve this problem in two ways. The first is to add a "scaling mode" to the application, which would involve changing the State field of our controller to

```
State {Idle, Selected, DraggingObj, DraggingSelect,
       DraggingControl, ScalingObj }
```

We would need to add additional screen buttons, menu items, or special keys to set the State to ScalingObj. With this additional state, we can add rules such as

```
ScalingObj, •MouseMove -> !Scale
ScalingObj, •MouseUp -> !StopScale, Idle
```

The other way to handle the specification of scaling is to use a different mouse button when dragging to scale as opposed to dragging to translate.

Scaling Relative to Other Axes   All of our scaling operations so far have been parallel to the *x* and *y* axes, which is by far the most common technique for interactive scaling but not the only one required. Frequently, objects have been rotated, and a user may want to scale an object relative to its own natural axes rather than *x* and *y*. Take, for example, the housing subdivision shown in Figure 11-19. This neighborhood does not have streets aligned with north, south, east, and west. Houses are placed relative to the streets rather than relative to the compass. If we want to change the size of one of these houses, we want to do so relative to the street, not *x* and *y*.

One approach to such scaling is to use a scaling rectangle that has been aligned with the object's axes. Such a rotated rectangle is shown in Figure 11-20. The rotated scaling rectangle gives us the handles we need to perform scaling relative to a different set of axes. We still need to develop the correct transformation. The problem is that the scaling matrix is defined relative to *x* and *y*. To resolve this, we need to transform our problem to the *x*, *y* axes, scale it, and then put it back where it was. As an example of how to do this, let's

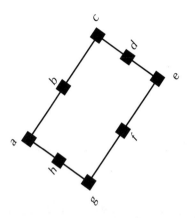

Figure 11-20   Rotated scaling rectangle

consider the case where the user is dragging point c in Figure 11-20. In this case, point g should be the origin for scaling and should remain fixed. We can compute the total transformation using the following technique:

1. Translate point g to the origin:
   translate$(-gX, -gY)$
2. Rotate the line e-g down to the x axis. Note that this is a negative rotation. We can compute the rotation angle from its tangent, as follows:

   $$R = \tan^{-1}\left[\frac{eY - gY}{eX - gX}\right]$$

   rotate(R)
3. We now want to compute the scale factors from c and c'. The problem is that after the translation and the rotation, the scaling is computed in a completely different coordinate system from the one that c and c' were defined in. We must compute new points t and t', from which we can compute our scaling matrix:

   $t = c \otimes translate(-gX, -gY) \otimes rotate(R)$
   $t' = c' \otimes translate(-gX, -gY) \otimes rotate(R)$

   $$scale\left[\frac{t'}{t}\right]$$

4. Undo the rotation:
   rotate$(-R)$
5. Undo the translation:
   translate(gX, gY)

The entire transformation matrix for dragging point c to scale that corner is

$$translate(-gX, -gY) \otimes rotate(R)$$

$$\otimes scale\left[\frac{c' \otimes translate(-gX, -gY) \otimes rotate(R)}{c \otimes translate(-gX, -gY) \otimes rotate(R)}\right]$$

$$\otimes rotate(-R) \otimes translate(gX, gY)$$

Similar transformations can be developed for the other corner and edge points in the rotated scaling rectangle.

Rotation

Rotation has similar problems to scaling in that it must be performed around some center point. Rotation, however, need not be concerned about where the axes are. As with scaling, we can ask the user to click on a point for the center of rotation and then to drag some other point to the desired rotation angle. We can also assume rotation about the center of the object. Regardless of how we acquire the points from the user, we must have an origin o, a starting drag point d, and an ending drag point d'. To compute the rotation, we rotate about o to put d on the x axis and then rotate the x axis back to d', as follows:

$$translate(-oX, -oY) \otimes rotate\left(-\tan^{-1}\left[\frac{dY - oY}{dX - oX}\right]\right)$$

$$\otimes rotate\left(\tan^{-1}\left[\frac{d'Y - oY}{d'X - oX}\right]\right) \otimes translate(oX, oY)$$

Note that our mouse has two degrees of freedom and our rotation only has one. We can exploit this by also providing uniform scaling in addition to the rotation. Uniform scaling is where the scale factors for both x and y are the same. Uniform scaling requires only one scale factor and is independent of the axes. To compute our scale factor, we can use the ratio of the distances between the drag points and the drag origin. The resulting transformation would be as follows:

$$translate(-oX, -oY) \otimes rotate\left(-\tan^{-1}\left[\frac{dY - oY}{dX - oX}\right]\right)$$

$$\otimes scale\left[\frac{\sqrt{(d'X - oX)^2 + (d'Y - oY)^2}}{\sqrt{(dX - oX)^2 + (dY - oY)^2}}\right]$$

$$\otimes \ rotate(\tan^{-1}\left(\frac{d'Y - oY}{d'X - oX}\right)) \otimes translate(oX, oY)$$

11.5.3 Snapping

The interactive techniques discussed above are based on the dragging of points to particular positions with the mouse. A problem arises, however, that with modern displays, mice, and ordinary people it is very difficult for a user to position the mouse with total accuracy. It can be done but it is very time consuming. This can be alleviated with a technique called *snapping,* in which the program will round the actual mouse position to some more appropriate position. These snapping operations can take several forms.

The simplest form of snapping is to a grid. The resolution, or distance between grid points, can vary. If we assume an integer coordinate system where the grid resolution is g pixels, then for a mouse point (mX, mY) the drag position actually used is

$$dX = floor\left(\left\lfloor\frac{mX + \frac{g}{2}}{g}\right\rfloor\right) \cdot g$$

$$dY = floor\left(\left\lfloor\frac{mY + \frac{g}{2}}{g}\right\rfloor\right) \cdot g$$

The above equations must be in integer arithmetic. This rounding to a grid technique makes it much easier to align points with each other because fine-hand accuracy is not required to get the same point. This same technique can be used when rotating. The rotation angle can be snapped to a resolution of 15-degree increments. Rotating to standard angles with some accuracy becomes very easy.

The advantage of using rounding for our snapping technique is that it is easy to calculate and it solves a variety of interactive alignment problems. There are, however, a number of alignment problems that it will not solve. Take, for example, the drawing of a house shown in Figure 11-21. Notice that the bottom corners and the top of the chimney all connect quite cleanly. All of the connections to the slanting roof, however, miss. The problem is that the intersection point between the left wall and the roof does not lie on one of the grid points. What the user really wants is for the wall point to snap to the roof line rather than to some arbitrary grid.

Figure 11-21   House drawn to a grid

Such snapping can be done using the formulas for distance to a line and nearest point on the line that were discussed in Chapter 9. The technique consists of checking the distance from a point to an object. If the distance is less than some threshold (say, 3 pixels), then we compute the nearest point on the object and replace the mouse point with that nearest point. Such a snapping mechanism is sometimes called a "gravity field" because it creates an area around an object such that any point inside that area is drawn to the object.

The drawback of such gravity fields is their cost of computation. To be effective, such computations must be completed within 1/5 of a second so that the dragging operation feels continuous to the user. What is required is that the mouse point be compared to all objects in the drawing within that 1/5 of a second. On a large drawing, this can become costly. The first speed improvement is to check the mouse point against the bounding box for an object; the bounding-box check can eliminate most of the costly nearest-point calculations. Snapping speed can be further improved by various caching schemes. For example, in very large drawings the application can maintain a list of those objects that are currently visible in the window. This list can substantially cut down the number of objects to be checked. A further approach would be to divide the window into large rectangular "buckets" and to maintain a list of those objects that intersect each bucket. It is then easy to determine which bucket the mouse point is in and to check the point against only the objects in that bucket.

11.6 Grouping Objects

One of the great powers of using a computer to create images is the ability to group objects together to form larger objects. In most drawing systems, grouping is done by selecting several objects and then invoking a Group command. The Group command takes the individual objects and assembles them into a single composite object that can then be manipulated as if it were a whole object unto itself. Any good system also has an Ungroup command that will take the group apart, leaving the individual objects in place. Note that groups can themselves be members of larger groups. This forms a tree of objects as the model, instead of just a flat list. As an example, the drawing in Figure

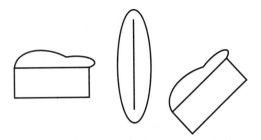

Figure 11-22   Drawing with grouped objects

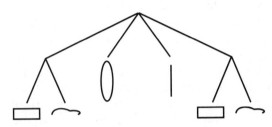

Figure 11-23   Drawing model from Figure 11-22 as a tree

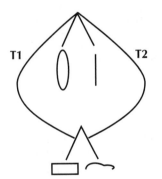

Figure 11-24   Drawing model from Figure 11-22 as a DAG

11-22 is represented by the tree in Figure 11-23. Note, however, that it may also be represented by the directed acyclic graph (DAG) in Figure 11-24.

One group in Figure 11-22 has been used twice in the same drawing. The difference between the two instances of the group is a translation and a rotation. To create the model in Figure 11-23, the first group is copied and then transformed. In such models, the transformation is applied to all objects in the group to create a new set of transformed objects that make up the group. This is the way that most drawing programs handle groups. However, many

CAD/CAM systems provide a model/instance mechanism for handling groups. In such a system, the group is not copied but a new instance is created. The difference between the two instances is defined by their two instance transformations **T1** and **T2** (Figure 11-24). Given that the left instance was drawn first and then grouped, **T1** might be the identity matrix. Transformation **T2** would then be a matrix formed from the concatenation of translation and rotation matrices.

There are two benefits from using model/instance as the grouping mechanism. The first is the savings in space from not duplicating the group objects. The second is that the group objects themselves can be edited, which will then change all instances of the group. For example, the rectangle could be changed to gray; this would make both instances gray automatically.

Note that in a DAG or model/instance design, when the rectangle is changed to gray the areas around all instances must be damaged to provide a correct redraw. In the tree model, each changed object appears in only one place on the screen; the transformations are applied to the objects one at a time, the group is transformed, and then the member objects are saved in their transformed states. There is no explicit storage of the transformation. All of this makes the redraw and the model much simpler because there are no transformations involved.

When a model is transformed to create a new instance in the DAG approach, the transformation must be stored. The redraw method must transform the model using the appropriate instance transformation each time an instance is to be drawn. In the case of groups within groups, these transformations must be concatenated together, as described in Chapter 10, Geometric Transformations.

11.6.1 Selection in a Hierarchical Model

The first interactive behavior that we need for a group is to select the group. A group is selected by a mouse point if the mouse position is over one of the objects in the group. An important optimization of the selection process is to compute and store a bounding rectangle for the entire group. This rectangle is computed as the maxima and minima in x and y of the bounding rectangles for all objects in the group. If the mouse location does not fall within the bounding rectangle, then the group cannot be selected and can be ignored. Since a given mouse point is usually outside of the vast majority of objects on the screen, discarding whole groups without checking their member objects can greatly speed the selection process. If the point is inside, then the objects in the group are checked for selection in front-to-back order, taking the first one found. If a group is encountered, the group-selection algorithm is applied recursively.

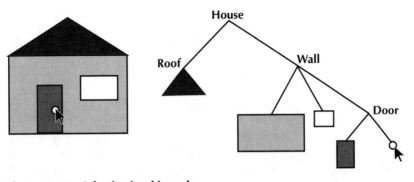

Figure 11-25   Selection in a hierarchy

If groups are represented as trees, the selection process is performed in world coordinates for the entire drawing, because all group members were transformed into world coordinates at the time the group was transformed by the user. In the DAG model, however, the selection point must be transformed by the inverse of the instance-transformation matrix. This brings the selection point into model coordinates, where it can be compared against each member. In our example, selection for the two instances is performed on the same objects in the same model coordinates but with different selection points, each transformed from the original selection point but with different instance transformations.

11.6.2 Level of Interaction in a Hierarchy

When a model is represented as a tree or a DAG, the user is faced with the problem of how to interact with the members of a group when necessary. Many drawing packages that use the tree model simply do not allow interaction with group members. If the user wants to change the members of a group, the group must be ungrouped, the members edited, and the group reformed. This approach greatly simplifies building the user interface because most of the drawing package's editing mechanism can ignore group members. In more advanced drawing packages and in DAG-based systems, the user must be able to interact with members of the group.

The first problem when we are interacting with members of a hierarchical group is to decide what a user is actually working on. Consider the drawing in Figure 11-25. The mouse pointer is over the door knob, but it is not clear whether the user is interacting with the knob, the door, the front wall, or the house as a whole. The mouse position could be interpreted as pointing at any of these. What we need is an interactive means for clarifying this selection.

One strategy is to support the notion of a group being "open" or "closed." Suppose that the user wanted to interact with the knob. Pointing at the house would select that group. Double-clicking, or some other interactive mechanism to indicate that a group should be opened, would open the group so that the user could interact with the group members; the members (roof and wall) would now be available for interaction directly. The fact that the house group is open must be visually indicated; this is frequently done by putting up a special border around the group's bounding box. Selecting any point that is not part of the group will close the group and it again will be treated as a complete whole. In Figure 11-25, we could open the wall group by double-clicking on one of its members. At this point, the roof, wall rectangle, window, and door are available for interaction. Note that the house is still open with the roof available. Selection of the roof, however, would close the wall group. If, instead, we double-click on the door, its members become available and we can now move the knob to a new position.

An alternative to the group open and close strategy is to use a selection reject key or button. When the user clicks on the doorknob, the house is highlighted. By hitting the reject key, the system will try another selection from the same point, such as highlighting the front wall. A second reject will highlight the door and a third reject will highlight the knob. The advantage of this mechanism is that it takes many fewer events to reach the knob that the user wanted to move.

11.7 Summary

In this chapter, we have taken the basic graphical geometry and transformations and described how a user can use them to interact with a variety of geometric objects. The techniques described are representative of the most common approaches; however, there are many variations to be found in existing applications. It is important to note that these concepts do not apply only to drawing programs. These techniques are used in CAD/CAM systems for machine, chip, or airframe design; flow charts; organizational charts; flow diagrams; control systems design; and user interface layout tools. The same fundamental mechanisms are used in a variety of situations; the primary difference among them is that instead of circles and rectangles, the primitive objects might be tasks, bolts, memory chips, or scroll bars. In interacting with such world-based objects, the techniques are built from the geometric objects that visually represent them.

We have discussed basic interaction techniques for creating objects whose geometry can be represented by control points. In working with the scaling rectangle, we saw that dragging a particular control point not only expresses a change in geometry but also can specify which part of the geometry is being manipulated by the user. In many systems, there are a variety of control point forms, each of which causes a different behavior when the user drags it. Such handles on the geometry give the user a direct way to grab and change objects on the screen.

We have also examined ways for the user to interactively express the basic geometric transformations that form the foundation for most drawings. By combinations of these techniques, the user can express a wide range of object manipulations.

Finally, we discussed interacting with objects that are modeled as composites of simpler objects. Of particular importance is the transformation of mouse positions created by a user into the coordinates in which the model is defined. This is essential for correct interaction in the presence of geometric transformations.

12

Drawing Architectures

In previous chapters, we studied the geometry of individual shapes as well as a basic set of linear transformations that can be used to manipulate geometry. We also studied how to express interactive behavior in production systems. The model-view-controller architecture gives us a framework for constructing user interface software. In this chapter, we will look at how all of these pieces can be brought together into a complete application.

The software architecture concepts described here are not restricted to drawings alone. Similar concepts can be used in a variety of situations where collections of individual objects are being manipulated on a 2D surface. A prime example of this architecture is the basic drawing application shown in Figure 12-1. The same architecture used for the drawing application can also be used for the circuit-layout application in Figure 12-2, the PERT chart editor in Figure 12-3, and the user interface layout editor in Figure 12-4. All share the same palette of objects to create, area to lay out the objects, and palettes of object attributes that can be changed. In addition, some of the objects have text that can be typed into them and various ways in which they can be manipulated.

12.1 Basic Drawing Interface

Before discussing the software architecture, an overview of the interactive behavior of these interfaces is in order. There are a number of basic things that every such interface must support. It must be possible to

■ create new objects of several primitive types
■ select one or more objects so that other commands can be applied to them

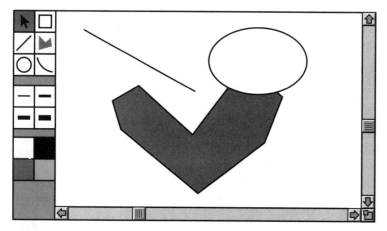

Figure 12-1   A drawing application

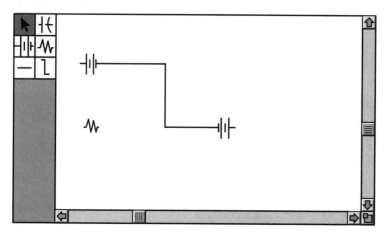

Figure 12-2   Circuit layout

- delete objects
- change the attributes of some objects
- transform objects
- assemble objects into groups

Objects are created by selecting the type of object from the palette and then drawing such an object in the drawing area. There are various ways in which the interface will echo the object being drawn. The interactive technique for drawing is almost always defined by a single •MouseDown, •MouseMoves, •MouseUp sequence or by clicking on a series of points to define all the control points of the object. Once objects have been created, most operations on

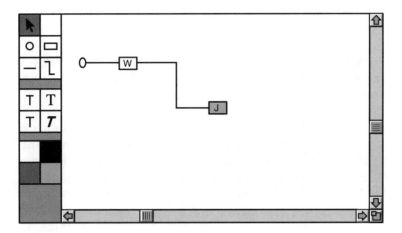

Figure 12-3   PERT chart editor

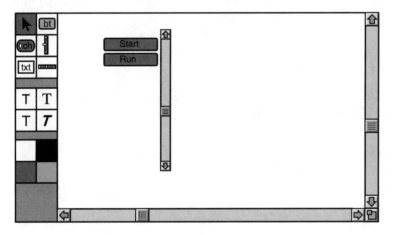

Figure 12-4   User interface layout editor

those objects are defined in terms of a selected set of objects. Usually only one object is selected, but in good interfaces it is possible to select several by using the interactive dialog discussed in earlier chapters. To differentiate between object creation and object selection, the objects palette almost always contains a selection icon to indicate that the user is selecting rather than creating.

Once a set of selected objects has been defined by a user, various commands can be applied to those objects. An important command is to delete all objects in the selected set. Another very frequent set of commands is to change some attributes of the selected objects. For example, one might select the "Start" button in Figure 12-4 and then click on the white area in the background color palette to change the color of the button.

One of the key functions that the interface must perform is to echo to the user the current attributes of the objects in the selected set. Suppose in Figure 12-1 that both the polygon and the circle have been selected by the user. In this case, the very skinny line icon is highlighted because both objects share that attribute value. There is no fill color icon selected, however, because there is no consensus among the selected objects as to what the value of that attribute should be.

Transforming the objects is usually done by selecting an object or set of objects and then specifying through a menu or button that some transformation is to be performed. While in this special transformation mode, the cursor is typically changed to reflect the alternative mode and the mouse events are interpreted by the transformation dialog rather than by the normal selection or creation dialogs.

Grouping is usually done by a pair of commands Group and Ungroup. The Group command will take the set of selected objects and form them into a single group object. The Ungroup command will take all selected groups and break them apart into their component objects.

12.2 Interface Architecture

The architectural model that is being used here is a variant of that developed by McNeill et al.[1] The drawing interface architecture consists of six main components:

1. drawing or work area
2. primitive drawing objects
3. selected set of objects
4. object palette
5. attribute palettes
6. commands to perform

The primary component is the drawing or work area. Within this area, a set of primitive objects is laid out. These primitive components are the raw material that the drawing is built from. Careful examination of Figures 12-1 through 12-4 shows that the primary differences in these applications are the set of primitive objects that things are built from.

In all of the examples shown above, the objects are laid out on a 2D plane. The drawing or work area need not simulate a piece of paper, as these examples show. The Macintosh finder view shown in Figure 12-5 shows the primitive objects (files and folders) laid out in a tree. Other applications may use lists or tables for their layout. Regardless of the layout mechanism used, the

Figure 12-5   Finder tree layout

drawing or work area consists of a space for interacting with a set of primitive objects or groups of objects.

A key component of the architecture is the currently selected set. This is simply a list of those objects from the drawing model that are currently selected. Many of the interface commands are defined to operate on this set of objects.

The final three components are types of palettes. There is a palette of primitive objects from which to create drawings. There are palettes of attributes that can be set on objects. Finally, there are palettes of commands or actions that can be performed on the currently selected set of objects. These palettes can be represented as sets of icons (as shown in our examples), as menus, or possibly they can be bound to particular keyboard buttons. The interactive technique used to select from a palette is not as important as the fact that such sets of selections exist, with each being handled in a different way.

In discussing this architecture for general drawing applications, we will first cover the model, view, and controller organizations and how they relate to the components of the drawing architecture. We will then look at the set of interactive tasks that must be supported and show how each is integrated into the architecture.

12.2.1 **Draw-Area Architecture**

In designing an architecture for the draw area, we want some general concepts for creating and manipulating objects that are relatively independent of the set of objects that can be created. The reason for this need for independence is that future versions of our program will likely add new types of objects. In addition, we want general concepts that we can apply to a variety of applications. Note that this drawing area is the primary display of the model. This is substantially different from the concept of a Canvas, which is the interface of a view to the underlying graphics system.

Draw Area

Our basic model for the draw area is a list of objects in back-to-front order. The objects belong to an abstract class, DrawObj, that defines the interface between the draw-area view/controller and the objects in the model. This abstract class allows a variety of object types to be used in the model without modifying the view/controller for the draw area. The applications shown in Figure 12-1 through 12-4 all use the same draw-area class because they all lay out objects in the same way. The differences between these applications are found in the subclasses of DrawObj. In Figure 12-1, the subclasses are Line, Circle, Arc, Rectangle, and Polygon while in Figure 12-4, they are Button, RadioBox, VScrollBar, HScrollBar, and TextBox. The functioning of the drawing area only depends on the interface defined by the abstract class DrawObj.

By ordering the objects in back-to-front order, we can draw the objects in the order that they appear in the list. This allows the frontmost objects to overlay the ones behind. If our application supports grouping, we can define groups as a subclass of DrawObj. This subclass can handle the issues of selecting and drawing the elements of the group. Thus our drawing model continues to look like a simple list of objects.

The model for the drawing would be as follows:

```
class Drawing: public Model
  {
  List of DrawObj objs;
    These are the objects in the model.
  List of DrawObj selectedSet;
    These are the objects in the currently selected set.
  void Select(DrawObj * selectedObj);
    Adds the specified object to the selected set.
  void UnSelect(DrawObj * selectedObj);
    Removes the object from the selected set.
  void UnselectAll();
    Removes all objects from the selected set.
```

```
void AddObj(DrawObj newObj);
```
Adds a new object to the model at the end (front).
```
void DeleteSelected();
```
Deletes all objects in the selected set from the model.
```
void SelectedToFront();
```
Moves all selected objects to the end (front) of the list.
```
void SelectedToBack();
```
Moves all selected objects to the start (back) of the list.
```
void ChangeObj(DrawObj * Obj);
```
Notifies all views that a particular object has changed or is going to be changed.
```
}
```

The Drawing class is a subclass of Model. We can assume that the Model class from Chapter 5 defines the methods for registering views and for notifying all of the registered views of any changes. In conjunction with such notification, the Drawing class defines the ChangeObj method, which will use the standard notification mechanism in Model to notify all views that a particular object is going to change or has changed.

The Drawing class contains a list of all objects in the model and a list of objects in the selected set. We will assume that the List class has the appropriate methods for managing the list and for allowing access to all of the items in the list in back-to-front order. How the List class is implemented is not particularly important here. The Drawing class has the Select, UnSelect, and UnSelectAll methods for handling selectedness; the AddObj and DeleteSelected methods for adding and deleting objects; and the SelectedToFront and SelectedToBack methods for managing the ordering of the objects in the list. Note that most manipulation of the objects in the model is done through the selected set. Also note that there are no methods on the model for changing the objects in any way. These methods are defined on the class DrawObj because they will be different for each type of object.

In addition to the Drawing model class, we must define a DrawView class that implements the view and the controller for the drawing as a whole. For the example applications in Figures 12-1 to 12-4, this DrawView class and the Drawing model can remain the same; the only differences are the set of objects in the drawing. For the example in Figure 12-5, a TreeView class might be the view/controller because objects in the model are laid out using much different geometry than in the drawing views. The model would remain unchanged. Retaining the same model would allow a drawing to be viewed both in the 2D layout form and in the tree form. This is exactly what is done in file systems like the Macintosh finder or Windows 95. The file system model is the same but multiple views are provided.

Drawing Objects

In considering the objects that make up our drawing, we must discuss both the models for these objects and their view/controllers. For every type of object in the drawing, we must provide a view/controller. The reasons for this are that not all objects are drawn in the same way, selected in the same way, or manipulated in the same way. We don't want to put this code in the DrawView class because it really relates to the individual object types.

Drawing Object Model   There are several general manipulations that can be defined for all objects, but they vary so widely in how they may be stored and how we may interact with them that we can really say very little about the class DrawObj other than that it can be created, destroyed, set, and that it can return its attributes and identify its type. We can define the abstract class DrawObj as follows:

```
class DrawObj
  {
  ObjTypeId ObjectType();
```
> *Returns an identifier of the type of drawing object that this one is.*
```
  DrawObj Copy();
```
> *Makes a new copy of this object.*
```
  void * GetAttribute(Id attributeId);
```
> *Returns the value of the specified attribute. If there is no such attribute, a NULL pointer is returned.*
```
  void SetAttribute(Id attributeId, void * attributeValue);
```
> *Sets the value of an attribute.*
```
  boolean isSelected;
```
> *This is true if the object is currently selected.*
```
  }
```

In keeping with the C++ design, we also assume that subclasses of DrawObj will define constructors and destructors to correctly create and delete objects. The Copy method will duplicate the object, for reasons that will be discussed later. The getting and setting of attributes will provide the general mechanism required by our attribute palettes. The set of attributes may change, but the general notion of manipulating the attributes of an object is common to all objects. In most applications, there are attributes such as color, line thickness, or font that are shared by a lot of the objects and thus should be handled in a common fashion. The ObjTypeId will vary among implementations. In some implementations, an integer is used; in others, a 4-byte code is used that uniquely identifies the type of attribute, or perhaps a string name is used.

The IsSelected field works in conjunction with the selectedSet field of the drawing. When redrawing objects, it is important to know if they are selected or not; this field provides that information. The methods on Drawing that manipulate the selectedSet must also manipulate this field on the objects to keep them consistent. The reason that we maintain the selectedSet field is that in large drawings it is very costly to search all objects for the one or two that have IsSelected turned on.

A given application will make subclasses of DrawObj for each type of object in the application. Such subclasses will add the additional information needed for such objects. For example, a Line subclass might have the following definition:

```
class LineObj : public DrawObj
  {
  ObjTypeId objectType() { return LINE_TYPE; }

  Point startPoint,endPoint;
  int thickness;
  RGB color;

  void * GetAttribute(Id attributeId);
  void SetAttribute(Id attributeId, void * attributeValue);
  }
```

Note that the model object class LineObj defines the information that must be saved about a line and the methods to set that information. The GetAttribute method will use the attributeId to decide whether to return thickness, color, or NULL (in the case of some attribute like Font that a line does not possess). The SetAttribute method will similarly use the attributeId to decide which field is to be set, if any.

Drawing Object Views   The remaining problem is that our general DrawView class does not know how to interact with anything but DrawObj so as to maintain its generality. DrawObj, however, provides little information about its various subclasses. What is needed is a view/controller implementation for each class of drawing object. Each such view/controller will know exactly how to interact with its own type of drawing object. We therefore define the DrawObjView abstract class, which defines how the view/controllers for individual object types interface with the generic DrawView class to provide our complete architecture. The DrawObjView class might be defined as follows:

```
class DrawObjView
  {
  DrawObj * myModelObj;
```
The model object for which this is a view/controller.
```
  void Redraw(Region DamagedRegion);
```
Draws the object if it is in the damaged region.
```
  Rect BoundingRect();
```
Returns the bounding rectangle for the object.
```
  int Ncontrols();
```
Returns the number of control points for this object.
```
  Point GetControl(int pointIdx);
```
Returns the value of one of the control points.
```
  void SetControl(int pointIdx, Point newPoint);
```
Sets the control point to a new value.
```
  void StartControlDrag(int pointIdx, Point selectionPoint);
  void MoveControl(int pointIdx, Point movePoint);
  void EndControlDrag(int pointIdx, Point endPoint);
  void StartCreationEcho(Point downPoint);
```
This will begin echoing the creation of the object where downPoint is the first point for the object.
```
  void MoveCreationEcho(Point movePoint);
```
This will echo the changing of the mouse while creating an object.
```
  void SetCreationPoint(Point newPoint);
```
This will add a control point to the object.
```
  boolean LastCreationPoint(Point newPoint);
```
Returns true if the new point will be the last creation point for this object.
```
  boolean IsHit(Point selectionPoint);
```
Will return true if the selectionPoint hits or closely hits this object.
```
  void StartObjDrag (Point selectionPoint);
  void MoveObj(Point movePoint);
  void EndObjDrag(Point endPoint);
  }
```

These methods provide the general mechanisms for drawing objects in a way that is consistent with the type of object. The BoundingRect method will compute from the model object fields the geometric bounds for the entire object.

There are six methods to handle control points. The first three provide the generic interface for setting and getting the control points. The second three are for dragging the control points. These methods for dragging control points must set up an echo that is appropriate to the object type and manage that echo on the screen while the control point is being made. For example, if the object is the LineObjView class, there will be two control points (one for each end). If the user selects one of these control points, the Drawing will notify the LineObjView by means of the StartControlDrag method. The Line-ObjView must echo a rubber band line for each call to MoveControl and then modify the model and remove the echo when EndControlDrag is called. Similarly, the three methods StartObjDrag, MoveObj, and EndObjDrag must handle the dragging of the entire object.

The four methods StartCreationEcho, MoveCreationEcho, SetCreation-Point, and LastCreationPoint must handle the creation of new objects. The problem here is that most objects require two points—•MouseDown and •MouseUp—while objects like polygons and splines require multiple points. These four methods provide a generic interface that can implement any creation mechanism. We will show later how the DrawView class can use these.

A most important method is the IsHit method. IsHit is our method for selecting objects. This method contains the selection geometry for a particular class of object. IsHit is where the geometric techniques from Chapter 9 are implemented.

Binding of Object Views to Object Models   For every object in a drawing, there must be a model object stored in a Drawing. The problem, however, is that we do not want to create a view object for every model object. This view-per-object approach can result in a tremendous space overhead. Instead, we add a TypeViewTable to our DrawView. This TypeViewTable is indexed by ObjTypeId and will return a DrawObjView of the appropriate type for that model object. The simplest form of this is to define ObjTypeId as a sequence of integers and then to use an array for our TypeViewTable.

When we have a DrawObj object that we wish to interactively manipulate, we can get its type by invoking its objectType method. We use this type to index our TypeViewTable to find the appropriate DrawObjView to use with this object. We then put the object into the myModelObj field of the view. We now have a view pointing to the correct model object and we can interact with that object through the view. This architecture greatly reduces the amount of space required for our drawings. This can all be simplified by adding the following method:

```
DrawObjView * DrawView::GetObjView(DrawObj * modelObj);
```
   Returns a view bound to modelObj that is consistent with model-Obj's type.

12.2.2 Palette Architecture

The architecture for palettes is much simpler than the draw area because their purpose is to make simple choices. Each palette has its own MVC structure. There are three fundamental kinds of palette in our drawing architecture. They are the object palette from which objects to be created are selected, the attribute palettes from which attribute values are selected and changes are made to objects, and the action palettes from which the user can select things to be done.

Object Palette

Let us first consider the object palette. The object palette provides a mechanism for specifying the kind of object to be created when the user performs mouse actions inside the draw area. The interactive mechanism for such a palette can vary widely. Many applications use the set of icons shown in our examples. Other applications have special windows with icons that can be moved around so as to be close to the work area. (Such a palette can also be represented by a pull-down menu.) In some applications, the palette selections are bound to function keys so that they can be selected from the keyboard. The interactive technique for making such selections is not relevant to our architecture. What is important is that a prototype object of the kind the user wants to create can be selected and placed where the draw area can find it. The model for this palette is a prototype object for the currently selected object type. For example, if the user has selected a polygon to be created, then the selected prototype will contain a polygon object.

The relationship between the object palette and the draw area is shown in Figure 12-6. Making a selection in the object palette will set the prototype. The draw area then uses the selected prototype to control what it should do. If the user selects the special selection object ▶ , then the prototype is set to empty and the draw area knows that selection is to be performed. Note that each button in the palette has an active and an inactive state. Each button also has a prototype object associated with it. When a button is selected, it sets its own prototype to be the selected prototype. For each button, if the selected prototype is the same as its own prototype, then the button is active; otherwise the button sets itself to inactive. This highlighting requires that the selected prototype (a model) notify all of the buttons (its views) whenever it changes so that they can update their active/inactive status.

Attribute Palettes

The second kind of palette controls attributes of objects. In Figure 12-6, such palettes are represented by the line-thickness and area-fill palettes. There are actually two ways of handling the setting of attributes. The first, as shown in Figure 12-6, is to display an icon or other selection for each value of

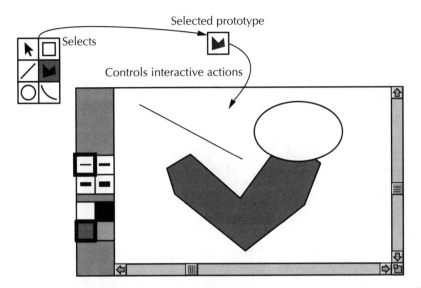

Figure 12-6   Object palette and draw area

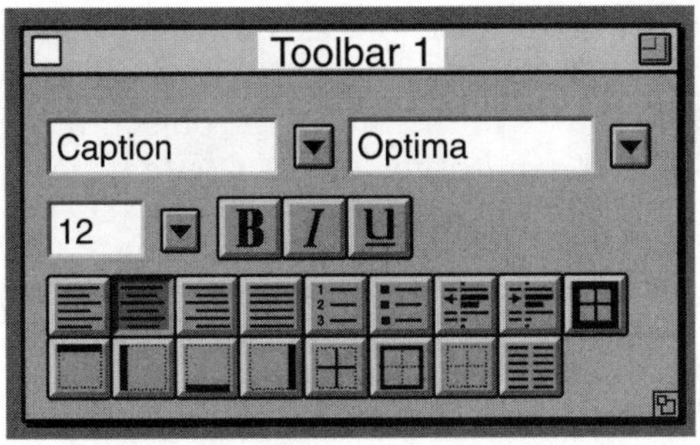

Figure 12-7   An attribute palette window

an attribute. For example, the line-thickness attribute has icons for thicknesses of 1–4 pixels. The area-fill attribute has icons for each of the fill patterns. In many cases, however, there are too many choices. For example, font sizes generally can range from 4 to 72 points. Many systems provide selections for the common sizes along with some widget, such as a type-in box, for the user to specify the exact size desired. Figure 12-7 shows a Microsoft Word tool bar window full of attribute icons for text editing. For purposes of this discussion, we will only cover simple selection of attributes. The techniques described here can be extended to other mechanisms for specifying attribute values.

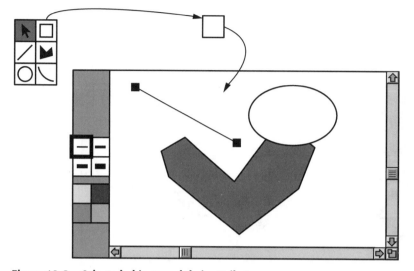

Figure 12-8   Selected objects and their attributes

There are two situations in which attributes must be settable. The first is where a prototype object has been selected for creation, as shown in Figure 12-6. In this situation, the line thickness of 1 pixel and fill pattern of half gray are highlighted because these are the attributes of the prototype object. If the user were to select the black fill attribute, the prototype object would have its area-fill attribute set to black. When a new object is created by the draw area, it copies the prototype object, including all of the current attribute settings for that object. Thus, in the situation shown in Figure 12-6, a new gray polygon will be created by the draw area when the user so specifies.

The other situation that the attribute palettes must handle is shown in Figure 12-8. In this case, the selected object is not a prototype object—there is none—but one of the objects in the drawing. The 1-pixel line-thickness attribute is highlighted because the selected line has that attribute. The area-fill icons are all disabled (grayed out and nonresponsive) because there is no area-fill attribute on lines.

When the prototype selection is empty, the attributes draw their values from the selected set of objects in the drawing model. The attribute palettes must also account for cases in which there is more than one object selected and in which the objects may be of differing types. The rules for attribute icon behavior are as follows:

1. If the prototype object, or selected set, contains at least one object that can accept the attribute to be represented by this icon, then this icon should be enabled. Otherwise it is disabled.

2. If the prototype object, or selected set, contains objects that all have this same attribute value, then this attribute icon should be in the active state (highlighted). Otherwise it is inactive.
3. If this attribute icon is enabled and the user selects it, then all objects in the prototype or selected set that can accept this attribute value should be set to the value associated with this icon.

If we give every attribute icon an identifier and an attribute value, then it is relatively easy to write view/controller code for such icons that implements the above three rules. In fact, the only differences among all such icons are the actual pictures shown in the icon, the attribute identifier, and the attribute value. All other code is the same. In addition, these icons must be registered as views of both the selected prototype object and the drawing model. Whenever the prototype object changes, the attribute icons must update themselves. This also must occur whenever the selected set for the drawing changes.

Action Palettes

Action palettes contain interactive techniques that are tied to commands to be executed. Such palettes consist of buttons or menu items that have code bound to them to perform actions such as to delete all selected objects, to rotate all objects 90 degrees to the right, or to paste objects from the paste buffer into the drawing. Generally, these are handled in the manner described in Chapters 6 and 7 on widgets.

12.2.3 Summary of Architecture

Our basic architecture consists of the drawing model, the drawing view, and the palettes. The Drawing model class is primarily a list of drawing objects along with a selected set of drawing objects. All of the drawing objects contained in a Drawing are subclasses of DrawObj, which defines the generic interface between the drawing objects and most of the rest of the architecture. Corresponding to the Drawing model class is the DrawView class that implements the view/controller. For each subclass of DrawObj, there is also a subclass of DrawObjView, which provides the view interface to that class of object. DrawObjView provides the interactive interface used by DrawView.

To prevent the creation of a view object for every draw object, we create a TypeViewTable, which maps a type of object to the correct view for that object. We can then attach a view to any draw object that we want to interact with, at the time of interaction.

The behavior of the draw area view is determined by the current prototype object, which is controlled by the object palette. The object palette and the current prototype object form their own MVC system.

The attribute palettes are controlled by the current prototype object, or by the selected set of objects if there is no current prototype. The attribute palettes use the set of attribute values and the set of possible attributes from the selected set to determine which items are active or inactive and enabled or disabled. Selection of palette items will either change the current prototype, and thus change the nature of newly created objects, or will change objects in the selected set.

12.3 Tasks

With our general architecture in mind, we can now address the set of interactive tasks that this architecture must support. A list of such tasks is as follows:

- redrawing
- creating a new object
- selecting objects
- dragging objects
- setting attributes on objects
- setting palette object attributes
- manipulating control points

12.3.1 Redrawing

A most important function of DrawView is to redraw the model whenever necessary. In general, the algorithm is quite straightforward:

```
For each draw object DO in the model list in back to front order
  {
  DOV = GetObjView(DO);
  If (DOV.BoundingRect() intersects DamagedRegion)
    { DOV.Redraw(DamagedRegion)
      if (DO.IsSelected)
        { for each control point C in DOV
          { draw handle for C }
        }
    }
  }
```

In this code fragment, each draw object is bound to the appropriate view object, depending on its type. The draw object view is used to check the bounds of the object and if the bounds are in the damaged region, then the draw object's view is used to actually draw the object. If the object is one of the selected set, then the object's control point handles are drawn.

12.3.2 Creating a New Object

The way a new object is created depends upon the kind of object it is. For a line or a rectangle, only two control points need to be specified, as discussed in Chapter 11. This can be done by a •MouseDown, dragging out the shape, and a •MouseUp. For objects like polygons or splines, an arbitrary number of control points are required. What we would like to be able to do is write generic code for interactively specifying control points and then let the draw object views handle the details of how to formulate the objects from those points. This would allow the DrawView to handle all of the interactive events, with DrawObjView handling the mapping between control points and the actual values of each object.

We can capture the state space of the draw area with the following fields:

```
DrawingState { Inactive, CreateDrag, ExtraCreate }
CreationPoint { ?AnotherCreationPoint, ?LastCreationPoint }
```
> *Calls the CreationPoint method to see if another creation point will be required.*

```
Prototype { ?NoPrototype, ?IsAPrototype }
```
> *Checks to see if there is a current prototype object or not.*

The creation dialog is driven by whether there is a prototype object and by whether the view of that object has received all of the control points that it wants. The actions used by our creation dialog are shown below (note that they use the generic creation methods provided by the view as well as copying the prototype object and when completed adding the prototype, with its control points, to the model):

```
Action {
  !CreateObj,
```
> *Makes a copy of the prototype. Binds it to a view object.*

```
  !StartCreationEcho, !MoveCreationEcho, !SetCreationPoint,
```
> *Invokes the corresponding method on the current view object.*

```
  !AddObject
```
> *Adds the copied prototype to the model.*

```
}
```

Having defined the state space, we can now address the dialog for creating objects; this is an enhancement of that given in Chapter 11:

```
1. Inactive, •MouseDown, ?IsAPrototype ->
      CreateDrag, !CreateObj, !StartCreationEcho


2. CreateDrag, •MouseMove -> !MoveCreationEcho
3. CreateDrag, •MouseUp, ?AnotherCreationPoint ->
      ExtraCreate, !SetCreationPoint
4. CreateDrag, •MouseUp, ?LastCreationPoint ->
      Inactive, !SetCreationPoint, !AddObject


5. ExtraCreate, •MouseMove -> !MoveCreationEcho
6. ExtraCreate, •MouseUp, ?AnotherCreationPoint ->
      !SetCreationPoint
7. ExtraCreate, •MouseUp, ?LastCreationPoint ->
      Inactive, !SetCreationPoint, !AddObject
```

This can be better understood by working through an example. Let us suppose that the current prototype object is a LineObj. When the first •MouseDown event is received, rule 1 fires. This moves the state to CreateDrag and invokes the !CreateObj action, which will copy the prototype line and bind a view to it. The DrawView object will save this copied line object and its view for use in the rest of the dialog. Rule 1 will also invoke !StartCreationEcho on the LineObjView object. Because LineObjView knows that it is drawing a line—DrawView has no idea what kind of object is being drawn—it will set the first end point of the line and then begin a rubber band line. Successive •MouseMove events will cause rule 2 to invoke the !MoveCreationEcho method on the LineObjView, which will update the rubber band line. When a •MouseUp event is finally received, either rule 3 or rule 4 could fire. However, a LineObjView knows that lines only need two control points and therefore its CreationPoint will always return true. The value of ?LastCreationPoint allows only rule 4 to fire, which will set the second creation point (which LineObjView stores as the line object's second end point) and will add the line object to the model.

When the line object is added to the model, all views of the model, including DrawView, are notified. When DrawView receives notification that a new object has been added, it must bind that object to a view, determine a bounding rectangle, and damage that rectangle. Note that DrawView still does not know about line objects and cannot assume that the object added was the last one that this view added. The reason this cannot be assumed is that another view of the same model may have added the object. DrawView must be careful to respond only to what comes from the model, not to its own stored information.

Suppose that the object in the current prototype is a polygon rather than a line. This time, on •MouseDown the polygon object is copied and a polygon view is bound to it. When the •MouseUp event is received, the polygon view will return false from its CreationPoint method. The ?AnotherCreationPoint condition tells DrawView that additional points are needed. This time rule 3 fires instead of rule 4 and the dialog enters the ExtraCreate state. As the mouse moves, rule 5 continues to fire, which invokes !MoveCreationEcho. The polygon view knows to update its rubber banding of the next polygon edge to be created. Any •MouseDown events are ignored. When •MouseUp is received, the CreationPoint method is checked. The polygon view will check this point against the first point. If it is close, then true is returned and the condition is ?LastCreationPoint. If the point is not close, then the condition is ?AnotherCreationPoint and the process continues. It is up to the draw object view to decide when enough points have been received and how those points should be echoed during creation of an object.

Note that all widgets in the object palette behave in the same way. The only difference among the widgets is their icon, their geometric position, and their prototype object. We can create a single class that handles each of these in a uniform way, as follows:

```
class ObjectSelector: public View
    {
    DrawObj Prototype;
    Icon myImage;
    Rect myLocation;
    DrawObj * CurrentSelectedPrototype
    . . . .
    }
```

Each of the object palettes in all of our examples can be created from objects of the class ObjectSelector. By setting Prototype, myImage, and my-Location, the object now knows everything it needs in order to correctly handle its task. By giving it a pointer to the selected prototype that is its model, it can work in conjunction with the other object selectors in the application.

12.3.3 Selecting Objects

Our DrawView differentiates between creation and selection based on whether there is a current prototype object or not. If there is no prototype, then object selection is indicated. The condition ?NoPrototype will trigger the selection dialog on •MouseDown. In previous chapters, we have discussed the dialog for selection by clicking or by a rubber band rectangle. In Chapter 11, we used the query field MouseLoc { ?MouseOverObject, ?MouseOverSpace } to determine whether to rubber band or to object select. In order to implement this query, we must test the mouse position against each object in the model. We can do this by adding the following method to DrawView, which will return the selected object or will return NULL for no object selected:

```
int DrawView::SelectObj(Point Mpt)
  {
  for each object DO in the model in front to back order
    { DOV = DO.GetObjView(DO);
      if (DOV.IsHit(Mpt))
        { return DO }
    }
  return null;
  }
```

Again, we use the views for each type of object to perform the actual geometry of selection. Using this SelectObj method, the dialog from Chapter 11 can perform most of its selection mechanism. The only remaining issue is the selection of all objects inside of a bounding rectangle. This is handled with the following method:

```
void DrawView::SelectInRect(Rect SR)
  {
  for each object DO in the model
    { DOV = DO.GetObjView(DO);
      if (DOV.BoundingRect() intersects SR)
        { add DO to the selected set }
    }
  }
```

Note that each of the draw object view classes must implement the selection and bounding-rectangle geometry discussed in Chapter 9.

Note that when objects are added to the selected set, the model must notify all views so that those views can damage the presentation of the objects. The action for damaging in DrawView is the same as that for adding an object. Note that the redraw will take care of drawing the controls for any selected objects.

12.3.4 Dragging Objects

In Chapter 11, we defined the following interactive syntax for dragging objects:

. . .

3. Selected, •MouseUp -> Idle
4. Selected, •MouseMove, ?IsLargeMove ->
     !StartDrag, DraggingObj
5. DraggingObj, •MouseMove -> !Drag
6. DraggingObj, •MouseUp -> !StopDrag, Idle

. . .

In our generic DrawView architecture, the !StartDrag, !Drag, and !StopDrag actions correspond loosely to the StartObjDrag, MoveObj, and EndObjDrag methods defined on DrawObjView. There are, however, some special problems that must be addressed. When an object is moved, the model must notify all views of this fact. For a view to correctly account for the movement, it must damage both the old location and the new location of the object.

The problem is that the object views must echo the changes while the user is dragging. One possible architecture is to notify the model of a change each time the !Drag action is invoked. The model can then tell each view of the old and new positions, and the redraw mechanism can move the object. This is a very nice dragging mechanism except that many workstations cannot get through the notify/damage/redraw cycle in the 1/5 of a second required for each mouse movement. In general, we need a simpler mechanism.

The draw object views can do a simple echo of their objects using XOR techniques, but this means that the position information for each object in the selected set must be saved by the view while the dragging is going on, because the model is not being informed of the changes. This XOR erasure technique requires that draw object views for all objects in the selected set must be saved during the dragging operation. Based on this requirement, we provide the following methods for each of the dragging actions (these actions assume that there is a DragViewList field in the DrawView):

```
void DrawView::StartDrag(Point Dp)
  {
  for each DO in the selected set
    { Add GetObjView(DO) to DragViewList }
  for each DOV in DragViewList
    { DOV.StartObjDrag(Dp) }
  }
void DrawView::Drag(Point Dp)
  {
  for each DOV in DragViewList
    { DOV.MoveObj(Dp) }
  }
void DrawView::StopDrag(Point Dp)
```

```
{
for each DOV in DragViewList
   { DOV.EndObjDrag(Dp) }
release space for DragViewList
}
```

Each object view is responsible for keeping enough information to correctly handle the dragging echo for its object. Each object view is also responsible for notifying the model of the changed geometry in its EndObjDrag method. At each such notification, the model has the old position stored in itself and the new position received from the object's view. With this information, it can give all model views sufficient information to damage both the old and the new positions of the objects.

12.3.5 Setting Attributes

The management of attributes involves the current prototype object, the selected set, and the active and enabled status of the attribute icons. The setting of attributes is quite straightforward. When an attribute value is selected by the user, the current prototype object is checked. If there is a prototype object, then its attribute is set to the selected value. If there is no prototype object, then each object in the selected set is checked. Each attribute selection widget must retain the attribute ID for the attribute that it manages and a value to be set. The DrawObj::SetAttribute method can then be used to actually set the new value. Note that if an object does not have such an attribute, SetAttribute will still work; however, nothing will actually happen. This greatly simplifies attribute-setting code in each widget.

Whenever the selected set is modified or a new prototype object is selected, the attribute palettes must be updated to reflect the new status. This palette highlighting means that all attribute palettes must be registered as views of both the current prototype object and the drawing model. Whenever a palette is so notified, it can then apply the rules for active/inactive status and for enable/disable to correctly reflect what the user can do.

As with the object selector palette, we can create a single class to handle all attribute palettes. Again, the only differences among these palette widgets are the icon, location, attribute identifier, and attribute value. In addition, each must point to the current selected prototype model and to the drawing model, as well as be registered with each. Note that sometimes attributes are set from the menu rather than from a palette. In such a case, we will need an attribute selector class for palettes and one for menu items. The information they require is the same, but their controller and view method implementations must reflect the differences in how users manipulate them.

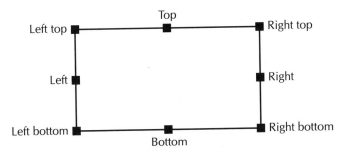

Figure 12-9   Rectangle controls

12.3.6 Manipulating Control Points

As pointed out in the description of the drawing architecture, each DrawObj-View has methods for inquiring about the control points on an object. Note that the object view, not the object model or the DrawView, manages the relationship between the control points and the object. The DrawView cannot manage this relationship because it is different for every type of object. The object models may store some of this information but do not know the exact geometry for where the control points should be placed. There is not necessarily a one-to-one mapping between control points and data in the object. Consider the case of the rectangle shown in Figure 12-9. The model for a rectangle contains left, top, right, and bottom. However, there are 8 control points that specify 16 different values. The view for a rectangle maps these controls to actual changes of the model values.

The input syntax for working with control points, object selection, and dragging was all worked out in Chapter 11. The key to that syntax was the query field MouseLoc. The rules for handling this syntax were defined as follows:

```
 . . .
10. Idle, •MouseDown, ?MouseOverControl ->
        !SetStartLoc, !SelectControl, DraggingControl
11. DraggingControl, •MouseMove -> !DragControl
12. DraggingControl, •MouseUp -> !SetControl, Idle
 . . .
```

The query condition ?MouseOverControl is implemented by the DrawView. We need to modify our general code for selection to also check for control points. Before checking an object to see if it has been hit, we need to first check to see if it is selected. If the object is selected, we then check all of its control points. The code is as follows:

```
for each object DO in the model in front to back order
  { DOV = DO.GetObjView(DO);
    if (DO.IsSelected)
       { Ncntls = DOV.Ncontrols();
         for (i=1;i++;i<=Ncntls)
            { if (MousePt is near DOV.GetControl(i))
                 { return DO as selected object with i as the
                      selected control
                 }
            }
       }
    if (DOV.IsHit(MousePt))
       { return DO as selected object with no selected control }
  }
return null;
```

The action !SetStartLoc can save the starting location in the drawing object's view. As with dragging in general, the DrawView needs to save the object view during the dragging operation. The !SelectControl action can use the DrawObjView::StartControlDrag method to begin the echoing of the moving control. On each •MouseMove, the !DragControl action can use the MoveControl method to actually do the dragging. Finally, the !SetControl method will use the EndControlDrag method. When each object view class is defined, these methods are written to provide the appropriate dragging echo for each of the control points. Using these methods, the input syntax can be placed in DrawView with the object views providing the custom behavior for each object.

12.4 Summary

A general architecture has been defined for laying out objects in a drawing area. By changing the set of objects that can be drawn and by providing view classes for each type of object, we can customize the architecture to a wide variety of applications. We can thus create the general classes DrawView, ObjectSelector, and AttributeSelector to implement almost all of the interactive behavior in a way that is general across all of the examples shown at the beginning of the chapter.

It is important to note that this general architecture is not specific to drawings. If we replaced DrawView with a 3D rendering system, we could provide a similar architecture. The DrawObj3DView class would be slightly different because selection would be in terms of 3D rays rather than mouse points, and the control point model would be different, but the same general approach would apply. We could also apply similar techniques to the editing of lists or tables of objects. In all of these cases, there is a model that consists of a set of objects, some of which can be selected and manipulated in terms of their geometry (in 2D control points) and attributes.

13

Cut, Copy, and Paste

One of the great contributions of the Apple Lisa and its more successful Macintosh successor was the notion of interactive programs being able to share information by the mechanisms of Cut, Copy, and Paste. This meant that interactive programs did not need to implement all possible features because the product of one program could be copied and pasted into another program. The programs need not know about each other; they need only follow the conventions of the windowing system's scrap manager or clipboard. By including this feature in the windowing system, application developers were free to focus on their particular niche and they could rely upon the existence of other programs to fill the user's complete needs. Users were free to mix and match capabilities from various programs as they needed.

In the presence of Cut, Copy, and Paste, a word processor can accept information from a variety of spreadsheets, databases, drawing programs, and other applications to create the final work product. Even if a single product contained all of these features, as some tried to do, they could not compete with the more flexible Cut, Copy, and Paste model. The reason is that any one of the features is subject to new innovative ways for creating them. If a word processor included a paint program for making pictures, its users soon wanted a drawing program with more features than simple paint. Even if the next version included a drawing facility as well as paint, some other company would then produce a ray-tracing product to produce images from 3D models, and again the all-in-one word processor was limited and behind. On the other hand, a word processor that could paste in images from any program could exploit the output of the ray tracer as soon as it hit the market. This flexibility was a most important development in the creation of usable systems that met the needs of the vast variety of users.

The first architectures of this type provided a simple clipboard on which programs could place information and then others could copy it. This clipboard architecture is quite flexible. The problem with the simple clipboard was its inability to keep up with changes in the source information. Take, for example, a spreadsheet with a budget projection. A user copies the budget projection and pastes it into a report. After reviewing the report, the user realizes that one of the assumptions in the spreadsheet was wrong and quickly corrects it. The spreadsheet recalculates the budget projection and all is well except that the copy of the budget projection in the report is the old one.

The next architecture in the progression was publish and subscribe, where applications could notify each other of changes in their published information. Thus the pasted information could automatically be kept current with the original.

When a user encounters the budget projection in the report, he may want to modify that projection. In the publish and subscribe model, the user must find the published original, start that application, and modify the projection. What would be more desirable would be to edit the spreadsheet fragment in place in the report. Direct editing of pasted material requires that the word processor be able to embed the interactive facilities of the spreadsheet, or any other such program, in its own windows. This embedding facility is provided by Object Linking and Embedding (OLE) in Windows and OpenDoc on the Macintosh.

The embedding architectures of OpenDoc and OLE still require that each application handle all of the interaction for its own data. What is required is some mechanism whereby new features can be developed and "dropped into" an application. These new features can operate on the application's data and extend the basic functionality of that application. A successful example of this facility is Adobe's Photoshop, which allows for any number of image-processing filters to be added to Photoshop by third parties to enhance the user's ability to manipulate images. Netscape plug-ins also provide this extensibility. Java applets extend the concept even further by allowing the code to be downloaded on the fly.

13.1 Clipboards

The notion of a clipboard is simply a place where programs can put information and other programs can retrieve it. It is not very complicated for an operating system to provide such a known place, but there are several issues that must be addressed for the concept to work, including the following:

■ What binary or textual format should be used for the information placed on the clipboard?

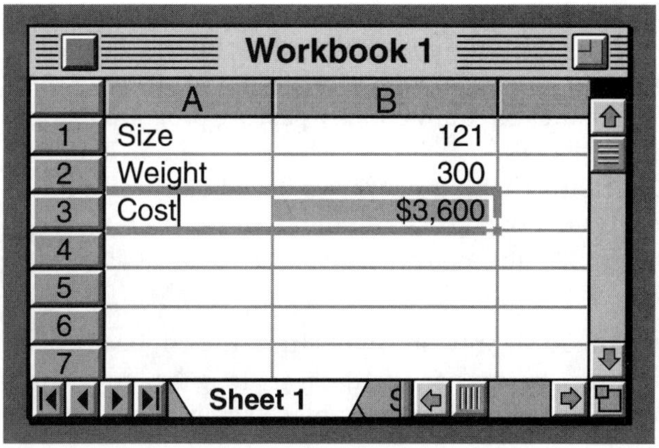

Figure 13-1   Example selected spreadsheet fragment

▪ How do we deal with the source program using one format and the destination preferring a different one?

▪ What do we do if the clipboard information is very large?

13.1.1 Simple Clipboard

The simplest implementation of a clipboard is a global memory item managed by the operating system where applications can store scraps of information. When information is stored on the clipboard, it must be stored with an identifier for the format of the information. Because the application putting information on the clipboard has no idea what the information is to be used for, it may place the information on the clipboard in several different formats. Take, for example, the selected spreadsheet fragment in Figure 13-1. This fragment could be pasted into another spreadsheet and therefore should be stored in Excel format. It may also be pasted into a simple text editor, in which case it should be stored in text format with tabs separating the columns. It may also be pasted into a diagram, in which case it should probably be placed on the clipboard in some picture format.

As we can see from this example, the clipboard must hold a variety of formats, with the pasting application being free to select one of the formats. In order for this communication to take place, both the source application and the pasting application must agree to an encoded identifier for the information formats.

On the Macintosh, all clipboard formats are assigned a unique four-character format identifier (e.g., TEXT, PICT, or EXCL). Such identifiers can be stored as 32-bit integers and thus are easily managed by the operating system. Apple maintains a central registry for developers to register their formats so that such identifiers will be unique. The Macintosh standards require that any source application must supply information in at least either TEXT or PICT format. This ensures that almost any pasting program can get useful information from the clipboard.

In the Macintosh system, items that a user wants placed on the clipboard are called *scrap*. In response to a cut or copy command from the user, an application can place its scraps of information on the clipboard using the following steps:

1. ZeroScrap is called to remove all previous items from the clipboard.
2. PutScrap is called, passing a pointer to the data, its length, and the format. PutScrap can be called several times to place scrap in alternative formats on the clipboard.

In our example, the spreadsheet would place EXCL, TEXT, and PICT versions of the selected cells onto the clipboard. If a simple text editor wanted to paste this information, it would call GetScrap, passing the format identifier TEXT. This would return the information stored under the TEXT format, which the editor could then insert.

Suppose that, instead of a simple text editor, Microsoft Word was trying to paste in the information. It would first try GetScrap, using the format ID for Microsoft Word information. Such information would include MS Word's formatting codes for bold, italic, and other such information; this is obviously the form that MS Word would prefer. In the case of our example, there is no scrap of this format on the clipboard. Microsoft Word might then try the EXCL format, because this is a companion product. In this case, there is success and MS Word can paste in the spreadsheet using EXCL information, which MS Word is programmed to understand.

In the example shown above, the scrap information is small and can easily be stored in memory where all programs can find it. In some cases, we want to cut, copy, and paste larger pieces of information. Such information can rapidly use up memory, particularly if multiple formats are stored. The Macintosh provides a simple mechanism for storing the clipboard on disk and releasing the local memory. Viewing the clipboard is also quite easy because either a TEXT or PICT version of the data is always available and could be displayed.

There are several problems with this simple approach to clipboards. The first is that clipboards still have to come into memory to be used. This is a particular problem if a source program wants to provide multiple formats. For example, Microsoft Word may want to provide its information to all of the word processing and drawing packages that it knows about. This will help in its compatibility with other products. Even a moderate-sized scrap will use up a lot of memory if 10–15 different formats of the information must be stored.

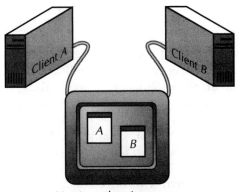

User's workstation server

Figure 13-2   X Windows from multiple clients

There is also a problem with generating unique 4-byte resource identifiers for the many different formats that may be used. This is a particular problem when there are multiple versions and upgrades of that format over time.

Clipboard Management in X Windows

The next step in clipboard management was taken in the X Windows system. This was forced by the unique client/server architecture of X. A user sitting at a workstation may be running two different programs on two different machines, as shown in Figure 13-2.

If a user wants to copy something from window *A* into window *B*, there is no shared memory for the two client programs *A* and *B*. In fact, the two clients may not even be running in the same operating system at all. The only thing that these two applications have in common is the server software running on the user's workstation. To make a clipboard work, there must be a common area where the scrap can be stored. In X, every window has properties that are simply named pieces of data. Such properties can be used to store scrap to be communicated between applications. For information from program *A* to be pasted into program *B*, program *A* must place this information in one of the properties of window *B*.

The problem is that at the time the information is selected in program *A*, the program has no idea what window may want the information and what format may be required. On the Macintosh, placing information on the clipboard simply required a few copies from memory to memory. In X, such copies involve network traffic between the client machines and the user's workstation. Such traffic must be minimized. What is needed, therefore, is a demand-based clipboard where only the information that a pasting application needs is actually sent.

In X, the clipboard is referred to as the *selection* and any application that wants to offer information must become the *selection owner* on a particular workstation. When a user selects a piece of an image or some text in application *A*, the client application calls XSetSelectionOwner for the particular display that the window appears on. (Note that in X, a client application can open windows on multiple workstation displays.) Program *A* says nothing at this time about what information it is offering, nor does it make any information available to the server.

When the user tries to paste into program *B*, the program will call XConvertSelection, specifying the format of the information that it wants. For formats (and other named objects), X uses *atoms*. To create an atom, a program takes a string name and calls XInternAtom, which will convert the name into a number that is unique for that string on a particular display. This number can now be efficiently used in place of the string. By registering such names with the workstation server, all applications drawing on that display can use identical numbers. These registered names eliminate the need for cryptic four-character codes while still having the same efficiencies.

When program *B* calls XConvertSelection, it not only specifies an atom for the desired format but also for the property on window *B* where the information is to be placed. When XConvertSelection is called, an XSelectionRequestEvent is sent to program *A*. Program *A* can find the format atom in the event and determine whether or not it can respond to the request. If program *B* asks for a pixel map when program *A* has text selected, program *A* can either attempt to convert the text to pixels or it can refuse the request. If *A* refuses the request, it must send an XSelectionEvent back to program *B* (using XSendEvent) indicating the refusal. Program *B* now can either resign itself to the fact that no information is coming or it can request a different format by calling XConvertSelection again. If the second request is for text, then program *A* will take the text and call XChangeProperty to put the information in the property that *B* designated. Client *A* then sends the XSelectionEvent to inform *B* that the job has been done.

In this mechanism, the server only keeps track of who owns the current selection. Information is only transferred when a program actually requests it. The source application (*A*) must maintain the information it has offered for pasting and then must attempt to convert the information into the desired format when requested. This demand-based mechanism not only reduces the network traffic but also reduces the work a source program must do to support multiple formats. Instead of doing the conversions to all possibly useful formats, as on the Macintosh, the source application only produces the format actually requested.

A last complication of this architecture is the fact that the source application (*A*) must maintain the selected information until requested or until some other application makes a selection. Once another selection is made (say, in program *C*), the old selection can release its selection information. When another program makes a selection and calls XSetSelectionOwner, the server software on the user's workstation will send an XSelectionClearEvent to the old owner (*A*), which reacts by freeing the information that it was saving for selection.

Demand-Based Pasting

The MS Windows system developers reviewed both of these designs to produce an effective compromise as well as to enhance the negotiation of formats. As with X, MS Windows uses string names for formats and provides a RegisterClipboardFormat routine that will convert the string name into a unique identifier that can be used with other calls.

Unlike X, MS Windows does have the luxury of all applications sharing the same display, processor, and operating system. However, there are still true asynchronous processes going on that must be accounted for when communicating between windows. Whenever an application wants to work with the clipboard, it must first call OpenClipboard, and when done it must call Close-Clipboard. This bracketing of the clipboard activity allows the operating system to resolve any conflicting accesses.

A window establishes that it has information for the clipboard by calling EmptyClipboard. In a method similar to X, EmptyClipboard will send a WM_DESTROYCLIPBOARD message to the old owner of the clipboard, allowing any information to be freed. A source program calls SetClipboard-Data to place information on the clipboard; it should make this call once for each format of information that it is offering. The order in which the calls to SetClipboardData are made is significant because it establishes the priority that the source program places on the various formats. In our Excel spreadsheet example from Figure 13-1, the first call would be for Excel format, the second for text, and the last for PICT, since that is the most meaningful order for spreadsheet information.

When an application calls SetClipboardData, it may either pass the actual data or defer until later. To actually pass the data, the program allocates some global memory, places the data in it, and then calls SetClipboardData with that information. If this information is not needed, the system can reclaim the memory. If, however, the data are large or the format is rarely used, an application can call SetClipboardData with a NULL pointer. This indicates to the system that the information for that format will only be generated on demand. This information-passing mechanism allows for the in-memory efficiencies of the Macintosh scrap manager as well as the information-on-demand model found in X.

A key idea in the MS Windows clipboard architecture is the negotiation of formats. When a program wants to paste from the clipboard, it has several mechanisms to negotiate the format. If the pasting program is rather simple and only supports one format, it can call IsClipboardFormatAvailable to see if the format it wants is on the clipboard. If not, it abandons the paste operation and informs the user. The next possibility is to let the source program decide the format. By calling the GetPriorityClipboardFormat routine, a pasting program gets the highest-priority format, according to the ordering of the source program. The most flexible negotiation is to call EnumClipboardFormats to access all of the available formats in priority order. The pasting application then takes the first format that it knows how to handle. This mechanism selects the best format, from the source's point of view, that the pasting program can effectively use.

When a pasting program has finally negotiated a format, it calls GetClipboardData to retrieve the information. If the information is actually on the clipboard, it is returned and the program can then make use of it. If the information is not on the clipboard, then the system automatically sends a WM_RENDERFORMAT message to the source program. This event notifies the source program that it must generate the information in the specified format. When a program receives a WM_RENDERFORMAT message, it must generate the information and then call SetClipboardData to post the information on the clipboard. The pasting program sees none of this message traffic; when the system returns from GetClipboardData, it has the desired information.

When a program is terminated, it may have information posted on the clipboard. The clipboard information must survive the program that created it. However, in the case of delayed information, the program will not be around to generate the information if requested. Before a program is terminated, MS Windows will send it a WM_RENDERALLFORMATS message if it is the owner of the clipboard. In response to this message, the program is expected to generate all of its information in all of its formats and to put the data on the clipboard using SetClipboardData. Note that because handles to global memory are used for clipboard information, the operating system is free to swap clipboard information out to disk and to reload it on demand from a pasting application.

13.2 Publish and Subscribe

The clipboard model for cut, copy, and paste provides for permanent transfer of information from one application to another. Sometimes, however, it is desirable to have an active connection between the source of the information and its destination so that whenever the information changes in the source, it is updated in the destination. One of the important issues is how often this updating should be performed. One option is to make notification of the update whenever the data change. Immediate update is one of the strengths of spreadsheets, but the cost of launching and updating programs whenever small changes occur can be large. A second option is to provide updates whenever the source file is saved, to prevent a lot of temporary changes from being propagated across program boundaries. A third option is to only make changes when the user explicitly asks for them. This gives the user a lot of control but pushes some of the tedium of tracking updates back on the user.

The Macintosh provides a mechanism called Publish and Subscribe. In some applications, such as our spreadsheet in Figure 13-1, a user can select a piece of information and request the application to publish it. This creates an *edition* file that contains the published information. It also makes a record in the source file as to what the published information really is. In the destination application, the user can select a place to put the information and request that a *subscription* be made to an edition. To subscribe to an edition is not only to paste the information from the edition, but also to establish a link to that edition so that each time the published section for that edition is changed, any subscribed sections will also be updated to reflect the change.

In many ways, an edition can be thought of as an active clipboard. There are several issues that must be addressed to keep publishers and subscribers synchronized with each other:

- The publishing application must record and inform the system of the existence of a publishable section.
- The publisher must create an edition file.
- The edition must be updated each time the publisher saves changes to the data.
- The subscriber must create a subscribe section and notify the system of its existence.
- The subscriber must be notified each time the edition changes.
- Both publish and subscribe applications must keep track of where their sections are located in the presence of editing actions in the rest of the document.

A user who wants to publish some information first selects that information and invokes a menu item or some other event to inform the application that the selected data should be published. The publishing application must create a section record that informs the system of the existence of the section to be published. A key part of this information identifies which data actually belong to the section. In the Macintosh system, each section is given a unique number by the application. The system uses this number to reference the section data in the application. The application must then maintain sufficient information of its own to identify what the information is. In our spreadsheet in Figure 13-1, the selected data might be identified as A3-B3, since those are the cell coordinates of the selected area. This information might be associated with section number 1.

Having created a section, the publishing application creates an edition file to contain the information that is being published. Putting information into an edition is very much like placing it on the clipboard. Editions support a variety of formats so that subscribers can locate information in the form that is most useful to them. With editions, however, there is no concept of delayed rendering. All of the data for all formats must be placed in the edition because at the time that a subscription to the information is created, the source program may not be running. Note that an application can publish many different sections, each in their own edition.

After having published a section, editing will probably occur in the source application. Each time such an application saves its data to a file, it must check to see if the information in any of its published sections has changed. If any has changed, the corresponding edition must be opened and new information must be written to the edition in all of the possible formats. Each writing to an edition is time stamped so that subscribers know when an edition has changed.

Editing can occur not only in the published sections of a file but also in other places. Such editing may change the way that section information is referenced. For example, if a new row is added to the spreadsheet in Figure 13-1, the section reference of A3-B3 no longer points at the correct data; the reference must be updated to A4-B4. If the application does not track such changes, the section information becomes inaccurate. A similar problem can occur if the published section is in a text file. Selections in a text file might be referenced by the file offset of the starting and ending points of the section. If any changes that add or delete characters are made earlier in the file, the start and end offsets will be wrong. In order for section references to stay stable in the presence of edits, either the file must have embedded section tags to identify where the section starts and ends or it must update section references whenever edits are made.

When an application wants to subscribe to an edition, the user must select a place in the document where the subscription should be pasted. The user can then request to subscribe and a dialog for selecting the appropriate edition is popped up. Having selected the edition, the subscribing application can check to see what formats are available in the edition. The formats must have been placed in the edition in highest-to-lowest priority order (from the publisher's point of view). The subscriber then selects a format and retrieves the information, much in the same way as pasting from a clipboard. In addition, the subscribe application must create a section record and section reference information to remember where in the document the subscribed information was placed. Maintaining this subscription section reference has the same problems in the face of editing as the publishing application had.

Whenever a subscriber application opens a file, it must locate all subscribing sections in that file and check their editions for changes since the file was last opened. In addition, a subscriber can receive Apple Events that inform it of section changes that were made since the subscribing file was opened.

The use of edition files ensures a separation between publisher and subscriber so that either can function without the other running and also reduces memory problems that result from publishing several formats of the same data. The notification on file save and load boundaries provides most of the automatic update that users want without unduly burdening the system.

On some occasions, the user will see subscribed information and will want to look at it in the context of the publisher. This mechanism is possible through the Event Manager, which can follow the links from a subscribe section to an edition file, to the publishing document, and to the publishing application. Using all of this information, the publisher can be launched and scrolled to the location of the published section using an Apple Event protocol created for the purpose.

A similar capability to Apple's Publish and Subscribe is found in Microsoft's OLE architecture. Instead of the creation of separate edition files, a pasting application retains links directly to the original source program. Such links are called *monikers.* The first part of a moniker is an absolute or relative path name for the file in which the linked information is stored. The remaining part of the moniker is a list of identifiers that reference the data within the file. These identifiers are freeform and it is up to the application that is managing the linked data to interpret the monikers. One mechanism for handling monikers is for the application to support *compound files*, which are Microsoft's mechanism for creating structured files.

Monikers have several problems. The first is that if the linked file moves, the links may be broken because the file names have changed. Monikers are not as robust as Apple's aliases in this regard. A second problem is that any editing of the source document needs to make certain that any monikers in that document are preserved, so that links into the document are not broken.

13.3 Embedded Editing

As we have seen, cutting and pasting is a powerful mechanism for integrating information from different applications. Unfortunately, once the data have been pasted, they are static and cannot change. In the case of linking or

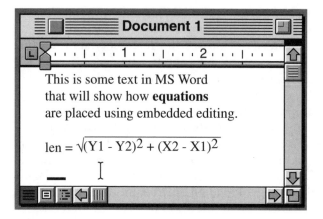

Figure 13-3   Embedded equation

subscribing, the data can change if the original application changes them. What is most desirable, however, is for the foreign data to be editable in place. Take, for example, the fragment from Microsoft Word in Figure 13-3. The text is handled by the word processor, but the mathematical equation is handled by a completely separate program.

The key here is that the *container*, in this case MS Word, does not know about all of the possible forms of live data that the user might want to embed in it. The editing and rendering of such information, therefore, must be general enough to allow any application to embed in another application, provided that they both conform to the appropriate protocols.

The two dominant architectures for such embedding are OLE from Microsoft and OpenDoc from Apple and partners. OLE reached the market well in advance of OpenDoc. The price of early introduction was that embedded objects must be strictly rectangular and cannot flow across page boundaries. OpenDoc provides such functionality as well as cross-platform capabilities, but it arrived much later.

13.3.1 Embedded Pasting

When live data are pasted into a container application such as MS Word, the first issue is exactly what should be pasted. In the case of our equations, they did not come from another file; they are an integral part of the text document. In our earlier example of pasting from a spreadsheet, the information may be a live part of the original document. In the case of our equations, the descriptive data for the equations must be stored in the MS Word document itself. In the spreadsheet publish and subscribe case, a link would be stored. Microsoft's Foundation Classes provide a mechanism for getting the data for an embedded object. If the object is stored in the container, then it is returned. If the container only holds a link, the link is traced down and the data are returned. In either case, the result is the object that describes the equations.

Because data from foreign applications of any kind can be embedded in a container document, it must be possible to save such foreign information to a file and to read it back. This necessity for applications to store foreign data led Microsoft to develop a compound file architecture that essentially supports files within files. The Bento facility in OpenDoc serves the same function.

These structured file systems need not be used, however, to accomplish the goal. All that is really needed is a mechanism whereby an application can convert some segment of its model into a stream of bytes and can later convert that stream of bytes back into the original model. In OLE, this conversion is done by requiring that models support a Serialize method that can convert the model to and from an archive stream. The Serialize method is also used for saving and loading models from files, as well as for debugging. The advantage is that the container application need only concern itself with streams of bytes. The Java language supports reflection, which allows code such as serialization to examine class definitions and to generate serializations automatically. This greatly simplifies the encoding problem for programmers.

Once embedded information is pasted into a container, the container must be able to present that information. The first issue is to negotiate the size and shape of the area where the information will be presented. In OLE, the shape is a simple rectangle. The source application must inform the container of the desired size, in x and y dimensions, of the embedded information. The container can then call the embedded information's drawing method, passing in the rectangle actually assigned by the container.

So far, the embedded information need only provide a Serialize and a Redraw method. The problem is that the code for these methods is in a different application from the container. Both OLE and OpenDoc provide mechanisms for launching the application associated with the embedded information, and by using lightweight remote procedure calls, the container can invoke the two required methods. This dynamic loading and linking to other applications is critical to embedding foreign data.

Such remote invocations of other applications are expensive in time and memory and should only be performed when absolutely necessary. In order to alleviate this problem, a container will call the source application's redraw with a special canvas (or, in OLE, a device context). This canvas does not represent a file but rather a storage for the list of drawing commands. In MS Windows, this is called a *metafile,* and on the Macintosh, it is a PICT data object. The advantage of such lists is that they can represent any image from any application and can always be reproduced in a window or on a printer without knowing anything about the application that produced them. The container can thus store the metafile produced by the redraw, along with the embedded data. Any redraw required on the part of the container can use the metafile without restarting the application that supports the embedded information. Although this requires more disk space, it is much faster.

13.3.2 Edit Aside

There are two ways in which a separate program can be used to edit embedded information such as our equation. The first and simplest is the *edit aside,* where a new window is opened to edit the information. The second, and more complicated, is *edit in place.* We will first consider the edit aside model found in OLE 1.0 and in the MS Office products delivered on the Macintosh.

When a user sees embedded information such as the equation in Figure 13-3, he can double-click on it. The container application bundles up the information that it has stored for the embedded object and has OLE launch the corresponding application, passing the data. The launched application puts up its own window in which the user can edit the information. When editing is complete or saved, the container application is notified. The container application then invokes the Serialize method to get the new embedded information, requests the new desired width and height, and invokes Redraw to get the metafile for the edited data. Other than serialization of data, negotiating the display rectangle, and getting the metafile redrawn, there is little communication between the container and the source application. Edit aside provides a relatively straightforward architecture.

13.3.3 Edit in Place

Editing in place is more complicated because two programs must now cooperate interactively. When the user double-clicks on embedded information, the source application must still be invoked. In OLE 2.0, the source application is given a window that corresponds to the rectangle allocated for the embedded information by the container. While editing is going on, there must be some negotiation between the container and the editor about the size of the rectangular area. This negotiation is even more complicated in OpenDoc, where the areas are not rectangular.

Because the editor has its own window, it will receive its own input events and can edit the information. There are problems, however, with menus and palettes of commands and attributes. In both MS Windows and the Macintosh, the menu is defined for the whole window. The embedded editor must merge its menu items in with the menu items of the container. Both systems provide protocols for negotiating such merging. With palettes, the embedded editor can simply put up additional windows of its own for the other tools and attributes that it needs. The problem is that these palettes can obscure information around the embedded data that may be important to the user.

13.4 Summary

Cut, Copy, and Paste are the basic mechanisms for integrating multiple interactive applications. They do for graphical user interfaces what pipes did for UNIX; they make the sum of the parts greater than the whole by means of a consistent model for interconnection. In order for pasting to work, the source and the destination must negotiate a format for the pasted information. It must be a format that represents the source information while being understood by the destination program.

A simple clipboard is a common memory location where scraps in all possible formats are placed. Pasting programs can select from this location the information that they want. More sophisticated clipboards can accept either data or simple format registrations. When a deferred format is requested, the source program can generate the information at that time. This reduces the amount of space required and eliminates the rendering of unused formats. In X, this is complicated by the fact that cutting and pasting must pass through the server because the client applications may be on different machines.

The cut, copy, and paste model can be extended to providing dynamic links between applications. In the Macintosh model, source applications keep edition files up to date with their latest information, and destination applications regularly check with the edition to paste in the latest information. In the OLE model, link records are stored in the source and destination files with message-passing mechanisms to keep the destination informed of source changes.

The highest form of cut, copy, and paste is when any data can be pasted into a container and then managed by their own creating application. This eliminates the format negotiations of clipboards and allows pasted data to be edited in place in the container.

14

Monitoring the Interface: Undo, Groupware, and Macros

In this chapter, we will consider software architectures for certain interface functions that must pervade the entire interface. Our previous discussions have involved single actions or commands on single objects or groups of objects. There are some facilities, however, that apply to all commands and all objects in the interface. Such facilities require fundamental changes to our MVC architecture.

The most important of these facilities is undo/redo. In a direct-manipulation interface, it is very important that it be possible to undo just about everything a user might do. For those actions that cannot be undone, such as saving to a file, the user should be warned and asked for confirmation before the action is taken. The presence of undo provides a feeling of safety to the interface. If a user knows that no permanent changes will be made without confirmation, then he will be more likely to explore the interface and try things out. The user is then secure in the knowledge that anything tried can be undone. Redo is simply the undoing of a previous undo.

To implement undo requires that every action, command, or model change must be monitored and sufficient information saved to permit the changes to be undone. This fact that all interactive behavior must participate in undo recording requires that it be handled specially within the software architecture.

The interfaces that we have discussed so far have all assumed that there is one user sitting at one workstation. This single-user assumption is not realistic. Working environments almost always consist of several people working at a variety of workstations. Users frequently need to cooperate with each other in the creation or modification of some document, drawing, or design. The single-user software we have discussed so far provides no support for such group activities.

There are two key ways in which multiple individuals can work together in some user interface. In the first case, multiple people are working on the same design product at different times (asynchronous collaboration). For example, there may be three people working together on a proposal document. When any one of them begins working on the document it is important to be able to see what changes the others have made. In the second case, multiple users may be working on the document simultaneously (synchronous collaboration). In this synchronous case, any actions taken by one user must immediately be propagated to the others; this requirement is sometimes referred to as WYSIWIS (What You See Is What I See). For either of these two cooperative situations, the user interface software must track all model changes, to either store them in a change log—which can be used by the interface later—or to forward them to other users so that their models can be updated to a consistent state.

A third capability of interest in this chapter is the recording of macros. In almost any user interface, there are a variety of commands provided that together can do almost anything the application domain requires. For some purposes, however, using these primitive commands may be too tedious for what needs to be done. The solution is to provide a macro capability whereby users can add new commands of their own. The problem is that a macro facility requires a language in which to program the macros, and users are generally not programmers. One solution is to allow the user to demonstrate the desired activity and then to record what the user has done. It is this recording process that is of interest here. Such a process requires that we monitor the entire user interface and record what is done as part of the macro.

These three capabilities—undo/redo, multi-user interfaces (or groupware), and macros—have a need to monitor all that the user is doing in order to provide some additional service to the user. In this chapter, we will discuss each of these capabilities in more detail. It is important to understand all of the issues related to each of these facilities before presenting a software architecture that will support them.

14.1 Undo/Redo

Almost all models for undo are built around the concept of a command, which has to do with the concept of closure. For example, when a user creates a line using a drawing program, the •MouseDown, dragging, •MouseUp sequence can be thought of as a complete conceptual unit. When the •MouseUp event occurs, a closure has been reached and the line is actually created. This complete unit is what we will refer to as a command. In another sense, each command or closure can be thought of as a permanent change to the state of the model.

14.1.1 Simple History Architecture

For purposes of undo, each command can be thought of as an atomic unit. We would not, for example, expect to undo all of the dragging operations that created a line. We would, however, expect that undo would completely remove the line just created. (There are architectures for which commands are not atomic, which will be discussed later in this section.)

There have been several formal models that define the meaning of undo.[1] In this chapter, however, we will take a more implementation-oriented approach. Undo is based on a *history list* of all of the commands that have occurred since the interactive session began. An undo can be thought of as removing the most recent command from that history list and restoring the interface to the state it was in before that command was executed.

A simple-minded approach to undo would be to remove the last command from the history list, reinitialize the model to its original state, and then re-execute the history list from the beginning. Such an approach has two problems. The first is that it would be very slow to perform the undo and the second is that storing the entire history list would take too much space.

The usual approach is to store up to a fixed number of commands in the history list (in many cases, only one history command is stored). With each history command, sufficient information is stored to reverse the effect of the command.

There are two cases where interactive actions are not included as commands in the history list. The first involves irreversible commands. For example, it is not possible to retract a print command once the ink goes on the paper. There are no erasing laser printers. Actions such as saving to files may not be reversible, because it is generally considered too expensive to save the old file contents. There are some systems that save the old file contents, but there are many that do not. With irreversible commands, the user is given the opportunity to abort the command before it is actually carried out and the command is not placed on the history list.

The second set of nonhistorical commands are transient commands. These are commands such as scrolling or selecting windows to bring them to the front, and may also include object selection commands. In general, they are commands that do not change the primary model state. The exclusion of such commands is primarily a design decision. In large documents, being able to

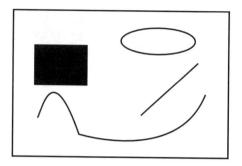

1. create white rectangle
2. create line
3. change rectangle to black
4. create ellipse
5. create curve

Figure 14-1   Example drawing and history list

undo a scrolling action may be very useful in finding an earlier place in the document. If complex selections or queries for objects are part of the interface, being able to undo changes to those selections may be of value. In terms of implementation, including or excluding such commands has little impact. This is primarily a design decision, based on user needs.

14.1.2 Selective Undo

In the simple history list model for undo, only the last command can be undone at one time. If the action to be undone occurred several commands ago, the user must step back through the history using successive undo commands. Consider the drawing in Figure 14-1 and the history list that created it. Suppose that the user wanted to restore the rectangle to its original color. Using the simple ordered undo, the user would need to perform three undo operations (5 through 3) in order to remove the command that changed the rectangle to black. In the process, the curve and the ellipse would be discarded, which is not what the user wanted at all.

We can also consider this problem from the user's perspective. What the user wants is to undo the last action on the rectangle. The implementation, however, is not defined in terms of what the user sees or wants but rather in terms of the order of actions. Most users would not have kept track of the fact that the ellipse and the curve came after the setting of the rectangle's color.

Careful examination of the history list shows that if command 3 were removed, the resulting history would be exactly what the user wants. This is called selective undo. However, there are problems with selective undo. Consider the drawing and history list in Figure 14-2. Suppose that the user again wants to restore rectangle *a* to white. Deleting command 3 from the history creates a problem because command 4 is dependent on command 3. What should the color of rectangle *c* be? It could be white, because without command 3 the color of the copied rectangle would be white, according to the history.

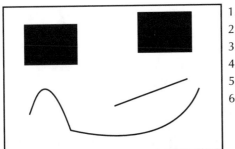

1. create white rectangle *a*
2. create line *b*
3. change rectangle *a* to black
4. copy rectangle *a* to create rectangle *c*
5. create curve *d*
6. move rectangle *c*

Figure 14-2   Example drawing and dependent-undo history list

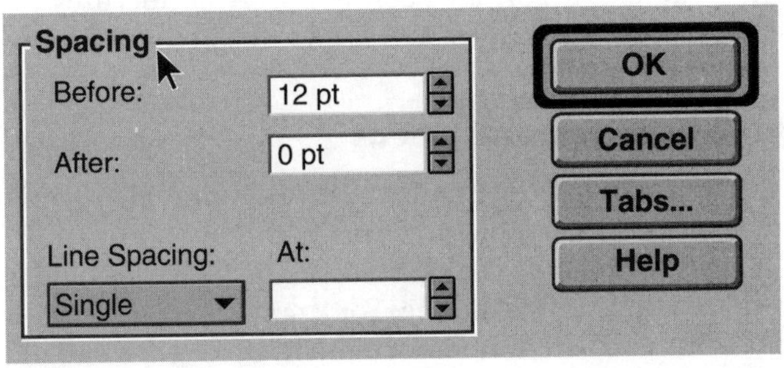

Figure 14-3   Dialog undo

Suppose that the user wanted to undo the creation of the line by removing command 2. This also has an impact on the implementation of undo. Without line *b*, the rectangle created in command 4 would be object *b* instead of object *c*. The curve in command 5 would be object *c*, and command 6 would now be moving the curve (*c*) instead of the rectangle that it originally moved. A selective undo mechanism must be able to resolve these dependencies in some manner that is reasonable and understandable to users.

14.1.3 Hierarchical Undo

As mentioned earlier, commands are generally considered atomic for purposes of undo, that is, the complete command is undone. Consider the dialog box in Figure 14-3.

Suppose that the user changes the "Line Spacing" followed by the "Before" field. The user then selects OK. There is actually a hierarchical command structure to this set of actions, as shown in Figure 14-4. Having done these actions, the user may want to restore the paragraph to its original state, in

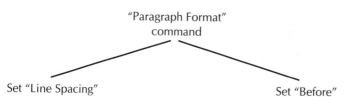

Figure 14-4   Command hierarchy for Figure 14-3

which case undoing the entire "Paragraph Format" command is the appropriate action. Suppose, however, that the user only wants to undo the "Before" setting. In that case, the undo should operate at the finer-grained level of the actions that make up the "Paragraph Format" command. Architectures for such hierarchical undo have been pioneered by Myers and Kosbie.[2]

14.1.4 Review of Undo Architectural Needs

In order to implement undo, our software architecture must provide several basic facilities. It must be possible to capture and save all historically significant user commands. When saving these commands, we must save sufficient information to allow the commands to be undone. For example, in the case of the "Paragraph Format" command, the undo mechanism must save the old values of "Line Spacing" and "Before," as well as a reference to the paragraph that was changed. It must be possible to instruct such commands to undo whatever they did. It must also be possible to instruct such commands to redo whatever they did so that redo can be implemented. If we are going to allow selective undo, it must also be possible to resolve any dependencies.

14.2 Groupware

This section will take only the most cursory look at groupware. This is a large field in and of itself.[3] It is useful, however, to consider some of the basic architectural needs. This discussion will highlight the use of command objects for supporting group work but will not discuss the implementation details.

14.2.1 Asynchronous Group Work

Let us first consider the asynchronous situation, where multiple people are working on the same design object, possibly at different times. (They may also be working on it at the same time.) The key here is that they are not directly aware of what the others are doing. In such a situation, they each take their own copy of the work product and modify it. For example, the application may be a VLSI design application. Each user is working on part of the design as they collectively construct an entire chip. The problem is that their work is interconnected and they must at some point integrate what they have done. In general with design efforts, there is also an approval process where others must evaluate the work before it becomes a permanent part of the design. If there is some problem with the work, it may need to be completely withdrawn or undone.

The most common place where programmers would encounter these problems is in managing the source code for large software products. There are many people working on the product whose work must be coordinated and tested before being allowed into the final software release. Everything a user has done to the model must be saved as a separate entity. In source code control and in other disciplines, such entities are called *patches*. A patch is a representation of a set of changes to some model that have been collected together for some purpose. Frequently, a user does not create a patch all in one work session.

Problems arise when there are conflicts between two patches. Such conflicts are very similar to the dependency problems in selective undo. Suppose in a drawing that one user changes a rectangle from white to black, while another changes the same rectangle from white to red. Before a final release of the drawing, this conflict must be resolved in some way. Or suppose that while the first user changes the rectangle from white to black, the second user deletes the rectangle.

A more complicated example is where one user deletes an object and the other does not. Then both users create new objects. In many systems, the objects are given consecutive numbers or positions in a list, and they are identified by such. Since one user has changed the ordering in a way that the other has not, the identifiers of the two new objects may conflict in subtle ways.

One way to resolve these conflicts is by locking portions of the work product to a particular user. In programming, this is typically done on a module level, where the source file for some module is locked so that nobody else can edit it. This prevents two programmers from working in the same area at the same time. Note that this does not prevent them from making semantically incompatible changes; it only guarantees that the state of the model is always well defined even if it is not appropriate to the project goals.

Another approach that is of interest to us is to provide some integration mechanism for resolving conflicts among patches. We will consider this approach in more detail later.

Of key importance to the user interface is that the changes stored in a patch must be presented to the users in such a way that they can understand what has been changed, understand what others have changed, and understand how they can resolve any conflicts that have arisen. Such change presentation issues, however, are application specific and not currently treatable by a general architecture.

14.2.2 Synchronous Group Work

In the synchronous situation, two or more users are working on the same work product at the same time, in cooperation with each other. In this situation, all of the users must be aware of the changes made by other users to the model that they are sharing. This notification is an expansion of the view notification problem in our MVC architecture, only now views and other copies of the model are on different workstations distributed over a network.

Since in many ways synchronous work resembles a discussion, there are a variety of social issues that must be resolved so that such users can cooperate with each other. Because such users usually cannot directly see each other, many of the social cues or conversational techniques we use to prevent too many people talking at once are not possible. There are a variety of enhancements to the user interface that have been proposed to fill in these gaps. This discussion will restrict itself to the problem of how to make sure that all of the users who want to can manipulate the shared model and that all of the other users can see the result.

One approach to this problem is to take a command history similar to the one used for undo and to propagate that history to all users. By propagating this history, each user's model of the work product can be synchronized. Remember, however, that for n users there are n command histories. Not only must the commands be propagated to each other but the conflicts must be resolved such that all users share the same history and thus have the same representation of the model.

In multi-user interfaces, there are some considerations that must be made in defining the command history. Suppose, for example, that we represented a command for selecting a piece of text by the mouse position at the start of the selection and the mouse position at the end. This representation would work if all users were using the same font. Suppose, however, that one of the users is visually impaired and is using a font twice as big as everyone else. The commands defined in terms of mouse position now have different behavior in the interfaces of different users. Our command model must have a consistent interpretation across all users, regardless of the surface differences in the interfaces presented to each user.

14.2.3 Groupware Architectural Issues

In order to support asynchronous group work, we must have mechanisms for capturing and saving commands or model changes. It must be possible to collect together such command or change lists to form patches. Where two patches overlap in the same work product, it must be possible to identify and resolve conflicts between patches. It must also be possible to visually present such changes to the users so that they can understand what has happened to their work product.

In the synchronous situation, we must be able to capture from and distribute to all of the simultaneous users all of the commands or changes. It must be possible to resolve the conflicts that can arise when multiple users can independently change the model.

14.3 Macros

Graphical user interfaces rarely come with all of the features that a particular set of users may want. In fact, many applications have too many features, confusing users with features that are unrelated. One approach to solving this is to allow users to create new commands of their own by building them out of the basic commands provided by the original implementors. Such user-defined commands are usually called *macros*.

The goal of a macro facility is to collect together a set of commands so they can be executed as a group. These commands can be named and added to the interface. One of the powers of UNIX—and other systems like it—is that they provide a scripting language that allows users to add new commands to the operating system.

In UNIX and other operating systems, the scripting language is almost identical to the command-line language. Most scripts will string together successive command lines. Some additional control commands and parameter syntax are added, but essentially the language is the same as the command-line user interface. One of the problems with graphical user interfaces is that, unlike command-line interfaces, the scripting language is not a natural extension of the interface.

One of the ways to provide macro extensions to a user interface is through a macro-recording facility. In such an approach, the user can turn on macro recording, and everything the user does is saved until recording is turned off. This recorded session can then be saved as a macro. Each time the saved macro is invoked, the same set of actions is performed again.

There are some problems with the simple recording approach, however. If the recorder simply saves the input events and repeats them, the result is not a very interesting macro. Mouse events, for example, would occur in exactly the same place, producing exactly the same results as last time. Take, for example, the drawing in Figure 14-5. Suppose that the user wants to create a number of ×s in boxes. The user turns on recording, draws the two lines of the × in the left box, and then turns off recording. If the recording saved all of the input events exactly as they were received, then invocation of the macro would draw exactly the same image in exactly the same place. This is not very helpful. The user wanted to be able to quickly draw an × in each of the other boxes. The problem is that what the user wants is not an exact copy but rather a general procedure that can be applied in other situations.

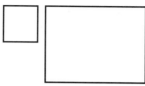

Figure 14-5   Drawing an × in a box

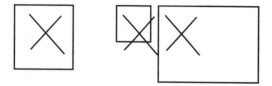

Figure 14-6   Point-relative macros

The first step to such a generalization is not to save the inputs but rather to save the commands that the inputs invoked. This representation allows our macro system to work with the user's intentions rather than his actual behavior. For example, while drawing the lines of the ×, the user moved the mouse a variety of places in the process of getting the lines right. These mouse movements are not essential to repeating the user's intentions. By saving the command that draws the line rather than all of the mouse movements that produced it, we have simplified and clarified our macro.

The next step is to parameterize the commands. For example, we may take the first point in the first command and use it as a parameter to our macro. We then take all the points in the other commands and define them relative to the original rather than in absolute coordinates. Before invoking the macro, the user can select a point in the small rectangle and then invoke the macro. The invoked commands are then executed relative to the new point and the × is drawn in its new position on the small rectangle. The current selection point is used as a parameter to the macro so that it can be applied in a variety of settings.

There is still a problem, however, because drawing the original × in the small rectangle produces the result shown in Figure 14-6. The problem is that the user wants the × to be sized according to the box that it is drawn on top of.

Suppose that before recording the macro, the user selects the box. The macro commands are then saved in terms of the selected object instead of the selected point. Before each macro invocation, the user selects a new box. The macro then resizes its commands relative to the selected object. The result is shown in Figure 14-7.

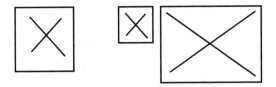

Figure 14-7   Object-relative macros

The object-relative result shown in Figure 14-7 is closest to the user's original intentions. There are a number of problems, however, in trying to figure out what the user actually intended. In Excel's macro-recording facility, commands are saved relative to the selected range of cells and macros can be invoked on a new range of cells. Another approach to our ×s is to have the user record the macro in the first box and then record it again in the second box. By comparing the two sets of commands, a generalization is produced that can be used in a variety of new situations. Creation of macros by example is a rather hard problem with a great deal written about it.[4]

The key, however, to all user-defined macros is to be able to record the interactive commands that the user generates, to reason about those commands so as to produce a general macro, and then to reexecute those commands at a later time as part of the macro body. These are pretty much the same facilities required of undo/redo and groupware.

14.4 Monitoring Architecture

The software architecture for handling all of these monitoring duties is based on the concept of a *command object.* This concept was first introduced by Meyer.[5] This chapter's discussion, however, also draws from the more complete implementation found in MacApp for the Macintosh.[6]

14.4.1 Command Objects

The basis for the architecture is an abstract class called Command. This class has the following three methods:

DoIt
> *Execute the action for this command.*

UndoIt
> *Undo the action for this command.*

RedoIt
> *Redo the action for this command.*

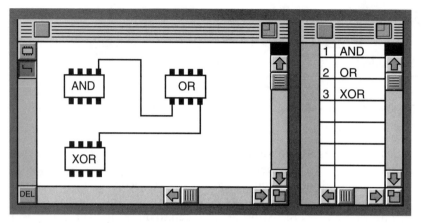

Figure 14-8   Chip-design program

Take, for example, the chip-layout program shown in Figure 14-8. From
Chapter 5, we take the following functional design for this program:

AddChip(CenterPoint)

AddWire(Chip1, Connector1, Chip2, Connector2)

SelectChip(ChipNum)

MoveChip(ChipNum, NewCenterPoint)

ChangeChipName(ChipNum, NewName)

DeleteChip(ChipNum)

SelectWire(WireNum)

DeleteWire(WireNum)

Each of these functional actions corresponds to a command that must be
implemented by the user interface. In order to provide the monitoring that we
want, we create a subclass of Command for each of these individual commands. For our example, we would have the following subclasses:

AddChipCmnd

AddWireCmnd

SelectChipCmnd

MoveChipCmnd

ChangeChipNameCmnd

DeleteChipCmnd

SelectWireCmnd

DeleteWireCmnd

Each of these subclasses would have its own implementation for DoIt, UndoIt, and RedoIt.

To understand how they would work, consider the AddChip command. In our user interface, the user would select the chip icon and then click someplace in the layout. The click would define the new center point for the chip. As an alternative, the user interface might put up an echo rectangle for the chip on •MouseDown and then move the echo around until •MouseUp, at which point the center of the chip would be defined.

After •MouseUp, the controller would create a new AddChipCmnd object that would have a public field CenterPoint. The controller would put the new center point into that field and then invoke the DoIt method. Since the Add-ChipCmnd class would have its own special implementation for DoIt, this method would first call the AddChip method on the model. The model would add the chip and notify the views. We need to modify the AddChip method, however, so that it returns the number of the chip that was created. In addition to invoking AddChip, the AddChipCmnd object will save the number of the chip that was created in one of its private fields. Having executed the DoIt method on the AddChipCmnd object, the controller will add that command object onto the history list for the user interface.

At some time later, if the user selects Undo, the top command object from the history is retrieved and the interface code invokes the UndoIt method on that object. The Undo code only understands the abstract class Command. It has no idea what kind of command this object actually represents. All the Undo code cares about is that there is an UndoIt method. If the top history object is an AddChipCmnd object, its UndoIt method takes the chip number saved in the object by the DoIt method and uses it to invoke the DeleteChip method on the model. This effectively undoes the action of the AddChip command.

After calling UndoIt on the command object, the user interface will add the object to the Redo list. If the user asks for a redo, then that object is retrieved and its RedoIt method is invoked. In almost all cases, the RedoIt method simply calls the DoIt method. There are some special cases where saved data structures must be handled differently between DoIt and RedoIt; this very much depends on the architecture of the application.

Let us consider the case of the DeleteChipCmnd. The controller will have selected a chip and will know its number. When the delete chip icon is pressed, the controller makes a new DeleteChipCmnd object and stores the selected chip number into that object. It then calls the object's DoIt method, which in turn calls the model's DeleteChip method to delete the chip. Before deleting the chip, the DeleteChipCmnd object must save the center point and name for that chip in the command object's fields. The DeleteChipCmnd is then placed on the history list. If the user tries to undo the command, the

UndoIt method is invoked. The UndoIt command could simply call the Add-Chip method, passing in the saved chip location, and then call the ChangeChipName method to restore the name. The UndoIt method could then save the new chip number of the added chip so that any RedoIt invocations could delete that chip again.

There is a problem with the AddChip mechanism for undoing a chip deletion. Consider the following sequence of actions:

1. `AddChip(point(10, 20)) -> Chip 6`
2. `ChangeChipName(3,"X12NC")`
3. `AddChip(point(40, 50)) -> Chip 7`
4. `DeleteChip(3)`
5. `undo(4)`

    This adds AddChip, which creates chip 8 and then changes chip 8's name.

6. `undo(3)`

    This deletes chip 7.

7. `undo(2)`

    This will try to restore the name of chip 3; however, chip 3 does not exist.

The problem with our simple AddChip mechanism for undoing the deletion is that it does not recreate a chip at the same number as the one that was deleted. If we continue to undo, we encounter the ChangeChipNameCmnd object, which will try to restore the name of a chip that no longer exists.

There are several solutions to the problem. The first is to have the model retain a stack of unused chip numbers and to have AddChip draw numbers from the stack before allocating new ones. This approach would have `undo(4)` create a chip at number 3 rather than number 8. Another alternative is to add a RestoreChip(Number, Center, Name) method to the model. This method could be called by the UndoIt method to completely recreate the chip that had been deleted.

There is a second problem with our implementation of DeleteChipCmnd, which is that deleting a chip will cause all of the wires attached to that chip to be deleted. The DeleteChipCmnd must save all of those wires so that they can be recreated when the chip is restored. Additional methods must be added to the model so that the DeleteChipCmnd object can find all of those wires.

In our discussion so far, the controller has created the appropriate command objects for each of the model methods. An alternative implementation is to have the model return a command object as the result of each of its methods. For example, the controller would simply invoke DeleteChip with a chip number and receive a command object in return. The model would take the responsibility to store what information is necessary in the DeleteChipCmnd object. This eliminates a lot of communication between the model and the controller. The controller then saves the resulting command object in the history list, where it can be undone later if necessary.

In this discussion, we have referred repeatedly to the history list. There are some important memory considerations with this list. If we save a history of everything that the user has done since the machine has been turned on, we may have a problem with space. There is also the issue that users cannot remember very many steps back in the history. For these reasons, the Undo history list is usually quite short. In some systems, only the most recent command is saved; in others, the history list is a fixed size, with only the last n command objects saved. In some systems, n is fixed, and in others, it is settable as a user preference.

Asynchronous Multi-User

Having shown how to use command objects for Undo and Redo, we can take the next step of supporting the concept of patches for asynchronous multi-user applications. Suppose that our chip layout was part of a large project in which many designers were creating circuits. A designer might open a circuit file and begin to make changes. If we were to save the history list of all changes since the file was opened, this history list would constitute a patch. When it comes time to save the file, we do not save the changed file. Instead, we save the patch, which can be used to produce the changes from the unchanged master file that everyone is sharing.

If we are keeping the unchanged original and saving the patch, which will produce the new circuit from the old one, we need to save all of the DoIt information from the command objects. When they are read in again, the commands can be redone on the model just as the user did them to create the patch to begin with.

An alternative, however, is to save the newly changed version and to retain the patch as a mechanism for restoring the circuit to its original state. In this case, we want to save the undo information for each command and to save the commands in last-to-first order.

The command-object history architecture gives us everything we need for creating such patches except for a way to save them. We need to be able to convert the sequence of command objects in the history list into a stream of data that can be saved in a file. This requirement poses a problem because each command object is storing very different things.

What we need in saving command objects is the concept of serialization, similar to that found in the Microsoft Foundation Classes. Let us assume that we are saving the DoIt information. We can then add three new methods to the abstract Command class, as follows:

CommandType
> *Returns an identifier of the particular subclass of Command.*

WriteDoItInfo(OStream)
> *Writes all of the DoIt information to an output stream.*

ReadDoItInfo(IStream)
> *Reads all of the DoIt information from an input stream.*

This implementation uses the stream abstraction in which objects can read and write from streams that may be files, strings in memory, network ports, or any other data-sequencing mechanism that conforms to the abstract classes OStream and IStream.

When we want to save a patch, we can create an output stream (OS) in which to save the patch. This output stream may be a file or it may be a sequence of bytes that will be stored in a patch database. The different options are not important to this implementation. We can then take the sequence of command objects that makes up the patch and do the following for each command object C in the patch:

```
{ OS << C.CommandType( ); // write type
  C.WriteDoItInfo(OS);    // write info
}
```

Using the WriteDoItInfo method, each command can write out whatever information it needs in order to be able to reconstruct itself later. Let us assume there is a function NewCommandObj that can produce a new command object of the appropriate class, given a command type. Using New-CommandObj, we can create the following code to read a patch in from an input stream (IS):

```
CType CT;
Command C;
do until IS is at end of stream
  { IS >> CT;                  // read type
    C = NewCommandObj(CT);
    C.ReadDoItInfo(IS);        // read info
    add C to the history list
  }
```

With these two methods, we can read and write history lists of user commands. Using a similar technique, we could write out the undo information to create a list of undo commands to restore our circuit to its original state. When the application reads in a patch, it can take each command object in the history list and perform that command's DoIt method, performing the patch as the user had done originally.

In Java, this extra work for serialization of command objects is not required. The Java reflection facilities allow general tools to inquire about all of the fields that an object may have and then to automatically write out those fields. This allows the serialization software to adapt itself to any object presented to it at run time. The dynamic loading of classes replaces the NewCommandObj method. Java provides a general serialization mechanism that performs all of this work with little or no effort on the part of the programmer.

This same serialization mechanism is also required for synchronous groupware situations. As each command is executed, it must be serialized so that it can be sent to all the other users, where it can be read and implemented. Serialization, however, is not enough because conflicts between the command histories of various users must still be resolved. This requires a more sophisticated command architecture.

Simple Macros

Given the serialization mechanisms of WriteDoItInfo and ReadDoItInfo, we now have enough to implement a simple macro-recording mechanism. Suppose that a user turns on macro recording. We can save the history list and start a new one. Everything that the user does is saved as command objects in this history list. When the user turns off macro recording, the macro history list is saved and serialized into a stream, which can be saved into a file. Whenever the macro is invoked by the user, this stream can be used to reconstruct the history list and the commands can be reinvoked using DoIt.

However, there is a problem with macro commands in that when the macro is invoked, the same objects may not be present. In our chip example, the numbers of objects may be different. This requires that when the macro history is serialized into a stream, all object references must be generalized. The simplest way to do this is to recognize that almost all object references in a command are actually references to the currently selected object. If such references are saved as a selected object reference and selection commands are also saved in the macro, then there is no problem because the selections will be reexecuted to create a selected object that the command can work on. These generalization issues, however, are best discussed in the next section.

14.4.2 Extended Command Objects

In the command-class architecture discussed so far, each command class is opaque. The undo, groupware, or macro systems using this architecture know nothing about the model objects that are actually being manipulated by the command objects. This causes some problems in implementing groupware and macro systems.

In a synchronous groupware situation, two users may simultaneously modify a circle to have two different colors. Each sends the command object to the other, which then changes the color on each machine. If the first user changes the circle to red and the second one to blue, after each has sent the command object to the other, the first user is surprised to see his circle turned to blue (by the other user's command object) and the second user is surprised to see her circle turned red. Not only does this surprise occur, but now the models are inconsistent with each other. The problem is that the groupware system cannot detect this conflict when the command objects are opaque and do not reveal the objects that they are working on.

In the macro implementation, we need to generalize or parameterize the recorded history so that it can be used in a variety of situations. With opaque command objects, this generalization is not possible.

Let us suppose that all command objects have a method GetObjectsUsed() that returns a list of identifiers for all objects used by the DoIt method of this command object. For this discussion, let us assume that objects are identified by integer numbers. (This need not be so, but it simplifies this discussion.) Using the GetObjectsUsed method, the groupware and macro software have a mechanism for examining the objects used by a command.

Groupware Conflict Resolution

Let us take the groupware problem first. Because command objects now reveal the model objects that they use, we can detect when two command objects are working on the same model object. The simplest mechanism for doing this is to have one workstation in charge (master) with the others serving as slaves. When the master receives command objects from user processes, it keeps track of how much of the history has been synchronized for all users. Any unsynchronized commands are compared with each other to detect conflicts. When conflicts are detected, the master resolves the conflict by selecting one of the options and then sending Undo commands to remove the effect of the discarded commands. This is a very simplistic discussion of what must occur, but the essential principles are to detect conflict and to use Undo to repair the problem.

Macro Generalization

If we have command objects that will reveal their model objects, we can do a number of things to generalize a macro. One option is for the macro recorder to remember the identifier of the currently selected object or objects at the time the macro was recorded. When the macro is invoked, any command using the old selected object can be modified to use the new selected object, requiring that the command class have a SetObjectUsed method for such changes. The result, however, is that the macro can now be applied to any selected object.

Another alternative is to compare two instances of a macro recording and then to insert parameter markers where two corresponding commands use different objects. When the macro is invoked, the macro system can ask the user for appropriate values for the parameters, set those values into the command objects, and then execute the saved command list. Because the model objects are available, such comparisons are possible and user-supplied parameters can be used each time a macro is executed.

14.5 Summary

This chapter has discussed the need for pervasive facilities that apply to all commands in an interface in addition to those approaches that treat each command independently. The concept of monitoring all commands has been presented as a means for implementing undo/redo, multi-user or groupware interfaces, and macro recording. This chapter could not possibly cover all of the issues in these three areas, but it has presented a general architectural starting point for adding such capabilities to user interfaces.

Endnotes

Chapter 1

1. Dix, A., Finlay, J., Abowd, G., and Beale, R. *Human-Computer Interaction*. Hemel Hempstead, UK: Prentice Hall International (UK) Limited, 1993.
2. Newman, W., and Lamming, M. *Interactive System Design*. New York: Addison-Wesley, 1995.
3. Eberts, R. *User Interface Design*. Englewood Cliffs, NJ: Prentice Hall, 1994.
4. Foley, J., van Dam, A., Feiner, S., and Hughes, J. *Computer Graphics: Principles and Practice* (2nd edition). Reading, MA: Addison-Wesley, 1990.
5. Norman, D. *The Psychology of Everyday Things*. New York: Basic Books, 1988.
6. Nielsen, J. *Usability Engineering*. Boston: Academic Press, 1993.
7. Mayhew, D. *Principles and Guidelines in Software User Interface Design*. Englewood Cliffs, NJ: Prentice Hall, 1992.
8. Birtwistle, G. *SIMULA Begin*. Philadelphia: Auerbach, 1973.
9. Goldberg, A., and Robson, D. *Smalltalk-80: The Language*. Reading, MA: Addison-Wesley, 1989.

Chapter 3

1. *PostScript Language Reference Manual*. Reading, MA: Addison-Wesley, 1985.
2. Salman, W., Tisserand, O., and Toulout, B. *FORTH*. New York: Springer-Verlag, 1984.
3. The UNICODE Consortium. *The UNICODE Standard, Version 2.0*. Reading, MA: Addison-Wesley, 1996.
4. Foley, J., van Dam, A., Feiner, S., and Hughes, J. *Computer Graphics: Principles and Practice* (2nd edition). Reading, MA: Addison-Wesley, 1990, pp. 592–593.

Chapter 4

1. Gosling, J., Rosenthal, D., and Arden, M. *The NeWS Book: An Introduction to the Networked Extensible Window System.* Palo Atlo, CA: Sun Microsystems, 1989.
2. Salman, W., Tisserand, O., and Toulout, B. *FORTH.* New York: Springer-Verlag, 1984.
3. Pike, R. "Graphics in Overlapping Bitmap Layers." *Computer Graphics* 17(3), July 1983, pp. 331–356.
4. Kruglinski, D. *Inside Visual C++.* Redmond, WA: Microsoft Press, 1993.
5. McCord, J. *Borland C++ Tools.* Carmel, IN: Sams Publishing, 1992.
6. Wilson, D., Rosenstein, L., and Shafer, D. *Programming with MacApp.* New York: Addison-Wesley, 1990.
7. Rosenthal, D. "Managing Graphical Resources." *Computer Graphics* 17(1), January 1983, pp. 38–45.
8. Linton, M., Vlissides, J., and Calder, P. "Composing User Interfaces with Inter-Views." *IEEE Computer* 22(2) February 1989, pp. 8–22.
9. Goldberg, A., and Robson, D. *Smalltalk-80: The Language and Its Implementation.* Reading, MA: Addison-Wesley, 1983.
10. Steele, G. *Common LISP: The Language* (2nd edition). Maynard, MA: Digital Press, 1990.
11. Ungar, D., and Smith, R. "Self: The Power of Simplicity." *OOPSLA Conference Proceedings*, 1987, pp. 227–241.

Chapter 5

1. Goldberg, A., and Robson, D. *Smalltalk-80: The Language and Its Implementation.* Reading, MA: Addison-Wesley, 1983.
2. Krasner, G., and Popo, S. "A Cookbook for Using the Model-View-Controller User Interface Paradigm in Smalltalk-80." *Journal of Object-Oriented Programming* 1(3), August 1988.

Chapter 7

1. Cardelli, L. "Building User Interfaces by Direct Manipulation." *ACM SIGGRAPH Symposium on User Interface Software*, October 1988, pp. 152–166.
2. Knuth, D. *The T$_E$Xbook.* New York: Addison-Wesley, 1986.
3. Linton, M., Vlissides, J., and Calder, P. "Composing User Interfaces with Inter-Views." *IEEE Computer* 22(2), February 1989, pp. 8–22.

Chapter 8

1. Jacob, R. "Using Formal Specifications in the Design of a Human-Computer Interface." *Human Factors in Computing Systems (CHI '82)*, March 1982, pp. 315–322.

2. Hill, R. "Supporting Concurrency, Communication, and Synchronization in Human-Computer Interaction: The Sassafras UIMS." *ACM Transactions on Graphics* 5(3), July 1986, pp. 179–210.
3. Hartson, H., Siochi, A., and Hix, D. "The UAN: A User-Oriented Representation for Direct Manipulation Interface Designs." *ACM Transactions on Information Systems* 8(3), 1990, pp. 181–203.
4. Olsen, D. "Propositional Production Systems for Dialog Description." *Human Factors in Computing Systems (CHI '90)*, April 1990, pp. 57–63.
5. Olsen, D. *User Interface Management Systems: Models and Algorithms.* San Mateo, CA: Morgan Kaufmann, 1992.

Chapter 9

1. Foley, J., van Dam, A., Feiner, S., and Hughes, J. *Computer Graphics: Principles and Practice* (2nd edition). Reading, MA: Addison-Wesley, 1990.
2. Hearn, D., and Baker, P. *Computer Graphics.* Englewood Cliffs, NJ: Prentice Hall, 1994.
3. Bartels, R., Beatty, J., and Barsky, B. *An Introduction to Splines for Use in Computer Graphics and Geometric Modeling.* San Mateo, CA: Morgan Kaufmann, 1987.
4. Burden, R., and Faires, J. *Numerical Analysis.* Boston: PWS-KENT, 1989.

Chapter 12

1. McNeill, T., Olsen, D., and Mitchell, D. "Workspaces: An Architecture for Editing Collections of Objects." *Human Factors in Computing Systems (CHI '92)*, April 1992, pp. 267–272.

Chapter 14

1. Berlage, T. "A Selective Undo Mechanism for Graphical User Interfaces Based on Command Objects." *ACM Transactions on Computer-Human Interaction* 1(3), September 1994, pp. 269–294.
2. Myers, B., and Kosbie, D. "Reusable Hierarchical Command Objects." *Human Factors in Computing Systems (CHI '96)*, April 1996, pp. 260–267.
3. See the conference proceedings series for Computer-Supported Cooperative Work (CSCW), published by ACM.
4. Cypher, A., ed. *Watch What I Do: Programming by Demonstration.* Cambridge, MA: MIT Press, 1993.
5. Meyer, B. *Object-Oriented Software Construction.* Englewood Cliffs, NJ: Prentice Hall, 1988.
6. Wilson, D., Rosenstein, L., and Shafer, D. *Programming with MacApp.* Reading, MA: Addison-Wesley, 1990.

Index

verage
gement